PRINCIPLES OF INTERNET MARKETING

PRINCIPLES OF INTERNET MARKETING

NEW TOOLS AND METHODS FOR WEB DEVELOPERS

JASON I. MILETSKY

COURSE TECHNOLOGY
CENGAGE Learning™

Australia • Brazil • Japan • Korea • Mexico • Singapore • Spain • United Kingdom • United States

COURSE TECHNOLOGY
CENGAGE Learning™

**Principles of Internet Marketing:
New Tools and Methods for Web
Developers**
Jason I. Miletsky

Executive Editor: Marie Lee

Acquisitions Editor: Amy Jollymore

Managing Editor: Tricia Coia

Developmental Editor: Mary Pat Shaffer

Editorial Assistant: Julia Leroux-Lindsey

Marketing Manager: Bryant Chrzan

Content Project Manager: Heather Furrow,
Jennifer Feltri

Art Director: Marissa Falco

Cover Designer: Cabbage Design Company

Cover Artwork: © CSA Images

Manufacturing Coordinator: Julio Esperas

Proofreader: Brandy Lilly

Indexer: Kevin Broccoli

Compositor: International Typesetting
and Composition

ISBN-13: 978-1-423-90319-2

ISBN-10: 1-423-90319-6

Course Technology
20 Channel Center Street
Boston, MA 02210
USA

Cengage Learning is a leading provider of customized learning solutions with
office locations around the globe, including Singapore, the United Kingdom,
Australia, Mexico, Brazil, and Japan. Locate your local office at:
international.cengage.com/region

Cengage Learning products are represented in Canada by
Nelson Education, Ltd.

For your lifelong learning solutions, visit **www.course.cengage.com**

Visit our corporate web site at **www.cengage.com**

Some of the product names and company names used in this book have been
used for identification purposes only and may be trademarks or registered
trademarks of their respective manufacturers and sellers.

Course Technology, a part of Cengage Learning, reserves the right to revise this
publication and make changes from time to time in its content without notice.

Printed in Canada
1 2 3 4 5 6 7 12 11 10 09 08

Brief Contents

Contents

CHAPTER 3

Social Media and Social Networking Sites **74**

CHAPTER 4

Blogging **119**

CHAPTER 8 **Planning and Developing the Site** **259**

CHAPTER 9 **E-Commerce Sites**. **298**

CHAPTER 10 Programs and Languages. **337**

CHAPTER 11 Driving Traffic: Marketing Strategies. . . . **362**

CHAPTER 12 Capturing and Keeping an Audience **404**

Preface

Principles of Internet Marketing: New Tools and Methods for Web Developers will help you understand the "why" behind the "how" of Web site development. This book will help you see sites not from the developer's perspective, but rather from the marketer's point of view. It will teach you about the importance of the brand and how that relates to Web site development, the reasons sites are developed, how they are used to build an audience, and most importantly, how companies use the Web to earn revenue and build recognition among their desired audience. You will learn the strategies used to drive traffic to a site, the tools that are available to keep audiences coming back (with a focus on social media tools), and the role marketing plays in the building of a successful Web site.

As traditional marketing and business growth becomes more integrated with the Web, and the Web becomes a more central part of every marketing strategy, the need for programmers and marketers to improve communication between them becomes increasingly important. Of all the Web languages you already know, this book will teach you one more: Marketing.

The Intended Audience

This book is meant to provide insight for anyone interested in gaining an understanding of marketing strategy as it pertains to the Web—with a particular slant toward the Web programmer. Although no specific code will be used or referenced in this book, it is helpful to have a basic understanding of how to program in HTML, or at least understand HTML's capabilities. Ideally, as you are going through this book, you will be continually relating what you are learning here with the various Web programming languages and techniques that you already know. You should also have a good familiarity with the Web, and some of the more popular Web sites, such as Google, MySpace, and YouTube.

Organization and Coverage

Principles of Internet Marketing: New Tools and Methods for Web Developers provides a comprehensive framework for understanding the best practices for Internet marketing and successful commercial-based Internet and Web projects. The first two chapters provide general overviews. Chapter 1 reviews the history of the Web as a commercial entity and the impact social media has had on the Web. Chapter 2 details the roles and responsibilities behind the development of a Web site as well as the different types of sites that can be found on the Web.

Chapters 3 through 6 highlight different social media applications. Chapter 3 reviews social media as a general concept and discusses the reasons for its popularity before exploring social networking specifically. Chapter 4 provides a comprehensive discussion on blogging and how blogs can be used in marketing. Chapter 5 focuses on streaming video and the increasingly important role it is playing in the lives of viewers and marketers. Chapter 6 rounds out the social media discussion with a look at other important tools including wikis, RSS feeds, mashups, and virtual worlds—what each of these is and how each fits into the social media universe.

Chapter 7 moves away from the topic of social media with a look at branding. Coverage of this important subject includes a discussion of a brand and why it is important, the elements that make up the brand, and where the Web fits into the brand picture. Chapter 8 moves the reader back to the Web with a look at the planning process including subjects that need to be considered before development starts, such as the concept, audience, design, navigation, and pros and cons of outsourcing development.

Chapter 9 examines e-commerce—with a look at the various sources of e-commerce revenue and how social media has changed the way consumers shop on the Web. Chapter 10 looks at the types of programs and languages used in Web development, while Chapter 11 examines the means and methods for driving traffic to a site through a variety of marketing methods including advertising, public relations, direct marketing, promotions, and viral campaigns.

Chapter 12 covers the importance of keeping users on the site for longer periods of time and enticing them to come back for future visits. Finally, Chapter 13 completes the story by taking a close look at the importance of measuring ROI (return on investment)—what variables need to measured and how best to go about determining success.

Features

Principles of Internet Marketing: New Tools and Methods for Web Developers is a superior textbook because it also includes the following features:

- Objectives—Each chapter begins with a list of objectives so you know the topics that will be presented in the chapter. In addition to providing a quick reference to topics covered, this feature provides a useful study aid.

- Interviews and Case Studies: Numerous interviews and case studies with professionals in and around the Web marketing field give expert insight throughout the book, and provide a first-hand look at important subject matter.

- Figures—Each chapter contains many figures, including screen shots to illustrate the various concepts discussed in the chapter.

- Tables—Numerous tables throughout the book support the concepts with recent and relevant Web and consumer-based statistics from highly regarded sources.

- Chapter Summaries—Following each chapter is a summary that recaps the programming concepts and techniques covered in the chapter. This feature helps you to recap and check your understanding of the main points in each chapter.

- Key Terms—Each chapter includes a list of newly introduced vocabulary. The list of key terms provides a mini-review of the major concepts in the chapter.

- Review Questions—Each chapter contains 20 multiple-choice review questions that provide a review of the key concepts in the chapter.

- Projects—Each chapter concludes with meaningful projects that reinforce the concepts you learned in the chapter.

Teaching Tools

The following list supplemental materials are available when this book is used in a classroom setting. All of the instructor resources for this book are provided to the instructor on a single CD-ROM.

Electronic Instructor's Manual. The Instructor's Manual that accompanies this textbook includes additional instructional material to assist in class preparation, including items such as teaching tips, quick quizzes, class discussion topics, and additional projects.

ExamView®. This textbook is accompanied by ExamView, a powerful testing software package that allows instructors to create and administer printed, computer (LAN-based), and Internet exams. ExamView includes hundreds of questions that correspond to the topics covered in this text, enabling students to generate detailed study guides that include page references for further review. The computer-based and Internet testing components allow students to take exams at their computers, and save the instructor time by grading each exam automatically.

PowerPoint Presentations. This book comes with Microsoft Power-Point slides for each chapter. These slides are included as a teaching aid for classroom presentation; teachers can make them available on the network for chapter review, or print them for classroom distribution. Instructors can add their own slides for additional topics they introduce to the class.

Solution Files. Password-protected solutions to all Review Questions and end-of-chapter projects are provided on the Instructor Resources CD-ROM and on the Course Technology Web site at www.course.com.

Distance Learning. Course Technology is proud to present online test banks in WebCT and Blackboard to provide the most complete and dynamic learning experience possible. Instructors are encouraged to make the most of the course, both online and offline. For more information on how to access the online test bank, contact your local Course Technology sales representative.

Acknowledgments

I would like to thank everyone at Cengage Publishing who helped make this book happen, in particular, Amy Jollymore, Tricia Coia, Anupriya Tyagi, Heather Furrow, and Jennifer Feltri. I'd especially like to thank Mary Pat Shaffer and Ann Shaffer—I know I wasn't the easiest person to work with, and I really appreciate the great job you did keeping me in line!

I would also like to thank all of the people who took time to interview with me and let me share their ideas and opinions with the readers. The insights that each of you shared represent some of the best information in the book, and I'm excited to have all of you be a part of it.

Thank you, Mom and Dad, for being supportive as always. If it wasn't for you both reminding me that I need to stop typing and have fun once in awhile, I might have become glued to the computer! The same goes for my good friends, Jackie, Chris, and Luz who are always understanding and supportive even when I can't spend as much time with them as I'd like.

Of course, I need to thank my business partner, Deirdre Breakenridge, who not only contributed to this book with an interview of her own, but has been a big part of shaping my own understanding of social media. (And thanks to her daughter, Megan, for giving me a hug when I needed one!) In addition, I want to express appreciation for the PFS team who work extra hard and pick up the slack when I'm off writing.

I am also grateful to each of the reviewers who provided their insight during this book's development, including Natasa Christodoulidou, California State University, Dominguez Hills; Vicky Hardin, Jefferson Community and Technical College; Steven McClung, Florida State University; and Denny McCorkle, University of Northern Colorado.

Finally, I want to thank Demitre and the staff at Eros Cafe in Rutherford, and Jerry and his staff at the Barnes and Nobles in Clifton, for keeping the Diet Pepsi's coming and letting me take up space for hours every night and never complaining about it.

This book is dedicated to Gabriella, Matt, Michael, and Kathleen.

CHAPTER 1

An Overview of the Web

In this chapter you will learn about:

- ◎ The rise of the Web from obscurity to commercial revolution

- ◎ The evolution of the Web after the Web bubble burst

- ◎ Social networking on the Web and its effect on social relationships and marketing

- ◎ Important trends and demographic differences in Internet usage

- ◎ Predictions for the future of the Web and how these developments might further impact society

2

In the 1950s, conversation centered on the dinner table, school dances, and chance meetings in the neighborhood. People socialized by getting together with old friends and meeting new people face-to-face. People shopped at stores in their hometowns and did their banking with a trusted personal banker. News from around the world took days, sometimes longer, before its impact was felt, and public opinion was most often found on the Letters to the Editor page. The world may not have been any more innocent, but for most people, it was certainly smaller. A lot has changed since then. In the years since Elvis Presley first rocked the world and sparked a cultural revolution, technological developments and events have worked to open the lines of communication around the world and bring us closer together (though some may argue further apart). Nothing has been nearly as powerful a protagonist in that change as the Web and its rapid commercialization.

According to a February 2008 *BusinessWeek* article, a full 2% of all new marriages in the U.S. are the result of relationships that started on just one online dating site, eHarmony.com.[1] Often, these new relationships are between people who, due to geographic, career, or schedule differences, would never have had the chance to meet if not for the Web. Similarly, the neighborhood bank has fewer visitors. According to a December 2007 survey of Internet activities by the Pew Internet & American Life Project, over 53% of all Internet users now engage in online banking.[2] On the surface, the Web has changed the way we buy, sell, research, and explore. Looking deeper, we see the true and lasting effect: as the Web has evolved into a single source for instantaneous, global communication, it has radically changed the way we live.

A Brief History of the Web Through 2001

In the 1950s, while the typical American was meeting his or her friends at the soda shop on the corner, ARPA (Advanced Research Projects Agency)—a division of the U.S. Defense Department—was launched in response to Sputnik, the Soviets' first venture into space. Most likely, the original ARPA members would not have guessed that the technology advancements they would soon make, including computer networking and the first hypertext system, would rattle the world just decades later. These innovations continued to come to life through the 1970s and 1980s, out of the public eye, until at last the commercial world was ready for them.

In June 1993, HTML was released and changed the world forever. For the remainder of the 1990s, the "Web Boom" brought with it rapid and dramatic changes both online and offline. Netscape, an early and popular Web browser, was released in October 1994. After its release, Netscape dominated the way people viewed the Web, diminishing in popularity only after Microsoft made a play for the throne almost two years later, when it released the first version of Internet Explorer.

The Web Boom sparked other developments in technology, as well. Computer usage, fueled by the commercialization of the Web, improving technology, and falling prices, exploded. According to the U.S. Census Bureau, by 1997, the percentage of households that owned computers had ballooned to 35% from only 15% in 1990, while the amount of money spent on computer-related equipment and associated hardware more than tripled.[3] Companies around the world were also quick to take advantage of the opportunities that the tech boom offered. Low interest rates made borrowing funds affordable, and companies of all sizes rushed to install new equipment, establish servers, and launch their own Web sites for marketing purposes.

In the mid-1990s, BBC News measured the number of Web sites in existence as fewer than 19,000[4]—a pittance by 2008's standard of nearly 176,000,000 (as measured by Internet research company Netcraft).[5] Still, that was enough to raise the eyebrows of investors worldwide. **Venture capitalists**, investors who invest cash in new and emerging businesses, rushed to fund new ideas and get in on one of the greatest technological growth periods since the start of the Industrial Revolution. This early crop of investor-funded sites included Cadabra.com and Auctionweb.com (now known as Amazon.com and eBay, respectively).

To understand the importance of venture capital and the effect the Web had on investors, one only needs to look at the statistics. According to a 1997 report by the U.S. Small Business Administration, the total amount of investments made by venture capitalists tripled from $3.4 billion in 1991 to over $10 billion in 1996.[6] In that same period, however, the average amount of money that venture capitalists invested into any one company only rose from $4.1 million to $6.8 million—meaning that the number of new projects being funded was expanding quickly year after year. The Web's impact on these statistics can't be ignored. In 1996, technology-based companies received the most investments, a full 60%, and software companies came in second.[7]

Thanks to the growing Web economy, low interest rates, easily available credit, and improving technology, the economy flourished. By the time the stock market reached its peak in early 2000, as shown in Figure 1-1, the U.S. unemployment rate stood at only 3.8%—a benchmark it hadn't seen since in over 40 years according to the U.S. Department of Labor, Bureau of Labor Statistics.[8]

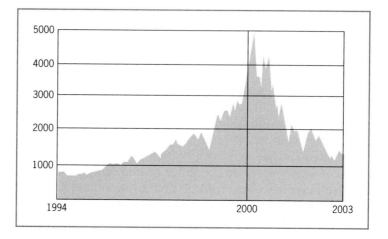

Figure 1-1   A graph of the NASDAQ exchange between 1994 and 2003. The dot-com bubble hit its peak in 2000. SOURCE: U.S. Department of Labor, Bureau of Labor Statistics, Aug. 2008.

And then, it ended.

The bursting of the Web bubble wasn't an instant collapse. It was a momentum-building process, and once the ball got rolling it picked up speed with ease. Investors became anxious to start seeing positive returns, which were few and far between as **burn rates** (the rate at which companies spend their available cash) were accelerating much more quickly than income was being generated. As venture capital money dried up, many **dot-coms**, the name given to the growing batch of new, investment-driven Web sites launched in the mid-to-late 1990s, quickly ran out of cash. Some struggling Web sites were based on outlandish concepts and had no business being funded in the first place. Other sites, while conceptually viable, simply didn't have sufficiently experienced management behind them. Even legitimate sites were struggling to pay operating expenses, such as salaries and leases. Inventory costs climbed, and due to an increasingly crowded marketplace, advertising expenses soared. These financial pressures mounted, while consumer skepticism toward online shopping remained high.

The stock market topped out in the early part of 2000, and one dot-com bankruptcy after another throughout the rest of that year sent investor optimism into a tailspin. When high profile sites like eToys and Webvan finally filed for Chapter 11 bankruptcy protection in February and July of 2001, respectively, the cracks in the wall could no longer be covered. The media, which had brought the Web so much positive attention during the 1990s, also rushed to report its demise, sending worried investors running for cover. Shares were sold, and stock prices plummeted. The bubble had finally burst.

There were many investment-funded sites that went under in the frenzy. Some of the more high-profile failures include:

- **Webvan** (1999–2001)—A company with a good idea that grew too fast, Webvan allowed people to order groceries online and have them delivered right to their door. Webvan expanded to eight cities with plans for 26 more, burned through more than $375 million, and began development of $1 billion in high-tech warehouses before it realized it was missing one key ingredient: customers.[9]

- **Pets.com** (1998–2000)—The famed Pets.com sock puppet mascot was so well known that it was featured in a Super Bowl commercial and as a balloon in the Macy's Thanksgiving Day Parade in 1999. After its initial funding, Pets.com raised $82.5 million in an IPO.[10] **IPO** stands for initial public offering, which is the first sale of shares from a private company on a public stock exchange. Unfortunately, the site was not able to draw enough customers and the company undercharged for shipping, causing it to lose money on almost every transaction. It barely lasted two years.

- **Kozmo.com** (1998–2001)—Like Webvan, Kozmo.com was actually a pretty good idea. Just log on and order practically anything—a DVD, a bagel with cream cheese, a deck of cards— and it was delivered to your door shortly after. But with free delivery, small items just cost too much to deliver, and after blowing through $280 million (plus an additional $150 million earned from a promotion deal with Starbucks), Kozmo.com was gone.[11]

- **Flooz.com** (1998–2001)—Cut up your credit cards—you won't need them anymore. At least, that's what the people behind Flooz.com thought, in one of the silliest ideas to hit the market. The concept was that users would buy Flooz—a new, online currency—and use it to make purchases at online retailers. Why? Neither initial investments of $35 million nor spokesperson Whoopi Goldberg could give consumers a compelling reason.[12]

- **eToys.com** (1997–2001)—The online toy retailer raised $166 million in an IPO and went on an advertising and technology spending spree.[13] However, eToys realized too late that it was spending a lot more than it was earning, and it closed its doors in high-profile fashion.

The ten years following the launch of the Web were eventful. Figure 1-2 provides a detailed timeline of important benchmarks in the Web's history between 1991 and 2001.

6

1991

AUGUST 6   **TIM BERNERS-LEE INTRODUCES THE WEB**

Tim Berners-Lee had developed a system meant to "allow links to be made to any information anywhere," by combining hypertext with the Internet. On this date, he introduces his Web project on the alt.hypertext newsgroup and releases all of the files necessary for people to duplicate his invention.

DECEMBER 12   **PAUL KUNZ SETS UP FIRST U.S. WEB SERVER**

After meeting with Tim Berners-Lee at the CERN Labs (CERN is the European Organization for Nuclear Research) near Geneva, Paul Kunz (of the Stanford Linear Accelerator Center (SLAC)) sets up the first Web server in North America. Using Berners-Lee's software, SLAC launches the first U.S. Web site.

1993

APRIL 22   **MOSAIC WEB BROWSER FOR WINDOWS IS RELEASED**

Developed at the National Center for Supercomputing Applications in the U.S., the first-ever Web browser, named Mosaic, is released. Mosaic allows the general public to navigate through the limited but growing amount of information on the Web.

APRIL 30   **CERN ANNOUNCES FREE USE OF THE WEB**

CERN is persuaded by Tim Berners-Lee and a colleague to provide Web technology and codes at no cost for anyone to use. This is a turning point, fueling the rapid expansion of the Web.

MAY   **'THE TECH,' PUBLISHED BY M.I.T. STUDENTS, BECOMES THE FIRST ONLINE NEWSPAPER**

JUNE   **HTML PROGRAMMING LANGUAGE IS RELEASED**

NOVEMBER   **FIRST WEBCAM GOES ONLINE**

Who says a watched pot never percolates? A group of coffee-drinking computer scientists at Cambridge University, annoyed at having to walk up many flights of stairs only to find the coffee pot empty, install the first Webcam to monitor the pot remotely.

1994

FEBRUARY   **YAHOO! ONLINE**

David Filo and Jerry Yang, students at Stanford University, launch "Jerry's Guide to the World Wide Web"—a hierarchical directory of other sites. It is later named Yahoo, which stands for Yet Another Hierarchical Officious Oracle.

OCTOBER 13   **NETSCAPE BROWSER RELEASED**

Figure 1-2   Timeline of the Web 1991–2001. SOURCE: "Fifteen Years of the Web." BBC News <news.bbc.co.uk/1/hi/technology> 5 Aug. 2006. (*continues*)

(continued)

OCTOBER 25 **FIRST MAJOR BANNER ADS APPEAR ON WEB SITES**

AT&T and Zima (a clear beer that never really caught on) are among the initial crop of banner advertisers.

1995

FEBRUARY **RADIO HK LAUNCHES FIRST FULL-TIME WEB RADIO STATION**

JULY 1 **ONLINE BOOKSTORE AMAZON.COM IS LAUNCHED**

Jeff Bezos launches Cadabra.com, an online bookstore later renamed Amazon.com, one of the first e-commerce sites.

AUGUST 9 **THE WEB BOOM HITS THE STOCK MARKET**

Netscape, one of many Web companies to go public, records the third largest IPO share value ever on the NASDAQ exchange.

AUGUST 24 **INTERNET EXPLORER RELEASED**

Microsoft launches Internet Explorer as part of Windows 95, igniting the so-called "browser wars." This signals the end of the Netscape era and ushers in a new series of headaches for site programmers.

SEPTEMBER 4 **EBAY AUCTIONS BEGIN**

Originally named AuctionWeb by founder Pierre Omidyar, eBay goes on to facilitate tens of thousands of transactions every day (the first sale is for a broken laser pointer sold for $13.83).

DECEMEBER 15 **ALTA VISTA IS LAUNCHED AS THE FIRST MULTILINGUAL SEARCH ENGINE**

1996

JULY 4 **HOTMAIL IS LAUNCHED**

1997

JUNE **DOMAIN NAME SALE FRENZY HEIGHTENS**

The high-priced game of selling domain names turns into a modern-day gold rush, as the domain name Business.com is sold for $150,000. Court cases over domain name ownership rights vs. trademark infringement begin to spring up.

DECEMBER 17 **LET THE BLOGGING BEGIN**

Jorn Barger, editor of *Robot Wisdom*, coins the term 'Weblog' (later shortened to 'blog') to describe the process of logging on the Web.

Figure 1-2 Timeline of the Web 1991–2001. SOURCE: "Fifteen Years of the Web." BBC News <news.bbc.co.uk/1/hi/technology> 5 Aug. 2006.

(continued)

1998

SEPTEMBER   **GOOGLE IS LAUNCHED**

From their California garage, Stanford University postgraduates Larry Page and Sergey Brin unveil their research project—a search engine designed to analyze the relationships between Web sites in order to rank their importance.

OCTOBER 19   **FIRST BLOG COMMUNITY, OPEN DIARY, IS LAUNCHED**

1999

MARCH 16   **EVERQUEST GETS ROLLING**

Although not exactly a household name, Everquest, a "massively multiplayer online role-playing game" preludes social networking.

JUNE 1   **MUSIC INDUSTRY GETS ROCKED**

Launched by college student Shawn Fanning as a way for him and his friends to find and share mp3 files, Napster becomes the first widely used peer-to-peer file-sharing device. Napster makes it easier for listeners to obtain music (for free) and raises the ire of the music industry. After a series of highly publicized court cases involving Napster, new laws helped shape modern copyright standards and paved the way for newer, legal forms of mp3 download programs, including iTunes.

2000

JANUARY 10   **AOL PURCHASES TIME WARNER**

The largest corporate merger to date, the sale of Time Warner to AOL would later become one of the most highly criticized as AOL eventually lost its luster.

JANUARY 14   **THE DOW JONES INDUSTRIAL AVERAGE REACHES AN ALL-TIME HIGH**

MARCH 10   **THE NASDAQ REACHES ITS PEAK**

The NASDAQ exchange, where many Web and technology stocks are traded, hits its high, thereafter losing ground as investors begin to take a grim look at their Web investments.

AUGUST   **NUMBER OF WEB SITES HITS THE 20 MILLION MARK**

Figure 1-2   Timeline of the Web 1991–2001. SOURCE: "Fifteen Years of the Web." BBC News <news.bbc.co.uk/1/hi/technology> 5 Aug. 2006.

(continued)

2001

JANUARY 11	**PODCASTING IS DEAD**
	The first ever podcast is demonstrated with a Grateful Dead song.
JANUARY 15	**WIKIPEDIA EMERGES**
	Jimmy Wales launches Wikipedia, an online encyclopedia.
FEBRUARY	**ETOYS.COM FILES FOR BANKRUPTCY**
JULY	**WEBVAN FILES FOR BANKRUPTCY**

Figure 1-2 Timeline of the Web 1991–2001. SOURCE: "Fifteen Years of the Web." BBC News <news.bbc.co.uk/1/hi/technology> 5 Aug. 2006.

A Brief History of the Web from 2002 Forward

The heyday of easy Web money and the expectation of a radical new economy were gone. In the aftermath, the Web community was left to reexamine itself and how it fit into a world that was now once bitten, twice shy. Newly minted college grads with big ideas but little practical experience no longer had the luxury of spending millions of dollars of venture capital money at a breakneck pace. Of course, the Web didn't go away or even diminish in its importance—it simply became more serious about its usefulness. For the next few years, few new Web IPOs generated significant media buzz, and the Web began to find its true comfort zone in a new business environment.

The turn of the century had brought with it significant improvements in technology. Full color monitors were now the standard, allowing designers to broaden their canvas beyond the 216 Web-safe color standard. Faster connection speeds through cable lines, dedicated T1 lines, and other broadband options made surfing the Web faster. As more businesses and homes adapted to these standards, developers could worry less about file size, allowing more information and interactivity to be present on their sites. Graphic designers finally got cheesy animated GIFs, bevels, and embosses out of their systems, Web programmers and graphic designers learned how to communicate with each other, and a new array of better, more marketing-relevant Web sites began to appear. Figures 1-3 through 1-9 highlight some surprising "before and after" sites. Security enhancements improved e-commerce functionality, and slowly but surely, consumers gained confidence in making purchases online (see Figure 1-10). Companies of all sizes began to understand better how to use the Web as a marketing tool. In short, the Web, and people's understanding of it, began to mature.

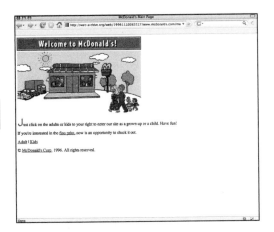

Figure 1-3 McDonald's was apparently going the more kid-friendly route with its first Web site, designing a page that looked like it came from a coloring book.

Figure 1-4 Pepsi's original designer pulled out all the stops, with bevels, embosses, and an extremely distracting background. Pepsi's newest site is about as cool as a consumer brand can get and definitely worth a visit.

Figure 1-5 NBC's peacock couldn't have been that proud of the original effort, which contained very little information compared to today's version which is a virtual dashboard of info.

Figure 1-6 Interestingly, Yahoo's original site design looked a little more like Google's current site looks.

Figure 1-7 It took years before the news media really understood how to best use the Web.

Figure 1-8 Apple's latest site is cool and sleek, representative of its brand. The same can't exactly be said for the newsletter style layout of its original Web site.

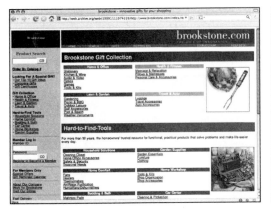

Figure 1-9 Brookstone's original site offered e-commerce capabilities, but didn't quite drive a user to action. Its latest site takes far better advantage of page space for marketing and moving product.

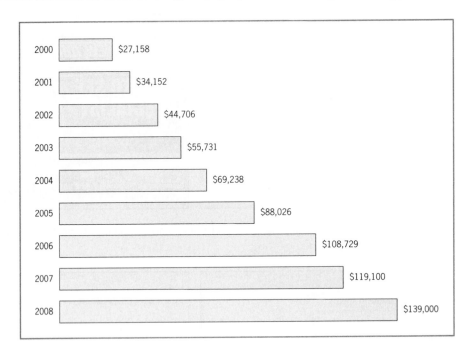

Year	Sales
2000	$27,158
2001	$34,152
2002	$44,706
2003	$55,731
2004	$69,238
2005	$88,026
2006	$108,729
2007	$119,100
2008	$139,000

Figure 1-10 E-commerce retail sales growth 2000–2008. Figures in millions.
SOURCE: U.S. Census Bureau, Department of Commerce, Aug. 2008.

More importantly, a new generation was growing up with the Web as an everyday part of their lives. They were learning to use it not only for basic research purposes, but for communication and entertainment, as well. Network television, long a leading source of family entertainment, suffered greatly. The four major networks, which commanded the attention of 90% of all TV viewers in 1980,[14] saw their audience share drop to 32% by 2005, while online video sharing sites like YouTube continue to grow.[15] (Web usage is only one reason that network TV viewership has declined. Increased DVR usage, console video game systems, and competition from cable networks are also contributing factors.)

As this new crop of "Webgeners" has entered the workforce, the Web has continued to become further ingrained in the development of relationships, both personal and business.

Figure 1-11 provides a detailed timeline of important benchmarks in the history of the Web from 2002 and 2007.

2002

MARCH 15   **MACROMEDIA FLASH PLAYER 6 RELEASED**

Released as part of Macromedia Flash MX, Flash Player 6 is the first version of the popular vector-based animation program that supports video files. Later evolutions would produce the FLV container format, and serve as the basis for popular video sites such as YouTube, Google Video, and MyPod Studios.

2003

APRIL   **SECOND LIFE LAUNCHES PUBLIC BETA**

Developed by Linden Labs, Second Life is a social media network set in a 3D landscape. Using Second Life currency, the Linden Dollar, users can purchase land, build homes and stores, and create virtual businesses. Although not as popular as other globally-recognized social media sites like MySpace, Second Life generates significant media attention because of its unique graphical approach to socializing on the Web.

APRIL 28   **APPLE LAUNCHES iTUNES**

With the support of every major music publisher, Apple changes the entire music industry with the launch of iTunes.

JULY   **MYSPACE LAUNCHED**

Tom Anderson and Chris DeWolfe lead a small group of programmers in building one of the first widely used social networking sites, allowing users to personalize their own pages, upload photos, music files, and videos, and write blog entries. By 2006 it has over 100 million users. *The Guardian* noted that if MySpace were its own country, it would be 10th largest in the world, right behind Mexico.

OCTOBER   **INFORMATION OVERLOAD**

A study by researchers Peter Lyman and Hal Varian at the University of California at Berkely determined that:

- An average of 800 MB of recorded information is produced per person each year (that's for the entire world—all 6.3 billion of us).
- The Web contains about 170 terabytes of information—17 times the size of the Library of Congress print collections.
- About 5 billion messages are sent via instant messaging—each day.

Figure 1-11   Timeline of the Web 2002–2007. SOURCE: "Fifteen Years of the Web." BBC News <news.bbc.co.uk/1/hi/technology> 5 Aug. 2006. (*continues*)

(continued)

2004

JANUARY 27   **AMAZON.COM POSTS A PROFIT**

Proving that heavily funded sites can generate a positive ROI, Amazon.com lifts investor confidence by posting its first full year profit.

FEBRUARY   **SOCIAL NETWORKING SITE FACEBOOK LAUNCHED**

APRIL 7   **VIRAL MARKETING GETS ATTENTION**

In what many people consider to be the first real example of a major brand utilizing the viral aspect of the Web to draw an audience, Burger King launches subservientchicken.com. The site, which allows people to give orders to a man in a chicken suit, underscores Burger King's "have it your way" message and garners over 46 million hits in one week, with an average visit time of 8 minutes.

AUGUST 19   **GOOGLE GOES PUBLIC**

Originally offered at $85.15, shares skyrocket to nearly $750 per share by November of 2007.

NOVEMBER 9   **MOZILLA FIREFOX WEB BROWSER LAUNCHED**

2005

FEBRUARY   **YOU ARE ON THE AIR**

Video-sharing site YouTube goes online as streaming technology comes of age and more people search the Web using faster connection speeds.

OCTOBER   **WEB GROWTH SURGES**

17 million new sites go online, as the Web grows more in 2005 than all of the years during the dot-com boom put together.

2006

AUGUST   **AOL SWITCHES GEARS**

Unable to gain traction as a service provider in the broadband world, AOL announces a dramatic shift in business strategy, eliminating its monthly fee-based services and concentrating on being a media provider with an ad-based revenue stream.

OCTOBER   **NUMBER OF WEB SITES SURPASSES 92,000,000**

2007

FEBRUARY   **APPLE REACHES THE ONE BILLION iTUNES DOWNLOAD BENCHMARK**

APRIL   **GOOGLE HOLDS TOP SPOTS**

FT.com ranks Google as the most valuable global brand, surpassing Microsoft. Google is also the most visited Web site.

Figure 1-11   Timeline of the Web 2002–2007. SOURCE: "Fifteen Years of the Web." BBC News <news.bbc.co.uk/1/hi/technology> 5 Aug. 2006.

Social Networking on the Web: Its Impact on Relationships and Marketing

If you're reading this book, chances are you have a MySpace or Facebook page, run your own blog, have commented on someone else's blog, left a review on a product or entertainment Web site, have a profile on a dating Web site, have posted a video on YouTube, communicated via e-mail, or sent an instant message to a friend. If you have, then congratulations—you're officially a part of the social networking revolution.

Of course, the Web didn't invent social networking. A **social network** can exist in the physical world in a variety of situations. Wikipedia (which itself is a social network) defines a social network, as of June 2008, as:

. . . a social structure made of nodes (which are generally individuals or organizations) that are tied by one or more specific types of interdependency, such as values, visions, idea, financial exchange, friends, kinship, dislike, conflict, trade, Web links, sexual relations, disease transmission (epidemiology), or airline routes.

Wikipedia then goes on to explain more about social networks:

Research in a number of academic fields has shown that social networks operate on many levels, from families up to the level of nations, and play a critical role in determining the way problems are solved, organizations are run, and the degree to which individuals succeed in achieving their goals.[16]

Figure 1-12 provides a visual representation of a social network.

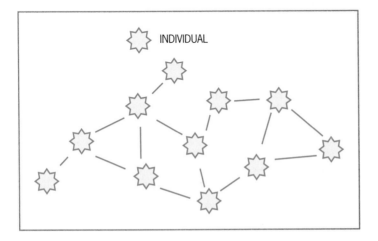

Figure 1-12   A visual depiction of social networking.

15

While social networks date back to the exchange of meaningful grunts at community cave gatherings, the term has increasingly become part of our vocabulary as more social media sites and applications have been introduced on the Web. **Social media** is the umbrella term used for all of the Web tools and applications used to socialize on the Web. These tools include social networking sites, message boards, blogs, wikis, podcasts, instant messaging, online forums, photo and video sharing, e-mail, and more. Social networking on the Web, however, differs dramatically from practically any other social networking community in history, in three distinct ways. First, it allows people to communicate with others while maintaining their anonymity. In many cases, this anonymity has allowed people to develop a separate "cyber life" persona, often times far different from the person they present themselves to be in a "real life" social setting. In his online book *The Psychology of Cyberspace*, John Suler, Ph.D., a clinical psychologist and professor at Rider University, writes:

It's well known that people say and do things in cyberspace that they wouldn't ordinarily say or do in the face-to-face world. They loosen up, feel more uninhibited, and express themselves more openly. Researchers call this the "disinhibition effect." It's a double-edged sword. Sometimes people share very personal things about themselves. They reveal secret emotions, fears, wishes. Or they show unusual acts of kindness and generosity. We may call this benign disinhibition.

On the other hand, the disinhibition effect may not be so benign. Out spills rude language and harsh criticisms, anger, hatred, even threats. Or people explore the dark underworld of the Internet, places of pornography and violence, places they would never visit in the real world. We might call this *toxic disinhibition*.[17]

Dr. Suler notes that there are many reasons that the anonymity of the Web permeates the individual user and alters their behavior, including the sheer invisibility offered by the ability to hide one's name, age, and other vital statistics; the cathartic effect of being able to vent one's feelings and then leave an online conversation or situation as quickly as it takes to close a browser window; and the equalization of status in an online environment.

You might ask, "So what?" So people's behavior changes when they go online. This isn't a psychology class; it's a Web marketing class. However, at its very heart, marketing *is* the study of behavior, and online marketers (and Web developers) need to understand the subtleties of behavioral change in their audience when trying to reach someone through an online effort.

INTERVIEW WITH...
John Suler

One of the most valuable assets a marketer has is information. Understanding their target audience and how they act is important in determining how to reach them most effectively with the most compelling message. But are groups and individuals the same online as they are in "real life," even within the same demographic categories? As social media networks and tools gain popularity, our social behaviors are changing, which ultimately may affect how we mold our marketing messages.

Dr. John Suler is a leading voice in the growing study of "cyber psychology"—the study of how individuals and groups behave on the Internet. He has authored numerous online books, including *The Psychology of Cyberspace*, and provides some insight into how, if at all, the Internet is changing human behavior and socialization.

Jason: Do you find that people use their online personalities to represent themselves as they really are, or in the way they want to be perceived?

John: Some people create online personalities that might be very close to their real world identity, while others present themselves as being much closer to their ideal identity. It's similar to a Halloween party. The costume that the person chooses is in some way a representation of some aspect of their identity, something that they wish to be. It's an interesting experiment in identity manipulation.

Jason: But a Halloween party comes around once a year. On the Internet, the masquerade party goes on infinitely.

John: That's right. Sort of like a parallel lifestyle for some people. For many people, it's literally their second life. They have their in-person lifestyle and then they have their online lifestyle. They create an online identity that can be very different from the way they are in their face-to-face life. You could argue about whether their online self is their really true self or a false self. It may be an expression of who they really are, or some underlying need or wish. Most people online really want to establish connections, correspondences, friendships, or even romances.

John: As people put in more hours on the Web and the Web becomes more of a social playground, are they losing their ability to interact in person?

John: For some people that does happen. Some people have so much trouble with in-person relationships that they are drawn to online fantasy environments or the safety of being able to click out of a relationship very easily. It's possible that they may even resort to that and become even more deficient in their face-to-face relationships. But in some ways, online interaction could possibly enhance our face-to-face relationships. For people who aren't naturally comfortable in real-life social situations—and there are a lot of people who fall into that category—going online and having an opportunity to interact with people through text gives them more control over what they're saying, and time to compose their reply. This allows them to feel better about themselves and how they relate to other people, and to develop skills in conversing with people.

JASON: That being said, JWT conducted a survey, and found that 28% of Web users say they spend less time with their friends in real life because of Web use. Do you feel that those numbers are representative of Web audiences, and if so, do you expect this to continue?

JOHN: It's a new form of entertainment—the Web is a complex environment with information, social opportunities, and buying. People are so drawn to the Web that it's taking up more of their time, and taking time away from other activities including their relationships with friends and family. I believe that will change over time. The Internet is here to stay. Over time I think people will get used to it, and there will be more of a balance in how people use it.

JASON: How strong are cyber relationships? Are they as strong and meaningful as relationships that have formed in real life?

JOHN: Some people will swear that their online relationships are more pure than an in-person relationship, and they are more powerful because it's people encountering one another without having to worry about how a person looks, talks, or smells. They feel like it is a mind meeting another mind online, and that's a very powerful and very meaningful relationship.

JASON: Based on the culmination of all of the research that you've done, give me a glimpse as to how you think human social behavior will change be as social media networks expand.

JOHN: The online world is going to be as complex, rich, deep, and nuance-filled as offline life, and people are going to choose the kind of online style that's right for them. Some people go online and they want to do sports fantasy games or shop. Some people want to go online because they want a second life and an imaginary world. I think we're going to see specialized alignments to address particular interests.

You see that already. I think that those things are going to become even more complex. You're also going to see a growth in communicating beyond the keyboard and through video conversing technology. There will be all sorts of remote interaction where you can cue your keyboard and move a physical presence in another environment, maybe to even interact physically with another person. We already have that technology in a primitive form. I think we'll see an increase in that sort of interaction among people.

The second aspect in which social networking on the Web is dramatically different from more traditional social networks is **reach**—the amount of people who may be exposed to a message or site. No other forum in the history of the world has allowed conversations to take place, ideas to be shared, and relationships to be forged on such a vast scale as the Internet. With the right effort, savvy marketers can harness the power of cyber social networks to spread their message to untapped audiences, often on a smaller budget than they might spend on more traditional marketing campaigns. **Traditional marketing** includes advertising in print publications such as magazines and newspapers, running TV or radio commercials, sending direct mail ads, or other such efforts.

For all of the opportunities that marketers have to spread their message over the Web, real and present danger lurks in the third distinct difference between Web and real world social networks, which is absolute permanence. While the right message can ignite a spark beneath a brand and dramatically increase sales and exposure, a single misstep spreads just as quickly. It also stays around for good, doing long-lasting and possible irreversible damage to the brand. As Chapter 7 explains in greater detail, a **brand** is more than just a product or a service or the company behind it (although we often use the term in those ways throughout this book). Ultimately, a brand is really the combination of reputation based on past performance and consumer expectation of future results. In the lifecycle of a brand, both of these elements will be positively or negatively impacted by a variety of things, including news reports. Negative news, transmitted via traditional media outlets like TV, radio, or print, can have a harmful, but typically limited, impact on a brand, given that people's attention spans are similarly limited. Once negative news finds its way onto the Web, however, not even a team of high-powered lawyers can make it all disappear. Once uploaded, it can haunt a brand for a very long time.

Later, we will examine brands that have faltered due to their misuse of social media and Web marketing.

Trends and Demographic Breakdowns

So who's out there? What are they doing? As a site developer, you're always going to want to keep the marketing aspect in mind. Understanding usage trends and **demographics** (the population characteristics such as age, gender, education, and others that define particular markets) is vital to the development of an effective Web site and to the formulation of a successful marketing strategy. Table 1-1 shows a wide range of relevant data for Internet usage during the year 2007. Figure 1-13 shows historic growth rates from 1995–2007, when it seems to have leveled off.

Gender	Uses the Internet
Men	71%
Women	70%

Age Group	Uses the Internet
18–29	87%
30–49	83%
50–64	65%
65 +	32%

Race/Ethnicity	Uses the Internet
White, non-hispanic	73%
Black, non-hispanic	62%
English speaking hispanic	78%

Geography	Uses the Internet
Urban	73%
Suburban	73%
Rural	60%

Household Income	Uses the Internet
Less than $30,000/yr	55%
$30,000–$49,999	69%
$50,000–$74,999	82%
$75,000 +	93%

Highest Education Level	Uses the Internet
Less than high school	40%
High school	61%
Some college	81%
College +	91%

Table 1-1 Internet user general demographics—2007. SOURCE: "Demographics of Internet Users." Pew Internet and American Life Project, 15 Jun. 2007.

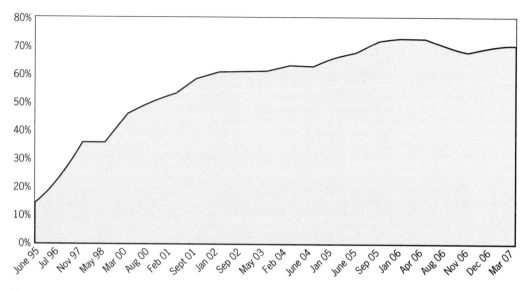

Figure 1-13 Historic growth rates in Internet usage from 1995–2007. SOURCE: "Demographics of Internet Users." The Pew Internet & American Life Project, 15 Jun. 2007.

From the data in Table 1-1 it is clear that while men and women use the Internet in equal amounts, on a percentage basis, the same can't be said about the age range, where younger people dominate. A dramatic drop in usage is seen in user over age 50, and an even more dramatic drop is seen in users over the age of 65. An inverse usage trend is seen when it comes to household income and education level, as Internet usage increases among households earning more income and individuals with higher levels of formal education.

Of course, different sites each have different demographics associated with them, as topics, content, and presentation attracts different audiences. Marketers need to plan their marketing strategies so as to get the most amount of attention from their most desired audience within a certain budget. In order to do so, they must consider the online demographic breakdowns of in order to develop an effective plan of action.

While Table 1-1 shows that Internet usage is high across the entire spectrum of demographic categories, deeper research shows that each set of users may use the Internet very differently from one another—a fact that marketers consider as they develop their sites and marketing strategies. In a December 2005 demographic report, for example, The Pew Internet & American Life Project noted interesting gender differences in Internet usage including:[18]

- Men tend to use the Internet more aggressively, logging on more often, spending more time online, and connecting via broadband more frequently than women.

- Women are more likely to use e-mail to stay in touch with friends and family, sharing personal news, stories, and anecdotes. Men tend to use e-mail more for work-related purposes.

- While men and women both use the Web in equal amounts to buy products and engage in online banking, men are more likely that women to go online to:

  - Pay bills

  - Engage in recreational reading

  - Obtain information on hobbies

  - Participate in auctions

  - Listen to online radio

  - Download music and videos

While distinct differences exist in how men and women use the Internet, other sharp and often profound differences exist between various age groups, with younger users having markedly different uses for the Internet than older users. In a January 2006 report entitled Generations Online by The Pew Internet & American Life Project, Web usage disparities between generations and age groups include:[19]

- Users aged 12-17 are far more likely than any other age group to use the Internet for online game playing. This group is also more likely to play games than do anything else online.

- Instant messaging becomes less frequent with each older age group. Three quarters of all 12-17 year olds use IM for regular communication, while only one quarter of online seniors over 70 engage in IM chat.

- Younger generations (under age 29) are more likely to spend time online downloading music, watching videos, or creating blogs, while adults over age 29 are more likely to spend their time online making travel reservations, searching for health related information, engaging in online banking, or doing job-related research.

And what about marketers? New methods of communicating have altered the way they have developed their strategies. **Public relations**, which is the branch of marketing that concentrates on spreading a message through mass media, has virtually reinvented itself. "PR 2.0" involves reaching out to a global market using social media tactics such as blog comments, e-mail, and **message board threads**. (A message board is a Web site on which people can post a comment or question on a variety of topics, and other users can post responses; a thread is the grouping of messages, hierarchically by topic.) Because of the potential geographic scope of a single online conversation, marketers have been proactive in trying to include their product names in these discussions as part of their frontline marketing campaigns.

Today's aggressive brands consider the Web a vital weapon in their fight to gain market share. In fact, a 2007 report by *Inc.* magazine reveals that two out of three companies on the *Inc.* 500 (which ranks the 500 fastest-growing private companies) consider Web-based social media as either "somewhat important" or "very important" to their future marketing strategies.[20] Figure 1-14 shows the breakdown of multiple Web tools and at what rate they are being adopted by companies in the *Inc.* 500 as part of their mass marketing efforts.

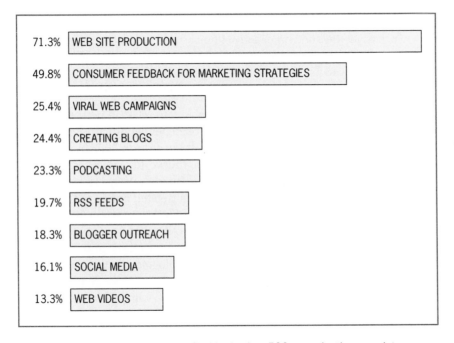

71.3%	WEB SITE PRODUCTION
49.8%	CONSUMER FEEDBACK FOR MARKETING STRATEGIES
25.4%	VIRAL WEB CAMPAIGNS
24.4%	CREATING BLOGS
23.3%	PODCASTING
19.7%	RSS FEEDS
18.3%	BLOGGER OUTREACH
16.1%	SOCIAL MEDIA
13.3%	WEB VIDEOS

Figure 1-14 How marketers profiled in the *Inc.* 500 are adopting a variety of Web tools. SOURCE: Schweitzer, Tamara. "*Inc.* 500 Companies Fast Adopters of Social Media." Inc.com 9 Feb. 2007 <www.inc.com>.

Where Do We Go from Here?

The future of the Web remains wide open. More powerful computers, advanced programming languages, and faster connection speeds have given marketers and developers a new landscape in which to explore creative ideas. This has, in turn, given rise to various predictions about what that landscape will look like in the future. This is especially potent in a world where conversations and ideas can be shared across divides that separate not only continents and countries, but generations, socio-economic classes, races, religions, and industries as well. If a single person can come up with a groundbreaking idea, the world will have to brace itself for the innovations that an ongoing global brainstorm session could potentially create.

One prediction for the future that is generating growing debate is that, thanks to the Web, English will become a global language, slowly but surely squeezing other languages out. Currently, an estimated 500 million to one billion people around the world speak English as their first or second language. That figure could balloon to two billion in less than a decade thanks to expanding American cultural influences and advertising and growing global social networks.[21] As reported by the *International Herald Tribune* in an August 2006 report entitled "English, Now the Global Language, Drifts from its Roots," the president of Iran tried to stem the tide by banning words like "chat" and "pizza." At the same time, native French speaker Jacques Levy, of the Swiss Federal Institute of Technology, was quoted as saying, "It's a lost cause to try to fight against the tide. It could have been another language; it was Greek, then Latin, French, now it is English."[22]

Another prediction is that society's ability to relate in personal settings will deteriorate as people become dependent on the comfort that a virtual environment offers. A survey done in 2007 by JWT (formerly J. Walter Thompson), one of the world's largest advertising agencies, found that only 18% of active Internet users claimed they could go a week or more without feeling isolated due to not having Internet access, while 36% could only last a day or two. A full 28% acknowledged that they spent less time out with friends in favor of more time online.[23] As broadband connection speeds find their way into more homes and social networking, blogging, and streaming video mature, it's reasonable to assume that our dependency on the Web and the role it plays in our relationships will only increase.

Similarly, it is likely that the Web will weave its way into our lives far outside the boundaries of a personal computer. **GPS** (Global Positioning System, a satellite-based navigation system often installed in cars or on cell phones to generate maps and directions) is already becoming a standard feature in many vehicles, as is Internet radio. That's just the tip of the iceberg. As you read this, your local Shop Rite supermarket may be changing forever how you shop for groceries. In a pilot program starting on the east coast, Microsoft has designed a shopping cart system that allows users to e-mail their shopping cart in advance, and with the help of an on-cart monitor, lays out a map of the store pinpointing where each of your items can be found.[24] This will open up new doors for advertisers, who can pay for the right to have the cart recommend their brand or alert shoppers to sales on certain items as they pass them on the shelves.

As savvier marketers see greater opportunity for reaching a global audience, site developers will begin to attract more advertisers through increased standardization. Traditional commercial television advertising, for example, whether on CBS, NBC, ABC, FOX, or a cable network, is standard across the board, with typical ad spots running in either 15 or 30 second increments. Similarly, print advertising in publications like *Sports Illustrated*, *Newsweek*, and *People* is standardized. While some minor specifications may change slightly from one title to another, by and large, the requirements are the same. This allows media buyers and ad content developers to create one ad for multiple outlets. Unfortunately, Web advertising has been plagued with a lack of standards. Yahoo, MySpace, Marketwatch, Facebook, and others have their own distinct criteria for banner ad dimensions, video length, file size, and cost calculations. (For example, using the **pay-per-click** method, advertisers are charged a pre-set amount every time a Web user clicks on an ad. With the **cost-per-impression** method, advertisers are charged a pre-set amount for each time an ad appears on a site, regardless of whether or not users click on it.) This means that media buyers need to look not only at the pricing structure, reach, and demographics of each site; they must also examine how each specific ad acts (whether it is static, an animated GIF, Flash-based, video, or other) and the unique specifications involved. The Internet Advertising Bureau, an organization supported by many of the largest advertising and media agencies, has been aggressively pushing specific Internet advertising standards for the various types of online ads. Slowly but surely these standards are changing the face of the Web as an advertising medium. Eventually, Web site owners, hungry for advertising revenue, will recognize the Web as a single media and standardize the technical requirements, making the Web a more attractive destination for marketers.

Entertainment will continue to grow with the explosion of streaming Web-based videos. As more people flock to the Web to watch everything from amateur videos to movie trailers, TV networks are feeling the pressure to reach audiences by putting pilots and full episodes of popular shows on the Web. In coming years, this trend will increase, moving beyond single episodes into full seasons of prime time shows. More studio releases will find their way onto the Web, as well, as Netflix and other companies that offer downloadable movies expand their reach.

As more entertainment makes its way on to the PC, the interactive nature of the Web will provide even greater opportunities for marketers through **product placement**, the subtle (and not so subtle) placement of specific brands into the scenes of TV shows and movies. Apple and Coca-Cola are masters of this form of advertising, staying in front of their audience without making a direct pitch. In an interactive arena, product placement will allow users to click on brands when they see them and visit their Web sites immediately.

Chapter Summary

- Since Tim Berners-Lee first introduced the means for links to be made between various pieces of information in 1991, the Web has been on a fast growth track, changing the way both people and brands interact with one another.

- The potential benefits to commerce were quickly noticed by investors, who rushed to fund many new Web site ideas, sending the stock market skyrocketing upward. In 2000, when most of these sites were unable to post a profit, the stock market crashed hard from its peak.

- After the bubble burst, the Web evolved into a more serious marketing tool. Site designs improved, as did technology, connection speeds, and companies' understanding of how to use the Web for marketing purposes. As more people logged on, and new tools such as blogging, streaming video, and social media networks gained popularity, the Web was transformed, facilitating the global exchange of ideas and opinions.

- With an increasing number of people using online social media tools, brands are beginning to include these tools in their marketing strategies. Individuals are also affected, as the Web begins to change the way we represent ourselves and the way we interact with one another offline.

- While the large majority of the U.S. is plugged in, it's clear that the Internet is used differently by people in different demographic categories. The predominant amount of new content is generated by younger users; women use e-mail to stay in touch with friends and family; and men get involved in paying bills and purchasing digital content online. Brands need to consider each of these demographic breakdowns in determining their marketing strategies.

- There are many views on how the Web will evolve in the future, including a prediction that the Web will be the source of a shift to English as a global language. More common predictions concern a paradigm shift in how audiences view entertainment, as online gaming and streaming video gains popularity while network TV viewership continues it steady decline. Online advertising will become standardized, as with TV and print advertising, and it will become easier for brands to purchase, thus improving ad revenues on popular sites.

Key Terms

brand—Can refer to a company, a product, or service that a company promotes, or the reputation that a company, product, or service has built over time.

burn rate—The rate at which companies spend their available cash.

cost per impression—A method of paying for Web advertising that charges the advertiser a pre-set amount for each time an ad appears on a site, regardless of whether or not users click on it.

demographics—The specific attributes that help define a particular audience. These include age, gender, income, education level, and others.

dot-com—Often used to refer to the large number of investment-driven Web sites that were funded and launched in the mid-to-late 1990s.

GPS—Global Positioning System, a satellite-based navigation system often installed in cars or on cell phones to generate maps and directions.

IPO—Initial Public Offering. The first sale of shares from a private company on a public stock exchange.

message board—A site on which people can post up a comment or question on a variety of topics, and other users can post responses.

pay per click—A method of paying for Web advertising that charges advertisers a pre-set amount for each time a Web user clicks on an ad.

product placement—The subtle (and not so subtle) placement of specific brands into the scenes of TV shows and movies.

public relations—The branch of marketing that concentrates on spreading a message through mass media.

reach—The amount of people that are exposed to a marketing campaign, message, Web site, etc.

social media—The umbrella term for the many tools that allow people to socialize on the Web, such as social networking sites, blogs, wikis, etc.

social network—A social structure made of individuals or organizations that are tied by one or more specific types of interdependency, such as values, visions, ideas, financial exchange, friends, etc.

threads—The grouping of digital messages in a message board, hierarchically by topic.

traditional marketing—Marketing that is not new media-driven, such as print advertising, TV and radio commercials, direct mail, etc.

venture capitalists—Investors who invest cash in new and emerging businesses.

Review Questions

1. Which of the following demographics is most likely to use online bill paying features?

   a. Men

   b. Women

   c. Teens

   d. Senior Citizens

2. What year did the stock market peak, and the original dot-com bubble burst?

   a. 1998

   b. 1999

   c. 2000

   d. 2001

3. Which of the following is least likely to be considered part of "social networking" on the Web?

   a. Having your own site on MySpace

   b. Checking Yahoo for local movie times

   c. Leaving your comments on a popular blog

   d. Meeting someone on a dating Web site

4. When it comes to online advertising, what is most likely to help increase overall revenues?

   a. Standardization of banner ad sizes

   b. Elimination of banner ads in favor of streaming video ads

   c. Improved ad design by graphic designers

   d. Limitations on banner ad animations

5. According to Dr. John Suler, the effects of socializing on the Internet can be most closely related to:

   a. Giving charity anonymously at Christmas

   b. Going to a costume party on Halloween

   c. Socializing on New Year's Eve

   d. Going wild on spring break

6. Which of the following contributed the least to the growth of the Web?

   a. CERN's announcement on April 30, 1993

   b. Improving technology

   c. Faster connection times

   d. Google's purchase of YouTube

7. In the 1990s, the "browser wars" were fought between:

   a. Netscape and Internet Explorer

   b. AOL and Internet Explorer

   c. Netscape and Firefox

   d. Mosaic and Internet Explorer

8. Cadabra.com was the original name of which of the following Web sites?

   a. Yahoo!

   b. MySpace

   c. Amazon.com

   d. eBay

9. The first Web browser was called:

   a. Mosaic

   b. AOL

   c. Internet Explorer

   d. Netscape

10. Women are more likely than men to:

   a. Listen to online radio

   b. Download music

c. Use e-mail for work purposes

d. Send e-mail to friends

11. Internet users under age 29 least often use the Web for:

a. Job-related research

b. Starting a blog

c. Listening to music

d. Watching videos

12. Which of the following demographic categories uses the Internet the least?

a. People with less than a high school education

b. People over age 65

c. People whose household income is less than $30,000/year

d. English-speaking Hispanics

13. Blog creation is in the marketing strategies for what percentage of companies?

a. 49.8%

b. 24.4%

c. 19.7%

d. 16.1%

14. Which of the following aspects of the Web is the biggest danger to brands?

a. News can easily get lost in a sea of information

b. Bad news can remain online forever

c. Web users take brands less seriously

d. People have a negative reaction to banner ads

15. Social networks on the Web differ from more traditional, "real life" social networks in which three ways?

a. Reach, anonymity, and ambiguity

b. Reach, permanence, and indifference

c. Reach, anonymity, and permanence

d. Indifference, anonymity, and ambiguity

16. According to *Inc.* magazine, roughly what percentage of the fastest growing companies considers social media a "somewhat important" or "very important" part of their future marketing strategies?

   a. 33%

   b. 50%

   c. 66%

   d. 75%

17. Put the following in the order in which they were launched, from first to last:

   a. MySpace

   b. Wikipedia

   c. Facebook

   d. iTunes

18. Which number is highest?

   a. Total number of Web sites online as of October 2006

   b. Number of instant messages sent in a single day

   c. Total number of MySpace users as of 2006

   d. Total number of iTunes downloads as of February 2007

19. How much would a single share of Google have cost you if you bought it when it first went public?

   a. $85.15

   b. $115.78

   c. $750.90

   d. $786.22

20. According to FT.com, as of 2007, which is ranked as the most valuable brand?

   a. Apple

   b. Microsoft

   c. Google

   d. McDonald's

Projects

1. Over the next week, keep an accurate log of everything you do on the Internet. Calculate the percent of time you spend:

   • communicating via instant messenger or e-mail

   • networking on a social media site like MySpace or Facebook

   • watching online videos

   • doing research for school

   • engaging in other online activities

   Compare your total time online to the total amount of time you spend doing offline activities, such as watching television, going out with friends, reading a book, etc.

   Based on these findings, write a one-page synopsis of the role that the Internet plays in your life.

2. Many business analysts have called the growth of social media sites, blogs, and streaming video a second Web bubble and have compared it to the original Web bubble of the late 1990s. Write a three-page report that explains whether you believe the social networking revolution represents a second Web bubble or if the media is creating baseless hype. Consider facts including stock market activity, number of new sites being launched, etc. Make sure to reference all findings.

3. Select one of the following dot-com companies that went bankrupt in the original Web bubble:

   • Webvan

   • eToys.com

   • Pets.com

   • Flooz.com

   • Kozmo.com

   In a report no longer than three pages, summarize the business concept on which the site was based, the market it intended to reach, and why you think it failed. Do you think that if the site you chose had launched after 2005, it would have had a better chance of succeeding? Why or why not?

4. Interview five of your classmates about their Internet usage. Develop a set of 5 questions, such as:

- How often do they use the Internet?

- What type of sites do they use?

- Do they use it for entertainment? Blogging? Research?

   Then interview five people over the age 35 and ask them the same questions. How, if at all, do the generations differ? Are there any differences in gender usage? What other demographic differences do you notice?

5. Using your programming knowledge and your own use of the Internet, write a two-page report on what you think the Internet will be like ten years from now.

Endnotes

1. Holahan, Catherine. "So I Married an Avatar." *BusinessWeek*, 14 Feb. 2008.
2. "Survey of Internet Activities." Pew Internet & American Life Project, Dec. 2007.
3. "Issues in Labor Statistics." U.S. Department of Labor, Mar. 1999.
4. "Fifteen Years of the Web." BBC News, 5 Aug. 2006.
5. "July 2008 Web Survey Results." *Netcraft*, Jul. 2008.
6. "Trends in Venture Capital Funding in the 1990s." U.S. Small Business Administration, Office of Advocacy, Aug. 1997.
7. Ibid.
8. U.S. Department of Labor, Bureau of Labor Statistics, Aug. 2008.
9. German, Kent. "Top 10 dot-com flops." *CNET* <www.cnet.com> 21 Aug. 2008.
10. Ibid.
11. Ibid.
12. Ibid.
13. Ibid.
14. "The big three's prime-time decline: a technological and social context." Entrepreneur.com <www.entrepreneur.com> 1 Mar. 2008.
15. "Alexa." <www.alexa.com> 1 Mar. 2008.
16. "Social Network." Wikipedia <http://en.wikipedia.org/wiki/Social_network> 17 Aug. 2008.
17. Suler, John, Ph.D., "The Psychology of Cyberspace." <http://www-usr.rider.edu/~suler/psycyber/psycyber.html> Jan. 2006.
18. Fallows, Deborah. "How Women and Men Use the Internet." Pew Internet & American Life Project, 28 Dec. 2005.
19. Fox, Susannah, et al., "Generations Online." Pew Internet & American Life Project, 22 Jan. 2006.

34

20. Schweitzer, Tamara. "*Inc.* 500 Companies Fast Adopters of Social Media." Inc.com <www.inc.com> 9 Feb. 2007.

21. Cohen, Noam. "English, Now the Global Language, Drifts from its Roots." *International Herald Tribune*, 8 Aug. 2006.

22. Ibid.

23. "U.S. Users Seriously Addicted to Internet, Cell Phones." *JWT*, Sept. 2007.

24. "Microsoft bringing ads to shopping carts." CNN.com <www.cnn.com> 14 Jan. 2008.

CHAPTER 2

Types of Web Sites

In this chapter you will learn about:

◎ The roles and responsibilities behind the development of a Web site

◎ The different types of sites that make up the Web, how each differs from the other, and how marketers can take advantage of each type of site

Within the interconnected tangle of links that makes up the Web, millions of sites vary from each other not just in how they are designed, but in their purpose. As you develop, program, and market Web sites, it is important to understand all of the different types of sites, the audiences they hope to reach, and how marketers can use different sites to build their brands.

The People Behind a Web Site

Before examining the different types of sites on the Web, let's take a quick look at the people behind a Web site. The cast of characters that come together to make a site come alive varies considerably depending on the site. In the following sections, we will discuss the roles and responsibilities of the people often involved in the development of a Web site.

Owners

These are the people who get the ball rolling. They have the initial idea. They own the company, and they organize the team of people who will come together to make the site happen. A successful site owner will wear many different hats. They are visionaries who have a clear idea of the type of site they want to build and the audience they want to reach. They are strong negotiators who can arrange the best deal with venture capitalists and secure the necessary funding to get the site up and running. They are good communicators, who can express their ideas clearly to the people who will put it all together. Finally, successful Web site owners are strong motivators and managers; they are able to assemble the best possible team and rally that team to do the best possible job developing the site.

Venture Capitalists

Most established businesses, like restaurants, retailers, and manufacturers, use their marketing budget to develop their Web sites, which are used to support and supplement their core business. Web-based companies that do not have an offline component often do not have the necessary funds to hire the staff to program the site, purchase necessary inventory, or effectively market the site. Venture capitalists provide the monetary resources necessary for getting some of these sites going. Many people have exciting ideas for new sites, and there is strong competition for a finite amount of money. Venture capitalists want to see a solid business plan for a site and will usually hold a series of investigative meetings with the company's owners before they will make an investment.

Creative Directors

The creative director works with the site owner to understand the purpose of the site and identify any specific features required. Creative directors then develop the vision for the site—the concept, look and feel, layout, mood, and message—before conveying that vision to other team members who will then execute it. Creative directors will usually develop a **site schematic** (see Figure 2-1), which is a diagram that establishes the navigational elements and organization of the site.

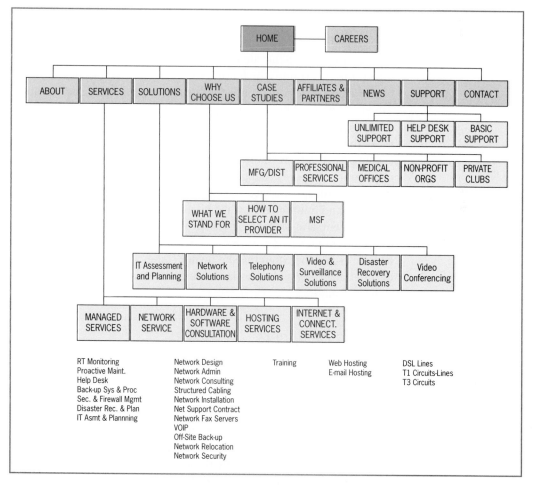

Figure 2-1 A sample schematic. The schematic provides the blueprint for how the pages of a site will link to one another and how content will be distributed.

Account and Project Managers

The development of any Web site involves a lot of moving parts that need to work together. Account managers act as the central point of contact for the entire team and manage the development process so that the final site meets the required specifications and is completed on time. Account managers ensure that deadlines and benchmarks are met, individual site elements pass quality control standards, and progress reports, approvals, and opinions are communicated among the team members. If the site is particularly large, a broader team may be required. In that case, project managers will be assigned to specific projects within the development umbrella and will report their progress back to the account manager.

Programmers

Programmers make the site happen. They confer with the creative director to determine which creative visions are feasible, based on financial and time constraints. Once the site needs have been established, the team of programmers determines the best programming languages to use (or how best to use the languages they know) to make the site come to life. Programmers also work closely with the account managers, who often do not understand the complexities of programming or the length of time needed to complete projects, in order to set appropriate deadlines. Programmers test the site for accuracy and functionality, warn of any potential problems with site development, and provide regular progress reports. It also falls to the programmers to determine how to adjust and alter the work they have already done when the site owner comes up with a new idea (as often happens with visionaries) and wants to make a radical, last minute change.

Graphic Designers

Graphic designers take the creative director's vision and interpret it artistically. Using programs like Photoshop and Illustrator, they make sure that all elements of the site properly represent the company for which the site is being developed (through careful use of colors, font treatments, and image styles). Graphic designers also produce the necessary graphics in the format requested by the site's programmers. Most commonly these formats are either .GIF or .JPG, depending upon the need for transparency, color accuracy, photography or illustration, file size, and other factors. If the site is to include Flash elements, then a designer trained in Flash development will provide graphics, animations, and interactive features in the appropriate Flash format. Usually, graphic designers will have to work closely with the programmers to understand how the site will be developed (for instance, the cell dimensions within a table), so that the designers can properly slice large graphics into the appropriate smaller segments.

Copywriters

Quality content is what makes a site interesting and informative. Sometimes the most time-consuming and daunting task in developing a new site is the creation of the content. Copywriters are assigned the responsibility of writing new and compelling content that will capture the audience's interest and deliver an appropriate message. Usually, copywriters work with either the site owner or the creative director to determine the content needs of the site. In addition, copywriters partner with the graphic designers to balance the amount of copy to be written with the available space for copy. This partnership is important in order to avoid a potentially frustrating catch-22: graphic designers are unable to design without knowing how much copy will be included, and copywriters are unsure how much copy to write without knowing how much space the graphic designer will allot for text.

Marketers

A site's marketers are responsible for promoting the site and driving traffic to it. How they go about this will largely be a function of the site's target market, and available marketing budget. The strategies and tools available to marketers in their efforts to drive Web site traffic are reviewed in greater detail in Chapter 11.

The size, complexity, and budget of a site will help determine the team required for its development. Not all sites will require all of the people listed above. For smaller sites, the site owner may also act as the account manager, and the creative director may fulfill the responsibilities of the graphic designer. No matter how large the site and the team of people assembled to create it, the needs that all of these roles fulfill will have to be met.

Types of Web Sites

Different types of sites serve different purposes; each provides a unique opportunity to marketers. The type of Web site you build depends on the purpose of the site, the market you want to reach, and whether the site will be used to support an existing business or function as a business unto itself. In the following sections, we will cover the primary types of site that currently exist on the Web.

Web Portals

A **Web portal** is a site that helps users locate information that is dispersed throughout the Web; a portal presents and organizes information regarding other sites. Typically, this is done through a **search engine**, which is a program that allows users to find documents based on keywords that they enter into a text field. The portal will scour the Web for pages that include the desired keywords and, almost instantaneously, present a list of relevant pages. Most portals do not divulge the specific weighting system used for compiling their search results or how sites are ranked. However, the indices are usually created using a variety of criteria, including information contained in the HTML code, such as the <title> and <meta> tags, copy found within the body of a site, the popularity (based on site traffic) of a given site, and links to and from a site. A search can return thousands of pages of results containing millions of individual Web pages that include matches to the requested keywords. Because of this, a niche segment within the marketing industry has arisen that provides services to help companies get their URL's listed in the coveted "Top 10"—the first ten results sent back by search engines (usually page one of the results).

In order to be categorized as a true Web portal, a site needs to provide easy access to other sites—not just information about its own site. Google, for example, is the largest and most visited portal[1], and each search for information results in the listing of sites from all corners of the Web. Online superstore Amazon would not count as a portal. Even though it has a powerful keyword-based search engine that visitors use to search for information, the results provided are links only to products that Amazon sells on its own site.

As the starting point for many Web users, portals have become more than just a means of finding information through search engines. Portals also serve as a one-stop resource for tools, information, and links. Some portals, such as Google, allow users to select the type of tools and information (if any) they would like to appear on the Home page of the site each time they return. Other portals, like Yahoo! and AOL, have a set offering of tools and information like e-mail, headline news, stock tickers, product sales, popular videos, and more already built into their framework. Figure 2-2 shows how Google offers the user numerous options for tools to include on a customized Home page, and Figure 2-3 shows the Yahoo Home page, which has a pre-set Home page with less user customization available.

Figure 2-2 Google allows users to select the information they want to appear on their personalized Home page.

Figure 2-3 The Yahoo Home page comes with pre-set information.

A standard Web portal collects and presents connections to other sites based on keyword matching or other links within its pages. A **distributed Web portal** collects information from Web sites and other portals based on a central theme. SimplyHired.com (see Figure 2-4), for example, gives visitors the opportunity to search for jobs posted by companies and organizations across the Web through a keyword-based search engine. A search on the Simply-Hired site returns links to job postings on individual company sites and other online job search sites.

Figure 2-4 Simply Hired is a distributed Web portal that collects job listings from individual Web sites and other job search portals.

Niche portals are similar to distributed Web portals in that they focus on a specific topic. However, niche portals largely provide their own content and allow users to search both on and off the site for relevant information. There are niche portals online for practically any interest that is shared by enough people to support a site. Figure 2-5 features ESPN.com, a niche portal for people interested in sports information.

Competition in the Web portal business has been fierce from the early commercialization of the Web. A large percentage of the online population visits a portal on a regular basis. According to Alexa.com, a rating site for the Web, three of the top four most popular Web sites based on traffic rates are portals as defined in this section.[2] The revenue generated on portal sites can be immense (Yahoo reported

Figure 2-5 ESPN.com is a niche portal specifically for sports-related topics such as major league and college level team information, scores, highlights, and commentary.

revenues of $6.4 billion in 2006), and acts as a strong lure for new entrants in the field.[3]

B2B (Business to Business)

One of the most common types of Web sites is a **B2B** (business to business) site. B2B involves one business marketing and selling products and services to other businesses. Many businesses generate their revenue solely by serving other businesses. Advertising agencies, for example, are not interested in reaching out to individual consumers. To make their money, they need to catch the attention of business owners and marketing directors. Payroll administration companies, insurance providers, trucking companies, IT management firms, original equipment manufacturers, employee recognition providers, event managers—the list of businesses that sell goods and services to other businesses is lengthy.

B2B companies typically have a very limited audience that they need to reach, which can pose a significant challenge. A company that provides payroll services, for example, might be able to serve a company with tens of thousands of employees. However, only a few of those employees represent the target market—the handful that work in the Human Resources department, in particular, the department director.

Because B2B sales are more relationship-based, and the sales cycle can be fairly long, B2B sites typically do not have e-commerce functionality. B2B companies tend to focus their Web resources on achieving the following goals:

- Reinforcing their brand name

- Establishing that they understand their clients' "pain points"—the critical issues faced by potential clients in their particular industry and those faced by the decision-making individuals within those companies

- Proving that they can deliver the products and services necessary to ease the aforementioned pain

- Showing themselves to be leaders in their industry

- Moving potential visiting clients to take action by contacting a sales representative

In order to reach these goals, B2B companies focus on creating sites that will capture their audience, present information that makes the company seem established and capable, and encourage users to take further action by contacting a company representative. In developing their sites, B2B companies take many specific and deliberate efforts, including:

- Utilizing copy and information more frequently than graphics and animation

- Using case studies and client testimonials to illustrate how their services can be beneficial to potential clients

- Scheduling educational video Webcasts

- Authoring white papers (authoritative reports) on key industry topics and offering free downloads of those papers via their Web site

- Providing informational brochures in PDF format for easy downloading

- Developing a cyber newsroom that shows how the company has been improving, growing, and evolving (cyber newsrooms are discussed in greater detail in Chapter 11)

- Including an About Us section that details the biographies of key management to evoke trust in the experience and knowledge of the company's leaders

- Offering a password-protected area where clients can log in to review invoices, company files, time sheets, and other account information

- Presenting company contact information, including e-mail links and phone numbers, on an easily accessible contacts page

Unfortunately, many B2B companies do not understand that while their clients are other companies, their target audience is made up of individual people in decision-making positions. In addition, many smaller B2B companies do not have the financial resources to hire the right designers and programmers; therefore, B2B sites have tended to lag behind other sites in terms of aesthetics and development innovation.

CASE STUDY: ERC Dataplus

ERC Dataplus is a B2B company that understands how to build an effective B2B Web site. Located in Norwalk, CT, ERC was founded in 1993 by current CEO, Paul Rathblott, and Vice President of Marketing, Joel Pelzner. Since then, they have been providing technology to help companies manage their application and hiring process for both hourly and managerial employees—a process that can be time-consuming and frustrating for job seekers and employers alike.

ERC's client base is made up of mid-to-large-sized companies that would benefit from services that expedite the interviewing and hiring process. ERC targets the decision makers within the human resources department of prospective organizations in order to sell their services.

To reach this highly specific audience, ERC integrates online and offline strategies, including pay-per-click online ad placement, print and online banner advertising in key industry publication magazines and Web sites, and inclusion in vendor directories. Ultimately, ERC's goal is to land an account through a personal interaction between a salesperson and a potential client. However, ERC's frontline marketing strategy is to drive human resources professionals to the ERC Web site for more information. "There are over 100 competitors in our industry," Pelzner explains, "By and large, most of the larger organizations that we would want as clients already have a technology solution such as ours in place, although not all of them are very happy with them. So there is change taking place. Once a company is committed to changing resources, the first action they'll take is to do research on who's out there, who's delivering the best price, performance, functionality, and so forth. And each time, that research begins on the Internet."

With that in mind, ERC has been careful to create a Web site that builds their brand and caters to a potential client's need for information (as shown in Figure 2-6). ERC does not anticipate that potential clients will be heavy repeat visitors, so the company does its best to capture the audience and deliver key messages as effectively as possible during each visit. To accomplish that, ERC included a variety of tools on the company's Web site, including: live online chat with a sales representative, online product demos, regularly updated corporate news releases, announcements of upcoming events, an online literature

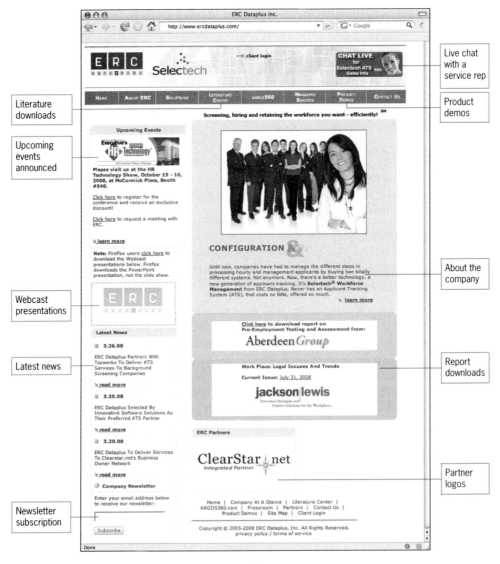

Figure 2-6 The ERC Home page, with important B2B features pointed out.

library for brochure and white paper downloads, and an option to subscribe to a company newsletter. Each of these tactics is meant to promote ERC as a thought leader within their industry, establish the brand as experienced and capable, and encourage a prospective client to take the next step in retaining ERC's services.

Because the Web site plays such a key role in ERC's marketing strategy and sales cycle, they are careful to keep it updated regularly, not only for the benefit of potential clients, but also for existing clients who visit the site to access account-related files through ERC's client admin area. As Pelzner explains, "We need to always make sure that the Web site stays fresh. Years ago, making content changes meant having to write everything in raw HTML, which is a rather laborious process. Now, with content management systems, the way the site's been set up and organized, and with a number of the programming tools that we use, it becomes a lot easier to make those content changes. We don't need extensive technology backgrounds, although we do have Web designers on staff who are in the process of redoing the entire site. I believe that it's important to change the site every year and a half to two years, to keep up with the times, keep the site fresh, and reflect some of the new content that's been developed."

As for many marketers, effectively communicating with the programming staff to create the ideal site has been an important and sometimes challenging task for Pelzner. According to Pelzner, "the designers and I have to come up with a common language. They can't talk to me in code, and I can't necessarily talk to them in non-technical terms. We use a lot of graphics and sketches to explain to the programmers what we're trying to achieve. We'll lay out what we'd like the Web page to look like, fill in some headlines to indicate what the content for each page may be, and thereby illustrate what we'd like. We then ask the programmer for feedback about what they think will work. There's a lot of give and take, but the programmers have gotten a lot more familiar with marketing, which has proven to be a big help in terms of site development."

B2C (Business to Consumer)

E-commerce, which is the nickname for "electronic commerce," is the buying and selling of goods and services over electronic systems, most notably via the Web. While bank transfers of electronic funds and other types of exchanges technically fall under the e-commerce umbrella, e-commerce is commonly used to refer to purchases made via a Web site, and this is how the term will be used throughout this book.

While some B2B sites do have e-commerce capabilities on their site (companies that sell ink and print toner to other companies, for example, might utilize e-commerce functionality, as might distributors with a large catalog of products that they sell to retailers), e-commerce is most often used by companies who sell directly to the consumer. **B2C** (business to consumer) involves a business marketing and selling products and services to a consumer.

In 2003, Amazon paved the way for a surge in e-commerce activity by posting their first ever yearly profit.[4] One of the few survivors of the dot-com collapse, Amazon's ability to get out of the red, even for just a year, proved that money could, in fact, be generated through e-commerce.

E-commerce has grown significantly year after year, both in terms of total dollars generated and as a percentage of overall retail sales. Shopping online has become so popular that one of the most popular shopping days of the year, Black Friday (the Friday following Thanksgiving), is now followed almost immediately by what is commonly called Cyber Monday (the Monday after Thanksgiving), when shoppers flock to their computers to buy their Christmas gifts from their favorite Web stores. Very often, however, consumer brands find that their e-commerce sites help boost revenue offline as well as online. According to a 2006 study by ComScore, a leading Internet marketing research company, 63% of people who searched for and researched a specific product on the Web completed their purchase offline; only 37% made their purchases online.[5] A similar study by Forrester Research in April 2006, found that 22% of all offline sales are influenced by the Web.[6] As the line between cyber shopping and in-store shopping continues to blur, e-commerce has expanded beyond the confines of the Internet and has integrated itself with traditional offline retail channels.

B2C companies count on consumers executing relatively quick online transactions (the length of time it takes a buyer to make a decision is typically proportional to the price of the item being purchased. For example, it will take buyers longer to decide which car to purchase than to decide which bar of soap to buy.) Therefore, B2C companies concentrate on the following goals when developing online sales and marketing strategies:

- Reinforcing their brand name
- Gaining a consumer's trust
- Building consumer loyalty to the brand
- Showing that their product or service fills a consumer's needs
- Differentiating their products or services from competing brands

- Making the decision-making process quick and easy

- Maximizing consumer dollars spent per purchase through add-ons

- Creating a pleasant overall shopping experience

- Providing quality customer service throughout the decision-making and purchasing process (this is usually a short-term interaction that ends upon completion of a given transaction, as opposed to the ongoing relationship necessary on the B2B side)

That is a fairly extensive list, and a lot for one Web site to accomplish—especially when targeting a consumer market that has many other options on the Web to choose from. To capture and keep their audience, B2C companies need to present themselves in an engaging way, motivate users to move through the site in a particular direction, and ultimately compel them to buy. To reach these goals, B2C e-commerce sites tend to do the following:

- Utilize images and product shots more frequently than long sections of copy.

- Personalize the site as much as possible, so that when shoppers return, the site offers them products they will be more likely to buy.

- Feature more popular products on the Home page where they are more likely catch the attention of a site visitor. (Many brick-and-mortar retailers, on the other hand, put the most sought-after products as far from the entrance as possible. In large supermarkets, for example, milk and eggs, which are staple household products, are almost always stocked as far from the entrance as possible, ensuring that customers walk past as many other products as possible on their way to get them. Because it is so easy for users to surf away from a site and shop at another, e-commerce sites do not have the luxury of making the more popular products harder to find.)

- Offer a wide selection of products to choose from, easily searchable based on price, popularity, availability, and other related criteria.

- Build in functionality that allows customers to read and write product reviews.

- Offer links to related products based on the products a shopper is reviewing (suggesting light bulbs after a shopper has added a lamp to his or her shopping cart, for example).

- Provide shopping cart and check-out capabilities that make shopping and paying as easy as possible.

- Provide easy to understand and easy to implement product return policies.

As e-commerce continues to improve and grow, so do the features e-commerce sites offer their shoppers. Chapter 9 of this book will analyze the various features of a typical e-commerce site and how they add to and improve the shopping experience.

C2C (Consumer to Consumer)

Drive through a typical suburban neighborhood on a sunny weekend day and you are bound to pass a garage sale or two, where homeowners have put used items that they no longer want in their yard and driveway so that other people can purchase them. The people running the garage sale aren't doing so as a profit-generating business. They are not turning their yard into a retail center in order to sell new products that they have bought at wholesale and marked up for profit. They are consumers who have bought products and are now selling them to other consumers. The sellers benefit from making a few bucks on products they no longer want, and the buyers benefit from paying lower prices, rather than retail prices which include a mark-up.

Garage sales are examples of **C2C** (consumer to consumer) marketing. C2C involves a consumer marketing and selling products and services directly to other consumers. The Web has its share of C2C-specific sites, and they are growing in popularity due to their potential for cost-savings and the near limitless selection of products and services available.

eBay.com is one of the most well known C2C sites. eBay users auction everything including used socks, houses, CDs, and corn flakes shaped like certain U.S. states. eBay takes a small commission for each sale and charges fees to make auctions more obvious, but beyond that there is little mark-up attached to products and services. Items are sold at the going rate. Because eBay is an auction site, products and services are sold to the highest bidder.

Another popular example is Cragslist.com (shown in Figure 2-7), which provides Web-based classified ads. Users visiting Craigslist can open a section specifically targeted to their geographic area and search through posts generated by other users for products to buy, rooms to rent, small services offered, and any one of a number of different classified categories. For the most part, posting ads is free (in some cities, Craigslist charges companies a nominal fee to post job offerings), so that consumers can easily connect with other users.

The drawback of C2C Web sites is that they rely in large part on the trust factor. There is no brand or reputation to count on and no customer service number to call. If you buy something from someone on Craigslist, for example, there is no guarantee you are going to get what you paid for, and there is very little retribution if the transaction goes awry.

Figure 2-7 Craigslist is a popular C2C site that provides mostly free classified ad postings, allowing consumers to sell to and interact with each other.

CASE STUDY: Turning a Red Paperclip into a House

Of the many classified ad categories on Craigslist, one of the most popular is the section called "Barter"—an area where people post items they would like to trade for something else.

To prove the power of C2C marketing, on July 12, 2005, Kyle McDonald launched a Web site called One Red Paperclip and posted a picture of a red paperclip in the Barter section of Craigslist, with the following copy:

> *This red paperclip is currently sitting on my desk next to my computer. I want to trade this paperclip with you for something bigger or better, maybe a pen, a spoon, or perhaps a boot.*

> *If you promise to make the trade I will come and visit you, wherever you are, to trade.*

> *So, if you have something bigger or better than a red paperclip to trade, email me.*

> *Hope to trade with you soon!*

> *Kyle*

PS: I'm going to make a continuous chain of 'up trades' until I get a house. Or an island. Or a house on an island. You get the idea.

Kyle got a response, and ended up trading his red paperclip for a pen in the shape of a fish. From there, his string of trades (14 total), would take some astonishing turns, earning him a house and a place in the Guinness Book of Worlds Records for the biggest online trade:

- *He traded the fish pen for a handmade, ceramic cabinet doorknob in the shape of E.T.*

- *He traded the doorknob to a guy who needed a knob for his stove top espresso maker in exchange for a Coleman stove.*

- *The Coleman stove was traded for a red generator, to a sergeant in the Marines who was driving across country and wanted to use the stove to cook along the way.*

- *The red generator was traded to a man in Queens, New York for an "instant party" - a beer keg, a neon Budweiser sign, and an I.O.U. for a keg's worth of beer.*

- *The instant party was traded for a snowmobile. The snowmobile was owned by Michel Barrette, a radio talk show host in Quebec, Canada, who had heard of Kyle's red paperclip project and announced the trade on his radio show. Suddenly, news outlets, including CNN, were covering the story.*

- *One of the news shows that covered the story was The Hour, a national TV program in Canada. The host asked Kyle if there was any place he wouldn't go to make a trade. Kyle replied "I'll go anywhere, except Yahk, British Columbia." The next day, a magazine located just outside of Yahk called and made an offer for the snowmobile: roundtrip airfare for two from anywhere in North America to Cranbrook, British Columbia, a day of skiing, meals, and a snowmobile trip to Yahk.*

- *The trip to Yahk was traded to a man who worked for the Cintas uniform company. In return for the trip, he gave Kyle a 1995 Ford Cintas Cube Van with over 200,000 miles on it.*

- *The van was traded for a recording contract that included 30 hours of recording time and transportation to and from Toronto, Canada from anywhere in the world, accommodations in Toronto, and the chance to have the final recording pitched to executives at Sony-BMG and XM radio.*

- *The recording contract was bartered to aspiring musician Jody Gnant, for a year's free rent in half of a furnished duplex in downtown Phoenix, Arizona, with roundtrip airfare for two from anywhere in North America.*

- *The woman who lived in the other half of the Phoenix duplex got interested in the trade. She was an employee for Alice Cooper's (the rock star) restaurant, and she arranged with her boss to trade an afternoon spent hanging out with Alice Cooper for the free rent for a year.*

- *The afternoon with Alice Cooper was traded for a motorized KISS snow globe.*

- *One of the biggest snow globe collections in the world is held by actor Corbin Bernsen, who got the snow globe in return for a paid, credited speaking role in an upcoming film, room and board during filming, and roundtrip airfare to and from anywhere in the world.*

- *Finally, Kyle traded the movie role to the town of Kipling, Saskatchewan, which, among other things, gave him a key to the town, built the largest red paperclip on Earth, and, yes, gave him a house.*

The power of C2C marketing![7]

B2E (Business to Employee)

B2E (business to employee) marketing involves a business carrying out online initiatives to communicate with its employees. Many medium to large companies have B2E sites, which help facilitate internal communications and provide information to employees. B2E sites can be used to provide a variety of resources and important information to employees, including:

- Important corporate announcements

- Access to employee information, such as benefits statement, 401(k) management, insurance information, etc.

- Special employee offers (trips, products, etc.)

- Campaign information (companies often run internal campaigns to incentivize their employees to reach certain goals)

- Employee requests for supplies

- Online training

Social Networking

Social networking is the interaction of people from a variety of demographic groups and geographic locations via the Internet. At its heart, through blogging, Web site feedback, reviews, message boards, RSS, and other tools, the Internet has become one large, ongoing conversation, with side topics being started and continued all the time. Think of it as a large party. The party itself is made up of a large group of people in attendance, all talking and engaging in conversation, meeting each other, exchanging ideas, debating, and so on. Throughout the night, small groups of people band together to engage in a variety of side conversations, usually open to anyone who passes by. Each of these side conversations evolves as different people enter and leave, moving from one group to another, perhaps taking the thoughts and opinions from a group on one side of the room and expressing them to a group on the other side of the room.

All of the tools that enable social networking fall under the umbrella term "social media," and can be found throughout the Web. Product reviews left by customers on a shopping site, for example, constitute social networking through social media, as does a stand-alone blog, and reader comments on a news article.

Social media involves all of the tools that facilitate the online conversation; however, the definition of a "social media site" is a site built specifically to facilitate a user's personal expression and interaction with others—such as MySpace, Facebook, and My Yearbook. Although different business models exist for each social media site, advertising, rather than e-commerce, is the primary source of revenue. Social networking sites are based on the ability of users to communicate freely with friends, family and strangers. These sites typically include blogging capabilities, photo, and video sharing options, message boards, chat rooms, and more. For marketers, the ability to reach users through social media networks creates a unique opportunity, both in increased awareness and perceived brand acceptance on behalf of the target market.

Chapter 3 details the power of social media and social networking sites, how they work, and the ways in which marketers can take advantage of these tools and sites.

INTERVIEW WITH...
ANTHONY LAMME AND CHAD HAHN OF FAMZAM.COM

Famzam.com is a rapidly growing social networking site that focuses on keeping family and friends connected (see Figure 2-8). Registered users spend their time on the site trading photographs, postings blog entries, sharing recipes, and more, allowing them to maintain relationships in ways they never could before.

I have had the pleasure of being involved with the development and marketing of Famzam from its early stages, when CEO Anthony Lamme first sat with me over sushi and talked to me about his idea.

Figure 2-8 The Famzam Home page.

In the true spirit of an entrepreneur, Anthony risked everything he had, selling his home to keep expenses down while pursuing his dream of launching his own company.

Famzam is now a major Web destination for friends and families, and Anthony and his partners have proven that marketing, ingenuity, and a little bit of risk can reap big rewards. I recently sat down with Anthony and his partner, Chad Hahn to discuss Famzam's start-up, marketing strategies, and future goals.

JASON: Tell me what Famzam is and how you came up with the idea for the site.

ANTHONY: Famzam is a social connection site. We like to use the term "social connection" rather than the more mainstream "social networking" title that's used for sites like Facebook and MySpace. The difference is we're really not about networking. Famzam is about connecting with your family members and your closest friends. Users aren't going to Famzam to meet new friends— they're going to the site to connect with people closest to them. Because we felt that this was an unfulfilled need on the Internet, my two partners and I created what we feel is the best platform to meet that demand.

I came up with the idea for the site in 2006. Originally, Famzam was going to be a memorial site, where people could go to honor the memory of a deceased family member by creating a Web page for them, lighting a cyber memorial candle, and telling stories about their lives.

My two partners introduced me to the social network phenomenon, and the Famzam concept moved in that direction.

JASON: So the site has gone through a major evolution since the initial concept. Walk me through the timeline and some of the other evolutions you went through prior to launch.

ANTHONY: We started building the site in June of 2006, and it took us about nine months to get a first beta version up. The beta version was private and available only to our friends, family, and certain investing parties. It was a core prototype with just the connecting mechanism in place. Shortly after that, we included the ability to share photos and to blog. At this point, it was family connectivity only - no friend connectivity yet. People could "sneak" friends into their network, of course, by calling them a cousin or a brother, but at the time, maintaining a network of friends wasn't really why the site was built.

After the beta version of the site was up, I went to an entrepreneur training program (which I strongly suggest any entrepreneur do). With knowledge and resources I received at the program, along with the successful launch of Famzam as a beta test, I was able to secure funding. That funding allowed us to build out the site, including the ability to invite friends, as well as family, so that users have a customizable friend network and a customizable family network that are completely independent from one another. We also created a calendar to store family events and dates with an automatic reminder feature, a recipe-sharing section, in-network private messaging capabilities, and other features that would interest the target market.

JASON: And who is the target market?

ANTHONY: Our primary target market is young women who are Internet savvy and are using the Web every day to share photos and communicate with friends and family. These women will be the catalyst for inviting those close to them to sign up with Famzam and spreading the word about our site virally.

JASON: What is the Famzam business model? What are your revenue streams?

ANTHONY: Every revenue stream is derived from something family-related. There is advertising, of course, which we have strategically placed to maximize ad revenue, without getting in the way of a user's enjoyment of the site.

In addition, we have a proprietary gift store where users can customize products like mugs and blankets with their own photographs. We also have Famzam Flowers, a proprietary flower store, and connections with major retailers like Best Buy, Zales, and others for online purchases. But from a marketing perspective, having these stores isn't enough. We have to compel the user to make a purchase. That's where the connectivity comes in. Let's say that a registered user invites his or her mother to the site. The mom accepts the invitation and joins. Her birthday now appears on the calendar of the person who invites her, and it will show up on the calendar of everyone she adds into her network. So when her birthday is approaching, Famzam will alert her network and prompt them to send her a gift from one of the Famzam stores. We leverage the users' information and relationships to create more personalized—and more effective—marketing.

JASON: In terms of programming, what languages went into building the site?

CHAD: We used the Microsoft .NET platform—C#.NET, SQL Server 2005 database, IIS 6.0, Windows Server 2003. We also used the ASP.NET AJAX Control Toolkit for some of the rich UI features.

JASON: Can you describe a particularly difficult programming hurdle you encountered in the programming of the site, and explain how you overcame it?

CHAD: The biggest programming challenge had to do with establishing the connection between family members and how the inverse relationship gets automatically established. For example, if you have a sister and you both invite your father, he is your "father." But in the eyes of your father, the inverse relationship is tricky. In one case, you are his "son," but in the other case, your sister is your father's "daughter." The inverse relationship is gender dependent, and the software logic to correctly identify this was difficult to build. We got through it by pure sweat and perseverance. With programming, a lot of solutions are found through trial and error.

JASON: When you developed the site, how difficult was it for you to communicate with one another? Was there a marketer/programmer language barrier? If so, how did you overcome it?

ANTHONY: That's a great question. It was actually pretty seamless. Our other partner, Mark Murphy, is the graphic designer who created the look of Famzam, and he put me in touch with Chad originally. Chad understood the importance of marketing as well as how to program a site—otherwise I don't think it would have worked.

There were five stages of development that we used throughout the process:

- The first phase is analysis. The three of us would talk about what we wanted to add, the different features to be included, and we would map out schematics.

- The second phase was creating it. Mark would create the mock ups and the overall look and feel of the service.

- The third phase would be its analysis and development. Chad would develop the framework and outsource to India for the coding to be done.

- The fourth phase was to test the new service on a test server, get all the kinks out, and fix the bugs. This was a joint effort among the three of us, and our community of about 200 sample testers who represented our potential audience.

- The final phase was deployment; we launched that service to our existing clientele.

JASON: How do you drive traffic to this site?

ANTHONY: We have a marketing agency that is helping us with our marketing and PR plan. Getting the name out through public relations both online and offline has really helped raise the brand profile and drive traffic.

As far as marketing the site, we have a very multi-tiered approach. As a social site, the viral nature of Famzam is the most effective marketing tool. We use other social networking tools like Facebook and MySpace to get the word out, and we stay active in the blogosphere. We also use a pretty active Google AdWord strategy [a popular method of running pay-per-click ads on Google search pages and third party sites that feature Google ads.]

Most importantly, though, we continue to market to our strongest audience—the people who've already registered. These people have already bought in and like the site, so we send them regular reminders through e-mail blasts to expand their network, invite more people, and visit the site often. Sometimes we use promotional tactics, like sending a Starbucks giftcard to users who sign on three new members. Too often, marketers assume that once you've captured an audience you no longer need to market to them, because they've already bought in. But it's exactly the opposite—these are the people you need to market to the most, as they'll be the best advocates for your brand.

JASON: What advice would you give to graduating students interesting in pursuing a career in Web development? What skills should they know in particular?

CHAD: It's most important to learn the software development lifecycle. Also, they need to be a generalist in terms of programming technologies but specialize in one thing—either back-end programming or Web programming, etc.

JASON: What's the end goal for Famzam? What does the future hold?

ANTHONY: Simple. To be the largest family-based Internet portal in the world. And I believe that in three to five years, we will be that.

Informational

Much like any other site category, the purpose of an informational site is to relate content to the users. The difference, however, is that informational sites do so as the primary reason for being, unlike a B2B site, which exists in order to generate new contacts and eventually increase sales, or B2C sites, which primarily exist to generate Web-based sales.

Informational Web sites include a variety of sites, reaching any number of different markets. Maybe your school offers online classes, or an area for campus clubs to post upcoming meeting or event dates. These types of sites fall within the informational category, as do concert calendars posted by radio stations, online gossip magazines, movie review sites or general media sites. Figures 2-9 through 2-11 provide screen shots of three different informational sites.

Figure 2-9 The *New York Post* Web site provides information on daily news events.

Figure 2-10 Rotten Tomatoes is a Web site that provides information about and reviews for current and upcoming movies.

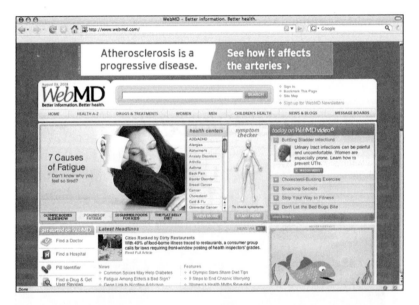

Figure 2-11 WebMD provides users with on-demand medical information.

Some informational sites may be created by hobbyists, or launched simply to support a certain audience. A Web site established to announce campus club events, for instance, is set up by the college to support organized student activities—it is unlikely that this type of site is meant to generate revenue.

For larger, more commercial informational sites, the main revenue stream is advertising. The key to generating higher advertising revenue is to show as many ads as possible, which means that traffic rates have to be high. In order to generate high traffic rates, informational sites need to ensure that the information they provide is:

- Interesting to the market they are trying to reach—not just in terms of content, but also in the way the content is presented. Copy writers must work hard to ensure that they produce copy in a voice that is specific to their readers.

- Updated on a regular basis. If long periods of time elapse between content updates, readers will be less likely to return. RSS feeds, discussed in Chapter 6, help alert the user when new content has been added to a site, so that they are more likely to return.

- Highlighted in a marketing campaign. In order to gain maximum exposure, developers of information-based sites need to do their own marketing to let their target audience know that their content exists.

Other revenue models for informational and educational sites include offering paid subscriptions for more in-depth information and articles. This is not a popular model, however, as it has proven difficult for subscription-based sites to find an audience with so many free resources available on the Web.

Entertainment

Entertainment-specific sites have grown in popularity—a simple glance at the most-visited sites on the Web proves that. Users continue to flock to YouTube, while new and established sites race to cash in on the streaming-video craze. Traditional forms of entertainment such as TV and board games have steadily lost their audience, while online video and gaming sites have seen steady and impressive increases. Flash, a program developed by Adobe, has played a large role in the popularity of both online gaming and video sharing, as more developers turn to Flash for its vector-based, interactive capabilities for complex game creation, and its cross-platform near lossless technology for video compression.

Perhaps more than any other type of site, entertainment sites enjoy a particularly valuable quality: user retention per visit. In 2006, each YouTube visitor, for example, averaged nearly fifteen 1/2 minutes per visit, according to the Pew Internet and American Life Project.[8] Because videos and online games provide a potentially longer user experience (once started, users tend to watch a video or play a game to completion), entertainment sites are able to keep visitors locked in, feeding them more advertising and offers to purchase products. (Using fifteen 1/2 minutes as an average retention time, a Web site that rotates a new display ad once every 30 seconds would feed 31 different ads to each visitor—an exceptionally high rate.)

Keeping content fresh is one of the highest priorities for entertainment sites, as most videos and games lose their ability to entertain after the first few times they have been watched or played. While user retention per visit might be higher than it is for many other types of sites, keeping users coming back to entertainment sites is more of a challenge. Much like an e-commerce site, which pitches its best products on its Home page, entertainment sites constantly need to seek out better ways to entertain and must frequently refresh their sites with new and exciting products.

The high user retention rates and increasing volume of traffic to entertainment sites make them a potentially explosive platform on which marketers can gain visibility among a large audience of potential customers. While standard display and video commercial advertising on these sites has perhaps been the most popular means of leveraging entertainment sites, some marketers take more creative approaches. On video sharing sites like YouTube, for example, some brands have posted their own videos, in the hopes of capturing attention (see Figure 2-12 and Figure 2-13).

Figure 2-12 Hewlett Packard posts instructional videos on YouTube that demonstrate the power of their product.

Gaming sites are increasingly offering games that are either sponsored by a particular brand or created by them, with the product playing the central role. Figure 2-14 shows an example of how one national restaurant chain has marketed itself by creating a game around their name and menu items. By such means, a company can create brand awareness subtly, but effectively, while entertaining users.

Figure 2-13 Another printer takes an entirely different approach. Pazazz Printing posted on YouTube this very funny and very popular video on how passionate they are about printing.

Figure 2-14 This game, which has been distributed through gaming sites for free online play, is centered on the menu of Denny's, a national restaurant chain. Notice the accompanying banner ad for Denny's at the top of the site.

INTERVIEW WITH...

JOHN VECHEY

Online gaming has become a popular pastime for Internet users of all ages, as faster connections and more sophisticated programs allow for programmers to develop better games. It is a highly competitive industry, where game providers struggle to capture the largest share of the game-playing audience—an audience that is notorious for getting bored easily and demanding new and better games.

Since 2000, one online game provider has executed a successful strategy, maintaining a strong position as one of the most highly visited gaming sites on the Web. PopCap Games, the brainchild of entrepreneur John Vechey, continues to be one of the most popular game providers (see Figure 2-15). Chances are that you've played at least one of PopCap's games, which include such perennial titles as Bejeweled and Zuma. PopCap remains popular by using a surprising business model—while most game sites allow free online play, PopCap Games earns its revenue by selling games. I spoke with John to discover the how and why behind PopCap's success.

Figure 2-15   The PopCap Games Home page.

JASON: What gave you the idea to start this site?

JOHN: We started PopCap Games in 2000. At the time, the big thing in online gaming was multiplayer games, where people competed against other online players, but there were no real single player games. So basically [my two partners and I] wanted to change that. Our original model was to create games and license them out, and because the games were going to be awesome, we were going to make a lot of money from the licensing fees. It didn't really work out like that. What we eventually discovered was that we could draw an audience by creating an online version of a game that's free to play and make a downloadable version with better art, better graphics, music and all that stuff, and then sell that. So we had this symbiotic relationship between a little Web game and a downloadable, deeper gaming experience.

JASON: A number of gaming sites offer games from a variety of developers. Does PopCap do this as well?

JOHN: We were distributing games made by other developers a while back, but eventually we decided to remove those games from the site because we realized that our audience really want PopCap games—they want that PopCap experience. Every other gaming site offers everyone else's games—including ours. The fact that we only offer our own games is one of the main ways that we differentiate ourselves for our customers.

JASON: Tell me about your background—is it more in marketing or more in programming?

JOHN: It's more in starting companies. In college, I met a friend, Brian Fiete, and we were studying computer science, so I suggested we make a game. We created a downloadable Internet action game, and we put it out there in 1997. We got people to come and play it by talking it up in chat rooms and stuff like that—our early efforts at marketing! Eventually the game got picked up by a company called the Toy Computer Network, which became ToGo. That's where we met Jason Kapalka, who became our third partner in PopCap, which we started after holding down other jobs and learning the trade. So my background includes a little of everything—development, sales, marketing—but my main focus has always been on building the momentum of products or a company, which falls on the sales and marketing side.

JASON: What is the basic marketing strategy now? How do you drive traffic to the site?

JOHN: Well, the trick isn't so much to drive traffic to the site as it is to distribute games through as many places on the Internet as possible. PopCap.com is just one place users can purchase and download our games. Our strategy has been to partner up with other companies and resources, like MSN, Yahoo, AOL—we work with everybody. It's these partners that market our products for us, so we actually spend almost no money on marketing.

JASON: Demographically, who is the target audience that you are trying to reach?

JOHN: We're about 65% female on most of our channels. They're mostly a little bit older, over 35, and college educated.

JASON: And what's the primary revenue stream?

JOHN: Advertising on PopCap.com is a healthy revenue stream; although, for us the majority is the downloadable sale of games.

JASON: How do you compete with sites like Bubblebox.com and AddictingGames.com that provide online play for free?

JOHN: Having a better game experience. We're careful to always have the best product on the market. Why is the iPod more successful than the countless other mp3 players, which have similar and sometimes more features than the iPod? It comes from the fact that iPod is better - it feels like a better product, you want to feel it, you want to touch it, and it's gratifying. From a game standpoint, if you say that all games are commodities, then your question makes perfect sense, and users would play the games that are totally free and browser-based. But we offer a better experience, a richer, deeper experience that's a lot more gratifying in the long run. For some people, the quality they get on a free site is good enough, but PopCap attracts customers who want a richer experience.

JASON: One of the things I've noticed on your site is a lack of popular social networking tools, like giving users the ability to review games. Most other online games sites that I've seen have included these capabilities. It there any reason why you've stayed away from that?

JOHN: As a company, our philosophy is to not add things unless we have a great idea for them, or there's a real need. People come to PopCap.com to play games, right? So why add something to get in the way of that? Just to do it, because it's kind of a neat thing? That's not what we're about. We want to give users what they came for, which is to play games. If a new feature won't add to that experience, in a very direct way, it's really not worth putting on.

JASON: As someone who has been highly successful with an Internet business for the better part of a decade, what do you think are some of the more important skill sets that graduating students need to know, if they want to build their career on the Web?

JOHN: Simple: Getting things done. I've seen a lot of people that try to start companies, and they just wallow in this world of trying to make it work. They have this big vision, but they don't have the discipline to get there. To be successful on the Web, or in any business, just get one thing done and move forward. And then get one more thing done and move forward. That's what builds momentum.

Don't try to be all things to all people, but try to be one thing for one segment and do it really, really well. So many people fail because they are trying to create some giant thing like the next YouTube, or the next MySpace, and that prevents them from doing something simple. If you want to build something, keep it simple, get it out there, and then expand on it.

Chapter Summary

- Web sites don't just appear out of thin air. A team of people, each with a different skill set, comes together and puts the pieces in place to develop a new site. A wide range of talents is required to develop a successful site. Ideally, a Web development team will represent a mix of financial, creative, programming, organizational, and communication-based skill sets. Each site will require a different blend of people and responsibilities, with larger and more complex sites naturally demanding greater resources of talent.

- Often, one of the most difficult hurdles to overcome in site development is the communication among team members who don't necessarily understand the unique challenges specific to each role.

- Web sites fall into a variety of categories, including portals, B2B, B2C, e-commerce, social networking, informational, and entertainment sites. What each type of site does, how it is built, and the way it is presented to the user are largely dependent on the combination of the human and financial resources available, the general purpose of the site, and the target audience.

- Each type of site brings with it its own challenges and opportunities for building an audience and making inroads into a target market. Business to business sites, for example, may concentrate more on gaining the user's trust and encouraging a potential client to make a phone call, download white papers and call for more information. E-commerce sites are more likely to try to encourage visitors to make an immediate purchase. The types of challenges a site might face will help determine how the site gets built and the team of people that are needed to build it.

Key Terms

B2B—Business to business. One business marketing and selling products and services to other businesses.

B2C—Business to consumer. A business marketing and selling product and services to general consumers, or end-users.

B2E—Business to employee. A business carrying out online initiatives to send messages to their employees.

C2C—Consumer to consumer. A consumer marketing and selling products and services directly to other consumers.

distributed Web portal—A portal that collects information from Web sites and other portals based on a central theme.

e-commerce—The buying and selling of products and services via electronic systems, mostly often via the Web.

niche portal—A Web portal that focuses on a specific topic. Niche portals largely provide their own content and allow users to search both on and off the site for relevant information.

search engine—A program that allows users to find documents based on keywords that they enter into a text field.

site schematic—A diagram that establishes the navigational elements and organization of the site.

Web portal—A site that helps users locate information that is dispersed throughout the Web and presents and organizes information regarding other sites.

Review Questions

1. For a large, Web-based company, who is most likely to provide the funding for the site's development and marketing?

   a. Creative director

   b. Venture capitalist

   c. Site employees

   d. Account managers

2. Which of the following would a graphic designer be primarily responsible for?

   a. Deciding which programming languages should be used to build a site

   b. Graphically interpreting the creative director's vision

   c. Developing the overall concept of the site

   d. Organizing all of the information regarding the site development and communicating it to the team

3. Which of the following would be mostly likely to require an account manager and project managers?

   a. An e-commerce site for a large retail chain that sells shoes and shoe accessories

   b. A site for a local B2B company that offers financial planning services to small companies

   c. A travel blog written by a world adventurer

   d. A site that shows the best places to find wildflowers in Massachusetts

4. Which of the following statements is false?

   a. B2B companies typically have longer sales cycles than B2C companies.

   b. B2B Web sites tend to favor graphics over content.

   c. B2B sites often feature downloadable PDFs of brochures and catalogs.

   d. B2B sites often have online biographies of key management.

5. Which of the following is not part of the ERC Dataplus site, as of the time of this writing?

   a. Online product demos

   b. Downloadable PDFs of brochures

   c. Live chat with a sales rep

   d. E-commerce functionality

6. According to 2006 data, what percentage of shoppers who searched for a product online actually finished their purchase offline?

   a. 24%

   b. 78%

   c. 63%

   d. 11%

7. A site that is used as the starting point to find other sites is called a(n):

   a. B2B site

   b. E-commerce site

c. Web portal

d. Search engine

8. A "distributed Web portal" provides:

   a. Capabilities for online shopping

   b. General online entertainment

   c. Information gathered from other sites and portals based on a specific topic

   d. Portals that can be licensed and distributed to private sites for internal use

9. Developers of most e-commerce sites would be least concerned about which of the following?

   a. Making shopping carts easy to manage

   b. Providing a large product selection

   c. Scheduling informational Webcasts

   d. Building their brand name and recognition

10. Famzam.com generates increased revenue through which of the following methods?

   a. Reminding users when to buy gifts for loved ones through a social calendar

   b. Maintaining an inventory of wholesale merchandise that they can resell at huge mark-ups

   c. Charging users a membership fee to be part of the site

   d. Selling their users' private information to other companies

11. Which of the following are examples of sites utilizing social networking tools?

   a. A site that provides restaurant information for major cities, and allows users to provide their own feedback

   b. A B2B site that runs its own blog about industry topics

   c. An e-commerce site that allows product reviews

   d. All of the above

12. The best way for companies to take advantage of informational sites in their marketing strategies is through which of the following?

   a. Posting streaming videos

   b. Public relations

   c. Writing blog entries

   d. None of the above

13. Which one of the following is a benefit of entertainment sites in terms of generating advertising revenues?

   a. Long audience retention times

   b. Ad agency executives are known to love entertainment

   c. They can charge more because there as so few entertainment sites on the Web

   d. The high ad click-through rate among visitors of entertainment sites

14. Companies can take advantage of video sharing sites like YouTube by doing which of the following?

   a. Posting informational videos about their products and services

   b. Posting humorous, entertaining videos about their products and services

   c. Both A and B

   d. Neither A nor B

15. For a new site, the size and make-up of the development team often depends on which of the following?

   a. Size, complexity, and budget

   b. Interest and market

   c. Marketing strategy and advertising messages

   d. Desired audience

16. The 14-step barter that turned a red paperclip into a house is an example of what type of marketing?

   a. B2B

   b. B2C

c. C2C

d. C2E

17. Which of the following is most likely to be a primary responsibility for a programmer developing a Web site?

   a. Establishing how much space should be left for copy

   b. Deciding which images should be used on the site

   c. Determining what language would best fulfill the site objectives

   d. Communicating the production schedule and associated deadlines

18. C2C sites are becoming popular because:

   a. They are easy to program

   b. Consumers don't trust marketers to be honest with them

   c. Prices are often lower because C2C sites eliminate retail mark-ups

   d. C2C is more social network-friendly

19. Which of the following is least likely to appear on a B2E site?

   a. Information regarding how much taxes have been taken out of an employee's gross salary to date

   b. Date, time, and directions to a company's upcoming employee picnic

   c. Movie reviews of new releases

   d. Lists of doctors in a corporate health plan

20. Programmers would often interact with account managers to do which of the following?

   a. Decide together which programs should be used

   b. Determine the best colors to use in the overall design

   c. Make sure the copywriters know the type of content needed

   d. Develop progress reports

Projects

1. For two of the different types of Web sites discussed, list the programming languages you think would most likely be needed for each. In a two- to three-page paper, explain why, and what potential programming problems might be faced with each.

2. Choose three B2B sites and three B2C sites. In a three-page paper, describe up to five differences between them. Consider messaging, how they are reaching their audiences, methodologies, strategies, even programming.

3. Over the next week, keep a log of all the sites that you visit, and how much time you spend on each site. Then divide the sites into the categories discussed in this chapter. In a one-page paper, describe your findings, and why you think you spent more time on certain categories of sites than others.

4. Visit YouTube, MySpace, and Yahoo. On each site, find three ways that companies are using those sites to promote their brands. Describe your findings in a three-page paper.

5. Find a product for sale on a C2C site. Find a similar product on a B2C e-commerce site. In a one- to two-page paper, compare and contrast the products in terms of price, condition, shipping offered, return policy, etc. Which would you be most likely to buy? Explain why.

Endnotes

1. "Alexa" <www.alexa.com> 17 Aug. 2008.
2. Ibid.
3. Knight, Kristina. "Yahoo Revenue Up for 2006." *BizReport*, 24 Jan. 2007.
4. Frey, Christine, et al. "How Amazon.com Survived, Thrived, and Turned a Profit." Seattlepi.com, 28 Jan. 2004.
5. "The Role of Search in Consumer Buying." *comScore*, 21 Mar. 2006.
6. Mendelsohn, Tamara. "The Web's Impact On In-Store Sales." *Forrester*, 1 Jun. 2007.
7. "One Red Paperclip." blogspot.com <http://oneredpaperclip.blogspot .com> 18 Aug. 2008.
8. Madden, Mary. "Online Video." Pew Internet & American Life Project, 25 Jul. 2007.

Social Media and Social Networking Sites

In this chapter you will learn about:

◎ What social media is

◎ How and why social media grew to play such an important role in the Web

◎ The demographic breakdown of social media users and how their use of various applications differs

◎ Various types of social networks, how social networking sites function, and how marketers use these sites to build an audience

After the stock market dropped in 2000, the rapid influx of new e-commerce sites that gave rise to the dot-com bubble subsided. Large-scale, investment-backed Web sites that defined the 1990s and brought the Web so much publicity during its early commercial growth were all but gone. In fact, according to a February 2006 article in *USA Today*, in the five years from 2001 to 2006, only 31 Internet companies issued an IPO—393 fewer than launched in just 1999 and 2000.[1] Businesses continued to launch B2B sites, and the Web continued to grow, but investors, stung from their earlier losses, were wary of getting involved with Internet stocks again. Even profits were not enough to lure investors back. In 2005, 48 companies in *USA Today's* "Internet 50" (the 50 most important Internet stocks), generated profits quadrupled what they had posted in 2000, but the average stock price for these companies gained only 1% compared to the S&P 500's 3% gain. Take Google's stock price out of the picture and the paltry 1% gain for the Internet 50 suddenly becomes an 8.2% loss—for a group of companies that were almost all seeing profits.[2]

With the bursting of the dot-com bubble still fresh in people's minds, it would take more than profits to re-energize the Web—it would take an almost complete make-over. So, after only a relatively short life span as a communication tool, media outlet, information resource, storefront, and general window to the world, the Web evolved and added one more title to its résumé: social media resource.

An Overview of Social Media and Social Networking Sites

Social media is the umbrella term for the wide variety of tools and applications that give the Web its social capabilities—capabilities that allow a community to come together, communicate, and build upon each other's opinions and ideas. Social media applications and tools are numerous and include:

- E-mail

- Instant Messaging

- Blogs and **Vlogs** (video blogs)

- Internet forums and message boards

- File sharing (music, pictures, videos, games, etc.)

- **Wikis** (online content created and edited by ongoing user collaboration)

- Social networking sites and applications

- **Virtual worlds** (computer-generated simulated environments in which users can engage each other through the use of avatars)

- **RSS feeds** (subscription to sites that alert Web users when new content has been uploaded)

- Product and service reviews

- **Mashups** (the combination of two or more social media tools into one application)

A **social networking site** is one that uses these social media tools for the primary purpose of promoting connectivity and interaction—to facilitate people communicating with other people. Social networking sites include generalist social networking sites, online dating sites, and **social bookmarking** sites, which allow users to remember and organize Web sites and pages to return to later. These bookmarks are usually made public and available on social bookmarking sites for other Web users to review. Not all sites that include social media tools are considered social networking sites. An e-commerce site that only allows users to purchase products is simply an e-commerce site. An e-commerce site that allows users to purchase products *and* read and publish product reviews on the site is an e-commerce site with social media functionality. It might have social networking capabilities; however, its primary purpose is not social networking. For the purpose of categorizing types of sites, the categorization of a site is typically based upon its primary purpose. (The Famzam.com Web site that was profiled in Chapter 2, for example, allows users to make purchases on the site, but it is not categorized as an e-commerce site. Rather, it's a social networking site with e-commerce functionality.)

Social media tools rely on the collaborative and continuous interaction of people in order to have relevance. This ongoing interaction also means that social media Web sites are in a constant flux. A Web site often layers on additional social media applications as it expands and attracts new audiences. A social networking site, for example, might decide to provide video-sharing capabilities. Web sites that utilize social media applications are also beginning to integrate with each other, further expanding the global conversation and offering more benefits for businesses.

The Rise and Dominance of Social Media

The question of when social media began to take its modern form will forever be a source of debate. E-mail and instant messaging are generally considered to be two of the earliest examples of social media applications. These tools allowed for direct interaction between multiple people over the Internet, although the communal capabilities of those applications were somewhat limited. Newsgroups and listservs were early precursors of today's social networking sites. **Newsgroups** facilitated discussions among numerous users via a series of posted message threads. **Listservs** functioned in a similar fashion but communicated users' comments to other list members via e-mail. More widely known was the 1990s incarnation of AOL, which at the time served as a means for users to access the Internet (it has since reincarnated itself as an online media outlet). Among other services, the AOL application provided access to popular chat rooms (see Figure 3-1) where users regularly congregated. These chat rooms, organized by topic and chat room name, allowed AOL members to join in a group conversation, or break away for private, one-on-one discussions. While these chat rooms represented the Web's early attempts at social integration, the experience was finite: once the room was empty, the conversation was finished, and no record of the exchange of ideas existed.

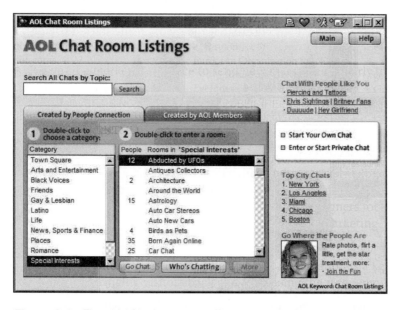

Figure 3-1 The old AOL chat rooms offered a sneak peak at how popular the social aspects of the Web could be.

While the masses were meeting in faceless AOL chat rooms and investors were focused on funding the first wave of e-commerce sites, a small but steadily growing movement was going on behind the scenes. Personal online diaries were being written by users wanting to record and share their day-to-day thoughts and activities. In 1997, Jorn Barger, an early adopter of this technology and editor of the often controversial site *Robot Wisdom*, coined the term *Weblog*, to describe the process of logging these diary entries on personal and public Web sites.[3] The term was later shortened to *blog*.

Also gaining momentum were a few Web sites that were laying the bedrock for future social networking sites. Classmates.com, which helps users locate and keep in touch with friends and acquaintances from kindergarten through college, and Craigslist, which features online classified advertising and discussion forums, both launched in 1995. For the first time, sites whose primary focus was socialization were being developed, although it would be years before this type of site would explode in popularity. (According to Web tracking site Alexa.com, in 2008, Craigslist was ranked as the 65th most popular site in terms of traffic. Classmates was ranked as the 1,697th most popular—an impressive ranking for a social network that requires a paid subscription to enjoy most features.)[4]

After the turn of the new century, blogs continued to gain traction and other social media sites began to appear. Friendster.com (a social networking site designed to help people make friends), Wikipedia, and others began to dot the landscape. However, it wasn't until MySpace became populated with users that the media really started paying attention, and the new age of socialization on the Web truly began.

Social media tools and Web sites have become so popular because the practical, social, and psychological benefits are numerous:

- Blogs, online forums, and other applications give people the ability to express their opinions or beliefs in an open and safe public setting.

- Online reviews by consumers put shoppers in a power position, allowing them to hold businesses accountable for the products and services they sell.

- Social media gives people the ability to stay in touch with many friends and loved ones.

- Social media helps individuals meet people they might not otherwise have. Some networking sites give users the ability to take ownership of their own page and use their creativity to express themselves through the design of their page.

- Through video sharing, popular blogs, or social networking sites, people seeking fame can leapfrog to center stage with content that captures widespread attention. With social media applications, anybody can be a movie star, director, artist, songwriter, journalist, or storyteller.

- Social media allows people to easily gather news and information from a wide range of sources.

- People who have inquiries about everything ranging from a simple programming problem to the mysteries of the universe can pose their questions via social media applications and receive answers and opinions from people across the globe.

- News that comes from a social feed or videos that have been viewed and rated highly by others provide users with a comfort zone. Because the community in general has already blessed these articles and files with a seal of approval, people are more likely to view them.

- Probably the biggest reason that social media has captured people's imagination is because it's fun to be out there, see what else is going on, and be part of the world without having to leave the comfort of home.

Another reason for the rise of social media is the increased emphasis placed by marketers on Web marketing, which can be segmented into two distinct methods outside of standard banner and video advertising: social media optimization and social media marketing.

Social Media Optimization

Social media optimization is a marketing strategy that encourages people, companies, and organizations to get their content distributed as widely as possible throughout the social media universe. This strategy is based on the idea that marketing is more effective when seen by more people; therefore, marketers and content developers work to spread their messages through a multitude of social media networks. To accomplish this, developers optimize their Web sites to include the ability to share text and video content, or provide links back to their site through popular social media networks. Figures 3-2 through 3-4 provide examples.

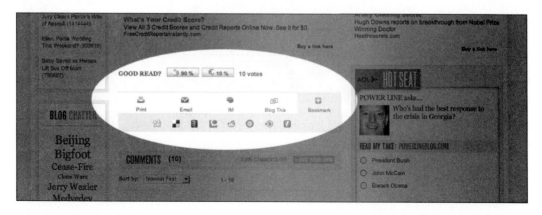

Figure 3-2 AOL readers can vote on the value of a news story and repost the article on a variety of social media news and bookmark Web sites.

Figure 3-3 The Web site for the band Train includes direct links to the band's MySpace and Facebook pages.

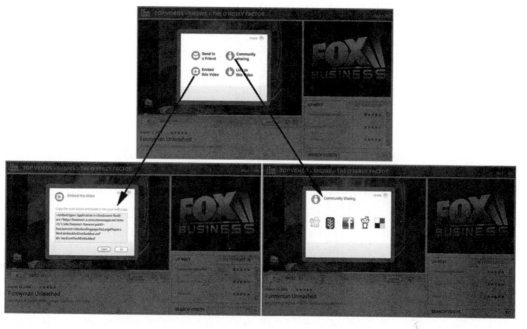

Figure 3-4 After watching a video on the FOX News Web site (top), users are given the option to e-mail, link to, or embed the video on their own Web site.

Social Media Marketing

Before the popularization of social media, reaching an audience through the Web was fairly straightforward. While marketers had options, the most prominent means of communicating a message was through banner and display ads placed in key areas of Web sites. Today, while banner ads are still a highly viable means of Web marketing, social media has created numerous other opportunities for marketers to identify and reach their audience. However, because the social media universe can be so rich and complex, setting the best, most effective marketing strategy can be a daunting task. **Social media marketing** is the utilization of social media specifically as a marketing vehicle, and typically falls into one of three categories:

PUBLIC RELATIONS: As more news is generated by users and traditional news is increasingly spread through online communities, public relations professionals are looking to social media to get their message to their target audience. To do this, news must be trustworthy and valuable to the reader, or it risks getting lost or ignored in the crowded social media universe.

MARKETING CONTENT GENERATION: Blogs, videos, and other content created for a marketing purpose need to be crafted in such a way that they will be relevant to the desired audience. Although not necessarily as news-oriented as the information distributed via traditional public relations methods, brand-generated content must still be compelling in order to capture readers' attention via social media networks.

VIRAL MESSAGING: Viral messaging campaigns are typically shocking or unusually entertaining videos (or sometimes, text) that pique such a high level of interest in an audience that people feel compelled to pass the file or information on through e-mail, social media networks, or other means. In instances where the content is particularly engaging or entertaining, viral messages can make their way to millions of people in an extraordinarily short period of time.

Social media tools and the power they yield in bringing communities together have been a boon for marketers. By adding these tools to their own Web sites and by marketing their brands through social media networks using site optimization techniques and the direct inclusion of new content, marketers have contributed to the rise of social media and have been able to expand the reach of their message.

Some of the many significant benefits that social media brings to marketers are:

- **Cost efficiency**: Social media tools allow marketers without large advertising budgets to reach a target audience. If a message is crafted correctly, marketers can often rely on the audience to spread the word for them, sparing marketers the high cost of ad placement.

- **Broad visibility**: If desired, marketers can reach a broad and general audience through social media.

- **Narrow visibility**: Similarly, marketers can reach more narrowly defined audiences through vertical or niche outlets that reach a specific market demographic.

- **Pulse of the market**: By paying attention to the blogosphere (the blogging community as a whole), social media trends, and user opinions, marketers can track how users feel about their brands. Marketers can take that information and develop their business and marketing plans to respond effectively.

- **Increased trust**: By allowing consumers to express public opinions—both positive and negative—about their brands through social media, marketers can gain the trust of their audience, who want to believe that the brands they buy will be responsive to their needs.

- **Self-made community**: Brands can use social media applications to create their own online communities. Marketers build strong connections to their brands by giving people news, product updates, information, and the ability to express themselves.

- **Increased revenue**: Ultimately, the increased visibility and inter-action with consumers should lead to increased sales and revenue.

- Social media allows audiences and marketers to interact in ways that they have never been able to before, leading not only to more effective marketing, but also to better service and an improved understanding about what each has to offer the other.

CASE STUDY: Full Metal Jackie

Full Metal Jackie is the host of Chaos—a metal music radio show that is syndicated throughout the U.S. Named "Metal Host of the Year" two years in a row by FMQB (a music industry publication), Jackie has built up a nationwide audience through hard work, perseverance, and a focus on spreading her name through social networking.

Jackie started Chaos on the Los Angeles radio station Indie 103.1 in 2004. The only all-metal music show in the Los Angeles area, Chaos quickly built a following. However, with the show limited to two hours a week (the 10:00 PM to midnight time slot), Jackie knew that the exposure Chaos would have was limited.

To expand her audience, Jackie turned to the Internet. Her first step was to use Internet radio as a tool to broaden her market. After obtaining the rights to distribute past shows, Jackie struck a deal with popular Internet radio station KNAC, allowing them to replay previous shows. While that gave new fans access to her show, it didn't solve the marketing problem she faced—Jackie still needed to let metal fans know her show was out there.

"My MySpace page (shown in Figure 3-5) played a big part in building a nationwide fan base," Jackie explains. "I was able to use it to reach out to people—what I call the Chaos Army. Once kids linked into my page as a 'friend' of the show, they helped spread the word to other people. It gave them a real taste of what my show is like. I post clips and pictures from band interviews I've done. I play some of the music I feature on my show and really make the page into a full metal experience. Plus, I'm constantly updating the page with new links to different metal bands, which gives my listeners access to new music that I think they'll go for. I also give them dates for upcoming metal concerts and appearances, and tell them where they can listen to my show. I get a lot of really positive feedback and suggestions about which songs I should play on my show. The comments that people leave on my page give me more of an insight into what bands and interviews my fans will respond to. That kind of interaction makes me more accessible, which is what my listeners want. I also stay in touch by sending out new bulletins on upcoming guests to the show, or concerts I'll be going to—anything to stay in touch with the audience.

"On my MySpace page, I have a Chaos banner, and I have provided the code so fans can copy it and use it on their own MySpace pages. So when their friends visit their sites, they see the banner, click on it, and come right to my page."

"My MySpace page links to my external site, fullmetaljackie.com, as well as to my online video shows at Hollywoodmusic.tv and Metal Edge Magazine's Web site, where I have another weekly video program. Each of these sites relies on the other to build an audience, and the social networking that I'm doing keeps that audience growing. I also spend time on the metal blogs out there, replying to posts and keeping my name in the mix. It's all pretty viral, and it's growing pretty fast."

In fact, Full Metal Jackie's popularity has grown so fast that in 2007 she hosted the first ever metal music concert on MySpace, appearing before over a million listeners. Thanks largely to her active presence in the social networking universe, Chaos continues to pick up steam and is becoming nationally syndicated.

Figure 3-5 Full Metal Jackie's MySpace site provides links to bands' Web sites, video and audio clips of interviews, updates on concerts and appearances, and code that allows people to place the Chaos radio show banner on their own page.

Who Is Using Social Media and How?

While social media use reaches across demographic age groups, there is no question that its growth has been fueled primarily by teens and young adults. In fact, content development is inversely proportional to the age of the user. Figure 3-6 is a graph that shows the percentage of Internet users in different age groups who have created social media content, such as blog postings, online reviews, bulletins, and artwork. As that figure shows, 12–17 year olds account for the greatest portion of social media usage.[5] Table 3-1 provides a laundry list of social media functionality and the popularity of each for each age group, according to the research organization Pew Internet & American Life Foundation in a December 2007 report on teens and social media.

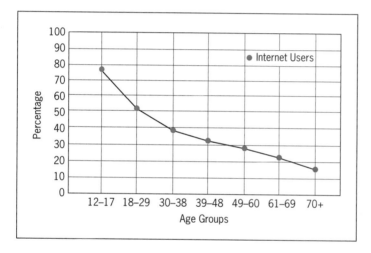

Figure 3-6   Nearly all teens on the Internet (which includes nearly all teens in the U.S.) create content via social media. Content creation decreases as age increases. SOURCE: Lenhart, Amanda, et al. "Teens and Social Media." Pew Internet & American Life Project, 19 Dec. 2007.

Social Media Application	Young Adults 12-29	Adults 30 +
Read Blogs	54%	36%
Download Podcasts	14%	12%
Write an Online Review for a Product or Service	37%	32%
Upload Photos	51%	37%
Upload Their Own Artwork, Stories, or Videos	39%	22%
Have and Post to their Own Blog	33%	12%
Create an Avatar that Interacts with Others	19%	9%

Table 3-1   A breakdown of various social media applications and the percentage of Internet users in each age group who have made use of each application at least once. SOURCE: Lenhart, Amanda, et al. "Teens and Social Media." Pew Internet & American Life Project, 19 Dec. 2007.

By reviewing this data, marketers can begin to understand the audiences they are likely to reach via a specific social media tool. Because marketers rarely benefit from reaching all age groups, understanding who uses what, when, and how helps marketers effectively hone their strategies.

Social media, therefore, is not only used by individuals. Where the individuals go, so go the marketers looking to turn them into loyal customers. In fact, over 54% of all major U.S. corporations (those with over 500 employees) use social media technology, as do 74% of companies with less than 500 employees.[6] Blogs are particularly popular among corporations because they are inexpensive to create, give a company the freedom to steer the conversation in a beneficial direction, and allow the blog editor to eliminate potentially damaging user comments. In addition, because reading blog postings ranks among the highest of all social media activities for both younger and older adults, marketers have the best chance of capturing audience attention by blogging.

Companies that deploy social media applications are doing so externally but are also using these tools within their organizations, as a means of improving internal operations. Internally, social media programs provide valuable benefits, including:

- Enriched employee communication and collaboration

- Identification of experts and individuals with key information within the company

- Improved knowledge management

Companies that utilize these tools report that the biggest hurdle in pursuing social media strategies is the lack of internal resources—most notably, developers that can implement these tools in a way that demonstrates a clear understanding of the audience.

Social Networking Sites: Types and Audiences

Just as in real life, where communities of people form around similar interests, demographics, or lifestyles, there are many different social networking sites. Social networking sites can be divided into three distinct categories: generalist, niche, and bookmarking.

Generalist Social Networking

Generalist social networking sites have something for everyone, and attract audiences regardless of age, race, gender, or interest. They seek to build the most broad-based communities. These sites are mostly used for staying in touch with large groups of friends, meeting new people, expressing artistic creativity, and other entertainment-based activities. It is not surprising, therefore, that younger adults make up the largest portion of the population on these sites.

The advantage of social networking sites is that developers of these sites do not have to generate any significant amount of content. Instead, they can concentrate on developing applications for interactive communication. They rely on their users to generate content through blogs, message and bulletin board postings, file uploads (such as videos, pictures, art, and music), comments on those files, and online group discussions. The formula for success is relatively simple: encourage users to generate a lot of interesting content, which will entice more people to come to the site. If the content is compelling enough, these new visitors will then invite their friends and family to come to the site, as well.

Generalist social networking sites provide users with their own unique page, or profile, which they can customize by adding their picture, headline, and personal information (age, gender, town and state, school, occupation, etc.). Some sites allow users to personalize their profile further by changing the page design, and by adding background colors, wallpaper, custom buttons, and highlights. Site users can upload photographs, artwork, or favorite songs and videos, post results of personality and trivia quizzes, and create personal blogs. Users can build their personal social networks by finding people on the site (usually a variety of search mechanisms are available) that they want to link up with or by inviting people who are not already site members to join and be part of their network. Once they have established a network, site users can use their profiles to communicate with people within that network through private e-mail or public bulletins. Users can also visit each other's profile, leaving comments on the items a user has posted.

While generalist social networks offer a number of profile personalization and communication options, not all of these are used equally. Figure 3-7 shows a sample page from Facebook, a large social networking site, and a breakdown of how people use some of the more popular features, such as sending public or private messages, sending a group message, or winking at, poking, or nudging someone (basically a quick way of saying "Hello").

88

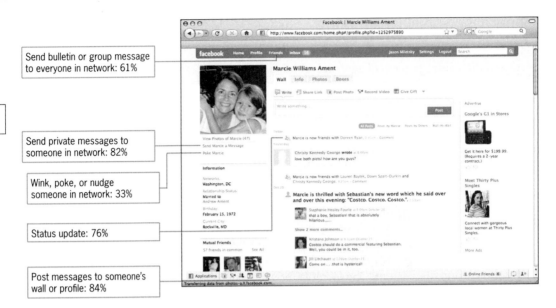

Send bulletin or group message to everyone in network: 61%

Send private messages to someone in network: 82%

Wink, poke, or nudge someone in network: 33%

Status update: 76%

Post messages to someone's wall or profile: 84%

Figure 3-7 A breakdown of a typical Facebook profile and the percentage of users that use some of the more popular features.

As Figure 3-7 shows, people who create profiles on generalist social networking sites are active in creating public communications with the people in their networks. This results in a tremendous amount of content being generated, as well as an increasing amount of time being spent by users online. Therefore, successful sites can point not only to a growing number of members and visits per member but also to a relatively high amount of time spent on the site (over 20 minutes per visit)—all key measurements for online advertisers.

However, unlike most industries, which have room for multiple competitors—sometimes hundreds in a given category—the generalist social networking sector has little tolerance for too many players. Because success relies on large groups of people visiting often and because there are only so many hours in a day for these people to maintain their network profiles, generalist social networking tends to be an "all or nothing" kind of business. This is underscored by the June 2008 market share snapshot of the social networking industry as reported by Hitwise, a research and data analysis company. MySpace dominates the field with the lion's share of the entire market, followed by the increasingly popular Facebook. All of the other top five most popular social networking sites held only a relatively tiny market share (myYearbook, which is profiled later in this chapter, is ranked number 3 and led the entire category in market share growth, with an astounding 40% increase over the previous year).[7] The dominance of the top two players is a testament to the reality of the social network business model: while small sites can prove profitable, this is not an industry where many large sites can compete for dominance. Table 3-2 provides a table of the top five most popular social networking sites as of June 2008 and their growth over last year.

Rank	Site	June 2008	June 2007	% Change
1	MySpace	71.92%	77.42%	– 6%
2	Facebook	16.91%	11.60%	40%
3	myYearbook	1.54%	0.33%	318%
4	Tagged	1.08%	0.69%	45%
5	Bebo	1.05%	1.52%	– 41%

Table 3-2   The top five social networking sites as of June 2008, compared with their market share from one year earlier. The dominance of MySpace and, to a lesser extent, Facebook, demonstrates that there is little room for multiple generalist social networking sites to gain massive audiences. SOURCE: "Summer Social-Network Traffic Still Sizzling, but Down from '07." Hitwise <www.hitwise.com> Jun. 2008.

INTERVIEW WITH...
CATHERINE COOK, FOUNDER OF MYYEARBOOK.COM

So what does a 15-year-old do when she looks at her high school yearbook and decides it's not very good? If that 15-year-old is Catherine Cook, the answer is simple: team up with her 16-year-old brother, Dave, and build a Web site—one that can be everything your printed yearbook can't.

In 2005, over spring break, armed with an idea, a fax machine, and some early funding from their older brother, Geoff, they set out to build a social networking site marketed toward high school teens. Founder Catherine Cook took some time out of her busy day at Georgetown University to sit down with me and talk to me about how myYearbook.com got started (shown in Figure 3-8).

JASON: How did you get myYearbook.com started? Did you raise a lot of money at the outset?

CATHERINE: Actually my oldest brother, Geoff, invested $250,000 into our idea at the onset. We used that money to outsource the

Figure 3-8   The main profile page of myYearbook.com.

programming to India. Though $250,000 is not a lot in the tech world, we made it last for over a year. In November 2006, we decided to reach out to some venture capitalist and raised $4.1 million in our Series A round. We used this funding to further grow the site and hire an ad sales team, and did not make our Series B of $13 million dollars until July 2008. Other networks have raised ten times as much funding as we have, but are still only half our size.

Programming began in March 2005. In order to launch by April, it would have been impossible to find a firm that could do it that quickly in the U.S. It was just much faster and much easier to go overseas. Right after we launched, though, we brought it all in-house.

JASON: Was it hard to manage a phased roll-out with the programmers overseas?

CATHERINE: Not really. We hand-wrote hundreds of pages and drew up the idea of what the site would look like, page-by-page, in exact detail, so that there really wasn't that much room for interpretation, and we faxed them all over. Of course, there were always some modifications to deal with later, but my brother Dave and I would work from midnight to around 3:00 a.m. each night going through all the pages, working and reworking everything.

Being in school during the day didn't help. But we got everything done in phases, which helped. The first stage, which was just the profile page, the group page, and classes, took about a month. The first phase of the site looked nothing like how it does now. It's completely different in all aspects except for the color scheme.

Phase two of the site came after the launch of phase one, and included applications that allowed users to upload music files, and features like "flirting," "admiring," and "high-five" and "forward a message" based on what we thought the site needed. We had our public launch in August 2005. Nine months later, we hit the million user mark.

JASON: How did you get so many people to the site so quickly?

CATHERINE: Word of mouth, mostly. The first thing we did was to get people from my high school to join. My brother Dave and I wore the same type of t-shirt to school every day for over two weeks. It had the myYearbook name and logo on it, and a funny quote on the back. Eventually people got curious and interested. Within a week of our launch a lot of the kids in my high school were signed up. After that, kids from other schools in our area started to join and the site was generating a lot of buzz.

Even though it was growing on its own, we knew we couldn't depend on buzz alone; word of the site might not spread in the same way from school to school. So we decided to send free T-shirts to users who referred five people—because they're cheap and easy to deliver, and everyone wants them. We ended up sending out hundreds in the first two months and only stopped sending them out in late 2007 because we started offering our members our virtual currency, Lunch Money, for referring friends instead.

Another thing we've done is use other social networking sites to market our own. At the time that we launched, Facebook hadn't really hit the high schools yet, but MySpace was widely used as were many blogging sites. We decided to engineer virality by making all of our features into widgets that could be posted and shared on other sites. For example, a user could post their quiz results on Xanga, and their friends could click the results and be directed to myYearbook.

JASON: Let's talk about MySpace and Facebook. From a marketing perspective, how do you deal with competitive pressures from those sites? Will users take the time to be part of multiple social media sites, or will they just choose a favorite and stick with that?

CATHERINE: I think everyone has their favorite, but they'll use all of them. I mean, myYearbook is my favorite, obviously, but I also have a Facebook page because I'm enrolled at Georgetown University and it just helps with college. They all have their own audience. Facebook and MySpace are a little more mass market, myYearbook is basically for teenagers, LinkedIn is for professionals, and so on.

JASON: The teenage market that you reach tends to be very fickle. How do you keep the site fresh so that users don't get bored and go somewhere else?

CATHERINE: We try to add a new feature every two weeks, or improve an existing one. The site is always changing. You'll always be able to log in and find a note from the founders saying, 'Oh, by the way here's a new feature,' or 'You can use your lunch money (our site currency) to get different things on the site.' With a social media site, you have to keep the site constantly changing and growing.

Also, I am always aware of what our users are doing and how they are using the site. I have to keep my finger on the pulse of the audience. I'm always on the analytics page and comparing the traffic and usage week-to-week.

It's also important to understand your users. The reason why the features are so dead-on is because I'm also young, so I know what my audience wants. And I listen to them—I get around 3,000 messages a day, many of them from kids telling me what features they want. We decide which ones make sense for the site. For instance, a "battle," which is our most popular feature, was a member's idea. He wanted to write a different way of doing superlatives. You have to listen to your market if you want them to stay loyal.

JASON: How do brands benefit from advertising on your site?

CATHERINE: We give them access to a highly targeted and valuable teen audience. We found our niche—we started the site out as a high school site, and we've kept it that way. We know our audiences, so we know what features are going to appeal to them. For advertisers, it's a very focused group. If they're looking to promote a product to clear acne, for example, they know they're going to be reaching their target market on our site.

Also, we believe we are successful with these advertisers because we allow our users to engage with advertisers by choice. Through a series of specially designed applications, our partners are able to truly connect with the teen audience. Featured gifts average over 20,000 gifts given and the average campaign profile generates over 50,000 friends, illustrating the success of these applications to appeal to teens. Our campaigns have been successful because of the level of engagement we offer our users with the brand.

JASON: How do you see myYearbook evolving?

CATHERINE: We expect to see a continued rise in user-generated content. We already have the largest teen magazine on the Web, and it's completely user-run. It's popular because the articles and issues come from them. That's the way the Web is moving, in general.

JASON: What do you think is the most important skill graduating programming students need in order to succeed in a Web business?

CATHERINE: Marketing. You have to know how to capture a user's attention and market to them in a way that will actually be helpful to them. Programming knowledge is fine, but what good is it if you don't know who you're programming for?

Because generalist social networking draws in a large young adult audience, advertisers who cater to this market are particularly drawn to these sites as vehicles for growing their brands. According to an October 2007 report by the research firm comScore, Inc., "heavy" social media users (defined as the top 20%, based on time spent on social networking sites) were more likely than the overall population of Internet users to visit online retail stores. (95% of heavy social media users reported visiting online stores versus 80% of all Internet users.)[8] Leisure-oriented retail sites such as those selling music, books, movies, event tickets, fashion, and technology products ranked high among active social networking audiences. Table 3-3 shows a breakdown of some of the more popular online retail categories visited by this market, according to the comScore report.

Retail Site Category	Total Unique Visitors (000)	Heavy Social Networkers (000)	Heavy Social Networkers as a % of Site Visitors
Music	23,985	6,825	28.5
Luxury Goods	17,125	4,531	26.5
Apparel	61,184	15,157	24.8
Tickets	42,893	10,520	24.5
Consumer Electronics	49,110	11,714	23.9
Sports/Outdoor	29,208	6,965	23.8
Software	24,132	5,716	23.7
Books	62,276	14,700	23.6
Movies	27,043	6,316	23.4
Hardware	67,449	15,288	22.7

Table 3-3 This table shows the most popular retail site categories as visited by heavy social network users. SOURCE: "Social Networking Sites Represent an Attractive Venue for Advertising Apparel Products." *comScore* <www.comscore.com> 15 Oct. 2007.

94

Typically, marketers reach out to social networking audiences through online banner and display ads, as well as sponsorships of network-run events, such as online concerts or movie previews. Because generalist social networks draw such a broad crowd, advertisers take advantage of site specific tools to segment the audience and display their ads to the most appropriate users—the ones most likely to be interested in and purchase their products. Figures 3-9 through 3-12 show the four-step process that Facebook uses to help advertisers drive more traffic to their sites. Facebook lets marketers control both the delivery of their advertisements (which member segments will see their ads) and their advertising expenditures (how much they want to spend per click).

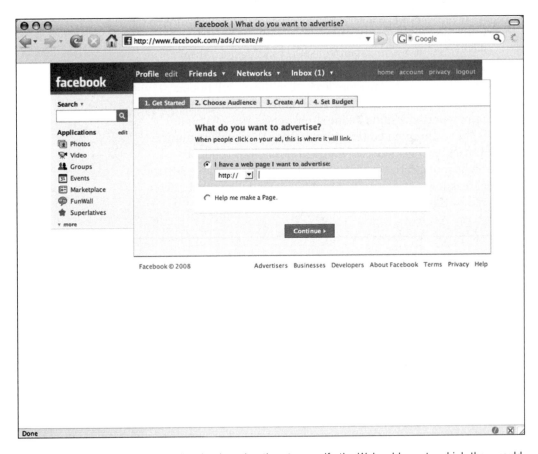

Figure 3-9   In Step 1, Facebook asks the advertiser to specify the Web address to which they would like their ad to link.

Figure 3-10 In Step 2, the advertiser gets to narrow down who their ads will reach by demographic metrics including geography, sex, age range, education, political views, relationship status, or keywords. Facebook calculates the audience size as each selection is made.

Figure 3-11 In Step 3, the advertiser can write the title and body copy for their ad and include a picture or graphic to go along with it.

Figure 3-12   In Step 4, marketers can set their daily budget, and how much they are willing to pay each time a user clicks through to their site (higher bids get better exposure).

Of course, larger-scale ad projects with more significant budgets are typically worked out through a negotiated deal between the advertiser and the specific social network site. These larger deals include not only wide-scale display advertising but also the development of brand-specific profiles that have greater flexibility in terms of page layout. Companies pay a fee to create a brand profile, which they can use to build a brand-specific community. These profiles, which are often created for new movie or album releases, often show video and audio clips and are used to announce release dates. As communities grow, brand-specific profiles work to move the audience to official, off-network sites where the companies can sell products, establish mailing lists, and provide further product information. Figure 3-13 shows the MySpace page that was set up for the May 2008 release of the new Indiana Jones movie (the fourth in the popular movie franchise). Along with promoting the movie's well-known colors, title, and imagery, this MySpace page shows advance video clips of the movie, offers downloadable Indiana Jones-themed wallpaper and icons, provides a link to the official movie site, and presents products for purchase. Their "friends" network includes characters from the movie, each of whom has their own MySpace profile page with bios, downloadable icons, and their own "friends" network.

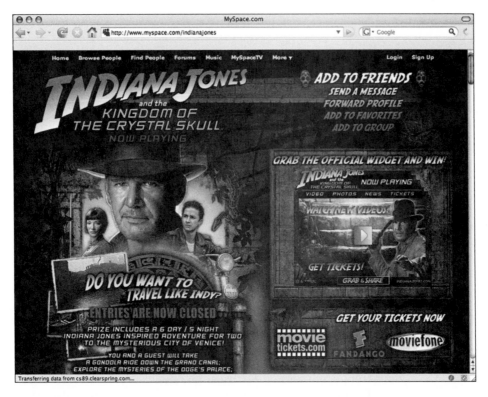

Figure 3-13 The MySpace page for the most recent Indiana Jones movie (released May 2008) is a paid profile that the studio used to build excitement for the movie.

Niche Market Social Networking

Niche market social networking sites are social networks based on a specific interest or topic, or geared toward reaching a specific demographic. These sites are less interested in reaching a broad range of users than in building a community of users based on a commonality of interests or needs. Because they are segmented, these communities tend to be smaller than generalist social networks but they are extremely beneficial to marketers who need to reach audiences with specific characteristics.

Because each niche site deals with different audiences and topics, the methods and applications that they offer their communities often vary considerably. For convenience, niche networking sites can be broken down into five broad categories:

- Interest and hobby
- Business
- Dating

- Shopping networking
- Family and lifestyle

Interest and Hobby Networking Sites

Social networking sites have been created for practically every interest a person can have. Naturally, the content of each site reflects the
subject matter at hand, and often, the social media applications provided are geared toward promoting interest in that subject. Users of
these sites tend to be so passionate about their particular hobby or
interest that building online relationships with like-minded people is
important enough to warrant signing up for and playing an active role
in the online community.

Examples of social networking sites centered on specific interests
and hobbies include SkiSpace.com and BaseballNooz.com, shown
in Figures 3-14 and 3-15, respectively. SkiSpace.com, a social network
created by world champion skier, Bode Miller, brings skiers from
around the world and of all skill levels together in one place to share
stories, give tips on techniques, post pictures and videos, review resorts
and mountains, and post blog entries about recent ski excursions. The
site also provides forums where the community can discuss everything from conditions on particular mountains to which equipment
provides the best value. SkiSpace.com also allows users to make travel
arrangement for upcoming ski trips directly from the site.

Figure 3-14 The SkiSpace.com Web site puts member skiers in touch with each
other, while providing valuable information on resorts, equipment, and techniques.

Figure 3-15 BaseballNooz.com is a social network for baseball fans looking to connect with like-minded fans, debate current baseball events, take polls, and post their opinions.

BaseballNooz.com plays heavily on the blogging aspect of social networking, bringing user opinion on all things related to baseball to the forefront. By placing the most recent baseball-related blog postings from across the Web directly on the BaseballNooz home page, the site encourages more people to reply to each blog. Personal profiles allow users to write about their favorite teams and players, share photos of games, and interact with other fans who share their passion. Other social applications on the site include baseball-related polls and fantasy leagues, as well as a listing of popular tags—keywords most often used by site members in their profiles.

Business Networking Sites

Business networking sites allow professionals to expand their business connections online. Recommendations and referrals are of significant value in business, particularly when looking for new clients, vendors, or employees. Online business networks create a more efficient means of expanding contacts. Personal profiles allow users to update online resumes and reach out to the community regarding business-specific issues.

INTERVIEW WITH...
KONSTANTIN GUERICKE, CO-FOUNDER OF LINKEDIN AND CEO OF JAXTR

Konstantin Guericke is a true innovator who has helped move the social media tide forward significantly. In 2002, he co-founded LinkedIn, one of the largest social networking sites and the predominant business-focused social networking site on the Web. Ranked the 217th most visited site by Alexa.com as of March 2008, LinkedIn has tens of millions of users and averages over 8.7 million visitors per month.[9] On LinkedIn, users have the ability to expand their business networks, making new connections with potential clients, vendors, employers, and job seekers through introductions and recommendations made by friends and colleagues. Figure 3-16 and Figure 3-17 show some of the key features of LinkedIn.

In December of 2006, Konstantin left his post as Vice President of Marketing for LinkedIn (staying on in an advisory role for the site), and took on the role of CEO for jaxtr. jaxtr bridges the gap between online social networking and voice communication by allowing users on jaxtr and other social networks to connect with other users via cell phone without having to post their private numbers online. jaxtr was one of the top 3,000 most visited sites as of August 2008,[10] but because its application can be used on any site, it is also one of the fastest growing communication tools on the Web. Figure 3-18 shows the jaxtr site.

Konstantin spoke with me about both sites and offered his insights on marketing and building online communities.

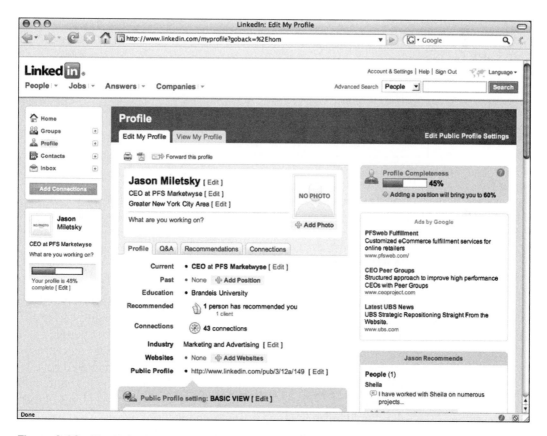

Figure 3-16　The LinkedIn Profile page shows who is in your network, how many people each of those people is connected to, and the most recent online activities of people in your network. Users fill in their profiles with details on their experience, skills, places of employment, and latest business dealings.

Figure 3-17   As with many social networking sites, LinkedIn relies on members to do the marketing for them by inviting friends and colleagues to join their network.

JASON: Let's start with LinkedIn. What gave you the idea for the site? How did it come about?

KONSTANTIN: LinkedIn was co-founded by five of us who shared the notion that we could build a successful Internet business where we could enroll users—not just users of our product, but people who would also become actual content traders who make as well as market the product. We figured if we could do that, than we'd have a very efficient business, because we wouldn't be paying for content creation or marketing. At the same time, we decided the focus of the site should be on building business connections, where users wouldn't join for fun and curiosity but would get a real benefit from it.

My role as vice president of marketing was to figure out how we could encourage people to contribute content to LinkedIn and encourage them to promote the site to people that they know. When the marketing comes from the users, the message is much more credible, because the users have first-hand knowledge of the site, and each person knows their friends and family and what they'll respond to.

JASON: How did you begin to build the community?

KONSTANTIN: We didn't do any traditional marketing. Each of the five of us invited 50 to 100 people. The idea was to focus on user-generated marketing from the beginning and encourage new interactions. The benefit of LinkedIn isn't really in reconnecting with people you already know; that's a nice thing, but the true value for people is the ability to tap into the network of their connections. That's really how business gets done. If you want to hire somebody, you usually go and get referrals from your employees or from people you know and trust. That gives you a much better flow of candidates than by just putting out a job listing.

If you're looking for the best information, it's not found on Google. The best information is in the heads of people. A random person isn't going to take the time to sit down with you and give you the best information. Why should they? But, if it's a friend of a friend, and your friend makes the introduction, you have a much better chance.

LinkedIn really comes down to the competitive advantages that users get from joining. Whether you want recommendations on new hires, to pursue new clients, or to access information that your competitors don't have, you need to tap into the network of contacts. Before LinkedIn, the only way to do that was to call people you know or meet up for lunch and ask them who they know, which is inefficient and labor-intensive. LinkedIn streamlines all of that. As people saw the benefits, they were encouraged to invite others to join.

JASON: How fast was the initial ramp-up of users after launch, and how fast has LinkedIn been growing since?

KONSTANTIN: In the first six months, we basically doubled every six weeks. Then growth gradually slowed down, and now we're doubling every year. Of course doubling from 10 million to 20 million is a lot more than doubling in six weeks from 40,000 to 80,000.

JASON: More recently you've gotten involved with jaxtr. Tell me a little bit about that.

KONSTANTIN: jaxtr is a communications product, and communications is one of the key parts of social networking. Social activities like dating and creating new business contacts—these exist outside of the Web, too. We're all connected by more than just the Internet. Mobile phones have been a great tool for keeping in touch and making contacts, but until jaxtr, nobody was able to bring the two worlds together. jaxtr is about linking your mobile phone with online social networks.

I went to jaxtr because I saw an opportunity to build something that could grow even faster than LinkedIn. Within the first year we expanded to ten million users, so jaxtr has grown several times faster than LinkedIn. The reason for the growth is that we've penetrated the existing social networks and reached people who already have a profile. If they want to call a friend or they want to be called through their social networking profile, then they simply add the jaxtr link to their profile. It lets people call them without them having to publicly post their real numbers online, and brings the two worlds together.

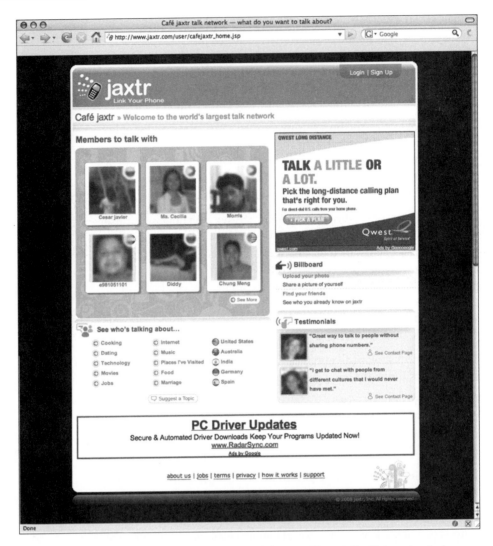

Figure 3-18 Jaxtr bridges the gap between social networking on the Web and cell phone usage by allowing people to move their online conversations to their phones without having to disclose their private numbers.

JASON: You seem to have a Midas touch when it comes to marketing. Do you have any personal marketing philosophies?

KONSTANTIN: I think on the Internet there are two ways to go, and both of them really involve a more analytical and quantitative approach to marketing than has been generally done. The first is to take more of a traditional e-marketing approach, where a company communicates directly with prospects through e-mail or online advertising. The Internet provides more precise targeting opportunities, so marketers can put the right ads in front of the right people and acquire customers for less money. It's about precise targeting—finding the right sites that can provide you with the audience you're looking for and then very quickly acting on the results of the ads because you have a lot more data and can track things all the way to the product purchase.

The second approach, and the one we use at LinkedIn and jaxtr, is to really focus on getting your users to do the marketing for you. I would say that you generally get about a ten-fold improvement in terms of cost and speed over traditional marketing. It's not something that you can do for just any product. "Word of mouth" marketing is fundamentally different from "viral" marketing. Word of mouth marketing means simply, "Hey, I bought a product, I like it; I'm telling other people about the product." That's nice, but it's not a tremendous benefit for the person who bought the product. They get some benefits by positioning themselves as the expert so that other people appreciate their input, but it's a pretty weak benefit.

With viral marketing there are very clear benefits to the person promoting a product to their friends because the product gets better as more people join. LinkedIn and jaxtr are both more useful the more of your friends are on it.

Where most viral marketers fail is that they don't look at their product from the user's point of view. You have to ask yourself what people will gain by recommending your product. Does it really improve the product? If it's not improving the product, then you haven't figured out viral marketing. Telling someone else how much I like the new brand of shirt I've bought doesn't make the shirt any better. There has to be a direct link, and it has to be realistic. There has to be a benefit to the consumer, and it can't be that they're getting paid a commission for marketing a product—that's just multilevel marketing and doesn't have the same endorsement value.

JASON: How important is it for programmers to understand marketing?

KONSTANTIN: It really depends on what kind of methodology you use. In certain situations, it's fine to just provide programmers with very detailed specs and then just give them the space they need to develop quickly and with as few errors as possible.

On the other hand, in many environments, there just isn't time to do detailed specs, and marketers just tell developers what needs to get done. Then you're leaving a lot of decisions up to the programmer, so they had better really understand the reason behind the site and what it's trying to accomplish.

JASON: What do you see in the future for social networking and for the Web, in general?

KONSTANTIN: All the applications that were created for the Internet, like shopping, online communities, e-mail, yellow pages, job boards—all of those things will become much more integrated with the relationship information provided by social networking. The current yellow pages on the Internet, for example, are the digital equivalent of the printed ones—they give you standard information. If you want a plumber, the yellow pages gives you names, numbers, and addresses. But people want recommendations—they want to know who their friends have used and liked. Social media has started the integration of that information, but I think in the future we're going to see this expand to even greater lengths.

Dating Sites

Online dating has emerged from the shadows, when users would meet online but were too embarrassed to admit it, and has become an accepted way for singles to meet potential mates. Online dating allows users to set up personal profiles, upload pictures, publish bios, and describe the type of person they would like to meet.

Where most dating sites tend to differ from other social networking sites is in the development of a personal "friends" network. Because dating is a one-on-one activity, and the object of joining is to eventually meet someone and remove oneself from the site, building large communities of friends that can interact with one another doesn't work for this model. Instead, users build private lists of favorites—profiles of people with whom they want to connect. Users of most dating sites can also join chat room discussions, leave relationship and dating-related posts, and send e-mails and instant messages to other users on the site.

These sites do receive revenue from advertising, although, for most, the primary revenue model is based on subscription fees for those who join. Advertisers on dating sites are usually targeting a younger, single audience with offers relating to everything from fashion and travel to services that help people create better online profiles.

Competition in this category is fierce, with a considerable number of sites offering services to singles. Match.com and eHarmony.com are two of the more popular dating sites, with tens of thousands of users. Less well known is Plentyoffish.com, shown in Figure 3-19, which takes on more of the traditional social networking properties. Besides being one of the few dating sites that is completely free (the site derives all of its revenue from extensive advertising on the site), Plentyoffish lets people publicly rate other users' pictures and leave comments as to why a particular individual would be a good person to date.

Figure 3-19 Plentyoffish.com takes on more of the traditional social networking methodologies than other dating sites.

Shopping Networking Sites

Social shopping sites have been on the rise, playing off of the increase in consumer product reviews and e-commerce. On these sites, users create profiles for themselves, post information on products they have purchased, make product recommendations, and invite friends into their network. Discussion forums cover topics ranging from design and fashion to the locations of the best sales. The social aspect of the site allows people to discuss various products and to immediately see which products are most popular and most-discussed.

Advertisers on these sites are typically retailers and consumer product marketers seeking to reach a community of people who take their shopping seriously and who are always on the lookout for the best products and deals. Display advertising is a primary tool for reaching users, as is the sponsorship of sections that feature specific products and promote upcoming sales.

Kaboodle.com, shown in Figure 3-20, is an example of a social shopping site. This site includes links to popular items, new member profiles, blog postings, and gift ideas; Kaboodle also allows users to post public polls, asking the community for help in deciding which products to buy.

Figure 3-20 The Kaboodle.com home page shows hot products, lists of individual users' favorite brands, active groups for members to join, and user-generated polls on what specific product a member should purchase.

Family and Lifestyle Sites

While making new friends and keeping in touch with old friends is the point of most generalist social networking sites, smaller social networks help people stay in touch with their family, or form a community based on common lifestyles.

Sites like Famzam.com, Famiva, and Famster bring families together and help distant relatives keep up with the events in each other's life. Like other networking sites, these sites typically allow picture and video sharing as well as blog postings. In addition, family sites often incorporate shared calendars, so that family members can stay on top of birthdays, anniversaries, reunions, weddings, graduations, etc. Other applications include recipe sharing and the development of a family tree showing how the members in a user's network are related to each other.

Other sites, such as BrandNewDad.com, shown in Figure 3-21, provide resources and community networking. This particular site transforms the community aspect into a virtual support system; expectant fathers can reach out to each other for advice, share pictures and stories, and get recommendations on the best products for the new baby, the new mom, and for dad, himself.

As with other niche social networking sites, advertisers can use family and lifestyle sites to reach a very specific audience through page sponsorships and display advertising. For many advertisers, reaching a precisely targeted audience is more valuable than reaching a mass of users through a generalist social site.

Figure 3-21 BrandNewDad.com is an example of one of the many social networking sites that focuses on family and lifestyle issues.

Social Bookmarking

Social bookmarking sites allow users to store, organize, and share bookmarks of Web pages that they find interesting and to which they may want to return. These bookmarks act much the same as the bookmark features of most popular browsers, except that the saved bookmarks are made public. Users who engage in social bookmarking can open their list of favorite pages to the community at large or to their private network. Another difference between social and browser-based bookmarking is that while browser bookmarks are organized in folders, most social bookmarking sites encourage users to save book-marks with **tags** (keywords associated with the page in question), so that other users can easily find them through search engines.

Users flock to social bookmarking sites such as Digg.com and del.icio. us (see Figures 3-22 and 3-23, respectively) because these sites give users the opportunity to see what information is relevant to other readers, as well as share information they feel is important. Social bookmarking sites have also begun to include other social networking applications including user profiles, RSS subscription feeds, and the ability to comment and vote on the relevance of each new posting.

Figure 3-22   Digg.com is a popular social bookmarking site that allows people to post and comment on Web pages and online news articles.

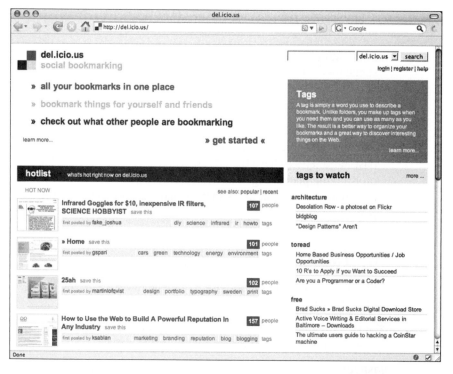

Figure 3-23 del.icio.us was the first social bookmarking Web site and coined the term "social bookmarking."

Marketers use these sites to reach an expanding, active, and information-hungry audience through display ads. However, these sites can also put a spotlight on a company's mistakes and missteps; even a small negative news story regarding a brand can be transformed into something much larger through social bookmarking.

Chapter Summary

- Social media is the umbrella term for the wide variety of applications that are used to bring online communities together. These tools include blogs, RSS feeds, forums, Wikis, bookmarking, and more. Social media tools rely on the collaborative and continuous interaction of people in order to have relevance. Social networking sites use these social media tools for the primary purpose of promoting connectivity and interaction.

- Social media rose to dominance as new sites and applications were introduced. Social media applications allowed users to connect with others, while expressing their thoughts, opinions, and experiences. Marketers saw social networks as a means of reaching large-scale audiences cost effectively.

- Although more age groups are joining the social media revolution, social media use is still dominated by young adults—a group that advertisers find particularly attractive. Social content development continues to be inversely proportional to the age of the user.

- There are many types of social networks: generalist social networks encourage people to communicate with each other on a wide scale basis, and tend to have the largest reach. Niche social sites focus on bringing people together who share interests or lifestyles. Social bookmarking sites let users share, organize, and comment on Web pages and online news.

Key Terms

generalist social networking site—A social networking site that attracts audiences regardless of age, race, gender, or interest.

listserv—An application that facilitated discussions by communicating users' comments to other list members via e-mail.

mashups—The combination of two or more social media tools into one application.

newsgroup—A site that facilitates discussions among numerous users via a series of posted message threads.

niche market social networking site—A social networking site based on a specific interest or topic, or geared toward reaching a specific demographic.

RSS feeds—Subscription to sites that alert Web users when new content has been uploaded.

social bookmarking site—A site that allow users to remember and organize Web sites and pages to return to later. These bookmarks are usually made public and available on social bookmarking sites for other Web users to review.

social media marketing—The utilization of social media specifically as a marketing vehicle.

social media optimization—A marketing strategy focused on getting content distributed as widely as possible throughout the social media universe.

social networking site—A site that uses social media tools for the primary purpose of facilitating people communicating with other people.

tags—Keywords used to describe a page or file so that other users can find it easily through search engines.

virtual worlds—Computer-generated simulated environments in which users can engage each other through the use of avatars.

vlogs—Video blogs.

wikis—Files and content that are created and edited by ongoing user collaboration.

Review Questions

1. Which of the following would not be a good example of social media?

    a. A blog on an automotive site about new environmentally friendly fuel options

    b. A B2B site that give users the ability to download company brochures

    c. An e-commerce site that gives users the ability to publicly review products after they purchase them

    d. A news site that allows users to post stories to their own Web pages

2. Social media optimization refers to:

    a. A social network user getting the maximum number of friends to their profile

    b. Marketers posting display advertising on niche networking sites

    c. Adding at least five new blog comments per day

    d. Marketers taking the steps to ensure that their content is as widely distributed over the social media sites as possible

3. Social bookmarking can be thought of as the social equivalent of:

    a. Browser-based bookmarking

    b. Using Google to search for information

    c. Setting up a private Web page

    d. Sending e-mail to a friend

4. One benefit that niche sites give to marketers is:

    a. Because they are smaller, they have to have lower ad costs

    b. They are easier to work with

    c. The provide a targeted audience

    d. Niche networking sites don't really provide additional benefits

5. Which site is not a good example of a niche social networking site?

    a. Facebook

    b. Famzam

    c. Digg

    d. Skispace

6. How long did it take myYearbook.com to reach one million users?

    a. 3 months

    b. 6 months

    c. 9 months

    d. 12 months

7. The most popular feature on social networking sites is:

    a. Commenting on a blog

    b. Sending private messages

    c. Send group messages and bulletins

    d. Post messages to someone's wall or profile

8. Pages that users create about themselves on a typical social networking site are usually referred to as:

    a. Blogs

    b. Profiles

    c. Tags

    d. Bulletins

9. One of the benefits that developers of social networks have is:

    a. Immediate revenue

    b. Little need for significant content generation

    c. Instant user popularity

    d. Simple to program

10. Companies often use social media applications for internal communications. True or False?

11. What percentage of companies with less than 500 employees use social media technology as part of their marketing strategy?

    a. 45%

    b. 54%

    c. 67%

    d. 74%

12. Which social media application is most popular among adults over age 30?

    a. Uploading photos

    b. Reading blogs

    c. Posting blog entries

    d. Writing product or service reviews

13. In which of the following age groups are over 30 percent of online users creating social media applications?

    a. 12-17

    b. 18-29

    c. 30-38

    d. 39-48

    e. All of the above

14. Which of the following is unlikely to be a reason why social media has gained popularity among marketers?

    a. Ability to sell products at a higher price

    b. Increased consumer trust

c. Broad visibility

d. Narrow Visibility

15. Which of the following is unlikely to be a reason why social media has gained popularity among users?

a. Artistic expression

b. Consumer power

c. Improved e-mail capabilities

d. Networking with others

16. Which of the following types of social networking sites is most likely to be "all or nothing" in terms of large-scale success?

a. Generalist social networks

b. Niche social networks

c. Business social networks

d. Social bookmarking sites

17. Which of the following types of social networking sites is most likely to have the largest number of members?

a. Generalist social networks

b. Niche social networks

c. Business social networks

d. Social bookmarking sites

18. The original term for "blog" was:

a. Weblog

b. Blogination

c. Interblog

d. Blogosphere

19. Three ways that brands engage in social media marketing are:

a. Public Relations

b. Adding profiles of the key management

c. Carefully crafted marketing-related content

d. Viral messaging

20. The primary purpose of LinkedIn is to:

    a. Help keep family members connected

    b. Help business people expand their professional connections

    c. Help users make new friends

    d. Help users create and upload new blogs

Projects

1. Find a niche social networking site that was not already discussed in Chapter 2 or 3. In a paper no longer than five pages, discuss the target audience, and detail the social media applications that are included on the site.

2. From a programming standpoint, what would be the most complex to build from scratch: a blog, social network, or file sharing site? Defend your selection and discuss which languages would most likely be used in development.

3. Pick three social networks other than MySpace or Facebook. On Alexa.com, determine the ranking of each. In a three-page paper, explain why you think one is more popular than the others, and what, in your opinion, the others could do to gain market share.

4. Social networking sites require significant marketing and programming capabilities. As a programmer, how valuable do you think it is to understand the marketing behind the sites you build? Explain your opinion in a paper no longer than 3 pages.

5. If you don't have a MySpace or Facebook profile, build one. Over the next two weeks, keep a log of the activities you engage in when you are on the site. Break down the amount of time you spend with each application (blogging, posting comments, posting photos, etc.). Explain why you think you spend as much time with each application.

Endnotes

1. Krantz, Matt. "Dot-coms' Song and Dance No Longer Entertains Investors." *USA Today* 2 Feb. 2006.
2. Ibid.
3. Barger, Jorn. "Top 10 Tips for New Bloggers from Original Blogger Jorn Barger." *Wired Magazine* <www.wired.com/culture/lifestyle/news/2007/12/blog_advice> 15 Dec. 2007.

4. "Alexa." <www.alexa.com> 16 Aug. 2008.

5. Lenhart, Amanda, et al. "Teens and Social Media." Pew Internet & American Life Project, 19 Dec. 2007.

6. "Trends in Adopting Web 2.0 for the Enterprise in 2007." *Awareness* <www.awarenessnetworks.com/resources/AN_WP_Web2.0.pdf> Dec. 2007.

7. "Summer Social-Network Traffic Still Sizzling, but Down from '07." Hitwise <www.hitwise.com> Jun. 2008.

8. "Social Networking Sites Represent an Attractive Venue for Advertising Apparel Products." *comScore* <www.comscore.com> 15 Oct. 2007.

9. "Alexa" <www.alexa.com> 16 Aug. 2008.

10. Ibid.

CHAPTER 4

Blogging

In this chapter you will learn about:

- ◎ Blogging and common elements of a blog site

- ◎ The growth of blogging

- ◎ Types of blogs and how they differ from each other

- ◎ The demographics of the blogging community and why people blog

- ◎ The benefits and potential pitfalls of using blogging as part of a marketing plan and the requirements for a successful marketing blog

The continuous exchange of ideas and opinions facilitated by the social media revolution has turned the Web into a massive, global conversation. In that conversation, blogs are the voice box. In rapidly growing numbers, Web users the world over are turning to blogs to publish their own content and explore the ideas and beliefs of others. Through this dialogue, the social aspect of the Web continues to expand.

What Is Blogging?

As you learned in Chapter 1, blogging is the online equivalent of writing down news, thoughts, and daily events in a physical journal. Unlike traditional journals, which are typically private, however, blogs are usually very public. Blogs present entries in chronological order (with the most current appearing at the top of the blog page) and allow people to comment on each entry. Moreover, blogs tend to be focused on a particular topic and maintain a theme that ties all of the entries together.

It is important to understand that the word "blog" can be used three different ways:

- As a noun to describe a Web site or an application within a Web site where entries can be made by the owner of that particular site or profile

- As a noun to describe a single entry made onto a blog site or application

- As a verb to describe the act of writing and adding content to a blog site or application

Blogs encourage social networking by inviting people in open, public forums to read postings and contribute their own ideas to the subject at hand. On particularly popular blogs, readers often comment on specific blog entries as well as other readers' comments. These online exchanges spark longer and broader discussions by people spanning global boundaries and demographic categories. Figure 4-1 shows a few pages from a typical blog site.

While the vast majority of blogs are strictly text-based, blogs can include images, video clips, audio files, downloadable reports, presentations, etc. Most blog sites contain many of the following elements:

- The blog title

- The name of the **blog editor** (the author of the blog) and sometimes a link to their bio

- The posting headline and date posted

- The posting itself

- Comments left by readers

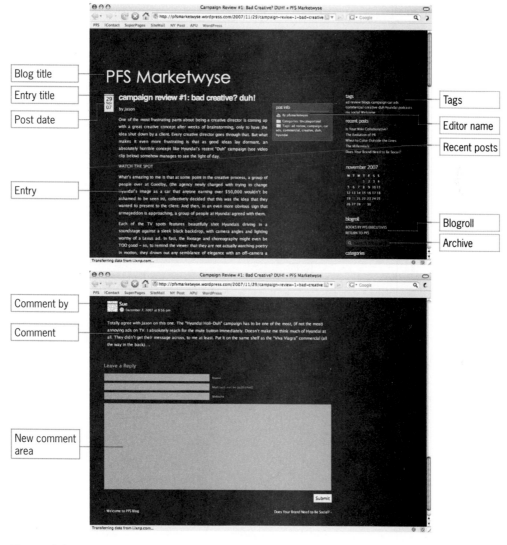

Figure 4-1 A typical blog site (from PFS Marketwyse, a marketing communications agency), with the key elements labeled.

- A response section for people who wish to log in and leave a new comment. The ability to subscribe to the blog (see information on RSS in Chapter 6)

- Access to archived entries

- A **blogroll** (a list of links to other blog sites that the editor thinks warrant attention)

- Links to related Web pages

- Tags for each entry; tags are keywords that describe the subject matter so that the blog can be found more easily in a Web search

The Growth of Blogs

The importance of blogging and its contribution to the growth of the social Internet can't be ignored. The **blogosphere** (the immense network of blogs on the Web) continues to grow. According to Technorati, an online resource that keeps track of the blogosphere, by December 2007 there were over 112 million blogs in existence, with over 120,000 new blogs created every day. That's almost 1.5 new blogs every second. In addition, 1.5 million new blog entries are made every day—17 posts every second.[1] That is remarkable growth from just four years earlier when the number of blogs was barely a blip on the chart. Figure 4-2 provides a chart outlining the growth rate of blogs over a four-year period starting in 2003.

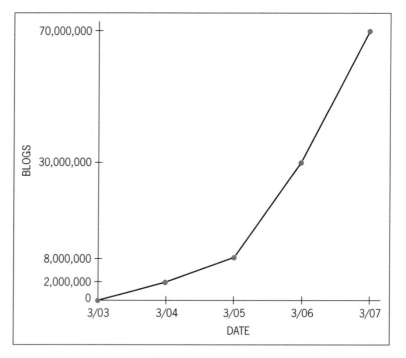

Figure 4-2 Blog growth chart from March 2003 to March 2007. SOURCE: "State of the Blogosphere." Technorati <www.technorati.com>, Aug. 2008.

Beyond the sheer numbers is a more striking statistic that reflects the trust being placed in blogs as a resource for news and information. In a list compiled by Technorati of the top 100 most visited online news sources in the fourth quarter of 2006—a list that includes such widely respected news sources as *The New York Times* and CNN—22 sites were blogs.[2] That's up from 12 just three months earlier. However, as more mass media news sources allow readers to comment on stories and repost them to social networking and book-marking sites, people are less able to distinguish a media site from a blog site. This is an example of the increasing convergence of all social media tools, which are coming together to create a more unified and integrated Web experience. If the early Web brought people together by links, today's social Web brings them together by content and contribution.

Types of Blogs

Just as a variety of social networking sites exist on the Web, a wide range of blog types also dot the Web. The content of each blog is dictated by the author who is writing it and the market that he or she seeks to reach. All of these types of blogs intertwine within the blogosphere to give readers a nearly limitless amount of content for virtually every possible interest:

- **Personal blogs**: Personal blogs are kept by individuals looking to record the happenings of their everyday life, thoughts on current events, etc. These serve as personal journals. Very often the blogger doesn't expect mass amounts of traffic but rather maintains the blog for his or her personal benefit and for the enjoyment of close friends and family. These blogs can include travel highlights, family updates, "state-of-life" postings, or musings on a variety of topics of interest to the blogger.

INTERVIEW WITH...
VICTORIA RENTZ

As blogs have sprung up across the Web, readers have begun to pick out their favorites based on topic, blog content, and writing style. Victoria Rentz writes and maintains a popular personal blog called Best Dates Now (see Figure 4-3), chronicling her adventures in dating. Victoria took some time from her busy social life to talk to me about her blog.

JASON: Why did you start writing the blog, and what inspired you?

VICTORIA: I'd been participating in a ton (too many, probably) of online dating sites and singles activities in New York City for about a year when I decided to start the blog. Because I'm on so many e-mail lists, I receive discount event coupons fairly frequently. I figured it might be helpful for others looking for similar activities to access these discount codes, and read reviews of the different dating events and sites I'd tried, and my experiences on them. Then I read about

124

Figure 4-3 'Best Dates Now', a personal blog by Victoria Rentz, profiling her online dating life.

a guy who made a lot of money each month by posting ads on his blog about cheap places to eat lunch in mid-town New York. I started my blog the following week.

JASON: What type of people are you trying to attract?

VICTORIA: Anyone who is single and looking to meet people. The events end up being pretty New York-centered, since that's where I happen to live. I try to mix it up as much as I can among reviews and discount codes of NYC events, national online dating sites, and humorous/horrendous (sometimes it's hard to tell the difference) personal tales of my own dating experiences. But surprisingly, people leave comments from all over the country. I guess people can have memorable dating experiences anywhere!

JASON: What do you hope to get out of writing it?

VICTORIA: Fame and fortune, of course! I'm just kidding. I do make a little money from the ads that are on the blog, but the real reason I do it is that I love to write. So if I can entertain people while giving them a way to access dating sites and events more inexpensively, then I'm pretty happy. It's a creative outlet for me. It makes the bad dates not so bad, because they serve a purpose as part of my blog, and it makes the good dates more exciting because I get to relive them in my writing. And who knows? It could eventually lead to more lucrative writing gigs in the future, and if it does, so much the better.

JASON: What have been the reactions from readers? Has it been hard to build an audience?

VICTORIA: I've received some funny and interesting comments on the blog itself. People have also told me directly that they enjoy reading it. At first most of the comments were from friends or people related to me, but over time I've started getting a dedicated and growing base of readers that look forward to each new entry. It takes time to build up an audience. I know other people that start a blog, and when nobody comes to read it, they get discouraged and give up on it. But there are a lot of blogs out there for people to read. It takes time and patience and persistence before people will find your blog and come back regularly. And of course, writing it is only half the effort. The other half is publicizing it, like getting onto other bloggers' blogrolls, including new posts in aggregate sites like Digg, tagging every new post appropriately, or just regularly e-mailing everyone I know when I put something new up.

As far as the comments go, once in a while I'll get someone who leaves an unpleasant comment, but when you run a public blog you have to expect that that's going to happen and have a thick skin about it. Mostly, though, the comments are all from people who have found themselves in the exact same position I've written about, and can empathize with my dating adventures. I think people like knowing that they aren't alone, that someone else "gets" them, and that they have an outlet to share their own stories or at least say "Hey, that happened to me, too!"

JASON: How often do you update your blog?

VICTORIA: I could probably attract a larger audience if I posted new content every day. But I'm an old-fashioned story-writer by nature, and since some of my entries are pretty long (sometimes closing in on 2,000 words, for instance), I've been posting new entries three or four days a week. If I were doing this for business purposes, or really to gain a lot of exposure, I'd write shorter blogs and post them more often. But I need to write my blogs in the way that I'm most comfortable with, because at the end of the day, my blog is my venue for self expression before anything else.

- **Media blogs**: Media blogs are like the op-ed columns of major newspapers or media outlets. Many journalists and columnists maintain blogs on mainstream media outlet Web sites (or they may maintain a separate personal blog site), offering their own thoughts and opinions on the news being reported. As noted earlier, many online mass media outlets allow readers to leave their comments directly on a news article itself, and the lines between what is news site and what is a blog are gradually blurring.

- **Business blogs**: Increasingly, businesses are maintaining blogs of their own, offering their insight and advice on the issues of interest to their customers. These blogs can help drive traffic to a company's Web site and establish the organization as an industry expert. While non-business blogs are usually an open forum for both positive and negative reader comments, businesses often police their blogs very strictly, deleting negative postings about their brand. This in turn puts the authenticity of positive comments in doubt, and can limit the effectiveness of the blog.

- **Vlogs**: Vlogs are video-based blogs in which the blog entry is provided in a video format as opposed to a text-based entry.

- **Blog search engines**: Blog search engines aren't blogs (although most contain blogs within them). Their main purpose is to help blog readers navigate the blogosphere in search of particular content by tracking a variety of blogs. The sites typically categorize blogs by subject type and highlight blogs and entries that are getting particular attention. The home page for Technorati, one of the more popular blog search engines, is shown in Figure 4-4.

- **Microblogs**: **Microblogs** are blogs made up of very short entries, often just a line or two to let friends, family, or coworkers get a quick glimpse of what the blogger is doing or thinking about. While standard blog entries can be long, like a journal entry or report, a microblog is purposely short, sweet, and to the point. Figure 4-5 shows a profile page on Twitter—a microblog site where users can write quick updates about what they are up to, and other users can sign up to keep track of their actions.

Figure 4-4 Technorati is a popular search engine that scours the blogosphere for blog content. The Technorati Home page lists popular blogs arranged by topic categories such as business, politics, sports, etc.

128

Figure 4-5 A profile page on the microblogging site, Twitter. Notice each blog entry (down the center of the page) is only a line or two—quick thoughts and updates. The thumbnails on the right side are other Twitter users who follow this microblog.

- **Flogs**: **Flogs**, or "fake blogs," are usually set up as marketing gimmicks to help promote a company or support an ad campaign.

- **Paid blogs**: Not exactly the worst sinners in the blogosphere (see next entry: splogs), paid bloggers post blog entries talking up brands and companies that sponsor them. Although these blogs may appear to contain only personal opinions, positive product mentions in these blog entries are actually paid endorsements from companies. Very often, **paid blogs** are established by sites that act as middlemen, connecting marketers with bloggers wanting to get paid for their writing. Fortunately, a very low percentage of bloggers engage in this practice, as it has the potential of undermining the honesty on which blogging is based.

- **Splogs**: The term "**splog**" is a blending of the words "spam" and "blog." Sploggers don't actually post any real content of their own. Instead, they open a blog site focused on a specific topic, grab headlines (called **scrapping**) from legitimate news sources, and publish those headlines on their site as actual blog posts. Much of this can be done automatically, with little hands-on work by the splogger. They then drive traffic to their splog by syndicating (publishing and distributing) it onto popular blog search engines. The sploggers usually fill the non-content area with pay-per-click ads, earning a few cents each time a person clicks on one of those ads. Splogs are frustrating for blog readers, who get fooled into thinking they are finding original source material rather than republished headlines designed only to bring in advertising revenue. An example of a splog is shown in Figure 4-6.

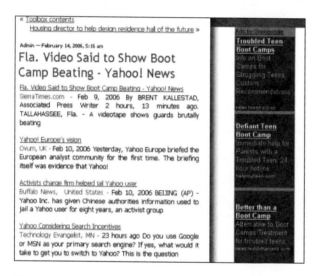

Figure 4-6   A typical splog's entries are just standard news headlines from around the Web. A splogger uses blog search engines and other means to drive traffic to their blog and makes money when people click on the paid ad links within the site.

Splogs are often confused with another annoyance, known as "spam in blogs," which are random comments left on legitimate blogs. The spam includes links to other sites, usually selling fake watches, counterfeit pharmaceuticals, or other scams.

Who Blogs, Who Reads Them, How, and Why

If the explosive popularity of blogs has shown us one thing, it is that people are hungry for information and anxious for an opportunity to express themselves. In fact, 54% of all bloggers have never been published elsewhere,[3] indicating that these people have had the willingness and desire to express themselves but lacked an appropriate outlet.

As with other areas of social media, blogs are dominated by younger Web users. Slightly over half of all bloggers are under the age of 30, with a fairly even divide between male and female.[4] Table 4-1 shows a number of popular reasons why people choose to blog.

Reason People Blog	Major Reason	Minor Reason	Not a Reason
Creative expression	52%	25%	23%
Document and share personal experiences	50%	26%	24%
Stay in touch with friends and family	37%	22%	40%
Share knowledge or skills with others	34%	30%	35%
Motivate others to action	29%	32%	38%
Entertain people	28%	33%	39%
Store important information	28%	21%	52%
Influence the opinions of others	27%	24%	49%
Network and meet new people	16%	34%	50%
Generate direct income	7%	8%	85%

Table 4-1 Table detailing the reasons why people blog. SOURCE: Lenhart, Amanda, et al. "Bloggers: A Portrait of the Internet's New Storytellers." Pew Internet & American Life Project, 19 Jul. 2006.

Bloggers are also proving to be a demographic all their own, as their behavior can vary substantially from other Internet users. Table 4-2 provides a table outlining some of the differences between the way that bloggers use the Web as compared to the Internet population as a whole.

Actions Taken	Bloggers	All Internet Users
Get news from the Internet	95%	73%
Share personal artwork, photos stories, or videos online	77%	26%
Go online for news and info on politics	72%	58%
Go online several times a day from home	64%	27%
Get news from e-mail newsletters	55%	29%
Get news from a blog	47%	9%

Table 4-2 Bloggers tend to act differently from all Internet users as a whole. SOURCE: Lenhart, Amanda, et al. "Bloggers: A Portrait of the Internet's New Storytellers." Pew Internet & American Life Project, 19 Jul. 2006.

With 95% of all bloggers looking online for news, and 47% of bloggers getting news from the blogosphere itself, it should come as no surprise that blogging goes hand-in-hand with current events.[5]

Bloggers are more apt to post during times when significant national and world events are taking place. The bar chart in Figure 4-7 shows some of the spikes in daily blog posts that coincided with important or well-publicized events between August 2004 and February 2007.

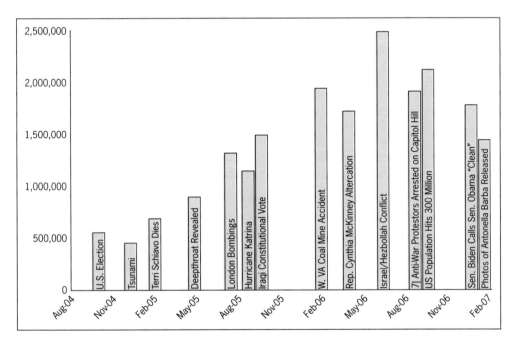

Figure 4-7 The number of blog entries typically spikes during important news and current events.

SOURCE: Technorati <www.technorati.com> Aug. 2007

Most bloggers don't view their own blogs as journalistic endeavors, but rather as personal pursuits, which is an especially interesting point of view given the very public nature of blogging and the increasing convergence of blogs and mass media. While only a third of bloggers consider their blogs a form of journalism, nearly two thirds spend time verifying facts, citing references and including external links to source information—actions typically associated with journalists. Table 4-3 breaks down the frequency with which bloggers take actions that would be considered over and above the call of duty for a private journal entry and that begin to overlap with methods used by traditional journalists.

Blogs have gained popularity in part as a response to concerns with the news coverage provided by traditional media outlet. According to a February 2008 poll by Zogby International (a leading polling and market research firm), nearly 70% of the U.S. public view traditional

Actions Taken	Often	Sometimes	Rarely	Never	N/A
Verify facts	35%	21%	14%	28%	2%
Add direct quotes	15%	25%	13%	41%	5%
Get copyright permission	12%	8%	11%	50%	17%
Include links to source information	35%	22%	14%	27%	2%
Post corrections	11%	27%	21%	38%	2%

Table 4-3 Even though a full third of bloggers don't consider their work to be a form of journalism, this table shows that very often, bloggers use methods that are employed by professional journalists. SOURCE: Lenhart, Amanda, et al. "Bloggers: A Portrait of the Internet's New Storytellers." Pew Internet & American Life Project, 19 Jul. 2006.

journalism as out of touch with what most American want from their news.[6] When you compare this to Pew's finding that nearly half of the Internet population is hungry for unbiased news, it is easy to see an opening for a new media to gain traction.[7]

The impression that major news sources such as CNN and MSN present news with a liberal slant and others such as Fox News have a more conservative bent is fueled by the blogosphere. As a result, even more people have begun to seek out news from blogs or generate their own content. Marketers need to recognize the consequences of this trend. Blog-reported information (both good and bad) regarding their products and services might easily be taken as fact or at least be given more credibility than it merits.

Blogging as a Marketing Strategy

While blogs have inspired millions of individuals to tap into their inner writer, blogs offer far more than simply a personal creative outlet. For businesses, blogs offer an opportunity to reach new and larger audiences in a unique way.

Businesses are drawn to blogs because of their accessibility. Blogs are inexpensive, and they are easy to get started. Programs and sites that enable the creation and publication of blogs are available from a variety of popular sources for free. Practically no programming skill is required to start a blog. Would-be bloggers simply sign-up with the selected blog provider, such as WordPress or Blogger, choose and customize the page design, and launch their blog. Once started, maintaining the blog is also simple, as adding content typically requires little more than writing the copy and pushing a "submit" button.

These are important features, especially for smaller companies that often don't have the resources or technical knowledge required for

Web marketing. For them, blogging provides an inexpensive way to get their name and message out to prospective audiences.

The Benefits of Blogging

For all companies, blogging provides opportunities that other on- and offline marketing tools do not. The following sections discuss some of the benefits of blogging for marketers.

Easy Provision of Information

Updating a blog does not require a highly coordinated effort. In fact, the only real time commitment is the time it takes to create the content. Compared to other forms of marketing communication such as print ads or brochures, which need to go through significant quality control checks, blogging is a relatively uncomplicated form of wide-scale communications.

Establishing a More Human Voice

Most companies speak to their audience through a variety of marketing materials, ranging from brochures, sale sheets, and corporate Web sites to radio and television ads. These vehicles are each unique, but they are all designed to deliver a specific message in marketing language that is carefully crafted but hardly conversational. Corporate blogs, however, give companies an opportunity to break away from traditional marketing language and speak to consumers directly, using a more informal tone. This helps to humanize the brand, making it easier to forge an emotional connection with the audience. Corporate blogs still need to maintain some semblance of their brand voice, but blogging provides significantly more room for relaxed communication than almost any other method of marketing.

Increased Credibility

Because corporate blogs give marketers the opportunity to support their products while allowing reader feedback, blogs can increase a brand's credibility with its audience. If misused, however, blogs can just as easily damage the brand, and reduce its credibility. This credibility doesn't just come from blog posts that hail the benefits of the company's products or services—in fact, just the opposite. Product and service claims made in ads are traditionally met with a degree of skepticism by the market, because they are viewed to have a single purpose: to sell. A blog, however, gives the marketer the opportunity to communicate with the market with a different purpose in mind: rather than to sell, their goal is to inform. This may come by blog posts that establish the author (a representative of a given company) as a thought leader or expert in a given field, in turn gaining reader trust and credibility with consumers.

Marketing Campaign Support

Large-scale marketing campaigns that use a variety of media outlets are typically centered on a unifying theme and promote a message from the brand to its audience. Often, large campaigns incorporate an online component that includes a campaign-based Web site (outside of a brand's standard, corporate Web site). The addition of a blog lets the brand further promote the campaign, explain the concept behind it, and involve the audience in the campaign by soliciting reader opinions.

Character blogs are one method of using blog technology to support a marketing program or increase the visibility of a brand. With character blogs, each entry is written from the perspective of a fictional character. Suppose, for example, that DC Comics developed a character blog in which Batman (one of their characters) described what was going on in Gotham City—new villains, politicians coming into office, current city happenings—letting readers really get into his head and leave comments on his entries. Obviously, readers would be aware that the blog entries are fictitious. After all, Batman is a fictional character and Gotham isn't a real city. However, that kind of blog could maintain the back story, build anticipation between movies, or help sell more comic books. These types of blogs are entertaining, and help promote a larger storyline. Figure 4-8 shows a blog kept by the "Banker," a fictional, shadowy, and brash character featured on the popular game show *Deal or No Deal.* His blog entries, each of which may get hundreds of responses, are blunt. They are written in such a way as to antagonize readers and establish the Banker as the villain in the show.

Improved Customer Service

Customer service is central to any company that needs to maintain long-term relationships with their customers. Because it is also an expensive endeavor that doesn't translate directly into increased revenue, many companies see customer service programs as a necessary evil. Because of this, some companies do what they can to decrease the cost of customer service, which can result in poor quality and unhappy customers. Blogs are an inexpensive and effective way for companies to improve their customer service. Blogs allow businesses to proactively tackle issues they know will be problematic and give customers a forum to ask questions that brand representatives can discuss in a public setting.

Figure 4-8 The Web site for the popular game show Deal or No Deal features a blog by the irascible Banker, a shadowy character who is the villain of the show. His blog is written in a snide, obnoxious voice, further developing his character and helping draw more people into the show.

Opportunities to Draw a New Audience

By promoting a blog through traditional marketing, tags, and listings in blog search engines, corporations can draw audiences they might not otherwise be able to attract. Blogs often include links to other company Web pages to drive traffic to specific areas of the main site for more information or to other pages where products can be purchased.

Improved Internal Communications

Although blogs are typically open to the general public, they don't have to be. Companies with a large number of employees or those with employees spread over a wide geographic range can improve communications by instituting an internal blog. These blogs can be used in a variety of ways, including as a digital "suggestion box," allowing employees to voice their opinions on how to improve the company. Blogs can also serve as a forum for key executives to update employees on company news and information that can help keep employees more closely tied to the company and improve productivity.

The Benefits of Staying Involved in the Blogosphere

Maintaining a blog is not the only way that a company can benefit from the blogging phenomenon. Marketers can also reap enormous benefits by paying close attention to other industry blogs and by actively posting to an assortment of blogs in their corner of the blogosphere. There is a wide variety of advantages to this active involvement in the blogosphere, including sensing the pulse of the market, increased visibility, and increased Web site and blog traffic.

Sensing the Pulse of the Market

The blogosphere is an ideal setting for gathering information on the market a company is trying to reach. Studying a variety of blogs and the comments left by readers can give marketers a keen sense of what's popular and what isn't, what trends are ending and which are developing, and how the market may or may not be adapting to changes in the industry. In addition, brands can get direct information about how people feel about their own products as well the competition. This knowledge allows marketers to be proactive in their efforts to introduce new products and effectively market existing products to their target audience.

Increased Visibility

Savvy marketers will also post comments on other blogs, where appropriate, to provide their brand's viewpoint on the subject matter at hand. This is a more subtle approach to spreading the brand name; however, building a voice in the blogosphere through comments on existing blogs does help to increase the visibility of the brand. There is a big difference between leaving comments and opinions on a blog from your brand's viewpoint (which people will accept and appreciate) and using someone else's blog to leave a blatant sales pitch or advertisement (which people will resent and which can slowly but surely damage your brand).

Increased Web Site and Blog Traffic

Playing an active role in the blogosphere can also help drive traffic to the brand's corporate site and blog. On most blogs, people who post comments can also include links to their own sites or other relevant Web pages. Therefore, marketers who make their voice heard via comments on other blogs can also expect to drive additional traffic to their own sites and blogs.

The Pitfalls of Blogging

While blogging can be a boon for companies in their marketing efforts, it also presents significant danger if not handled properly. As we'll learn later in this book, one of the keys to building a solid relationship with consumers is to gain their trust that the site in question and the company behind it means what they say, presents themselves well, is well organized and reflects the values and knowledge required by the market. Any missteps in these area can be potentially harmful and, if egregious enough, irreversible.

Lying

People see blogs as an honest expression of opinions and experience. They may vehemently disagree with the opinions that a blog editor expresses and will say so in comments, but at the very least, they believe those opinions are honest.

Marketers, however, sometimes create fake blogs in support of their campaign efforts. Flogs are established to trick people into believing that the opinions and stories they are reading are true, when in fact the postings are purely marketing-driven content written for the sole purpose of promoting a brand and its products. This can backfire dramatically, as blog readers do not like to be fooled and will hold the brand accountable for lying. Very often, if the brand that is perpetrating the deception is big enough, they can be persecuted in the media. The blogosphere will spread the word throughout the Web, potentially harming the brand image. The practice of creating a marketing campaign that leads the audience to believe it is something other than a marketing promotion is called **false transparency**.

Earlier in this section, we discussed character blogs, in which a blog is created and maintained on behalf of a fictional character, such as the *Deal or No Deal* Banker's blog. Some people think that character blogs are the equivalent of outright lying. After all, these characters don't exist in real life, so the content can't be true, right? It is a fine line, but two characteristics of character blogs make them less objectionable to most people.

The first characteristic is transparency. The transparency in the case of character blogs is not false. Nobody really believes that the Banker, Batman, Bart Simpson, or the Trix cereal rabbit are real. Blog readers visit these sites with the understanding that these blogs are there for both entertainment and marketing purposes. By reading and commenting, they are willing participants in the character and storyline. The second aspect of character blogs that makes them more acceptable is the nature of the blog entries. The postings on these blogs are true, from the perspective of that character. Darth Vader's blog about his frustrations with those pesky rebels would be made up of honest entries from his point of view. In these cases, blogs work to make the characters more real, and give them dimension, which is called good character development—not lying.

Substandard Execution

As with any marketing program, corporate blogs must be maintained and carefully crafted in order to build and keep an audience. Marketers need to pay close attention to the execution and development of the blogs. Companies can do themselves considerable harm by not fully executing their blogging efforts. Some potentially damaging practices include:

- Publishing a blog that is rarely or randomly updated. When a visitor comes to a blog only to see that the last entry was weeks or months ago, he or she will get the impression that nothing important is going on in the company. Obviously, no company would intentionally create such a negative impression.

- Poorly policing the blog and allowing comments to remain that are really just spam. Too many spam-generated comments will drive real readers away from the blog and reflect poorly on the brand, which can be seen as sloppy and disorganized.

- Posting poorly developed content that runs counter to the beliefs, promises, and personality of the brand, ultimately confusing readers as to what the brand is really about.

As mentioned earlier, corporate blogging is a commitment. Even though it is an easy and cost-effective type of program, blogs can be a digital lightning rod for audiences, and companies need to pay considerable attention to ensure that these audiences are fed information properly.

Longevity

Although specific entries can be deleted from a blog and blog sites can be shut down entirely, a simple copy-and-paste by a single blog reader can keep a controversial or damaging blog entry alive and in the blogosphere forever. Like a politician running for office, every brand has its enemies, looking for an opportunity to tarnish its image. Marketers should be sure that each entry they post will position their brand in a positive light, in both the short and long term, because very often, there simply isn't any going back to erase old mistakes.

Representation

Whoever does the writing for a corporate brand becomes the voice of that brand. Any opinions expressed by that representative will be seen by readers as the official position of the brand. A single misstep or a poorly worded blog entry can do untold damage to a brand.

Employees often host their own blogs outside of the office. Individuals may keep these blogs for personal reasons, but if the employees reveal where they work, they might be seen as a representative of that brand. Because of that, their blog entries could reflect on their employer. Companies that understand the power of blogs often set policies that limit the type of information that their employees can publish on their blogs, even during off hours.

Requirements for a Successful Marketing Blog

Companies that incorporate blogging into their marketing strategy need to make it a commitment, and consider six requirements in order to make their blogs successful: update content regularly, maintain a friendly but brand-oriented voice, keep content relevant, avoid ghost-writing posts, don't sell, and don't be too quick to delete.

Update Content Regularly

Once a company decides to maintain and promote a blog, it must make a commitment to keep the blog updated with new entries. The frequency of new entries is partially determined by the amount of traffic that comes to the site—the more traffic that visits, the more new entries should be posted. At the very least, new content needs to be added on a scheduled basis, so that readers know when to expect it. Posting entries on a seemingly random basis or missing scheduled updates is a sure way to lose core visitors who can easily become confused or indifferent, taking their blog-reading elsewhere.

Maintain a Friendly but Brand-Oriented Voice

Blogs offer companies the opportunity to communicate in a friendlier, more conversational tone. Marketers need to take care not to let this more casual style dilute the image and lifestyle that the brand represents. A tone of voice so informal that it runs contrary to the brand image can actually work against the company, detract from other marketing efforts, and drive away customers. For example, a blog set up by a luxury brand, such as Lexus, would benefit from being relaxed and intellectual, but would likely injure the brand if it included a lot of slang and inappropriate language. Successful marketing is about having control over the message. Blogging, with its conversational style and open forum for responses, can reduce the control a marketer has over the message, so extra attention needs to be paid to ensure that the blog is friendly but still brand-oriented.

Keep Content Relevant

For the most part, blogs are based on a central theme as determined by the blog editor. This makes it easier for readers to find the blogs that they are most interested in. Readers also develop an expectation of what type of entries they will see on a particular blog in the future. Corporate blogs are no different. Editors should be aware that readers will come to their blog because they are interested or curious about that particular brand or the industry in general. It is important for marketers to remain on topic and not deviate from the stated focus of the blog. This reassures blog visitors that they will find information relevant to the interest that drew them to the blog in the first place.

Don't Ghost-Write Blog Posts

While the content of a blog is important, so is the name behind the blog. Many people tune into a particular TV news network because they trust the news anchor. Likewise, the validity of a blog post will often rest on the shoulders of its author. It's not uncommon for readers to examine the blog author's biography. Therefore, it's important that if the author of the blog is listed as the CEO of a company, the CEO should be the one writing the blog - not his or her speech writer or public relations agency. Blogs by definition are meant to be more personal and intimate. Once readers (or worse, the media) catch on to the fact that a blog is being ghost-written, there can be a severe backlash, causing audiences to question any future statements or claims by that company.

Don't Sell

Blogs are meant to provide insight and opinion, personal thoughts, experiences, or expert advice that other people can benefit from. They are not meant to be straightforward sales pitches, which are best left for advertisements or the content on a company's primary Web site. Clearly, a blog on a company's site is meant to help increase sales (the blog provides expert insight on some industry-related topic, the reader makes the mental connection that the blogger is associated with that company, and that company is seen in a positive light, which in turn may lead to increased sales). Blogging can work in a company's favor as long as this subtle connection is allowed to unfold, and the direct sales route is avoided.

140

Don't Be Too Quick to Delete

Because blogs are meant to be a public forum where readers can comment on each post, it is important that bloggers allow negative as well as positive posts. While it's fine to delete rude and baseless attacks or spam-tinged comments, marketers have to be careful not to delete comments simply because they offer a dissenting opinion. Consumers want to judge the quality of the content themselves. They will put more trust in a company that presents all of the ideas available—including ones that work counter to the company's goal—than they will into a company that "stacks the deck" and only provides the comments it wants readers to see.

Chapter Summary

- Blogging is a method of maintaining an online journal where entries are listed chronologically, with the most recent entry appearing at the top. Blogs encourage social networking by inviting people to read postings and contribute their own ideas to the subject at hand. The blog title, the name of the blog editor, individual blog postings, and comments by readers are some of the common elements of a blog site.

- The importance of blogging and its contribution to the growth of the social Internet can't be ignored. Blogging has gained significant popularity over the past several years, and more people are turning to blogs as a primary source of information.

- Many different types of blog sites are present on the Web, including those for personal, media, and marketing purposes, as well as fake blogs and blogs set up by spammers to try and generate click-through ad revenue.

- Blogs are dominated by authors under the age of 30, with a fairly even divide between male and female. For the most part, bloggers write for their own creative expression, although an increase in blogging often coincides with major world news. Some bloggers are using approaches to research and writing that are similar to those used by professional journalists.

- When done correctly, blogging can be an effective tool for brands as a part of their marketing program, proving helpful in customer service, campaign support and increasing Web traffic and overall credibility. The blogosphere is an ideal setting for gathering information on a company's target. Blogging can also present significant danger if not handled properly.

Key Terms

blog editor—The author of a blog.

blogosphere—The immense network of blogs that exist on the Web.

blogroll—A list of links to other blog sites that the editor thinks warrant attention.

false transparency—The practice of creating a marketing campaign that leads the audience to believe it is something other than a marketing promotion.

flog—A fake blog set up as marketing gimmick to help promote a company or support an ad campaign.

microblog—A blog made up of very short entries, often just a line or two to let friends, family or coworkers get a quick glimpse of what they blogger is doing at the time, or what they are thinking about.

paid blog—A blog written by an author who is paid to write positively about the brand or company that sponsors the blog.

scrapping—When bloggers grab headlines from other sites and post them to their own splog in an effort to fool readers into thinking they are reading original content.

splog—A blog comprised entirely of headlines and content pulled from legitimate news sources set up to attract an audience and generate revenue when readers click on ads.

Review Questions

1. A blog can be most closely compared to which of the following?

    a. An online journal

    b. An interactive timeline of events

    c. A file sharing system

    d. An online bulletin board

2. Which of the following is not usually found on a typical blog?

    a. A blogroll

    b. The ability to invite others to visit

    c. The editor's name

    d. Access to archived entries

3. Tags in a blog serve what purpose?

    a. Give the blog a title

    b. Help readers search for content

    c. Let readers vote for whether or not they like a particular blog

    d. All of the above

    e. None of the above

4. With many blogs, readers that leave comments can also include links back to their own sites. True or False?

5. Which of the following can be included in a blog?

    a. Text

    b. Video

    c. Images

    d. All of the above

    e. None of the above

6. As of December 2007, how many new blogs were being created every day?

    a. 112,000,000

    b. 30,000,000

    c. 1,500,000

    d. 120,000

7. Which of the following is the most likely reason that people are relying more on blogs as a source for news?

    a. As TV viewership erodes, less news is being reported by the major networks.

    b. Many people see mass media as biased, and turn to blogs for more unbiased reporting.

    c. People only want to read news on which they can comment.

    d. Because blogs tend to be more informal, typically boring news stories are more interesting when in a blog format.

8. A vlog is a:

    a. Vertical blog - a blog that is written for a vertical market

    b. Verbal blog - a blog that is supported by an audio clip

    c. Video blog - a blog in a video format

    d. None of the above

9. Which of the following statements is most true when it comes to fake blogs and character blogs?

    a. Character blogs are the same as fake blogs-both provide false information.

    b. Character blogs aren't considered fake because it's clear that character blogs are fictional.

10. Which of the following is not a significant reason most people maintain blogs?

    a. To express themselves creatively

    b. To venture into journalism

    c. To document their personal experiences

    d. To document their professional experiences

11. Bloggers stand apart from the general Internet population in which way?

    a. Most bloggers go online for news and political information.

    b. Most bloggers are younger, under the age of 30.

    c. Most bloggers are male.

    d. Most bloggers use dial-up connections.

12. Through February 2007, which global news item spurred the most blog entries?

    a. Hurricane Katrina

    b. Israel/Hezbolah conflict

    c. Iraqi Constitutional Vote

    d. Space shuttle Challenger explosion

13. One reason that blogs and mass media are converging is:

   a. More news stories are written in a conversational tone

   b. More blogs are among the most popular news sources

   c. Mass media stories are increasingly allowing readers to leave comments

   d. Blogrolls are increasingly including links to mass media sites

14. Which of the following statements about corporate blogging is most true?

   a. Blogs are inexpensive to start but difficult to program.

   b. Blogs can be expensive to start but require very little programming.

   c. Blogs are inexpensive to start, but companies need to make a real commitment to maintaining them.

   d. Blogs are inexpensive to start, but can potentially cause a lot of damage to a brand and should be avoided.

15. Which two things do companies need to balance when creating and maintaining a blog?

   a. The number of entries made and the allocated blogging budget

   b. The length of each blog entry and the fact that people who read corporate blogs don't want to invest a lot of time reading them.

   c. The cost of blogging and the budget needed for other marketing campaigns

   d. The conversational tone that blogs allow and the brand personality

16. Which of the following would be the worst example of a character blog?

   a. Donald Trump maintaining a blog discussing issues regarding his show *The Apprentice*

   b. Bart Simpson keeping a blog about the things going on in Springfield

c. Zack Morris keeping a blog on what's been up with the *Saved by the Bell* gang since graduation

d. Hagrid keeping a blog about what's been going on at Hogwarts since Harry Potter graduated

17. Corporate blogs can help do which of the following?

a. Improve traffic to the brand's main Web site

b. Help with internal communications

c. Improve customer service

d. All of the above

e. None of the above

18. When blogging, companies need to make sure:

a. They update their blogs regularly

b. They never police the site, regardless of the comments that people leave

c. They write in the same carefully crafted voice that they use in other marketing tools

d. They don't provide links to their main Web site, so that readers won't think of them as too self-serving

19. Paying attention to the blogosphere can help a company because:

a. It can give company's employees something to do in their off time

b. It can let them in on their competitors' secrets

c. It gives them information on trends in their target market

d. There are no real benefits for companies to pay attention to the blogosphere

20. "False transparency" is best defined as:

a. A politically oriented blog that leans too far in one direction or another

b. A character blog

c. A blog that leads readers to think the blog is written by someone other than the real author

d. A blog that tells readers that a blog will be updated at certain times, when really entries are made more randomly

Projects

1. Pick three blogs within the same category (politics, sports, movies, etc.) and track them over a two week period. Compare and contrast the following:

   a. How often does each site upload new entries?

   b. How many comments does an entry on each site get on average?

   c. How interesting is each relative to the other?

   Briefly summarize each blog, and give your opinion as to why one might be more popular than another.

2. Find a B2B site that maintains a blog. In a two-page paper, describe how this blog differs from a personal blog in terms of voice, content, and other elements.

3. Pick a consumer product (a movie, sneakers, video games, etc.) and search the blogosphere for information and references to that product. In a two-page paper, describe general market trends and the feelings being expressed about the product you selected.

4. Research a blog campaign called "Walmarting Across America." In a paper no longer than five pages, describe the campaign, whether or not it was successful and why.

5. Research recent news stories as relayed through blogs on the Technorati Web site. Find similar stories as relayed in the general media, like CNN or Fox News. In a two-page paper, describe the following:

   a. Is the material and content presented differently in the blogs found on Technorati and the mainstream media? If so, how?

   b. Which comes across as more trustworthy?

   c. Which presents more relevant news?

   d. In the future, would you be more likely to go to Technorati or a mainstream news source for updated information? Why?

148

Endnotes

1. "State of the Blogosphere." Technorati <www.technorati.com> Aug. 2008.
2. Technorati <www.technorati.com> Aug. 2008.
3. Lenhart, Amanda, Fox, Susannah. "Bloggers: A Portrait of the Internet's New Storytellers." Pew Internet & American Life Project, 19 Jul. 2006.
4. Ibid.
5. Ibid.
6. "Zogby Poll: 67% View Traditional Journalism as 'Out of Touch.'" *Zogby International* <www.zogby.com> 27 Feb. 2008.
7. Lenhart, Amanda, Fox, Susannah. "Bloggers: A Portrait of the Internet's New Storytellers." Pew Internet & American Life Project, 19 Jul. 2006.

CHAPTER 5

Web-Based Video

In this chapter you will learn about:

- ◎ The various formats available for Web-based video, the factors that determine which one to use when, and why Flash is often the best option

- ◎ The demographics of the viewing audience, what they're watching, and why

- ◎ The reasons why people post videos to video-sharing sites, how video sites have incorporated other social media tools, and how video is used as part of other social media sites

- ◎ How and why companies are using Web-based video, and how audiences are responding to these efforts

- ◎ What goes into producing professional videos

Video is one of the fastest growing mediums on the Web. It has captured the attention of millions of viewers who tune in to watch everything from their favorite shows, newscasts, and music videos to movie trailers, home videos, and a wide range of amateur productions. Marketers have jumped on the bandwagon, getting involved in the online video market to help promote their brands to a growing audience that is hungry for new video content.

For video on the Web, the mid-2000s proved to be a perfect storm. Increased broadband adoption by homes and businesses, faster and more powerful computers, and a new, cross-platform Flash format by Adobe combined with the introduction of video-sharing sites to ignite a wave of excitement in online video. These factors, combined with declining TV viewership, could very well result in online video replacing television as the central means of personal entertainment.

Figuring Out the Format

Since the commercialization of the Web, Internet users have been eagerly waiting to see the promise of video at our fingertips fulfilled. Predictions of the family TV set becoming the primary source for television viewing and Web surfing seemed all but inevitable. However, with dial-up connections that were far too slow to showcase large video files and formats that were often incompatible with certain operating systems and browsers, video on the Web languished through most of the 1990s. The Web had the dream, but not the drive.

When the social media revolution roared onto the scene in the mid-2000s, however, online video came back with a vengeance. Now the Web was ready for it and so were the viewers. More importantly, the formatting problems that had plagued video developers wanting to provide the best possible video quality to the widest possible audience were finally solved—by the Adobe Flash player. The player, which has been around since the 1990s, did not hit critical mass until the 2006 release of version 9, when major upgrades and improvements made Flash the format (.flv) and player of choice for practically every major video site on the Web.

Before delving too deeply into the Adobe Flash player and why it has become the format of choice, it would be helpful to review the variables that should be considered when deciding on the best format for your needs. We will also take a look at the some of the other formats that are available.

The following points should be considered when deciding upon the best format for a Web video:

* **Platform compatibility**: To gain the widest possible audience, you need to use a format that can be seen by as many computer users as possible.

* **File size**: Even with broadband connections, videos files can be slow to download, which can cause viewers to lose interest and leave the site. In response to these concerns, developers have created two methods of delivering video: **streaming** and **progressive download**. Each method has its own distinct set of pros and cons; the specific requirements of each video project will determine which delivery option is the best choice. Table 5-1 provides a chart that defines and compares the two methods. Regardless of the method chosen, keeping files sizes as small as possible is beneficial for the viewer and the developer (large video files will use more server storage space).

* **Video quality**: Typically, as file sizes get smaller, the quality of the image deteriorates. It is important to balance the need to keep file size low with the desire to provide content that is sharp enough to keep viewers interested.

* **Accessibility and cost of conversion software**: Shooting the video is the fun part, but it still needs to be edited and converted. Producers need to consider the cost of editing and conversion software and whether their computer's operating system can run that software.

	Progressive Download	**Streaming**
How it Works	Video is housed on a standard Web server and served through an http request, the same way that any Web page would be loaded. The video is downloaded to the viewer's hard drive before playback, but it starts playing before it is completely downloaded.	Streaming video is not downloaded to a viewer's hard drive. Streaming videos reside on special streaming servers that must be set up in addition to a Web server. The streaming server creates a unique connection with each viewer and sends the video to the requesting client in small bits, which are discarded immediately after being viewed.

Table 5-1 Definitions and a comparison of the progressive download and streaming delivery methods for Web videos. (*continues*)

(continued)

	Progressive Download	**Streaming**
Pros	• The video ultimately resides on the viewer's computer so that he or she can watch it multiple times without having to wait for it to download again. This also allows the user to share the video file with others through e-mail or other methods.	• Streaming videos allow more advanced control, including the capability to detect the viewer's bandwidth (thus serving the video at the best rate for viewing) and the ability to automatically create thumbnails and short previews.
	• This format offers high-quality video and audio playback performance.	• Streaming videos begin playing very quickly.
	• The video can reside on and be served through lower cost Web servers.	• Producers that pay for bandwidth or hosting services by the amount of data that is transferred only pay for the bits that the client actually views.
		• Less disk space is required by the viewer, because the video is not downloaded to the hard drive.
		• Users can easily jump to any point of the video without having to wait for it to download, and it will begin playing immediately.
		• Analytics such as how long the video was viewed, whether the viewer jumped to a different point in the video, and how many times the viewer watched the video can be collected.
		• Live video can be delivered to viewers.
Cons	• Viewers are limited in their ability to fast forward the video until the entire video has been downloaded.	• Streaming video has significantly higher costs. It requires expensive streaming servers and a software license for each server.
	• Bandwidth is not allocated to individual viewers. As more people watch a video simultaneously, the video download will slow, resulting in a delayed start time for all viewers.	• It is harder for users to pass along streaming video, because the file is not downloaded onto the viewer's hard drive.

Table 5-1 Definitions and a comparison of the progressive download and streaming delivery methods for Web videos. (*continues*)

(continued)

	Progressive Download	Streaming
When to Use	• Progressive downloading is ideal for amateur videographers and sites with lower traffic and shorter videos. It should be used by sites that do not have a high concern about copyright protection (since the videos will be on the viewer's hard drive).	• Streaming is the best option for larger video files, so that users can jump around and navigate more effectively. Streaming should also be used when delivering live video, when the potential audience is large, and when advanced features and analytics tracking are desirable.

Table 5-1 Definitions and a comparison of the progressive download and streaming delivery methods for Web videos.

It is also important to gain an understanding of **media players** before discussing how to determine the appropriate video file format for a project. File formats are the way in which videos are encoded; media players are the software that plays the videos. Often, the media player and file format share the same name, thus creating the potential for confusion.

Popular and frequently used media players include:

- Flash
- Windows Media Player (WMP)
- QuickTime Player
- RealPlayer

Typically, media players come pre-installed on new computers (Table 5-2 shows which media player typically comes pre-installed on which computers). If a media player is not already installed, viewers can download and install it from the Web, usually for free. It is best not to rely on your viewers to download a new player—they are more likely to abandon that particular video altogether.

Media Player	PC	Mac
Flash	X	X
WMP	X	
QuickTime		X
RealPlayer		

Table 5-2 A breakdown of which media player is pre-installed on which type of computer.

Each media player works with different file formats. Table 5-3 details the most common file formats for video. Table 5-4 shows which player reads which format.

One last piece of the Web video puzzle is the **codec**, which is a program used to compress video files. In some cases, the codec and the format are the same, such as .wmv or .mpg. Other formats, such as .mov and .avi, are considered **container formats**, because they can play files compressed with a variety of codecs. Some codecs create smaller files that take up less space and are easier to transfer via e-mail or upload onto server at the expense of quality playback; other codecs retain a higher quality playback, but create larger files.

File Format	Description
.flv	The format name stands for Flash Video. .flv is the raw file created after converting a video from some other file format. As of the writing of this book, it is the format of choice because it is the most compatible and because more users have the Flash player installed on their computers than any other player.
.swf	.swf stands for ShockWave Flash. This is the extension used when creating standard Flash animations, buttons, and navigation bars. Users must have a Flash player installed in order to see .swf files.
.mpg	The format abbreviation of MPEG. This format will play on either the QuickTime player or WMP. MPEG has lost favor as Flash's popularity has risen, because MPEGs are usually larger files that cannot be streamed and cannot be created on a Mac without purchasing additional software.
.asf, .wmv	Advanced Streaming Format and Windows Media Video, respectively. These Microsoft formats only play on the Windows Media Player, which does not come preinstalled on Macs (Mac users can download WMV version 9, although Microsoft has stopped creating new upgrades for Macs). Mac users need to purchase additional software to convert other video formats into WMVs.
.mov	.mov is the QuickTime format, and plays only in the QuickTime media player. It is a container format, meaning that a number of different codecs can be used for file compression. PC users have to download the player to see QuickTime movies.
.mp4	The format name stands for MPEG-4. It can create very small file sizes, but the videos cannot be viewed by PC users unless they download the QuickTime player.
.avi	The format name stands for Audio/Video Interleaved, which is a container format that can contain video compressed by other codecs.
.rm	The RealMedia format. This format does not play on either the QuickTime player or WMV. Viewers need to download the RealMedia player; however, the free version is much less powerful than the fee-based version. There are very few RealMedia movies remaining on the Web.

Table 5-3 The different formats that are used for Web video.

	Flash	WMP (for Pc)	WMP9 (for Mac)	QuickTime Player	RealPlayer
.flv	X				
.swf	X			X	X
.asf		X	X		X
.wmv		X	X		
.avi		X		Depends on codec used	
.mov	X			X	
.mpg		X		X	X
.mp4	X			X	X
.rm					X

Table 5-4 A breakdown of which media player plays which file format.

The Flash (.flv) File Format: A Closer Look

Deciding which file format to choose might seem confusing and intimidating, but it is actually very simple. At the risk of sounding like a paid endorsement: Flash is far and away the best format choice. Practically every major video source on the Web utilizes the Flash format, including YouTube, Google Video, Yahoo! Video, and MySpace. This underscores the widespread acceptance of this remarkable format. To understand why the Flash player and format have gained such tremendous popularity, one just has to look at the benefits associated with it:

- **Wide-scale compatibility**: Because the Flash player comes pre-installed in both PCs and Macs, practically all Web users can see Flash videos.

- **Small file size**: The Flash format uses its own codec, introduced in Flash 8, to keep files sizes very small.

- **High image quality**: The FLV format is created using a **lossy** compression method, which means that data is eliminated during the compression in order to reduce the file to a much smaller size. However, Flash does an excellent job of reducing files sizes without causing too much image quality deterioration.

- **Multiple delivery options**: FLV files can be created for either streaming or progressive downloads.

- **Availability of custom controls**: With the Flash player, developers can create their own custom **player controls** (such as the progress bar that shows the progression of a playing video, the volume control, and the look, feel, and design of the player framework). This is a big benefit artistically and a big step up from players such as WMV and QuickTime, which only play videos in their pre-designed framework.

- **Full-screen capabilities**: With just the touch of a button on the player controls, viewers can switch to watching the video full screen (assuming the developer allows that option).

- **Friendly start-up screen**: While other players just show a blank screen as the video files begins to download, the Flash player allows you to customize a first frame, like "Hold on—video will start shortly", to let the viewer know that the video really is working.

The only true downside to using the Flash format is the extra step needed to convert original files from .mov, .wmv, or other formats into an .flv. Fortunately, this extra step is fairly simple and can be accomplished one of two ways:

- **Use an online service**: Popular video-sharing Web sites like YouTube and Google Video allow you to upload video files, which the sites will convert to .flv files and host for free. Each video-sharing site has its own pros and cons. Each has its own list of the types of files they can convert, how they will treat your videos (putting ads before or after them, for example), allowable file size, etc. Make sure you read the specifications for a video-sharing site before beginning the upload and conversion process.

- **Run conversion software from your computers**: With the appropriate software, you can also convert videos into the .flv format on your own computer. This option could be the best choice if:

  - You only intend to display the videos on your own site, and do not want to make them available to the potentially massive audiences of a video-sharing site.

  - You have a lot of videos to convert, and it would be too time-consuming to upload them to a video-sharing site.

Once converted, .flv files can still be uploaded to video-sharing sites. If you want to display them on your own site, you will need to install a Flash player on your server as well.

A variety of software applications can be used for converting files, with the best being the Adobe Flash Professional package. A full list of programs, their costs, and comparisons can be found at the blog site associated with this book. A list of available Flash players can be found here, as well.

Who's Watching What

Like blogging and social networking, Web video viewers have specific demographic characteristics, and online audiences are involved in video in a variety of ways. As with any other traditional or online tool, it is important for marketers to understand and analyze these audiences in order to reach them effectively.

The sheer numbers of online viewers is staggering (see Figure 5-1), and is especially remarkable when viewed as a percentage of Internet users as well as a percentage of the entire population (see Figure 5-2). According to eMarketer, a leading source of marketing research and information, by the end of 2007, nearly 80% of all U.S. Internet users viewed video online at least once a month—that's over half the population of the United States, or 154 million people.[1] While this figure is impressive, the reality is that viewers' hunger for online video is greater than their ability to properly receive it. As discussed earlier in this chapter, even when compressed, videos can be large files—at least when compared to standard graphics and animations. Broadband connections have no doubt contributed greatly to the mainstream adoption of online videos. However, according to the Pew Internet & American Life Project, less than 45% of all homes had a broadband connection as of February 2007, as shown in Figure 5-3.[2] Also according to Pew, a full 31% of those with no access to broadband at home or at work can be counted among the video consuming audience.[3] This means that many people are viewing online videos in less than ideal circumstances.

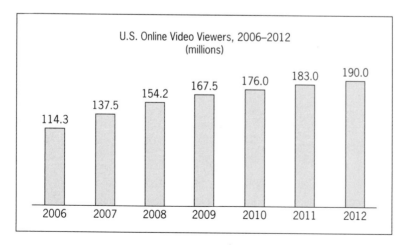

Figure 5-1 The number of online video viewers, projected through 2012. SOURCE: "Internet TV Audience Hits Critical Mass." eMarketer <www.emarketer.com> Feb. 2008.

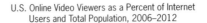

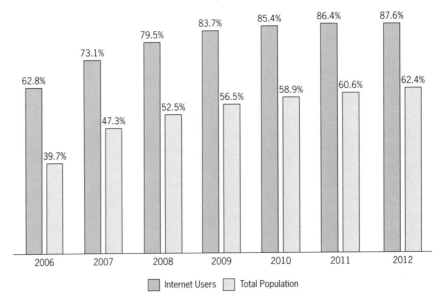

Figure 5-2   The number of online video viewers, projected through 2012. SOURCE: "Internet TV Audience Hits Critical Mass." eMarketer <www.emarketer.com> Feb. 2008.

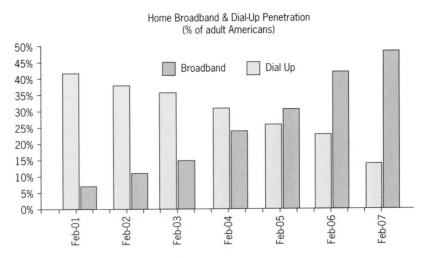

Figure 5-3   As of February 2007, less than 45% of all homes had a broadband connection. SOURCE: "Increased Use of Video Sharing Sites." Pew Internet & American Life Project, 9 Jan. 2008.

These are powerful numbers that make a strong case that online video will eventually replace television as our primary source of entertainment. In fact, people are already beginning to engage in online multitasking. Nearly 80% of online adults have gone online while watching TV, and more than a third do so often or always—most often to search for content completely unrelated to the broadcast they are watching.[4]

Like social networking and blogging, the dominant viewing demographic is made up of younger males between the ages of 18–24, 80% of whom watch online videos at least once a week.[5] Table 5-5 shows the frequency with which men and women in different age brackets view online videos. Although younger males lead the way, almost 50% of viewers in all the categories watch online videos once each week or more.[6] These statistics, which many experts predict will continue to show an ongoing shift toward more frequent viewing, show the power of combining two of the most powerful mediums ever invented—video and the Internet.

Frequency	Males 18–24	Females 18–24	Males 25+	Females 25+
Once per day or more	33.7%	17.0%	25.4%	13.3%
A couple of times per week	28.8%	26.0%	28.1%	25.9%
Once per week	16.9%	14.4%	12.4%	8.9%
A couple of times per month	10.0%	17.1%	17.1%	21.2%
Once per month	7.5%	15.8%	10.7%	17.5%
Less than once per month	3.1%	8.9%	6.3%	13.3%

Table 5-5   The frequency with which U.S. online video viewers (male and female across age groups) view online videos. SOURCE: Hallerman, David. "Online Video Content: The New TV Audience." eMarketer <www.emarketer.com> 24 Feb. 2008.

Online viewing audiences can also be segmented into demographics other than age and gender. Defined strictly by frequency of viewership, they can be split into groups of heavy, moderate, and light viewers that each have their own habits and similarities.

- **Heavy viewers**: Heavy viewers, which make up the top 20% of all online viewers, watch an astounding 841 minutes (just over 14 hours) of online videos each month—11 times more than moderate viewers and 140 times more than light viewers.[7] Interestingly, while YouTube is the top destination for viewers in all three categories, heavy viewers spent much of their time on small niche video sites—sites that serve less than 1% of the entire online population. It is likely that this audience is very discriminating in their video selection.

- **Moderate viewers**: Moderate viewers, which make up the next 30% of all on online viewers, average 77 minutes of online video viewing each month.[8] This group spends much of its time watching videos on broadcast TV sites, such as CBS and ABC. Moderate viewers also visit YouTube frequently, but they do not spend as much time on other general video-sharing sites.

- **Light viewers**: Light viewers, defined as the remaining 50% of online viewers, spend less than 6 minutes per month watching videos on the Web. Light consumers of online videos tend to be the heaviest consumers of TV, with 46% watching 13 or more hours of TV each week (compared to 39% of moderate viewers and only 30% of heavy viewers).[9]

Marketers have a better chance of sending the right message to the best audience when they fully understand who is watching what, where, and how often. This brings up the next obvious question—with so many different people online watching videos, what are they all watching?

To call the selection of online video diverse is to dramatically understate the true wealth of online video content. Hundreds of channels of cable or satellite television once seemed overwhelming; however, those viewing options pale in comparison to the 65,000 videos that are uploaded to YouTube alone every day.[10] Online videos fall into many of the same categories as would be found on television, such as news, comedy, sports, music, drama, cartoons, politics, and lifestyle. Some categories, however, are unique to the Web. Amateur videos, movie trailers, live concerts, educational/how-to videos, and on-demand clips from a variety of sources help drive audiences online. Table 5-6 shows a table detailing the most popular genres of online videos, and the percentage of online viewers that expressed an interest in each.

Video Genre	% of Online Users
News clips	36%
Short video clips or segments	33%
Music videos	32%
Full-length TV shows	28%
Full-length movies	27%
Other people's personal videos	23%
Live concerts	18%
Live sporting events	16%
Product demonstrations	15%
Some other video category	11%
On demand sporting event	11%
Advertising	4%

Table 5-6 The different genres of online videos, and the percentage of viewers who watch them. SOURCE: "The Importance of Delivering a Great Online Video Experience." JupiterResearch, 11 July 2007.

Reviewing these figures carefully, one can begin to paint a picture of the average Internet user. Online video viewers are most interested in watching news clips to catch up on current events, which is also the primary interest expressed by readers of blogs. Web users, particularly those who utilize social media applications, are hungry for information and want to get to know the world around them. This creates opportunities for savvy marketers to reach new audiences by putting their messages where online news is located and by presenting social media users with news and updates about their brands.

Video watchers are also among the most active Internet users in terms of leaving comments online. In 2007, nearly 27 million comments were left on video-sharing sites—averaging 12.6 comments for each new video posted that year (over 1.2 million).[11] These numbers are more than just an interesting peek into the activities of online video watchers—they are part of a larger roadmap that helps direct marketers and gives them further insight into their audiences. When people leave comments on a video—or a blog—it means that they are engaged. The comment may be positive, negative, jubilant, or angry, but it indicates that the video has captured the viewer's attention and spurred them to take some action. Brands and marketers can use information and users' feedback to help shape their campaigns and craft their messages, which can include more well-defined means of triggering an audience to make a purchase.

Video as a Social Media Tool

Online video has become an important part of the social media revolution, infiltrating sites in practically every category and expanding into its own industry. One reason for the popularity of video-sharing sites is that most provide free storage space, so that producers do not need to pay to upload their content. The cost of servers and the potential complexities of developing a site capable of showing videos could be an insurmountable barrier for the average user. Video-sharing sites virtually eliminate the costs and hassles for producers and create a central place where viewers can come to watch a variety of videos. The increasing volume of videos being uploaded to these sites has also been advanced by the growing number of cell phones and computers with built-in cameras and a reduction in the price of handheld semi-professional video cameras.

People post videos on various sites for many reasons, including:

- **Marketing**: Video has long been a mainstay of marketing campaigns, with television commercials being the most common application. These commercials often make their way onto video-sharing sites, where people seek out their favorites to watch repeatedly. Marketers also use online video for training purposes, news releases, product announcements, and corporate overviews (videos that show the company history, what they do, and why a consumer should buy from them).

- **Education**: Online video provides an effective means of educating people on any number of topics. How-to videos typically provide step-by-step instructions on topics such as using a specific product or how to program a Web page. Classroom style videos can teach people about specific topics important to the marketer's audience. For example, a pharmaceutical services company might produce and post educational videos about the importance of secure packaging for potential clients.

- **Fame**: With video sharing, anyone can be a star. Through the Web, people have rushed to find fame using every possible gimmick from producing home music videos and comedy bits to puppet shows and animations. Amateur video has created modern day social media icons such as the Obama Girl, who sang about her crush on U.S. presidential candidate Barack Obama, and Chris Crocker (shown in Figure 5-4). Crocker's now infamous video-taped cry of "Leave Britney alone!" in response to the media's constant hounding of singer Britney Spears became one of the most heavily viewed videos on YouTube and was shown on practically every news broadcast and late night talk show.

Figure 5-4 The YouTube video of Chris Crocker crying, "Leave Britney alone!" made him an overnight sensation.

- **Re-broadcast**: Television is finding a new home on the Web, with many popular networks creating sites to rebroadcast popular shows online after they have aired on TV. This attracts more viewers to these shows, helping networks increase their appeal to advertisers. Figure 5-5 shows a page of Fox On Demand, where viewers can watch previously run episodes of practically any show in the Fox lineup. With 65% of audiences preferring to watch professionally produced video content on the Web (as opposed to amateur content),[12] re-broadcast is a rapidly growing segment that is servicing a growing need.

Figure 5-5   The Fox On Demand Web site allows viewers to watch previously aired episodes of their favorite shows. A clip from the popular show *Family Guy* is shown in this figure.

- **Street journalism**: With a cell phone camera in hand, anyone can be a reporter. Amateur journalists who happened to be in the right place at the right time (or the wrong place at the wrong time, depending upon the situation) have uploaded videos of everything from freak tornados to crimes in progress. In many instances, these street journalists have captured footage that made national and even international news, including the 2007 clip shown in Figure 5-6, in which a heckler was arrested at a John Kerry speech, yelling "Don't tase me, bro!" as police tried to subdue him.

Figure 5-6   An amateur journalist taped and uploaded this video of a college student being arrested at a John Kerry event. This video became famous for the college student yelling "Don't tase me, bro!" as police tried to subdue him.

These reasons and more have brought a herd of viewers to video-sharing sites, and in turn, more sites of this nature have been launched. The nascent video-sharing industry took center stage of the media spotlight in 2006 with the heavily publicized purchase of YouTube, the clear leader in video-sharing Web sites, by Google for $1.65 billion.[13] That was an impressive amount to pay for a company that, as of August, 2006 had yet to generate a profit.[14]

Video-sharing sites take advantage of social media tools by allowing viewers to leave comments on each video, maintain a list of their favorites, and develop their own profile page that other users can visit. At the same time, other Web sites have used video as part of their social media offerings. Social networking sites like MySpace allow members to upload video to their profiles. In fact, videos have become a primary feature of MySpace. In 2007, MySpace officially began a rivalry with YouTube when it launched MySpace TV—a video-sharing network that has a permanent place in MySpace's primary navigation bar. MySpace TV allows users to upload their videos, which can also be embedded in the user's own MySpace profile, and it features a series of channels with more professionally produced content from both outside sources and MySpace itself. As would be expected in a social media setting, viewers are able to rate and leave comments on all videos, add their favorites to their

MySpace profile or blog, e-mail a video to a friend, or save it to a personal favorites page to watch again at a later time. Figures 5-7 and 5-8 show screen shots from MySpace TV.

Figure 5-7 The home page for MySpace TV allows users to upload their own videos, watch other user videos, browse videos from a variety of channels, and insert videos into their MySpace profile.

Figure 5-8 The Prime Time page for MySpace's video sharing platform lets viewers watch professionally produced content fed in from a variety of other online video sharing sites or from MySpace-produced content.

Web-Based Video as a Marketing Tool

In 2007, over 13% of U.S. companies had plans to include online videos as part of their marketing strategy. While this is not an extremely large number, it is impressive when compared to the 2006 figure of only 4%.[15]

Companies often upload videos to video-sharing sites as well as to their own sites. These firms gain significant benefits from this marketing strategy, including:

* Better audience retention: People are more likely to stay engaged and remain online if the message is actively communicated to them rather than being presented as copy that must be read.

* More effective messaging: Video gives marketers the opportunity to present a more complete picture. A single video can illustrate points through more than just scripted words. The inflection and enthusiasm in the presenter's voice, the graphics, animations, camera angles, scene changes, and music all contribute to the overall message. In short, online video allows marketers to generate an emotional connection between the marketer and the viewer.

* Improved marketing support: Companies are beginning to build entire Web sites around video-based concepts rather than just incorporating videos into portions of their sites. Clever programmers, designers, and producers are working together to develop more engaging and interactive experiences for their visitors. By doing this, they create sites that do far more than promote a product—they make visitors part of that product's culture. Often, these video-driven sites include other social media applications. Figure 5-9 shows the video-based Web site for the Geico Cavemen, a popular TV commercial that was spun off into a short-lived TV show. The Web site stars the cavemen in their home, against scenery that is interactive. Users can click on various items around the house for additional applications. Geico Insurance information is quietly woven throughout the site. Figure 5-10 shows the accompanying social networking site created to allow cavemen to interact with each other (real people, of course, are invited to create profiles, as well).

Figure 5-9 The home page of cavemanscrib.com—a video-based site that is part of the Geico Insurance advertising campaign. Most of the content is presented via video, although portions of the screen are clickable for more information.

Figure 5-10 Part of the Geico caveman concept is a sister site located at iheartcavemen.com. This social networking site allows cavemen and real people to create profiles and interact with one another. The large caveman pictured with the arrow over it (top left) is a video profile; a Geico ad appears on the right.

INTERVIEW WITH...

BRIAN PHALEN: ASCO POWER UNIVERSITY

ASCO Power is a business-to-business company owned by Emerson Electric. ASCO manufactures power generators for hospitals, Internet data centers, shopping malls, and other facilities that require a constant flow of electricity without interruption.

In a competitive market driven by highly educated engineers, ASCO takes an aggressive approach toward maintaining its role as the industry leader. Most recently, ASCO has taken this effort to the Web, where they have set up ASCO Power University (shown in Figure 5-11), a video-based educational resource. The site is designed to educate engineers about ASCO and other critical engineering topics that many universities fail to cover.

Brian Phelan is the Director of Marketing Services for ASCO Power, and spoke with me about the online university, its value, purpose, and future.

Figure 5-11 ASCO's Power University is an online video-based educational resource meant to inform audiences while establishing ASCO as an industry thought-leader.

BRIAN: ASCO Power University is an online educational resource for new engineers who have recently graduated, as well as veteran engineers that could benefit from a refresher course or want to see some of the latest innovations and methods in the electrical industry. Unfortunately, many of the engineering schools have stopped teaching the basics that lay the foundation for our entire industry. We're trying to fill that gap, provide insight, and pass on our accumulated knowledge and expertise. From a marketing standpoint, we're not taking the obvious route of uploading promotional videos about our products and services, why potential customers should choose ASCO, or why our brand is superior. There's a little of that, but the real value of the University is to establish ASCO as the thought and innovation leader in our industry. If an engineer is going to come to us to learn, it stands to reason he'll come to us when it's time to buy, as well.

The University is free for anyone to use, but we do require visitors to register with us before they can watch any of the educational segments. That registration gives us a powerful marketing advantage—we know who's coming, how often they visit, how long they stay, and we know how and where to reach them. It's an audience that we know is interested in these topics, and their registration information tells us where to find them. From a marketer's perspective, you can't ask for anything better.

JASON: How unique is this to your industry?

BRIAN: As of now, the Power University is the only one of its kind in an industry that has significantly lagged behind the times. This tool puts us far ahead of the curve and confirms the innovative nature of our company.

JASON: Why did you choose to use video to establish yourself as a thought-leader?

BRIAN: There's more to the Power University than video, although video is the central driving force. We went this route because video can capture people's attention unlike any other medium. These are pretty intricate topics, and having them explained through video is far more effective than having someone read flat copy. The fact of the matter is that we're an entertainment-based society, and video—even educational video—can be entertaining. It also gives us the opportunity to weave in illustrations, Flash animations, 3D models, and other resources to make these courses easier to understand.

It's something that we wouldn't have been able to do a few years ago, but with the advancements made in online video and the fact that most, if not all, of our prospects and clients now have broadband connections, the time is right for us to take advantage of these tools.

JASON: How difficult is the University to maintain?

BRIAN: The maintenance of the site itself is quite simple. We're using a design and database structure developed by MyPod Studios, which is a Web-based company that generates video-based channels for companies. The page structure stays the same, but we can use our own logo and colors to make it our own—much more cost-effective than building a site like this on our own. MyPod Studios gives us quite a bit of control over the look and feel of the site, and an easy-to-use back-end administration area that lets us post new content and edit information pretty easily.

The hardest or most time-consuming part, really, is the development of the content. The difficulty of content development is inversely proportionate to the benefit received from it. With video, the benefit is quite high, but it's that much harder to produce. For each video—most of which are between 15 and 30 minutes—we need to determine a viable topic and write content about that topic, which takes research and editing. That content needs to be turned into a script, speakers need to be hired and scheduled, as do camera and lighting crews. We need to set a location, which may involve travel. Once the shoot is done, the raw footage still needs to be edited, compressed, and converted to a Flash format for use on the University site. It's worth the effort, but it is effort.

JASON: The University uses other social media tools along with video. Tell me about those and how they enhance the user experience.

BRIAN: Not all the presentations are video. Some of them are Flash animations with a voice-over explaining the content, and some are just PowerPoint presentations that use a voice-over. For each video, users are allowed to post reviews for other users to read, which helps the audience decide which segments are the most valuable to them. Registered users can also save videos into a 'favorites' list so that they can return to them easily or send links to friends and coworkers leading them to certain videos. All of these tools work together to create a better, more educational user experience. RSS feeds also let users know when new content has been uploaded.

JASON: What's the future of the University?

BRIAN: Our first goal is to continue building content. Once you start gathering an audience, you have to keep the momentum going by adding new content as quickly as possible. What takes 30 minutes for someone to watch can take weeks or months to put together, so it's a chore. Beyond that, we're seeing opportunities to expand the University into a true 'university,' with accreditation programs, certificates of course completion, and other such features.

Companies also need to understand that marketing through online video can injure a brand if not done properly. Online video watchers have quickly adapted to the methodologies of online video; they have formed strong opinions about how video-sharing sites provide advertising and what they find most frustrating. Web surfing and frustration often go hand-in-hand, as users who have grown accustomed to receiving information quickly and clearly can easily lose patience when a site does not immediately yield those results.

Marketers who want to use video-sharing sites as a means of advertising should be aware that audiences have clear views on the types of ads that they are willing to tolerate. According to a study by JupiterResearch, 80% of all online video watchers are comfortable accepting ads as a necessary means of keeping the content free to view.[16] However, it is also clear that the ads they are most willing to accept are those that are the least intrusive. Table 5-7 outlines the types of ad that video watchers like the most and least. Keep in mind that although each video-sharing site will determine its own advertising model (when and where ads are shown), viewers are likely to take any negative feelings out on the brands they are seeing advertised.

Types of Ads on Video Pages	% of Viewers that Find this Type of Ad Acceptable
Banner ad next to every video clip	32%
Video ad after every video clip	21%
Video ad before every video clip	14%
Small ad in the corner of the currently playing video	9%
An interactive game ad after every video clip	4%
Will only watch online video if it has no ads at all	20%

Table 5-7   Types of online video ads viewers are most and least willing to tolerate. SOURCE: "The Importance of Delivering a Great Online Video Experience." JupiterResearch, 11 July 2007.

These results make it clear that viewers do not want their viewing experience interrupted. The ads people are most willing to accept are the ones that have the least impact on the videos themselves.

The viewing experience is of utmost importance to online audiences, and marketers need to carefully consider the quality of their content or risk permanently losing their audience. Sixty percent of all viewers will quickly leave a site if the viewing experience is poor, and a quarter of those people are unlikely ever to return to that site.[17] Table 5-8 details the most common reasons why people become dissatisfied with video sites, whether corporate run or video-sharing. Here too, the biggest reasons have to do with the interruption or delay of the video.

Source of Frustration	% of Viewers Who Indicate This Is a Source of Frustration
Video was interrupted (stopped for buffering)	44%
Video took too long to begin	35%
Picture quality was poor	32%
Site mandated registration	27%
Video was too slow during playback	22%
Ads inside video were too long or frequent	18%
Playback was interrupted and didn't automatically restart	16%
Site crashed or froze	15%
Error message received	14%
Viewing required payment	10%
Portions of video were skipped	10%
Figuring out how to play video too confusing	6%
Other reasons	3%
Never felt frustration with online video	15%

Table 5-8   The major sources of frustration viewers have with video sites. SOURCE: "The Importance of Delivering a Great Online Video Experience." JupiterResearch <www.jupiterresearch> 11 July 2007.

Off the Web: What Goes into Video Production

Professional video production can be among the most complex and exhausting undertakings when it comes to the development of content. Amateur videographers can put together a simple video by sitting in front of a Web cam, hitting the 'Record' button and talking, but marketers who want to take advantage of video have a much longer and harder road to travel. Entire books and classes are devoted to teaching the process of video production; the following section provides just a brief glimpse into what it takes to produce a video for the Web:

1. **Concept creation**: Varying amounts of concept creation will be needed depending on the type of production. TV commercials, which usually tell a complete story in just 30 seconds, can require weeks or months of creative concept development to determine the storyline, the messaging, scene, characters, etc. Videos that are more straightforward, for example an announcer or host speaking directly into a camera, take far less creative development.

2. **Script writing and story boarding**: Once the concept has been settled, marketers need to write a script. Typically, scripts not only provide the dialog, they also explain the scene, the reactions of the characters, and their movements. Once approved, a **story board**, which is an illustrated representation of the script, is developed to show how the video should look and feel. Figure 5-12 provides a sample storyboard.

Figure 5-12   A sample story board for a video shoot.

3. **Casting**: Usually the people in videos, whether they appear onscreen or perform off-screen as narrators, are paid actors. Finding the right person to hire can be an arduous task, and it sometimes takes days of seeing numerous models and actors to determine the right person for each role.

4. **Location scouting**: Most often, video shoots take place in a studio, which is specifically meant to accommodate video and film productions. These studios can be adapted to recreate almost any background or scene necessary, and they provide all the equipment needed. In many cases, due to specific needs or budget issues, videos must be shot someplace other than in a studio, such as in a warehouse, park, office, or city street. In these cases, the video producers need to scout the location in advance to determine any potential problems that may arise, such as noise from a nearby highway or lighting issues.

5. **Shooting**: The day of the shoot is usually long and hectic. With the script and storyboard in hand, and actors on site, the crew gets ready for the shoot. The crew usually involves one or two cameras and cameramen, lighting engineers, and audio engineers. A make-up artist will often be at the location, to put the proper make-up on the actors and help with make-up and wardrobe issues throughout the day. The director will also be present to tell the actors what to do, how to do it, and tell the camera operators how to shoot each scene. Finally, assistants will be present to help with all of the details and issues that will inevitably come up, arrange for snacks and lunch, help prep actors, etc. Often, shooting for an entire day might yield little more than a small amount of usable content.

6. **Digitizing**: Once shot, the video tape created must be digitized—brought into the computer for editing.

7. **Graphics**: Any graphics that are needed for the video are designed and brought into the computer that will do the editing.

8. **Editing**: The editor takes all of the footage, and, along with the director, decides which scenes to keep and which to discard. When this process is complete, the editor puts the remaining scenes, graphics, and music together into a completed story.

9. **Compressing and converting**: Once edited and completed, the video is compressed into a small file size and converted into the proper format (most likely an .flv).

10. **Uploading**: The converted file is uploaded to the site, referenced in the code, and it's ready to roll.

This list barely scrapes the surface of the effort that goes into a video production, but as a rising star of the Web, the effort is consistently proving worth the effort.

Chapter Summary

- Many different formats and players are available for presenting online videos. Since 2006, however, the Flash (.flv) format has been far and away the favorite of video-sharing sites because of its ability to reach a broad audience and compress files to small sizes without significantly harming the playback.

- Like other forms of social media, the largest audience for Web-based video is younger males, however every other age group watches significant amount of videos, as well. As with blogging, news and current events again top the list of the reasons why people watch online video, underscoring people's thirst for up-to-date information.

- Video has become an important part of the social media revolution, appearing not only on video-sharing sites, but on B2B, B2C, and other types of Web sites as well. There are many reasons why people post videos online, including education, marketing, street journalism and the desire for fame, however fleeting.

- Amateur video has flooded video-sharing sites like YouTube, but marketers must be careful to create high quality, professional productions. These productions can be very complex, but the results are often worthwhile.

Key Terms

codec—A program used to compress videos into a small size.

container format—A format that can play files compressed with a variety of codecs.

lossy—A compression method that eliminates information from a file in order to compress the file into a smaller size.

media player—The software that plays videos online.

player controls—The functionality, such as play, pause, stop, and volume, that allows a viewer to control the playback of an online video.

progressive download—A less-expensive way to serve online videos. Progressive download requires that the video be downloaded to the viewer's computer; the video will start playing shortly after download has begun.

story board—An illustrated, literal interpretation of a video script.

streaming—A method of delivering videos on the Web. Streaming video is delivered via a specialized server that creates a unique connection with each viewer and sends the video to the requesting client in small bits.

Review Questions

1. Which of the following is the least likely reason why video on the Web is growing so quickly?

    a. The rise of broadband connections in the home

    b. The popularity of cameras built into computers and cell phones

    c. The Flash video format

    d. The decrease in the number of computers loaded with the Real Media Player

2. Which of the following is the least important to consider when deciding on the best video format?

    a. Platform compatibility

    b. Video content

    c. Video playback quality

    d. File Size

3. Which of the following is the best delivery method if you expect a large number of people to view your video?

    a. Streaming

    b. Progressive download

    c. AVI

    d. Real Media

4. Which of the following is the best delivery option if you want to keep server costs down and allow people to pass along your video to others?

    a. Streaming

    b. Progressive download

    c. AVI

    d. Real Media

5. Which format is native only to Macs?

    a. .wmv

    b. .mov

    c. .avi

    d. .rm

6. What is the main function of a codec?

   a. To ensure that corporate videos accurately promote the brand

   b. To ensure that the video will play on as many computers as possible

   c. To reduce the file size of a video

   d. To convert files to the proper format

7. Once you convert a file to the Flash (.flv) format using software on your own computer, you can no longer upload it to video-sharing Web sites. True or False?

8. The percentage of people who watch online videos at least once a month is:

   a. Higher than the number of people who have broadband connections in their home

   b. Roughly the same number of people who have broadband connections in their home

   c. Lower than the number of people who have broadband connections in their home

   d. Not relevant to the number of people who have broadband connections in their home

9. "Heavy" viewers of online video are the:

   a. Top 10% of all viewers

   b. Top 20% of all viewers

   c. Top 30% of all viewers

   d. Top 50% of all viewers

10. One important similarity that the online video audience shares with bloggers is:

   a. A heavy interest in sports information

   b. A heavy interest in news and current events

   c. Slower connection speeds

   d. Mostly female

11. The fact that people tend to leave a lot of comments on specific videos indicates that:

    a. People who spend time online are largely bored and have nothing better to do

    b. People really enjoyed that video

    c. People felt engaged by the videos they have watched

    d. More video-sharing sites are encouraging viewers to leave comments

12. What percentage of online viewers would prefer to watch professionally produced content?

    a. 35%

    b. 50%

    c. 65%

    d. 80%

13. Which is the least likely benefit for a company that uploads videos to its own site or to video-sharing sites?

    a. Improved marketing support

    b. Better audience retention

    c. Reduced product cost

    d. More effective messaging

14. Once a video is compressed, companies cannot use it on their own site - they need to rely on video-sharing sites to support the upload. True or False?

15. In the online video that made him famous, who did Chris Crocker want the media to leave alone?

    a. Paris Hilton

    b. Nicole Ritchie

    c. Britney Spears

    d. None of the above

16. What was the main reason for using video as a driving force in the Power University?

    a. Video's ability to capture people's attention

    b. Reducing development cost

    c. The ability to explain complex topics

    d. Ease of creation

17. Which of the following is the main purpose of the ASCO Power University?

    a. Education

    b. Entertainment

    c. Establishing ASCO as a thought-leader

    d. Seeking out new, potential employees

18. Viewers do not mind seeing some advertising on video sites, however they do not like it when the ads:

    a. Get in the way of the video-watching experience

    b. Appear as banner ads around the video

    c. Promote products that they do not use

    d. Use the color red, which tends to look blurry on computer monitors

19. A large percentage of viewers who have a bad experience on a video site will:

    a. Stick with it, but are unhappy about it

    b. Write negative comments, even on videos that they like

    c. Leave the site and surf elsewhere

    d. Playing the videos repeatedly in the hopes of slowing down the site

20. In video production, the importance of location scouting is:

    a. To find the best actors for the roles

    b. To determine any issues that might arise in advance of the shoot

    c. To determine which format would be best prior to uploading

    d. To prepare the tape for digitizing

Projects

1. Start the video process from scratch. Using a cell phone camera, computer camera, or standard digital camera, take a short video of something you find interesting, and upload it to YouTube or some other video-sharing site. Write a two-page paper detailing each step in the process.

2. Using the same video that you shot in Project #1, create either an .flv, .mov, or .wmv using free conversion software. Program a Web page that allows others to view your video.

3. Find a video-sharing site other than YouTube. In a paper no longer than three pages, analyze the site in terms of:

   a. Types of videos (content)

   b. Media player and format used

   c. Audience you believe it attracts

   d. Other social media tools involved on the site

   e. How advertising is presented

   Critique the site—what do you like about it? What could make it better?

4. Provide lines of code for each of the following:

   a. A .jpg graphic

   b. An .mov movie

   c. A .wmv movie

   d. An .flv movie

   How do they differ from each other?

5. Find a B2B Web site that uses videos. In a two-page paper, describe the company and the site, how the videos are used, and how they improve user experience.

Endnotes

1. "Internet TV Audience Hits Critical Mass." eMarketer <www.emarketer.com> Feb. 2008.
2. "Increased Use of Video Sharing Sites." Pew Internet & American Life Project, 9 Jan. 2008.
3. Ibid.

4. "Double Dipping, Typers vs. Talkers and Media Multitasking Stand out as Common Activities." Harris Interactive commissioned by Blinkx <www.harrisinteractive.com> 28 Feb. 2008.

5. Hallerman, David. "Online Video Content: The New TV Audience." eMarketer <www.emarketer.com> 24 Feb. 2008.

6. Ibid.

7. "Online Video Users Segments' Viewing Behavior Varies Widely." comScore and Media Contracts <www.comscore.com> 14 Feb. 2008.

8. Ibid.

9. Ibid.

10. "Google Closes Acquisition of YouTube." YouTube <www.youtube.com> 13 Nov. 2006.

11. "User Generated Video 2005–2008: Metadata Metrics." AccuStream iMedia Research <www.accustream.com> 25 Jan. 2008.

12. Madden, Mary. "Online Video." Pew Internet & American Life Project, 25 July 2007.

13. "Google Closes Acquisition of YouTube." YouTube "<www.youtube.com> 13 Nov. 2006.

14. "YouTube could be a steal at $1 billion." *CNET* <www.cnet.com> 24 Aug. 2006.

15. Schweitzer, Tamara. "To Gain Competitive Edge, Companies Turn to Blogs, Video, and Social Networks." Inc. com <www.inc.com> 10 Aug. 2007.

16. "The Importance of Delivering a Great Online Video Experience." JupiterResearch <www.jupiterresearch.com> 11 July 2007.

17. Ibid.

CHAPTER 6

Wikis, RSS, Mashups, and Virtual Worlds

In this chapter you will learn about:

◎ Wikis and how they harness the collaborative nature of a user community

◎ RSS feeds, how people use them to stay up-to-date with new content, and how an increasing number of businesses are using them to keep current and potential customers updated on company activities

◎ Mashups and how they give marketers a unique opportunity to present features and information pulled together from other social media tools

◎ Virtual worlds, how people communicate using avatars, and how marketers pursue marketing opportunities by building and promoting a virtual online presence

While social networking sites, blogs, and video-sharing sites continue to weave themselves into the daily lives of countless Web users, the popularity of many other social media tools also continues to grow. Wikis and RSS feeds are two tools that have proven invaluable to marketers, developers, and Web users alike. Mashups and virtual worlds play a lesser but still important role in the ever-growing social media world.

Wikis

In the growing universe of online social media, wikis tend to command little media spotlight or developer attention. This is ironic, however, since of all social media tools, **wikis** (Web sites or pages that visitors can edit without needing to know any programming code or languages) most embody the essence of what social media is all about.

Wiki sites are collaborative by nature. They are built by community involvement; the community is made up of any site user that wishes to contribute information or edit content already on the page. These users do not need to know programming—they just need to be willing to share their information with others.

The best way to explain a wiki site is through example. Suppose you and some friends, John and Mary, decide to throw a party. Since you live miles away from each other and have different schedules, it is difficult to organize everything in advance. You try e-mail, but quickly find out that this is inefficient. People are e-mailing at different times, and for each e-mail sent to the group, a different document exists in each person's inbox. You all decide that it would be much easier if there was one central place where everyone could go to get and share information about the party, so you decide to use a wiki site. You start with a page called "Party Planning." You click the "Edit" button and create a list showing what you will need for the party: 'food,' 'drinks,' and 'dance music.' When you are done, you click the "Save" button, and the page is published for all to see.

Soon John comes to the page and decides to add some information. He clicks the "Edit" button, and he adds 'invitations' to the list. He also changes the word 'food' to 'potato chips and pretzels' to be more specific. He clicks the "Save" button, and the new updated list is published.

Mary later visits the page, and she too clicks the "Edit" button, adding party games to the list. She also highlights the 'dance music' entry, and clicks the "Link" button. This creates a new page called "Dance

Music" where a list of suggested dance CDs can be created. She clicks the "Save" button, and the updated page, with its new addition and new page link, is published.

Of course, John, Mary, and you are not the only ones who can see this page. It turns out a lot of people are organizing parties, and other people start visiting the page to help in their own planning. Some people just stop by to read the page. Others add items like 'party games' to the list; a few visitors add entire articles about different types of parties or tips for entertaining. Still others create links to different sites that offer more party-planning advice. Thus, the page and the site grow through online collaboration by the community of people who have interest in and knowledge of the topic.

Wikis first came into being in 1995, on a site called WikiWikiWeb, developed by renowned computer programmer Ward Cunningham. By 2005, it had grown to over 30,000 pages,[1] underscoring the power in the collaborative efforts of a community of online editors. In his book, *The Wiki Way: Quick Collaboration on the Web*, Ward describes the heart and soul of the wiki technology:

- A wiki invites all users to edit any page or to create new pages within the wiki Web site, using only a plain-vanilla Web browser without any add-ons.

- Wiki promotes meaningful topic associations between different pages by making page link creation almost intuitively easy and showing whether an intended target page exists or not.

- A wiki is not a carefully crafted site for casual visitors. Instead it seeks to involve the visitor in an ongoing process of creation and collaboration that constantly changes the Web site landscape.[2]

Ward Cunningham created the wiki; however, it was Jimmy Wales who made it a household word. His site, Wikipedia, is not only one of the most popular sites on the Web, it also has helped provide wide exposure to the organizational and communication benefits that wikis can offer.

Wikipedia, shown in Figure 6-1 and Figure 6-2, is an online encyclopedia launched in January 2001. Wikipedia content is developed by a large community of site users who add their own research, thought, and knowledge to wiki pages that cover virtually any topic imaginable. According to Wikipedia's own figures, as of April 2008, over 50 million people visit the site each month. Content is spread across over 10 million pages, in 253 languages.[3]

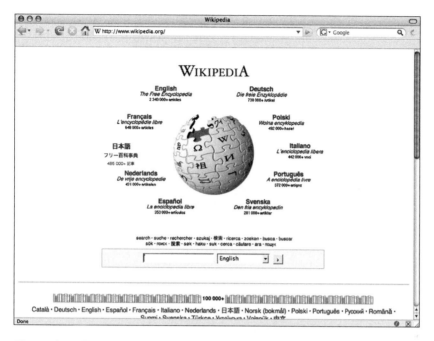

Figure 6-1 The home page for Wikipedia, the site that made wikis famous. Wikipedia is an online encyclopedia collaboratively developed by any users wishing to edit or add content.

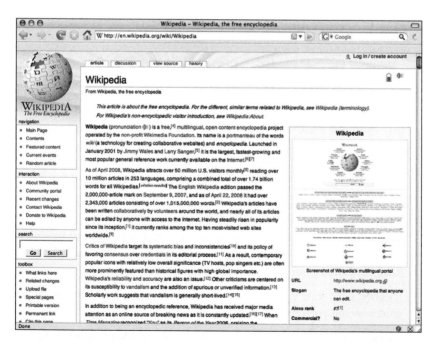

Figure 6-2 The category listing for Wikipedia. Users can gather information or be part of developing the content themselves.

Wikis closely embody the ideals of social media, in the sense that they allow for community-developed content. However, outside of sites like Wikipedia and AboutUs.org, wikis are often left out of mainstream social media conversations. Nonetheless, they are increasingly being adopted by companies for both internal and external purposes—in 2007, wikis were used by 37% of companies.[4] Some organizations develop and run their own wiki sites; others contribute marketing-related content to existing sites. Internally, companies use wikis to help plan meetings, establish protocol, develop marketing strategies, and connect with their employees in a wide variety of ways. In these situations, clients and other outside entities are typically not invited to contribute or edit content.

Large companies find wikis especially valuable for internal use, as employees spread across different facilities and departments can use wikis for collaboration and content development. This content can include corporate policies, information on technology, marketing material, corporate history and background, and suggestions for team building—absolutely anything on which company employees can collaborate. With internal wikis, coworkers can brainstorm and collaborate in ways that were not possible before, easily communicating with each other regardless of position or geography.

INTERVIEW WITH...
WARD CUNNINGHAM AND RAY KING

AboutUs.org is a wiki-based site that connects Web sites and businesses to each other through millions of user-editable pages. I was pleasantly surprised by how easy it was to get in touch with site founder, Ray King, and how accommodating he was in speaking with me about his site. As we started to talk, Ray gave me one more shock: he asked if I'd like to include Ward Cunningham in the interview. A little stunned, I asked, "You can get in touch with him?" to which Ray replied, "I think so. He's sitting ten feet from me."

Needless to say I jumped at the opportunity. To have the founder of one of the best sites on the Web, along with one of the Web's most influential and innovative programmers, together for one interview is immensely exciting—especially given the value that Ray and Ward's insights can provide to both programmers and marketers.

JASON: Let's start with the basics. Ward, in your words, what is a wiki and how did you come up with the idea for it?

WARD: I think of wiki in a lot of different ways. Mostly when I created it, I was trying to create a place on the Internet where a group of people can work together and make a new kind of document—at the time we called it a new kind of literature—that people could use to write about things that were important to them in a collaborative way. The problem we were facing was that my field of computer programming was being directed by textbooks and by the trade press in a direction that just seemed wrong. It didn't jive with people's experience, and programming is really a style of writing that honors practical experience. Before then, scientific literature was the model to be admired and it favored new invention; everything had to be novel to be publishable. We thought that the well-worn things that everybody should know—but not everybody did—were important. So we needed to connect a bunch of people. I actually sat down and tried to write something like that by myself, and I realized that I simply didn't have enough experience.

We held a conference on the subject of how to change the literature of computer programming in the fall of 1994 at the University of Illinois, which was where the Mosaic browser had been written. I was hanging around after the conference, talking to graduate students. They told me that this new thing called the World Wide Web and the whole notion of hypertext is how we can express this new literature. They just looked at me and said, "Ward, we think you can build the site that hosts new literature."

JASON: Did you have any idea when you created this that it would have such an impact on the future of the Web?

WARD: I could tell I was on to something right away. One reason was that it was easy to do. It was easy to have kind of scattered thoughts and just start putting them in and then connect them later, and it worked. Of course that's how our experience is. My focus was on experience. Remember something and remember something else and you could weave it together after the fact. But at the time, every collaborative medium we had was a firehouse. We would just get more information than we could possibly process. If we took a week off and went on vacation we'd be completely out of touch by the time we got back. I could work on wiki, and I could feel really into it. I could go away for a week and come back, and it would be different. But it wasn't so changed that I couldn't pick up the threads. This was especially important for bringing new people into our community. They could find something that they sort of understood. New visitors could link from this and that and go in progressively larger circles. They would end up coming back to the same page, but would read it again because other people had added content. They would get a little more out of it on a second, third, or later reading.

JASON: Are you finding the community is made up of a core group of users, or is it a fluctuating and growing base?

188

WARD: My original site, WikiWikiWeb [see Figure 6-3], has actually kind of served its purpose. We've changed the way people think about computer programming, and I had some of the most inventive and vocal people as part of the early community. It was probably a core of 15 to 50 people, and those people have kind of gone on to other things. Most of them have become famous as part of this transformation and write books now instead of wiki pages. Regardless, even people with the most obscure knowledge still had a place to write.

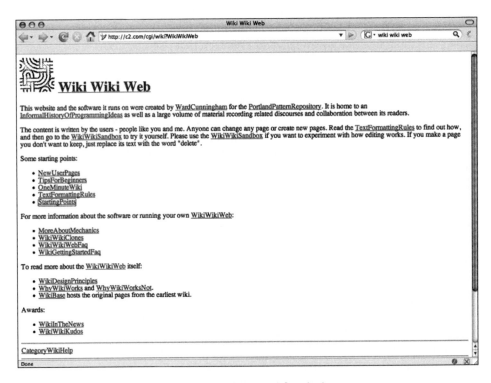

Figure 6-3   WikiWikiWeb—the original wiki by Ward Cunningham.

Now, let me just say that [the original wiki site] was created with an activist agenda—we wanted to change computer programming. That's very different from Wikipedia. The purpose of Wikipedia is to transmit knowledge, not to cause change. Of course, transmitting knowledge is going to cause plenty of change in its own right, but they don't want to change the knowledge. They just want to distribute it. We wanted people to talk about what they knew to be true. Wikipedia asks that people do no primary research and that entries only be summarized or explained in plain language, which makes Wikipedia an encyclopedia instead of an adventure in new literature. But this whole idea that you can go away for a week and come back and still find your way is very true to both my original wiki site and Wikipedia.

So, I had a purpose, and Wikipedia has a purpose. However, the concept of wiki itself as a medium has properties that influence both in identical ways. That's an interesting confirmation that something as simple as wiki can create a style of behavior among communities that is transferable.

JASON: Where did the name "wiki" come from?

WARD: I dubbed the technology 'WikiWikiWeb'—'wiki wiki' being Hawaiian for very quick. Hawaiians will double a word for emphasis so wiki means quick and 'wiki wiki' means very quick.

JASON: Talk to me a little bit about the growth of wiki as a Web medium.

WARD: I was five years into my site when Jimmy Wales [founder of Wikipedia] was trying to make this new Web-based encyclopedia that kind of floundered. One of my regular community members, Ben Kovits, was having dinner with the fellow who was running Jimmy's project and suggested they try wiki. They gave it a try, and it took off for them. Part of it is that wiki had been cloned [different versions of the original wiki had been created]. There were probably 30 versions at the time Wikipedia started, which were all derivative of my version.

Wikipedia is quite an accomplishment. They adjusted some of the principles that I adopted, and appropriately so, but the decision-making on that site has always been in recognition of the unique properties of wiki. In other words, the people who were running Wikipedia realized that it was also a work that would outlive its authors and that the community of authors was a very important part of the dynamic by which it was being created. So they're always very careful to make decisions to not damage that relationship.

JASON: Are you happy in general with how wikis are evolving and being used?

WARD: I'm really pleased with Wikipedia. I think other wikis could do a lot more if they had a different attitude about the people they use. When you have a community of people creating something for you, you really owe them something. Paying attention to your user community and treating them with respect is very important. Wikipedia gets five stars for that. I think I might only get three stars for mine. I haven't been perfect, but there are plenty of one star, no star sites out there that are simply exploitive. That frustrates me. But people fool around with those for a while, and then they'll walk away when they realize they are being exploited. Some people just put up a wiki site and think, "Gee, I just put up this site, and people come and create stuff for me and then I capitalize on it." That's not the right way to think about it.

JASON: How do wikis fit into the larger social media universe of blogging and social networking and sharing sites?

WARD: Probably the biggest difference between blogging and wiki is that blogging is very much about the self. However, by the time you have everybody looking at each other's blog, you get this blogosphere phenomenon. The blogosphere seems a lot like wiki, but at its core, the blogosphere is a community first. If it happens to produce something of lasting value, that would be secondary. I don't think that they actually do. There's a lot of information, but its back to that firehouse again. Wiki is a work first. It's a collection of writings that's worth reading, and it's a work on its own. Community is a necessary part of it, but the community is there because they care about the work. I think that's really important.

I also think blogging is like a market economy of information—the wisdom of the crowd. I think of it as complicated way to do averaging. You want to get a little bit of everybody's voice and combine that into some sort of average. A wiki is not so much about the average. It's about finding the person or the few people whose voices just happen to have the missing part that we can all resonate around. A single individual can have a tremendous influence by just saying the right thing at the right time and the right place on a wiki. There's no averaging going on there. That makes it a very different medium. When you stand back, all three social media tools—the blogosphere, social networking and sharing sites, and wiki—are all enabled by the fact that we have a reasonably literate population in the world that has enough free time to contribute.

JASON: That being said, wikis seem to lag behind other social media tools like blogging and social networking sites, grabbing less of the spotlight. Why do you think that is?

RAY: I think that wiki is intuitively harder for people to grasp. The minute you say, "Hey, this Web site is open for anybody to edit," everyone immediately assumes that it can't work because people will destroy the site, and you'll have no control. I think that was the prevalent thinking for a long time. When Wikipedia emerged and it was obvious that it was going to be a success, people started taking notice. Wikipedia is just one wiki project, but it has proven that wiki technology works. That will open the doors to new projects and tons of stuff that we haven't thought of yet. They're coming down the pike.

JASON: Let's switch gears a little and talk about AboutUs.org [shown in Figure 6-4]. What is it, and why did you decide to build the site on wiki technology?

Figure 6-4 The Home page of AboutUs.org, a wiki-based site that connects and chronicles other Web sites and companies.

RAY: The goal of AboutUs.org is to provide a resource to users who may be interested in a particular organization. We give users the opportunity to see how that organization is connected to the rest of the world and what it's doing right now. We mainly focus on information about other Web sites. If a Web site is out there it means that one or a group of people trying to accomplish something—build a business, sell things online, or change the world in some way. They all want to do something to make the world different, so AboutUs is very forward-looking. The majority of data on our site really describes Web sites. We're more interested in knowing that this particular organization is a subsidiary of that company, and that company supplies to this other company, and this blog tends to write about this industry for which that company belongs. We're interested in that type of information and helping to connect the dots.

As for why it's based on wiki technology—I've always been a big fan of collaborative technologies. I think that it's so much easier to do good work when you have got more than one head working on it, and wiki allows you to do that. When I first saw the technology, I immediately gravitated towards it. I've always been the guy within other organizations that thought about internal communications and Internet type systems, and wanted better ways to collaborate. And wiki . . . it was just sort of obvious to me that I wanted to work in this area.

JASON: Since AboutUs.org relies so heavily on community involvement, how did you get the site up to speed? What steps did you take to get people on the site and contributing content?

RAY: What I found was that when we asked people to come to the site and self-identify or make a page for themselves, describe themselves, describe their company, people for the most part all thought it was a great idea, said they would do it, but they never actually did. It's a new project, and people had to learn and start from a blank page, which can be a tough sell. We found that if we went ahead and started the page, and said, "Here's what we know about you, and it's probably not a lot, but I'm prepared to put something up there," then people were much more likely to edit the page, because it was already started for them, but might not be exactly right, or they'd want to add to it. That was kind of the key to building AboutUs—we would get pages started for people and in that way invite a lot more editing.

JASON: How can traditional companies benefit from using wiki technology as part of their marketing strategies?

WARD: We've been talking about wikis that find an underserved niche and serve it. I think another question is—if you're already a going brand, you have customers with whatever interest they have, and your job is to serve those customers while realizing that those customers are changing—how do you continue to serve those customers and maybe even reach out to serve more?

For the most part, companies provide information to their customers. They write a newsletter, for example, and they post it up on their site for people to download. It could be beneficial to a company to let their customers contribute their own thoughts to an online, customer-facing newsletter. I think that wiki offers some formulas that are worth examining. Customers would probably like getting to know more about their peers than your brand. That is, people would benefit in learning, in a non-exploitative way, about who else is using your product. For a company, that will be powerful information, because they'll discover things that are outside of their ability to even consider.

Another area where wikis can benefit companies is a little counterintuitive to how most companies think. For most companies, their motivation is to extend the product to do more of the same.

Customers, however, tend to use the product as it is but often want to combine it with other products. My vision is always of the guy buying scientific equipment and hooking it up in complicated ways to do something new—something that none of the manufacturers or marketers would have thought of because they are not scientists, or maybe wouldn't have really liked because their products are being combined with competing products. People are innovative and will find ways to do new things with existing products. Wiki can create a community where people can share these ideas even if it's risky from the point of view of the company itself. I would say this to companies: better to be a participant with your customer community than to be abandoned by them; better to find that out early what your customers do and what they want and ask your customers to help you evolve.

JASON: How important do you think it is for a programmer to understand the marketing aspects of the sites that they are building?

WARD: I think it's really important, because if you just build a site that has some mechanism that you think is cool, three of your friends will tell you it is cool, and then that's done. Programmers have to have an understanding of what people are going to do on the site and what's going to motivate them to do it.

As a programmer, you could take an artistic approach and say you're going to program what you want and not care if people like it. But if you're programming a site and you expect to have growth and you want to make something with general appeal, then you have to understand people in general, not just assume you're making this for people just like you.

That's really important in building a business. I think anybody who's built a business beyond 30 customers knows that you have to understand your customers. If you're not customer-oriented, you're not going to survive. In that sense you can have a computer programmer who just says, "Tell me what to do and I'll do it." But that's not somebody who's creating; that's somebody who's just using a small amount of programming knowledge. If you're a developer that understands [the customer], you're developing a business at the same time you're developing technology.

RSS Feeds

Visually, RSS needs no introduction. Its bright orange and white icon has permeated practically every media-related site and blog on the Web (see Figure 6-5).

Figure 6-5   The symbol for RSS feed.

RSS is a Web feed that makes it easy for people to stay up-to-date with new content that is posted on a specific site. Although there is some debate as to what the letters RSS stand for (most sites and users have settled on Really Simple Syndication), few would debate how useful RSS can be.

For example, let's say a user clicks on the RSS icon on the New York Post's Web site. By doing so, they create a free subscription for themselves to that site. Of course, that doesn't mean that the paper will start arriving on their doorstep. It means that through the use of an XML (Extensible Markup Language) file they will get the digital equivalent. The feed will provide the most current headlines that the Post has added—without the user having to go directly to its site.

RSS has its roots in the Netscape browser, which developed an early version of the tool in 1999. It was not widely distributed until 2005, when, after years of revisions, updates, and controversy over publishing rights, Microsoft Internet Explorer, Outlook, and the Opera Web browser all adopted the icon shown in Figure 6-5. This icon had originally been introduced by the Mozilla Firefox browser. (Other icons do exist, but this remains the prominent means of identifying a feed.)

RSS feeds can be offered by any site (although traditionally they are offered by sites that update content often). These include blogs and file-sharing sites. On sites with a large volume of content or content that is segmented into a number of different categories, RSS feeds are often set up to allow users to subscribe to very specific information. Users can even customize their subscriptions based on keywords. The video-sharing site YouTube, for example, allows visitors to narrow the scope of their subscriptions. Users can subscribe to specific channels, most-watched videos, most-recently updated, etc. In addition, because each video is tagged with specific keywords for search purposes, users can subscribe to videos based on keywords, receiving, for example, a feed on all new videos tagged with the word "guitar." RSS feeds can usually be scheduled to scan for new information at any interval—every few minutes or every few days. They can be turned off or deleted if the user loses interest in the topic. Figure 6-6 shows the RSS page for BusinessWeek's Web site. Users can subscribe to any number of feeds from stories, blogs, podcasts, or videos.

Figure 6-6 *BusinessWeek's* site allows users to subscribe to RSS feeds based on the category of information they are most interested in, and it provides links to various RSS readers for download.

Most large media sites have already adopted RSS feeds into their sites, and marketers are finding it useful as well. Distributors, for example, can alert retailers when new products have been stocked, and medical researchers can use RSS feeds to let doctors and other interested parties know about breakthrough techniques and findings. There is even an RSS feed for the Amber Alert, which provides information on missing children in an effort to locate them.

RSS is built using the XML programming language, and it reads headlines, titles, or short site summaries provided by the site developer. On the user side, these summaries are displayed through a program called an RSS reader, which accepts the feeds and displays them to the subscriber. RSS readers come preinstalled in most browsers; however, dozens of other readers are available for download. Some readers are free, while others require either a one-time payment for their software or a monthly subscription. Each has its own features, ranging from creating a running ticker in the browser window to more sophisticated customization options. Newsdesk, a reader shown in Figure 6-7, comes pre-installed with subscriptions to over 50 popular news sources and organizes feeds in a similar fashion to Microsoft Outlook's popular e-mail program.

Figure 6-7 An RSS reader, pulling in feeds from a large number of subscription sources.

With this and similar applications, users can create "watches." A user enters keywords, and the reader searches all RSS feeds in its subscription base, returning content based on those words. This can be a fun feature for hobbyists or those interested in specific news content, and it can prove particularly useful for marketers. Companies can use RSS feeds to keep up with competitor news and activities and, through subscriptions to blogs, stay abreast of movement and ideas within the marketplace. It can even help marketers keep track of rumors or news about their own company, saving valuable research time and giving them new insights.

Mashups

A **mashup** is exactly as it sounds, a blending together of information from multiple sources into one tool or site. Mashups blend multiple tools into a single offering that is often more powerful or useful than any of the tools would be on their own. For example, a music-based information Web site might pull concert locations for touring bands through RSS feeds and mash that information up with Google maps to show where the performance is taking place.

Figures 6-8 and 6-9 show screen shots of a mashup on the 2008 Gillette Young Guns (Gillette's NASCAR team) Web site. This mashup uses Google Maps to pinpoint NASCAR tracks across the country. It then allows users to zoom in for a close-up satellite view of each track, and it blends each location map with information and statistics about the specific track. In doing this, Gillette gives fans information about NASCAR racing, presented in a way that they otherwise couldn't have easily accessed through Google Maps or other NASCAR-affiliated sites.

Figure 6-8 The Gillette NASCAR racing site includes a mashup that shows all of the racing tracks in the U.S. as pinpointed on maps fed in from Google.

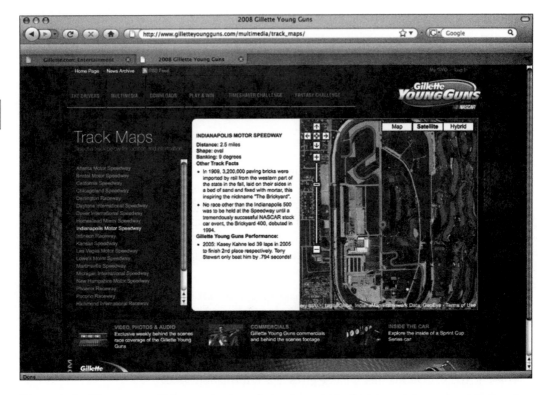

Figure 6-9 When a user clicks on a track marker and zooms in, they see a close-up aerial view of the track and additional information about the track.

Mashups are quickly gaining popularity as more tools to create them are popping up around the Web. Google, Yahoo, and Microsoft have each launched beta or completed versions of sites that help users create mashups. These sites also include social networking areas where visitors can share their mashup ideas with others. Figure 6-10 shows the home page for Popfly, Microsoft's proprietary site, which helps users create mashups (Popfly also helps users develop Web sites and games). Figure 6-11 shows how a mashup comes together. Like many other mashup creation sites, Popfly gives users an easy-to-use toolbox of sites and applications to pull information from and a highly visual approach to combining this information. Figure 6-12 shows the final result, in this case a mashup that combines mapping tools with traffic news updates to show location and information about traffic in and around the Seattle area.

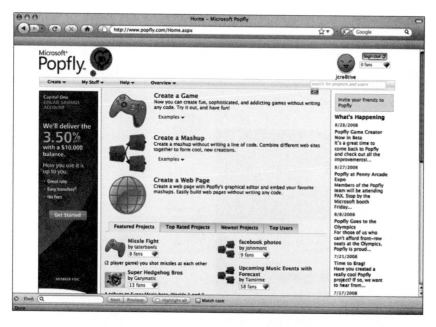

Figure 6-10 The Home page of Microsoft's Popfly.com gives users the tools to easily create and share applications, including mashups.

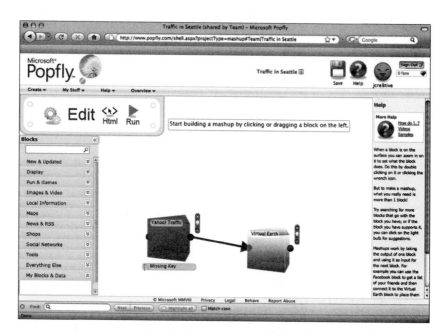

Figure 6-11 Once in Popfly, users can create their own mashups by connecting social media tools and information from various sites to develop a unique application. With Popfly, these connections are made using object-based graphic representations of individual tools, eliminating the need for programming.

Figure 6-12 The result of the mashup being created in Figure 6-11, this tool blends local news with a third-party mapping program to display traffic problems in the Seattle area.

From a marketing perspective, mashups allow companies to provide a unique offering that rival sites might not present. An e-commerce site that sells books, for example, could create a mashup that combines recently reviewed and bestselling books with an online calendar of when and where the author of those books will be signing copies (and, of course, include links for shoppers to buy those titles online). An online media site could create a mashup by pulling tags from multiple sources (including popular blogs) and representing them in a graphical interface unique to that site. While the individual parts may not be original, the end result can be a lure that keeps people engaged and coming back.

Virtual Worlds

Virtual worlds are like social networking sites on steroids. A **virtual world** is an online environment built to reflect either the real world or some type of fantasy realm in which users can interact and explore. By using an **avatar** (an icon or model used to represent a user), a person can meet and interact with other people. Often, these environments are three dimensional. Some virtual worlds are created for the purposes of online gaming. In an MMORPG (Massively Multiplayer Online Role-Playing Game), large numbers of players compete with each other in a virtual world, strive to reach new levels, or amass points in an attempt to win the game or complete specific tasks. (Figure 6-13 shows a scene from Disney's popular *Pirates of the Caribbean* online MMORPG, in which users can create their own pirate avatars and go on quests and adventures.)

Figure 6-13 A scene from the online MMORPG, "Pirates of the Caribbean," where users from all over the world pursue adventures through their pirate avatars.

Other virtual worlds, like Second Life (shown in Figure 6-14) are not games at all, but are social platforms in which people can meet other people and use virtual currency to build homes, shop at virtual malls, or start in-world businesses. Like a hybrid between a real-life social setting and an online social network, virtual worlds often bring people together in virtual dance clubs, arcades, beach parties, concerts, and other similar events.

Figure 6-14 The inside of a home in Second Life. Using personalized avatars, users explore, communicate, shop, and build homes and businesses in the 3D virtual environment.

As of July 2008, Second Life is the largest and most populated virtual world, with about 550,000 unique visitors per week.[5] Although this is still relatively small compared to standard social networks like MySpace or Facebook, marketers and the media are starting to pay close attention to virtual worlds as an up-and-coming resource for bringing people together. As Figure 6-15 shows, press coverage for Second Life has increased significantly.[6] It is likely that this attention will continue and traffic to Second Life and other virtual worlds will continue to build as more homes add broadband connections (virtual worlds are often very cumbersome, and require powerful computers and faster connections to work properly).

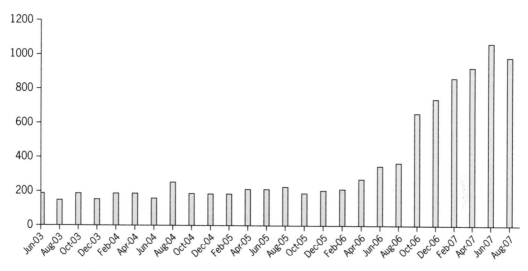

Figure 6-15 Mentions of Second Life in the press. Once the media took notice of Second Life, it quickly gained significant attention. SOURCE: LexisNexis <http://w3.nexis.com>, Jan. 2007.

This increase in popularity hasn't gone unnoticed by companies who are quickly seeking potential marketing opportunities. For some marketers, these opportunities have come in the form of advertisements within Second Life and sponsorships of pre-planned events, such as the Coca-Cola stage shown in Figure 6-16. Other companies have built entire corporate presences in Second Life, where consumers can come to find out more information about products, talk to customer service representatives, or just stay in touch with the brand. Larger companies, whose employee base is spread across the country or throughout the world, have also been finding valuable internal uses for Second Life by creating virtual meeting places where everyone can congregate (individually represented by their avatar) and sit in on a meeting to review sales, marketing, or other important issues. Figures 6-17 shows the Second Life presence for Sears, while Figure 6-18 shows how a meeting can be held in the virtual world.

Figure 6-16 A concert stage sponsored by Coca-Cola, one of the many advertisers that uses special events in Second Life as a marketing vehicle to promote their brand.

Figure 6-17 The inside of a Sears in Second Life, where visitors can find out more about Sears products.

Figure 6-18 A meeting held in Second Life. Employees from around the world attend by having their avatars sit in on the meeting.

While there are many reasons to believe that virtual worlds have promising futures as social networks and tools for marketers, there are some reasons for concern, with much of this concern falling on the shoulders of market leader, Second Life. For as much as Second Life has helped generate vast interest in virtual worlds as a social and marketing platform, as of the writing of this book there are equally compelling reasons to believe Second Life may falter and set the virtual world movement back. In July 2007, Time Magazine listed Second Life as one of the five worst sites on the Web, noting, "Visually, this vast virtual world can be quite impressive, but it's notoriously slow to load (it runs on free software you have to download) and difficult to navigate, even with a broadband connection . . . The corporate world's embrace of the place as a venue for staff meetings and training sessions does seem to lend Second Life a layer of legitimacy. But maybe it's a case of some CEOs trying too hard to be hip."[7] While some companies are still exploring and investing in opportunities to market themselves in Second Life, others are closing up shop in the nascent platform, with companies like American Apparel and BMW abandoning efforts due to lack of tangible results. Like the Web itself, which had to go through a period of rapid growth followed by a spectacular collapse before it could really define itself, the future of virtual worlds has yet to be written.

INTERVIEW WITH...
JODY DEVERE: ASKPATTY.COM

Jody Devere is the president of AskPatty.com, a Web site that provides car advice to women, and she sits on the board of directors for the United Spinal Association (USA), a non-profit organization dedicated to helping people with spinal cord injuries and disorders. Jody heads up USA's Motorability Island (see Figures 6-19 and 6-20), a Second Life island with race tracks and other racing-related activities where people can come to watch or participate in a series of scheduled events. Jody recently talked with me about Motorability Island and how Second Life has helped them reach a new a growing audience base.

Figure 6-19   The outside of USA's Motorability Speedway race track. Users can buy Second Life cars for their avatars (using real money that is donated to USA), meet other racing enthusiasts, or watch scheduled races.

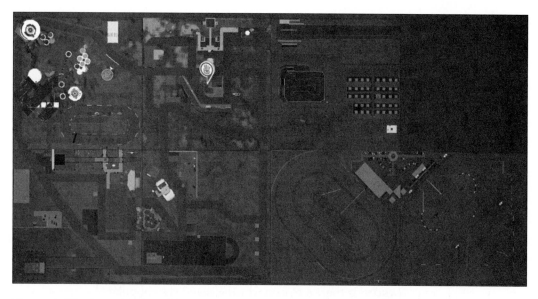

Figure 6-20 An aerial view of Motorability Island. The island has numerous racing tracks, go-cart tracks, a dance hall, and roadways for casual driving. It also features homes for volunteers and sponsors, and provides information on USA and how people can make donations.

JASON: How did you come to have an association with United Spinal Association?

JODY: We were a car-related business dedicated to women, and we've adopted United Spinal as our charity due to their motor sports program as well as their motor safe program. My own son is paraplegic, so they've helped me and my family a great deal. I am very dedicated to the great work that they do, especially for veterans; my son is a veteran.

I took AskPatty and United Spinal into Second Life at the end of 2007. Pontiac had an island with a racetrack, but decided that they wanted to end their marketing efforts in Second Life and were going to close the island. We were all notified, because we had sponsored the island. During that time we had become very close to the core residents of the island [virtual homes had been built there], and had really built a great racing community. There were a lot of synergies with the island community, and I felt really bad it was closing. The residents were up in arms. On a fluke I went to Pontiac, and I said "Hey, would you donate the island to my charity—United Spinal? We will carry on the car culture and support the residents." They said, "Yes."

JASON: That's a great idea.

JODY: Pontiac had created a community rather than just put up beautiful buildings hoping that people would come. It was a very active community and still is. There is the main racetrack, but there are also dances and events. All the residents were very actively involved in the community, promoting it, and making it a place that people would want to come to. Anyway, I took it over under the banner of United Spinal Association. Most of the core residents stayed on, and the island has developed into a very active and popular place in Second Life. Plus, we've added an NHRA (National Hot Rod Association) style straight track, and we have cart racing. There is also the United Spinal Walking Center, which is a mirror image of all of the services available to spinal cord-injured persons or persons with spinal cord disease through United Spinal Association. We just have so many things to do. We even have podcasts of the Action Online Magazine [the USA official magazine], which is very cool in podcast version.

JASON: Is there a reason why the island is so popular?

JODY: There is a very large disabled community in Second Life, because it allows people to get a 'Second Life' especially if they spend way too much time at home. In my son's situation, because he's not well enough to go out, it enables him to create relationships and have some activities that don't require mobility.

JASON: What's the benefit to USA? What do they gain by maintaining a presence in Second Life?

JODY: The benefits are endless. Of course, it's a public relations platform. The media outside of Second Life is always interested in what's going on in the metaverse [virtual universe], because it's still such a curiosity. Within Second Life, we've gotten a great deal of exposure and have done multiple interviews in the virtual world.

The main benefit is in securing donations. Not the 'in your face, send me money' kind of donations, but by community participation. For instance, when you buy a virtual racecar from the racetrack [paid for with real money], a portion of that goes to United Spinal. It's very clear that that's happening around the island, but it's not in your face until we hold fundraising events like events over the weekend. People have been very generous.

And the events are not just for people who are disabled. In fact, I wouldn't want it that way. I think that's one of the great things about Second Life is that it has supercharged public relations for United Spinal. It is also sort of an older charity, and Second Life has given them a boost as a more up-to-date kind of charitable organization innovator. Those are some of the branding images that they would like to have going forward as they do more things online. This newly minted brand image isn't just for people with disabilities, it's for everybody. We have a large population of people without disabilities coming to the island to participate in scheduled events and becoming more aware of the USA brand.

JASON: When you say "scheduled events," what does that mean? Is it a scheduled race or open race time? Are there concerts on the island?

JODY: We have all of those. If you go to Motorability.com you can view a Google calendar [mashup] of weekly scheduled events. We'll also have special occasion events like a summer concert series or the Veterans and Memorial Day weekend events. We even have a club on the island called Parcade that's holding almost daily dancing events.

JASON: And when you have one of these events, how many people come on average?

JODY: It's hard to say, because every event is different. But in general we average between 10,000 and 15,000 visitors a month, which is really outstanding.

People come to Second Life to do stuff. They want a job. They want to have something to do. They just don't want to walk around. Some of them are more gamers; they want stuff to keep them active and engaged. You know, they want a race; they want to have fun. They want to get skills. They want to learn to build their own virtual cars or homes. In fact, I have a place called Motorability Springs that teaches people how to become builders. In different months we promote different things to come and do, but then there are regularly scheduled events. You don't come to Second Life just to sit around, and I think new users need to join groups. They need to get reading the Avistar and the Metaverse Messenger, which are the Second Life newspapers, to catch up on all the things there are to do and where to go and the calendar of events—not just on Motorability Island, but everywhere within Second Life. By the way, my racetrack is on the calendar of events in those magazines. And it's a very popular place to come. So, you know that's the secret of success. You just can't have a building or store, expect people to show up, and tell them to buy something. You have to give them something to do and look for other ways to benefit from the virtual presence.

Chapter Summary

- Wiki sites are made up of pages written and edited by an online community. Users have the ability to edit and add information to a wiki page, and link those pages to other relevant pages on the site. Although Wikis are not always thought about in the same arena as other social media tools such as file-sharing sites, blogging, or social networking sites, they are gaining in popularity. Wikis are particularly useful for marketers looking to improve communications among their own employees.

- RSS feeds are an easy way to keep track of updates, headlines, and site summaries. Users can view feeds via RSS readers, many of which can be downloaded for free. Large sites typically provide opportunities to subscribe to RSS feeds by category or keyword. While most major media outlets already provide RSS feeds from their sites, an increasing number of businesses are using them to keep current and potential customers updated on company activities.

- Mashups pull together different tools and information to create a unique application or offering. Mashups are increasing in popularity, and numerous sites that facilitate the creation of mashups are beginning to appear online. Marketers can use mashups to engage their audiences in ways that competing sites don't.

- Virtual worlds allow users to represent themselves with an avatar to play games, meet other people, market their brands, and build businesses. While there is still some question as to whether market leader Second Life will propel the metaverse to greatness or crumble, it is clear that marketers see potential in virtual worlds and will continue to seek ways to harness their vast marketing power.

Key Terms

avatar—An icon or model used to represent a user in a virtual world.

mashup—A blending together of information from multiple sources into one tool or site.

RSS—A Web feed that makes it easy for people to stay up-to-date with new content that is posted on a specific site.

virtual world—An online environment built to reflect either the real world or some type of fantasy realm in which users can interact and explore.

wiki—Collaborative Web site or individual pages that visitors can edit without needing to know any programming code or languages.

Review Questions

1. The growth of wikis depends mostly on:

   a. Creativity in page design

   b. Content written by site developers

   c. Community involvement

   d. Successful linking to the blogosphere

2. How many pages are wiki sites limited to?

   a. 20

   b. 30,000

   c. 5,000,000

   d. Unlimited

3. Users who visit a typical wiki site are usually allowed to add new content, but usually are not allowed to edit existing content. True or False?

4. Wikipedia has content in:

   a. 20 languages

   b. 100 languages

   c. 200 languages

   d. Over 250 languages

5. In 2007, what percentage of companies used wikis?

   a. 37%

   b. 49%

   c. 59%

   d. 69%

6. The literal translation of the Hawaiian word "wiki" is:

   a. Quick

   b. Unlimited

   c. Wide

   d. Trick question—"wiki" is actually a Spanish word, not a Hawaiian word.

7. The early seeds for wiki were first planted during a conversation between Ward Cunningham and graduate students at the University of Illinois, which was also the home of which invention?

   a. The Netscape browser

   b. The Mosaic browser

   c. The first MySpace page

   d. The first blog

8. The first wiki site was created with an activist agenda, for the purpose of:

   a. Promoting commercial use of the Web

   b. Changing the literature of computer programming

   c. Lobbying the government for increased Web funding

   d. Reducing online pornography

9. The primary difference between WikiWikiWeb and Wikipedia is that:

   a. The purpose of WikiWikiWeb was to cause change, while the purpose of Wikipedia is to transmit knowledge.

   b. Although Wikipedia has the word "Wiki" in its title, it is actually based on a completely different technology.

   c. The purpose of Wikipedia is to cause change, while the purpose of WikiWikiWeb was to transmit knowledge.

   d. Wikipedia is a public site, while WikiWikiWeb was only open to a select few users in the community.

10. AboutUs.org's primary purpose is:

    a. To connect job seekers with employers

    b. To provide profile pages for up and coming celebrities

    c. To connect Web sites and business to each other

    d. To compete with Wikipedia as another online encyclopedia

11. According to Ward Cunningham, which of the following is based on the averaging of information?

    a. Wikis

    b. Social networking sites

    c. Blogs

    d. Product reviews on e-commerce sites

12. Wikis can help companies by:

    a. Acting as inexpensive blogs

    b. Getting their customers to discuss the brand rather than just read information about it

    c. Allowing people to post profiles of themselves

    d. Find information on job openings more easily

13. The RSS icon is typically:

    a. Red

    b. Orange

    c. Green

    d. Animated

14. RSS is built on which of the following programming languages?

    a. HTML

    b. C++

    c. XML

    d. Java

15. RSS gained widespread distribution when:

    a. It was first unveiled in 1999

    b. The logo developed by Firefox was adopted by IE, Outlook, and others

    c. CNN and Fox News began using it to distribute their news

    d. YouTube first featured a video on how to use it

16. YouTube allows visitors to narrow the scope of their RSS subscriptions using which of the following criteria?

    a. Specific channels

    b. Most-watched videos

    c. Specific keywords

    d. All of the above

17. Mashups are best defined as:

    a. A number of blogs combined on one site

    b. More than one person contributing to a wiki

    c. A blending together of information from multiple sources into a single tool or site

    d. A software programs that organize numerous RSS feeds

18. Mashups are fun applications for hobbyists, but they provide no real benefits to a company looking to market itself on the Web. True or False?

19. In most Virtual Worlds, people identify themselves with:

    a. Their photo

    b. Their avatar

    c. Their digital signature

    d. Their wiki entry

20. According to Jody Devere, the best way to be successful in Second Life is:

    a. To have pre-planned, scheduled events

    b. To trust that people will find your brand online over time through word of mouth

    c. To build bigger buildings than any other brands

    d. Virtual worlds are still so new, there's no way for brands to be successful there yet

Projects

1. Suppose you worked for a company that wanted you to build a wiki. How would you do it? What languages or software would you need? Research and write a summary of your findings.

2. Using AboutUs.org, do a "six degrees of separation" analysis. Start with one entry, and follow it through to a related site, and then another related site, until you show six sites in total. In a two-page paper, write about how these sites are connected.

3. Write the code needed to produce an RSS feed from a Web page.

4. Find a social media tool or application that has not been discussed in this book. Write a one-page summary of the tool and how it could help marketers.

5. Using Popfly, create a functional mashup. In a one-page paper, discuss the different elements that you combined, and how your mashup could benefit users more than any of the elements alone. Would the mashup you created have any value to a marketer? If so, explain how and why.

Endnotes

1. WikiWikiWeb <http://c2.com> Aug. 2008.
2. Cunningham, Ward, Bo Leuf. The Wiki Way: Quick Collaboration on the Web. Boston: Addison-Wesley Professional, 2001.
3. Wikipedia <www.wikipedia.com> Aug. 2008.
4. Guglielmo, Karen. "Waiting for Wikis to Break Through." FastForward, Jul. 2007.
5. "Why Is In-World Spending Up Even As Population Plateaus?" New World News, Jul. 2008.
6. LexisNexis <http://w3.nexis.com> Jan. 2007.
7. "5 Worst Websites." *Time*, Jul. 2007.

CHAPTER 7

Understanding the Brand

In this chapter you will learn about:

◎ How marketers define a brand

◎ Why the brand is important, and the role it plays in building marketing and generating revenue

◎ The elements that go into a brand, and how they come together to create a compelling case for consumers to make purchases

◎ How the Web is different from other marketing tools and the added value it can provide to marketers in developing brands

Social media tools are great. They give users increased opportunities to communicate with each other as well as the companies from whom they buy products and services. For marketers, however, tools are only a means to an end in an effort that begins with developing and promoting the brand. To promote the brand, marketers first must understand it—what it is, how it works, and why it is important.

Breaking Down the Brand

Understanding the brand is vital to the success of any marketing campaign, whether online or offline. In fact, the brand is the foundation upon which marketing programs are developed. What exactly is a brand? The answer often depends on who you ask and the context in which you are asking. The best way to arrive at a comprehensive definition, for marketing purposes, is to break the word down, starting from the beginning.

Visit any cattle farm and you are likely to see cows with letters or icons burnt into their hides with a branding iron. These burn marks help farmers determine which cows belong to which farm, should herds become intermingled while grazing. This topic might seem like a strange introduction to a marketing discussion, but the practice of marking animals is at the very root of branding. Because cows pretty much all look alike, farmers needed a way to tell which cows belong to which farmer. To solve this problem, farmers started to burn a mark on their cattle, so that they could tell them apart. The mark (brand) helps to tell one cow (product) from another. Therefore, one definition of a brand is:

Brand: An icon or mark (logo) that helps distinguish one product from another.

So then, is the brand a product? By this definition, no—the brand *represents* the product. Pepsi Cola is carbonated water, sugar, and caramel flavoring. The brand is the red, white, and blue circle, the Pepsi name, and the distinctive lettering used. When you see it on the shelf, you immediately know it is different from the bright red and white Coca-Cola bottle on the shelf next to it.

However, there is a slight disconnect with this definition. Let's revisit the farmer. The farmer brands his cows to prove ownership—not so that you, the consumer, can pick out his cows from those of another farmer. By the time his cow ends up on your plate, you are thinking far less about which farm it came from than you are about whether you will still have room for dessert. That is a very different scenario than the one in which a consumer is choosing to drink Pepsi instead of Coke. For many people, the choice comes down to taste, which is more than just the basic ingredients. Taste is a feature of each product that makes it unique. That brings us to a different definition:

Brand: A specific characteristic or unique quality that distinguishes one product from another.

The Pepsi logo lets you know that inside that particular bottle is the specific taste you are looking for. What if every time you opened a bottle of Pepsi, it tasted different? What if sometimes it was bitter and other times it was sweet? Chances are you would stop buying it. The red, white, and blue logo, the specific typeface, and the product name would no longer mean anything. As a consumer, if you see a bottle with the Pepsi logo on it, you know exactly how it is going to taste, whether you are in New York, Boston, Los Angeles, or any one of a million other towns. This brings us to the single most important definition of a brand from the perspective of a marketer:

Brand: The sum total of all user experiences with a particular product or service, building both reputation and future expectations of benefit.

From a marketer's standpoint, this is the definition that really matters. Notice that in breaking down the word, we have taken the brand from being tangible (an icon) to being intangible (reputation). We have also taken it from being a one-way communication (this icon tells you what the brand is), to a two-way relationship with the consumer (based on reputation, we expect something of the brand). If something seems familiar here, it should. Involving consumers directly in a brand is something we have discussed in the Social Media sections of this book. Blogs, online consumer reviews, and other social media tools allow consumers to take a more hands-on approach to a brand. However, the fact that brands and consumers are inextricably linked is nothing new; it is, in fact, inherent in the very definition of a brand.

Distinguishing the Brand from the Company

Before we go any further, we should discuss the question of whether or not there is a separation between the company and the brand. It is a fine line, and there is not always a clear answer. Our last definition of a brand referred to *"the sum total of all user experiences with a particular product or service."* It is not unusual, however, for companies to have different audiences than their products. Take Disney, for example. Anything with the Disney name associated with it, such as the Disney World and Epcot Center theme parks, movies like *Finding Nemo* and *High School Musical*, and TV shows like *Hannah Montana* and *That's So Raven*, all help to confirm the Disney consumer brand as kid-friendly and family-oriented. However, there is another Disney that rarely gets seen by most consumers—that is the corporate side of the company, the side that makes the big money deals, negotiates contracts and copyrights, and handles the inner workings of the business that make the consumer products come to life. That side of Disney has its own reputation among its market of vendors, producers, and talent as an extraordinarily tough negotiator and often difficult business partner. The corporate side of Disney is a brand unto itself, with a reputation for being extremely demanding, while the customer-facing properties work to bolster the family-friendly brand image.

Any one brand can have multiple sub-brands associated with it that are separate but whose reputations can impact the family brand. In the Disney example, nagging rumors of subliminal sexual messages hidden in the cartoon movie *Aladdin* threatened to tarnish Disney's squeaky clean brand image, as did racy photos taken in 2008 of Miley Cyrus—the 15-year-old star of *Hannah Montana*, a multi-billion dollar Disney property and successful brand in her own right.

In other instances, brands within a brand family do not always reflect the parent brand. Along with family-oriented sub-brands, Disney also owns Miramax Films, which produces R-rated feature films, as well as ESPN, which is dedicated to sports and sports-related news. It is hard to conceive how these sub-brands could injure the family-friendly reputation of the parent brand, because their audiences are very different and the sub-brands are not closely identified with Disney.

The Importance of Branding

Brand building is such an important element to success that most large companies hire people with the title of Brand Manager, as well as look to outside agencies for help building brands. Successful brand building involves paying constant attention to user enjoyment of a given product or service, setting sufficient budgets for marketing, and evolving the brand over time as markets and opinions change.

Companies invest in building and marketing their brands for a number of reasons, including:

- Increasing recognition

- Establishing trust

- Building brand loyalty

This last point, brand loyalty, is of particular importance, and worth looking into further. **Brand loyalty** is achieved when consumers stay faithful to a given brand and, whenever possible, take pains to continue their use of that brand. We will explore this concept later in this section.

Consumer behavior dictates how important brands are to driving increased corporate revenues. According to the Grocery Manufacturers of America, which studies consumer trends in grocery stores, half of all consumers consider the brand to be either the first or second most important element when deciding which product to buy (other important factors include nutritional information, cost, and nostalgia for products they remember using from childhood).[1] In addition, 13% first try a brand because it was recommended to them by someone they trust—further establishing the importance of brands in building a loyal following of customers willing to pass the word on to others.[2]

Brand Loyalty

Marketers do not expect consumers to spend time consciously contemplating their brands. However, they do know that strong branding helps forge emotional connections between their brands and the targeted consumer. Marketers hope the brand association will translate into brand loyalty. Brand loyalty is a consumer's commitment to a brand, and it occurs when a consumer will go out of his or her way to buy specific brands that they trust, even if they are harder to find or more expensive than other available options. After brand loyalty has been established, it can be difficult for competitors to sway that consumer from his or her preferred brand.

A good example of brand loyalty can be seen with some computer users, especially proponents of Macintosh computers. Although the Mac has significantly less market share than its Microsoft Windows counterpart, Mac has managed to build such brand loyalty among some members of its core market that dedication to these computers sometimes reaches a cult-like status. Focus groups run by competing computer manufacturers have shown that if a new Windows-based computer were introduced that ran twice as fast as the focus group's current computer and was priced competitively, Windows users would quickly switch to the faster one. Of the Mac users, almost none agreed to make the switch. When the Mac users were offered the faster Windows-based system for half the price of their Macs, they still refused to switch, a trend that continued regardless of how low the price for the PC dropped. Mac enthusiasts have such a strong emotional connection to the brand that convincing them to switch to a different brand can be an extraordinarily steep, uphill battle.

The Mac example is an extreme illustration of brand loyalty; however, the example does underscore how strong an emotional connection can be between a brand and its consumer. For a competing Brand X to win over a consumer who is enamored with Brand Y, it may take a combination of giveaways, enticing promotional offers, rave reviews of Brand X by trusted friends and family, and a prolonged marketing effort to get the consumer to even try the product. Even then, there is no guarantee that the consumer will make the switch and make it permanent.

Attachment to a brand is built through a number of factors, including overall benefit to the consumer, relative value versus price, accessibility, and emotional connection. Each of these variables, when changed, can positively or negatively affect how a consumer relates to a brand.

Brand loyalty is the jewel in the marketing crown; however, there are several levels of commitment that consumers can make to brands. In their relationship with brands, consumers can fall into one of the following categories:

- **Brand loyal**: Consumers who are committed to one brand, so much so that they will travel out of their way to get it. Very little will take them away from a brand that they trust, and these consumers are typically eager to tell other people about their favorite brands. In the Grocery Manufacturers of America study, 76% of all shoppers said that they would leave the store and shop elsewhere or live without the product until their next shopping trip if their favorite brands were not available, rather than buy a competing brand.[3]

- **Brand preferred**: These shoppers prefer certain brands over others and will go a bit—but not far—out of their way to get them. Slight price differentials or reduced accessibility are not enough to make them change brands, but significant changes in either variable may cause them to convert.

- **Brand aware**: These shoppers may like one brand over another—enough to recommend that brand to others—but they would not go out of their way for it. Slight differentials in price or accessibility compared to competing brands might sway their purchasing decisions.

- **Brand conscious**: These shoppers do not have a preference of one brand over another, and they would not go out of their way for any one brand. Price and accessibility are often the determining factors in deciding which products to buy. These shoppers still prefer to choose among brands that they know or about which they have formed an opinion (either through direct use or reputation). They stay away from brands that they don't know and avoid generic, unbranded products.

- **Brand indifferent:** Shoppers who base their decisions strictly on price and convenience. They are open to brands that they do not know and are also open to generic, unbranded products.

Any one shopper can fall into more than one—or even all—of the categories. A consumer who is brand loyal to BMW cars, for example, may not care one way or another about what brand of dish soap he or she buys. A consumer's reaction to certain brands is not always such a conscious decision—a shopper in a grocery store might look for Tropicana brand orange juice, for example, and not even bother looking at the price. To that shopper, nothing can substitute for the Tropicana brand. If the store is out of it, he or she might not buy any orange juice. That shopper is brand loyal to Tropicana, but he or she might not even realize it. Brand loyalty does not always involve the same fanaticism that we discussed earlier with Macintosh computers; few people wander the streets thinking longingly about their choice of orange juice.

INTERVIEW WITH...

MIKE HAND: THE HERSHEY COMPANY

Mike Hand began his career with BMW North America in 1994, helping to build one of the industry's premier automotive and motorcycle brands. Since that time, he has gone on to lead integrated marketing teams at some of the world's most recognized brand building organizations including M&M Mars, General Motors, and the Miller Brewing Company, where he was named by industry publications as one of the top ten most influential people to watch in retail activation.

Most recently, Mike has taken over the role of Director of Consumer Promotions, Hispanic and Sports Marketing at The Hershey Company, developing initiatives for brands such as Reese's®, Hershey's Kisses®, Kit Kat®, and Twizzlers®. He currently leads a team that has partnered with major sports leagues, motion picture/entertainment properties, and top selling musical acts to connect with consumers. As a well-established professional with significant experience, Mike shared with me his thoughts on brand building and the importance of "the brand" in terms of building a market.

JASON: In your words, what is a "brand" and how does it contribute to growth?

MIKE: The word brand is so hard to define; everybody has some unique way of serving it up and communicating what it is. I guess to me a brand is "a product with a unique identity." Anybody can make products, and some are certainly better than others, but it is the company/individual who creates an emotional connection and establishes an identity for that product that ultimately wins with the consumer. For example, I am an extremely passionate sports fan and love to look at the athletic shoe category for inspiration—on a personal and professional level. When I was in middle school, I was a dedicated Nike kid. At the time I had no idea what a special inner sole technology would do for me or how motion controlled sensors would stabilize my ankles; I simply loved the "Just Do It" campaign. The advertising and slogan spoke to me on a personal level. Reebok made good products—I guess. Converse made good products—I guess. But nobody could give me the emotional boost that Nike could give me. I trusted they made great shoes, not just because Bo Jackson wore them, but because everywhere I looked "athletes" were wearing them. I literally thought I could run faster, jump higher, whatever I needed when those shoes were on my feet. Looking back I know I was somewhat foolish, but as I begged my Mom to save more money for sneakers, it was clear that they had won me over. I even ran for Student Council President with "Just Do It" as my campaign slogan (Side note: I lost by seventeen votes—what's up with that?). I know that I wasn't the only kid in America watching Michael Jordan dunk or in later years watching Brandi Chastain tear off her uniform jersey to reveal a Nike sports bra for U.S. Women's Soccer—and watching Lance Armstrong overcome things a lot more intense than brand positioning issues.

The interesting thing about this example is that I am no longer a Nike guy. Past my college football playing days and likely done with my marathon running, as well—I've found that certain aspects of what I need can be found in other manufacturers' products. I still have a soft spot for the Nike brand and the attitude they bring to the table, but brands like Under Armour are fast becoming the "Nike of the next generation." I have a new-found respect for taking on a goliath head-on, and I think it will be interesting to see the results as UA gets deeper into footwear and cleats for athletes. This proves that brand contributes to growth, but also that you need to keep your brand fresh with consumers or you will not be able to sustain the growth. You can never forget that brands live in the heart of "individuals"; they don't live in a focus group and they certainly don't live in a conference room. The reasons brand contributes to growth is because simply seeing that trademark/logo can inspire consumers to purchase and repeat purchase. Brand becomes a symbol of a promise that something will deliver consistently and be something you can trust.

JASON: How have your personal experiences shaped your brand philosophy, and your ideas of how a brand contributes to value in an organization?

MIKE: While working at Miller we did more head-to-head consumer taste tests than I can remember of Miller Lite versus Bud Light. Bud Light remains the top selling beer in America despite the majority of consumers sampling both products and liking the taste of the Miller product more. Talk with those consumers and they admit that it's crazy, but the Bud umbrella of products is who they identify with on a personal level. Even when confronted with "sub-standard" product they would not switch brands. That's brand value. Don't get me wrong— Miller Lite did chip into the market share lead, but the fact that people admit their favorite brand is not as good but still stick behind it is quite impressive.

JASON: What are some of the specific challenges marketers have to be aware of as they grow and evolve a brand?

MIKE: The biggest thing marketers need to acknowledge is that the world is an ever-changing place. When you are evolving a brand you need to grow and adapt with it. Brands fail when they get complacent and aren't ready to adjust when the market conditions demands it. Brands also need to recognize and monitor their core user base. For example, if today's current buyer is a 20-year-old male, do you really expect to keep offering him the identical product experience as he grows up, or do you need to find another 20-year-old male to fill that void as he moves on? At the same time do you have an offering for that former 20-year-old male to grow into? And when looking at changes in the market, never take your eye off of what your key competitor is doing. However, be aware that it is very easy to become reactive instead of proactive in the marketplace when you are looking over your shoulder. Finally, you need to be very careful how you extend the brand into additional products. The biggest consumer companies in the world have become infatuated with creating 20 different flavor varieties and an additional 20 different package sizes of every leading product.

JASON: As a branding expert, what variables do you look at on a regular basis when managing a brand?

MIKE: Most marketers tend to fall into one of two buckets, you tend to be either a "creative driven" guy who leans into instinct and reading people for marketplace dynamics or you are an "analytical driven" guy who lets the numbers tell the story. As the world goes "green," I guess you could call me a bit of a hybrid. I tend to go more on gut feeling, but I always like to have some sense of the numbers to make sure. I like to focus on brand health measures. I want to know where I rank in top-of-mind consideration, top-of-mind awareness. I want to monitor the demographics of my core users to see where my brand has the most room to grow. When you have limited budgets you can't afford to fragment and try to mean something to everybody. You need to drill down with a laser and win. Budget is an interesting thing. I feel too many people get hung up on having big budgets. Some folks believe you need lots of money to find success. I disagree. Smart decisions with clear business objectives will win over a bigger budget 99% of the time. One thing that I do prefer to isolate is return on investment where/when I can. If I know that I spent $X on a sponsorship and the associated costs, how much can I assume I sold as a direct result? I like results. Show me actual transactional data when you can and you've found a way to my heart. This is still the area with the most opportunity for growth—showing clear returns.

JASON: Has the Internet changed the way you think about building a brand?

MIKE: Absolutely. The Internet has changed a ton of things about building a brand. It's changed the dynamic of how you interact and deliver your brand experience. So many consumers today are not just running into a store to buy a big ticket item and simply asking the salesperson a few questions to make that decision. They almost always go online first and start the homework process. The world of the Internet has shifted the buy/sell relationship power completely to the consumer. They can get reviews of the product online and hear what millions of people think and feel about it. Consumers are also much more aware of the wealth of options they have across product categories. People are no longer walking into car dealer "A" and saying, "My Dad drove a Cadillac so show me a Cadillac please." They are looking at 20 options across trucks, cars, hybrids, and others while listening to what their peers have to say. They can also visit any number of Web sites to gather expert opinions on areas that range from gas mileage to average cost of ownership. All of these things change the way your brand is perceived.

The Internet has also become a place where consumers can watch your ads again and again to relive a moment—whenever they want. Or better yet, they can create their own ads for you and post them on your Web site. The world of "user-generated content" making it all the way into Super Bowl ads [during a 2007 Doritos campaign] tells you something about the role the Internet continues to play in marketing programs. As you develop brand plans now, the Internet is not an outside extension that you reluctantly add to your plan. The Internet market gets a seat at the big kids' table, and it plays a critical role in planning and decision-making. It is not just banners and buttons, and it has to be more than just a Web page with basic information. The Web has become the home of very unique material that enables the customer to engage your brand in a more intimate way.

Every promotional effort that is run these days on my teams gets a strong interactive component. For example, say we're running a contest. The Web component can range from the simple—placement of full contest rules and entry pages—to the more complex—developing a promotional prize structure based on Web activity. It can even include custom Web items like screensavers, wallpapers, ring tones, and MySpace elements. As far as I'm concerned, we've only just scratched the surface on the role the Web will continue to play in brand building.

JASON: What brand efforts do you admire? Which do you think have failed?

MIKE: It pains me to say it in my current job at Hershey, but I've always been a fan of M&M's work. For the past 15 years, they have stayed true to who the brand characters are. You can envision Red or Yellow walking in a room and being that guy you see from TV ads.

They would have that same wit and sarcasm; they would be somebody you would identify with. They deliver it in the various seasons. They deliver it at retail. They deliver it at the race track. They deliver it at their retail stores. This is hard to do in a big organization, but they continue to be successful. It makes you feel like a kid every time you see it.

I also admire the work of Mountain Dew. It wasn't long ago that colas ruled the world and flavored soda was an afterthought. It is hard to walk anywhere today and not see a green bottle, especially with the under-20 set. They have made that brand very cool but not to the point of being unapproachable to the mainstream guy. The recent addition of [race car driver] Dale Earnhardt Jr. to the marketing stable only adds more cache to the brand. Not cool for the sake of cool, but again a little bit of confidence and swagger that feels fun.

The brand I am most concerned about today is Starbucks. Years ago I read the book "Pour Your Heart into It" by Howard Schultz, the founder of Starbucks, and I fell in love with the brand. The more I knew, the more I liked it, and the funny thing is I don't drink coffee. I loved their idea of employee benefits and the magical allure of stopping by your local coffee any time of day. Before I knew it, a store was on every single corner, and nothing felt special. I was being sold CDs and full meals while simply trying to order a hot chocolate with whipped cream (I forget the fancy name). They stopped smiling and being nice. They started barking instructions to a barista and then going to the next person in line while asking me if I wanted to add a gift card to my order. What is the deal with that? I hope Mr. Schultz getting involved again will return them to the roots that made them famous. Underneath it all, the DNA is still there and the employee care is still around. They need to feel the love for coffee again before every other small coffee shop in America steals it back. More companies also need to do a better job of rewarding loyalty—consumers have too many choices today. You need to grab hold of your user and never give them an opportunity to leave.

JASON: You've always been good for a few parting thoughts on topics I didn't cover. What do you have for me?

MIKE: I might have a few things I can add. One of the best ways to really understand the emotional impact a brand has is to make a list for yourself. List three to five brands that you think best describe who you are and ask some friends to do the same. It's amazing that people can provide detailed context on why they chose a certain brand. For example, my buddy is a BMW, Apple, New Balance guy— what does that say about him? He says he likes BMW for the sense of technology and precision in engineering he feels when he drives the car (note he does not own one, but has a girlfriend who does). He likes Apple because he thinks they simplify his life with products that are tech-advanced but easy to use. He is a runner and lives for New Balance—they just feel right and he knows they will last forever. Do you think these brands have formed an emotional connection and moved from being a simple "product" to having a unique identity? Damn right they have. The question to ask yourself as a marketer is how to you get your brand into that conversation. Your goal should be to create a passionate following for your brand that could sell out a concert tour strictly on the promise of showing up—because consumers know you won't deliver crap. It doesn't happen overnight, but that, my friend, is a solid brand foundation.

Elements of the Brand

Brands are complex entities that are made up of both tangible and intangible ingredients, all of which play an important role in speaking to the consumer, communicating a message, and building an audience. Brand managers are responsible for building trust, communicating a message, and forging an emotional connection with their market. All of that takes the careful fostering of promise, personality, unique qualities, and representative icons and elements. Figure 7-1 shows the major elements of a brand, and the part each plays in the development of a successful brand.

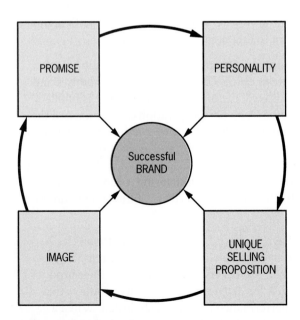

Figure 7-1   The elements that make up a brand.

The Brand Promise

If most marketers were forced to designate one element as the most important part of the brand, it would likely be the promise. Simply stated, the **brand promise** is the benefit the brand will deliver to consumers, and fulfilling that promise is one of the most important actions a company can take.

Suppose you visit a Web site that provides travel information. According to the site, they can give you more comprehensive information on remote destinations than any other travel site on the Web. So you search through the site to help you as you plan your upcoming vacation. After searching for a while, you settle on the island of St. Maarten in the Caribbean. The site details the exciting night life, a championship golf course, and award winning restaurants that make St. Maarten one of the most highly rated island destinations. You're sold! You book your flight, pack your bags and head out, anxious to play a round of golf and dance the night away.

There's only one problem—the Web site forgot to mention that a hurricane that hit the island over three years ago destroyed the golf course, which was never rebuilt. They also left out the fact that the night life consists of bars and clubs that are only open during specific months of the year, and they are all closed during the time that you're there. So much for "comprehensive information."

The site did not do what it promised. It promised you comprehensive information, but the information it actually provided was old and incomplete. The next time you are planning to take a trip, it's highly doubtful you will return to this site for information.

Fulfilling the brand promise is key to building trust for the brand. Initially, the consumer can only go by what the brand promises and assume that that promise will be fulfilled. If the promise is fulfilled, the brand is strengthened. A positive reputation has begun, and the expectation of positive returns during future use is increased, making it likely that the consumer will use that brand again. Break the promise, and the brand has been breached, raising doubt and diminishing trust. While trust can be difficult to build, losing it can be fairly easy. Regaining trust is often impossible, regardless of how much money is spent on advertising.

Do consumers really give the brand only one chance to fail? It depends on the brand in question; it often comes down to longevity and history. Nike makes sneakers; the sneakers are their product. Their brand reputation is for delivering high quality products that will enhance athletic performance with a stylish design. When a consumer purchases a pair of Nike's the expectation is that they will be comfortable and last a long time, even after aggressive use. For decades, Nike has fulfilled that brand promise and met consumer expectations. Now, suppose a consumer purchases a new pair of Nike's and they fall apart just two days later in the middle of a basketball game. That consumer will be annoyed, but their confidence in the Nike brand won't have taken too much of a hit. Chances are it was just one bad pair of sneakers off the assembly line. Nike has built enough trust equity to overcome a single bad experience. So, the consumer goes back and buys a new pair of Nike's. A few days later, his ankles hurt while playing tennis; the sneakers aren't proving the proper support. Will this consumer buy another pair of Nikes? Maybe, but his trust in the brand has been shaken, and he just may look at a pair of Reebok's the next time. Sometime in the future, when enough time has passed, the consumer will likely write-off these negative experiences and buy the Nike brand again, but there is no question that on some level, damage will have been done.

Unfortunately, most brands do not have the time, money, or exposure that Nike has to overcome isolated negative experiences. Brands must be careful to fulfill their promises each and every time in order to develop the trust necessary for gaining and retaining consumer loyalty.

While the brand promise often has to do with the quality of a product or service, that is not always the case. McDonald's does not try to claim that eating there is akin to dining in a five-star restaurant. Their promise is to provide you a quick meal that is inexpensive and tastes good. Women don't buy products from Juicy Couture because of their promised high quality. The promise (and promises are often subliminal, rather than expressly stated) is that if you own Juicy products, you will be part of an elite, fashionable crowd. The promise in this case is a promise of lifestyle rather than product-related factors, such as speed or quality.

The Brand Personality

When we think about personalities, we think about the people we come in contact with everyday and not so much about the brands we use. In reality, personalities in the brands we buy have an impact similar to the personalities of people that we meet.

Think about the people you meet on a daily basis. Some are super funny. Some are really good listeners. Some tend to be more serious. Still others are terrific conversationalists or have a depth of thought that makes them unique. Some people are obnoxious. Others are shy. Some are depressing, and some are generally upbeat. Chances are the people that you gravitate toward are people with whom you share similar personality traits.

It is likely that you will gravitate toward brands that have personalities similar to your own, as well. Like people, brands have their own personalities, and they use that personality to relate to a market that shares similar traits. Volkswagen, for example, comes off as fun and irreverent, while Lexus comes off as serious and elegant. Each brand has developed a personality meant to attract a specific audience.

Often times, consumers judge personality by first impression, usually based on aesthetic presentation. Go to any crowded place that attracts all different types of people, such as a mall. Find a bench, sit back, relax, and observe. Watch the people walking by. See the woman with the heavy make-up, pink hat, and loud pink pants? What do you think her personality is like? What about that guy with the comb-over, wearing the sweater vest, and walking timidly behind his wife, his head down and his hands deep in his pocket? How about the teenager riding the escalator, with the black Metallica t-shirt, baggy jeans, and half of his hair shaved off?

Right or wrong, people often make an immediate assumption about an individual's personality just by the way he or she looks, the colors that they wear, the style of clothes they choose, and other visual elements. Brands are no different. Brand personalities are often immediately judged by how they present themselves to the public through visual elements (discussed later in the chapter) and marketing efforts.

Brand personalities are vital to forging an emotional bond between brands and consumers. Customers who believe that a brand understands them and their lifestyle, and provides products and services with those understandings in mind, will feel a stronger bond to that brand. To create this emotional connection, a brand needs to carefully balance how it looks and acts so that everything is in synch. Think back to the guy with the comb-over and sweater vest. What did you assume about him from how he looked and acted? How would your image of him change if you later saw him in the music store, jamming away on an electric guitar? What if you saw the kid in the black Metallica t-shirt sipping a cappuccino while discussing the economic ramifications of further European Union expansion?

Chances are your assumptions about their personalities have changed a bit. You may not know what to think, because their image and actions contrast with each other. When it comes to judging people, this type of contrast may be little more than a mild curiosity. However, when it comes to brand, a disconnect between aesthetics and action can be the difference between brand loyalty and brand indifference.

The Unique Selling Proposition

Consumers make purchases based on need, desire, or both. Brands can make all sorts of promises and exude tons of personality; however, each brand still needs to offer a **unique selling proposition (USP)**—something that can differentiate the brand from their competitors—or brand loyalty will be impossible to achieve.

Assume that every bar of soap on a grocery store shelf looked exactly the same. Each was a plain white bar in a colorful box, with each box saying that this particular soap was guaranteed to get you clean. That is pretty much what soap is supposed to do, so it doesn't really tell you very much. Beyond that, the only thing that separates one product from another is the name and the logo. If the prices were exactly the same across all products, there wouldn't really be much of a choice to make. You could grab any bar of soap and feel relatively confident that it would do just as good of a job as any other bar.

Brands must look for ways to distinguish themselves from one another—to give consumers a reason to gravitate toward them. Maybe one brand adds the scent of exotic flowers to their soap, another develops a unique formula that gets users even cleaner, and still another shapes their soap in fancy designs. In doing so, they distinguish themselves from one another, giving consumers added reason to choose their product over competing products.

It is possible, of course, that competing brands will base their unique selling proposition on the same claim—a statement which might seem to be counter to the idea that the selling proposition is "unique." Coke and Pepsi each base their unique selling proposition on the taste of their product—similar claims, but each taste is unique in its own right. Jolt Cola differentiates itself by providing increased energy with "twice the sugar and twice the caffeine." Advertising agencies often differentiate themselves to potential clients by claiming to be the most creative. Again these are similar claims, but drastically different unique selling propositions; a quick portfolio review will show that each agency has its own creative approach, leaving it up to potential clients to decide which style is the best fit for their brand.

If there is no unique selling proposition, and a brand cannot find a way to distinguish itself from competitors, then that brand must determine whether there is really room for it in the market. With the growth and popularity of YouTube, numerous video sharing sites such as Heavy.com and others began appearing, anxious to cash in on Web users' sudden interest in online video. The unique selling proposition for most of these, however, appears negligible,

232

and as of the writing of this book, none have found a YouTube. com level of success. According to Nick MacShane, founder of Progress Partners, a business consultancy that helps companies develop their business plans and attract investors, "Investors are starting taking a 'wait and see' attitude to business plans involving video-sharing, to judge how the most recent crop of sites performs. Everyone and his brother are submitting a business plan now to launch new video sharing sites, and there's not a lot to differentiate them from each other."[4]

Image

While intangible features such as the promise and personality live at the heart of the brand, consumers need a visual way to identify, distinguish, and recall these messages. Image elements such as logos, taglines, and colors and fonts lend tangible and visual elements to intangible concepts, giving consumers an easier means of mentally categorizing each brand.

Logos

Like the burn mark on the farmer's cow discussed earlier, the **logo** is a unique, visual means by which people can instantly recognize a company and understand its product, promise, and personality.

Typically, logos are designed to be relatively simple, made up of no more than a couple of colors and lacking fine detail. There are a number of reasons to maintain simplicity in a logo, including:

- Simpler logos allow for easier and quicker audience recognition.

- Less detail makes a logo easier to replicate at smaller sizes such as on business cards or embroidered on shirts.

- Fewer colors are less expensive to reproduce.

Figure 7-2 shows a number of highly recognizable logos. Along with striving for audience recognition, companies will often try to develop a logo that tells something about them, even if it's a subtle, more subconscious inclusion. The Nike "Swoosh," for example, gives the impression of speed and activity. The CBS "Eye" logo represents CBS looking at the world.

Perhaps one of the most interesting logo stories revolves around one of the more boring corporate logos. FedEx's logo is well known and instantly recognized for its big, bold, colorful letters (Figure 7-3). What makes it so interesting is the "hidden" icon in the logo—the subtle arrow that's formed when the "E" and the "x" are put together. According to Lindon Leader, who created the logo:

Figure 7-2   A sample of recognizable logos.

Figure 7-3   The FedEx logo at the top as it appears in general marketing. The logo at the bottom outlines the subliminal arrow that many people never notice.

"If you put a lower-case 'x' to the right of a capital 'E' (Ex) you can begin to see a hint of an arrow, though it is clumsy and extremely abstract. I thought that, if I could develop this concept of an "arrow" it could be promoted as a symbol for speed and precision, both FedEx communicative attributes.

An arrow, in and of itself, is one of the most mundane graphic devices in visual communications. Truly, there is nothing unique or particularly strategic (marketing-wise) in using an arrow as a brand identifier.

"The power of the hidden arrow is simply that it is a 'hidden bonus.' It is a positive-reverse optical kind of thing: either you see it or you don't. Importantly, not 'getting the punch line' by not seeing the arrow does not reduce the impact of the logo's essential communication. The power of the logo and the FedEx marketing supporting the logo is strong enough to convey clearly FedEx brand positioning. On the other hand, if you do see the arrow, or someone points it out to you, you won't forget it."[5]

Leader's words not only provide an insight into this particular logo, they provide a glimpse of how much thought and consideration can go into the development of a logo, its look and feel, and ultimately, its meaning.

Taglines

The **tagline** is a brief statement used by most brands to send a quick message of brand promise or core competency summation to the audience. Typically, the tagline is closely associated with the logo, and they appear together on everything from business cards and letterheads to advertising and marketing campaigns.

Developing the right tagline for a brand can be an arduous task, and because it is the one line of copy that audiences will most closely associate with a brand, its importance cannot be overstated. Effective taglines typically serve one of six primary functions:

- **They serve as a call to action**: With just a few words, a strong tagline can inspire its audience to take some sort of action, while also telling you something important about the brand. Consider Apple Computer's famous two word tagline, "Think Different." The line suggests to people that they should change their way of thinking and open their minds to less traditional ideas, but it also establishes Apple as a company whose ideas, technology, and products are more innovative than their competitors'.

- **They relay the benefits of the brand**: As discussed earlier in this chapter, for a brand to be successful, it must provide some benefit to their target market; a brand needs to improve or enhance their life in some way. Without this benefit, there's virtually no reason for consumers to make a purchase. These taglines, like Miller Light's old but famous "Great Taste . . . Less Filling," take a direct approach and tell their market quickly and simply what benefits their brand will provide to customers.

- **They reconfirm the promise**: The promise is one of the most important elements of a brand; it lets consumers know what they can expect from their involvement with a brand. Taglines, such as Geico's "15 Minutes Could Save You 15% or More" or UPS' "We Deliver For You," reinforce the promise in succinct and memorable fashion by wrapping it into the tagline.

- **They associate their product or service with an intangible need or idea**: These taglines tend to be more vague and less communicative, establishing the value or importance of a brand by linking it to an intangible concept. Outback Steakhouse's tagline, "No Rules. Just Right," positions the brand as serving quality meals in a fun environment through an intangible tagline.

- **They point out the risk of not using their brand**: In order to make their product or service seem more like a necessity, brands will often use their tagline to make audiences consider the negative results of not using their brand. Ireland's (yes, countries are brands, too) 2008 U.S. travel campaign used the tagline, "Can You Afford Not to Go?" to highlight the value packages they offer in the face of the weakening dollar.

- **They link the tagline to their logo**: Because the tagline and the logo are usually closely associated, many taglines are written in such a way that they form a close association with the logo. Allstate Insurance's tagline, "You're in Good Hands with Allstate," reinforces their logo of two open hands, while still stating a promise to take good care of their customers.

Logos tend to go through minor evolutions and sometimes dramatic changes over time. Taglines get changed a bit more frequently in order to keep pace with changing times and market environments and changes in core competencies. Taglines also need updating to maintain a fresh, young feeling about the brand.

Colors and Fonts

Color plays an enormous role in the decisions we make as consumers and in how we feel about everything from companies and products to colleges and sports teams. Different colors hold different power and meanings for people, and entire sciences have been dedicated to studying how colors can affect both individuals and audiences, en masse. In the U.S., for example, colors have some very definitive associations, such as:

- **Black**: Dignified, sophisticated, powerful
- **White**: Innocent, optimistic

- **Gray**: Steady, stable, disciplined

- **Blue**: Loyal, responsible, conservative (blue is the most popular color for brands, and is considered a relatively safe choice)

- **Red**: Exciting, passionate, aggressive

- **Green**: Natural, balanced, healthy

- **Yellow**: Happy, warm, alert

- **Purple**: Regal, wise, celebratory

- **Orange**: Vibrant, energetic, playful

The feelings that colors elicit in people, and the reactions they can cause (hospitals dress nurses in light blues and pinks because patients relax more around these soothing, calming colors), are taken seriously by companies establishing and marketing their brands.[6] The colors used will resonate and create a strong association with the brand. The orange and green of every Crayola crayon box and the red and white of Coca-Cola are standout examples of the way colors play a role in consumer brand recognition. A turquoise gift box with a white ribbon lets a person know immediately that the gift is from Tiffany & Co.

The Web can put a wrinkle in the association of colors for a brand, because of the possibility of enormous reach. The earlier list of colors and the feelings associated with them is at best very general; colors are often interpreted differently depending upon culture, class, age, gender, and other demographic categories. For example, while white symbolizes purity and innocence in Western cultures, some Eastern cultures associate white with death and funerals. Younger audiences are drawn to brighter colors, while muted and pastel colors are more likely to attract the attention of adults. Men tend to be drawn to cooler colors like blues and greens, while women often appreciate warmer colors like reds and oranges. Because the Web gives companies access to larger audiences, there is a higher likelihood that the colors they have chosen will turn off some visitors or be ineffective.

Similarly, fonts are important in establishing the brand. Like colors, fonts may be compromised due to the Web. Fonts can help promote the brand personality, as each one of the thousands of fonts available has its own unique way of evoking an emotion and can speak volumes about the brand simply in the way the letters are formed.

It is important to understand the five basic styles of fonts and what type of feeling or mood each portrays:

- **Serif**: Serif fonts are fonts with non-structural details or ornaments on the ends of the some letter strokes. These fonts have a pretty serious look to them, and can be used to denote strength, sophistication, and establishment.

- **Sans serif**: Sans serif fonts are fonts without the non-structural details. They look much more sleek and are considered more modern and youthful. While they are not as serious as serif fonts, they are not necessarily frivolous, either.

- **Script**: Script fonts are exactly what you would expect them to be. Some are simple script; others are very fancy and ornate. They can denote class and sophistication, but can be difficult to read if not used properly.

- **Handwriting**: Handwriting fonts look like handwriting.

- **Artistic**: Artistic fonts range from the understated to unreadable. There is a wide variety of artistic fonts on the market, and they can be valuable in establishing a particularly whimsical, playful, or edgy brand personality.

Figure 7-4 provides a sample of each of these fonts.

Serif

San Serif

Script

Handwriting

Artsy

Figure 7-4 Samples of different font styles.

Brand developers should be aware, however, that on the Web, only fonts that reside on the Web viewer's computer can be seen in their browser. Exotic fonts that might not be widely available will not be seen. In these cases, the viewer's computer will substitute the desired font with a font already loaded into its system, which can cause unanticipated layout issues. One way that brands get around this problem is to provide their copy in graphic format, rather than HTML text. This approach is not recommended as it can make future editing difficult and diminish the chances of the copy being found through natural searches on most search engines. Typically, copy on sites is presented in either Times, Arial, or Verdana fonts, which come preinstalled on most computers. Brand developers, in deciding the font faces for their logos, taglines, and other marketing material, must develop these with the forethought that very specific font styles are likely to be used on their Web sites.

Consistency

When it comes to marketing the brand, the most important rule is to remain consistent. Companies may spend a good part of their marketing budgets on **brand management** (efforts to promote a brand and ensure it is being used properly and effectively) to make sure that the integrity of the brand is upheld throughout all forms of public dissemination. The larger the company, the harder it is to maintain consistency because larger companies tend to have a global reach, use multiple marketing and promotional agencies, and be involved in a large number of promotional efforts at any one time.

Consider the following scenario. Someone who visits a B2B Web site immediately gets a sense of that company's brand from the layout, navigation, and copy of the site. If he or she is interested in what the company has to offer, the visitor might e-mail a request for more literature. When it arrives, the colors used in the materials are different from the colors used on the Web site. In addition, the Web site uses photographic imagery in dark backgrounds, while the printed pieces have cartoon-style illustrations against stark white backgrounds. The tagline "Build it Better. Build it With Us," which appears on the site, is nowhere to be found on the literature. Potential consumers might not notice the discrepancies, but from the company's perspective, an opportunity to drive the brand message home has been lost. If the difference is noticed, the company could appear disorganized or not well-established.

Without consistency between materials and messages, no brand message can be established, and the company becomes just another in a sea of competitors. Sure, there's a logo, but there's hardly a brand because the message hasn't been properly communicated.

Remaining consistent throughout each medium a company utilizes is vital to ensuring strong penetration of the brand into the minds of its target market. In every aspect of life, from training a dog to learning to fly an airplane, consistency and repetition affect our behavior and help us form associations. The same is true for brands. Messages have to be repeated often and sustained without wavering. This means that if your company's logo is a specific shade of blue, it should appear in that shade on everything you do to promote your company. If the message is "We give great service" in radio commercials, the basic message should remain the same in the TV commercials. If the design style used in the print campaign is light and airy, it should be light and airy on the Web site. With the abundance of information that is constantly available, repetition is a key factor in reinforcing the message. It's the reason why you know that when you see a restaurant with a big red roof, it's a Pizza Hut, and you know the taste will be the same whether you eat in one in Paramus, New Jersey or Pasadena, California. Consistency. Whether customers love you or hate you, at least they will know that you exist, and they will know what you stand for.

Maintaining consistency in a brand is not an activity best left to chance. Brands consist of both tangible and intangible elements, each of which can be heavily dissected into considerably smaller parts. Because there are so many media that may be used to communicate the brand, each of these elements needs to be carefully detailed and recorded so that over time the brand doesn't lose its focus or sense of organization. Companies that understand the value of the brand and the importance of maintaining consistency do so by developing a **brand guide**, sometimes called a **style guide**. The brand guide is a book that details all of the elements of a brand, and can vary in length from just one or two pages for a small company, to hundreds of pages for large, multinational brands. Information found within the guide includes brand colors and how those colors break down into CMYK, RGB, and HEX values, font styles, how not to use the logo and more. Figures 7-5 and 7-6 show samples of two pages that would be found in most brand guides. These guides become more important as more people are responsible for handling the brand, including printers, designers, and Web developers. The potential for errors increases as more people become involved. As a general rule, brand guides are meant to be a strict rule of law to people outside of a company's core marketing group, such as sales people and vendors. The guides are meant to act as a guideline for people inside the core marketing group, who have greater insights to the brand and may be able to know better where and when liberties can be taken.

COLOR PALETTE
CENTURY BRANDING GUIDE

The Century colors are listed below. If you are using a program that does not allow for the use of specific Pantone colors, use the CMYK or RGB mixes indicated below to simulate the correct shade. The HEX numbers indicated are for Website use.

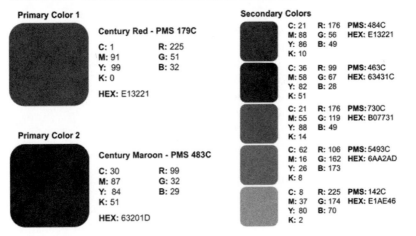

Primary Color 1

Century Red - PMS 179C

C: 1   R: 225
M: 91   G: 51
Y: 99   B: 32
K: 0

HEX: E13221

Primary Color 2

Century Maroon - PMS 483C

C: 30   R: 99
M: 87   G: 32
Y: 84   B: 29
K: 51

HEX: 63201D

Secondary Colors

C: 21   R: 176   PMS: 484C
M: 88   G: 56   HEX: E13221
Y: 86   B: 49
K: 10

C: 36   R: 99   PMS: 463C
M: 58   G: 67   HEX: 63431C
Y: 82   B: 28
K: 51

C: 21   R: 176   PMS: 730C
M: 55   G: 119   HEX: B07731
Y: 88   B: 49
K: 14

C: 62   R: 106   PMS: 5493C
M: 16   G: 162   HEX: 6AA2AD
Y: 26   B: 173
K: 8

C: 8   R: 225   PMS: 142C
M: 37   G: 174   HEX: E1AE46
Y: 80   B: 70
K: 2

TYPOGRAPHY

Logo Font
The Centurylogo font is:

BANK GOTHIC

This font should only be used for the logo itself, as well as for Web, PowerPoint and printed brochure headlines, titles and accents. Titles required for MS Word and other such documents should refer to the body copy section below.

Body Copy Font
Various forms of Verdana font should be used for body copy in all areas, including Web and other elecronic media.

Titles in MS Word should use
Verdana - Forced Bold - 12pt

Body copy in all areas should use
Verdana - 12 pt

Figure 7-5 A page from a style guide that details the color breakdown and the font styles of this particular brand.

LOGO USAGE
CENTURY BRANDING GUIDE

Size

Two versions of the logo have been created for use at different sizes. The larger version should be used when it will be greater than 4." The smaller version should be used when space is restricted and the size is less than 4." The logo should never be less than one inch in width when produced.

1.00"

Formats

Please refer to the charts below for correct resolution and format usage. Logos should **never** be scaled up in size - this will compromise the integrity of the logo.

	Lo-Res	Hi-Res
Print		X
Electronic	X	

	Print	Web	MS Word	Excel & PPT
JPG		X	X	X
TIF	X			

Isolation Area

Keeping a minimum amount of clear space around the logo, separating it from headlines, text, imagery, or the outside edge of a document is key to preserving its presence and legibility.

The isolation area is equal to half the width of the symbol. This is a universal proportional measuring system that applies to all sizes.

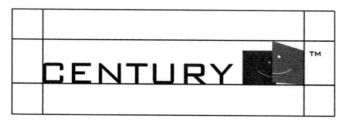

Figure 7-6 This page from the same style guide shows the sizes and formats of the logo, and how they should be used.

INTERVIEW WITH...

TONY MEOLA

Although it later took a serious hit, during the early to mid-2000s, the U.S. housing market was booming. Mortgage banks across the country were in fierce competition for borrowers, anxious to cash in on a housing craze that, at the time, seemed limitless. During those years, my agency, PFS Marketwyse, developed internal marketing campaigns for Washington Mutual to help motivate their sales force to reach quarterly sales goals.

Tony Meola was Washington Mutual's Executive Vice President of Sales and Marketing during those years. Having worked closely with Tony on the development of these campaigns, I came to respect him as having a very unique understanding of branding and the importance of aligning internal operations with the external brand. I caught up with Tony, now the CEO of Saxon Mortgage, the mortgage arm of Morgan Stanley, and asked him to discuss his thoughts on branding with me.

JASON: Tony, you've had a good deal of experience doing internal marketing and branding within large organizations. Have you been able to see these efforts impact external sales and influence audiences?

TONY: Absolutely. I would say as an operator, productivity is your first indication that the brand is successful. Employees are more productive because they're working for an image and a reputation that becomes their own. When I was with Citibank, the slogan that we built our brand around was 'The Citi Never Sleeps.' It was more than a tagline—we really wove it into our operation through our providing of 24-hour coverage. Every time we thought about access from a customer, we thought about it in terms of 24 hours. Employees are much more productive when their environment and the brand are in alignment, because they produce to support the environment and the environment is conducive to productivity.

JASON: So, at Citibank, the tagline really summed up the brand and the corporate environment. You also had a pretty powerful brand and tagline when you were with Washington Mutual. Talk to me a little about that.

TONY: At Washington Mutual we branded the mortgage business around 'The Power of Yes.' When we thought about loans, we thought about how to make that loan from each constituent's point of view: borrowers, shareholders, and regulators. We thought about how to say 'yes' in all of those worlds, and we really did a phenomenal job of bringing that brand to life internally and externally. It was successful because it was more than just a tagline. With most mortgage lenders, the mortgage application is filled out and the lender tries to assess whether or not you give that borrower money by asking a lot of follow-up questions, and going back and forth. With 'The Power of Yes,' our only question was, 'what would this loan have to look like for it to be approved?' We brought that information back to the borrower and would say "yes, we'll give a loan, if you give us this documentation"—a much different concept than anything in the industry, and a much more efficient process for everyone involved. Washington Mutual was one of the best examples I've seen of how the brand really influences an organization and vice versa.

JASON: It sounds a lot less like a tagline than a corporate philosophy.

TONY: I think that the great company brands reflect their values. For a brand to be strong, a company can't just arbitrarily decide what the brand is. For the Washington Mutuals, the Citibanks, and companies like those, their brand is who they are, their value system.

Going back to 'The Power of Yes' line that we used at Washington Mutual, the brand was born from the fact that we had a very sales and market-share focused company. We knew that the only way to generate sales and profitability was to give quality loans to people faster than other companies. I believe the values that drive the organization and its competencies come first and out of that, comes the brand.

JASON: When my agency worked with Washington Mutual, our work reflected the brand personality. Washington Mutual's personality was different than Citibank's, which is different from Morgan Stanley, where you currently work. How does the personality of each brand affect the way you approach your job and marketing efforts and sales efforts?

TONY: I think it's huge. I really think the values of a company dictate their operating environment. With Washington Mutual, part of their value statement is to get things done and to have fun doing them— fun that comes from expertise and teamwork and helping people. They pride themselves in the fact that they create an environment where employees enjoy what they're doing. Washington Mutual's brand is a brand that kids itself about the industry it's in and its approach. It does it, though, with a certain swagger that says they can perform better than the competition. It takes a knock at the industry because it has a lot of self pride as an innovative company. And that personality permeates into external marketing efforts as well as the internal culture.

JASON: Talk to me a little bit about the promise of a brand, and its place in influencing audiences.

TONY: If you don't have a promise, you don't have a brand, and if you can't keep your promise, you can't maintain consumer trust. The worst thing that could happen to a company is when their brand doesn't connect with their operating mechanisms. What happens then is that you can't fulfill the brand promise, and that's key to a consumer. People look at McDonalds with reverence because they've delivered a consumer reliable experience consistently throughout the world. When you go into a McDonalds, just look at all of the equipment in the kitchen that's designed for speed and efficiency; that's who they are. Now look at any company that's gone downhill, and you can usually trace it back to a brand that made promises it can't deliver. 'Ford Tough' isn't reflective of their record, so they're not tough. Once you break a consumer promise, it's very difficult to get that trust back. At some point, Panasonic ceased to "slightly ahead of our time."

JASON: On that note then, how is a brand affected when the market environment changes? You're in the mortgage industry, which has gone from extraordinary highs to crippling lows. Earlier, we discussed how part of Washington Mutual's brand personality is to have fun. It's easy to have fun when you're riding the bubble up, but how do you have fun when the industry is in a state of disaster? Or does the brand change to reflect the market environment?

TONY: I think that's a great question and frankly one they are struggling with. When the external environment changes, organizations have to tap strengths that they use differently in those types of environments. With the state that the mortgage industry is in today, the market doesn't want fun. Even if it did, it would be hard for Washington Mutual to maintain that attitude when "fun" isn't something their internal environment is feeling right now. So they tap into other values and competencies and use the power of advertising to send a different message. They no longer communicate their brand as 'The Power of Yes,' but rather promote a message that they are there for their customers in troubled times and that knowledgeable representatives can be reached by phone to discuss delinquencies and other issues. And Washington Mutual employees do take pride in helping people, so as the internal environment reflects that feeling, so does the external brand.

Companies need to be in tune with the marketplace around them, stay malleable, and be able to change to reflect the needs and sensitivity of that marketplace. Look at the rise and fall of Krispy Krème [donut chain]. People would go into a Krispy Krème store because they'd see the donuts coming off the conveyor. It was a lively, fun place to get a donut, but then Krispy Krème got smacked by a health craze that kept people from eating their donuts. They missed the boat on the coffee craze, which helped build Dunkin' Donuts into a gigantic brand. Krispy Krème didn't see the market changes, and so they didn't evolve their brand in time.

The external factors of a market are supply and demand. So companies have to look at the demand side of the equation and ask themselves if what they are supplying the market is still in demand. If it's not, what do they have to supply that will fit in with their core competencies. If you alter the brand in such a way that it's outside of your core competencies, then we're back to the earlier problem of not fulfilling the promise.

JASON: So what you're saying is that the brand and operations really rely on each other.

TONY: Absolutely. The question is often posed: is the brand born of the operation or is the operation born in the brand? As far as I'm concerned, it doesn't matter—they just have to be aligned. If you want to change the brand, you have to change your operations.

JASON: As students graduate and enter the workforce, what do you think the one skill is that they would need in order to be successful?

TONY: I would say communication. I think it's a skill set that is completely underrated. I don't mean communication from a standpoint of giving a speech, but from developing and delivering a message sent. What the intricacies of specific communication are, what's visual, what's audio, how does it work, what's the best remedy. There's a real entertainment value in all the commercials and advertisements and Web sites that is growing constantly. People want to be entertained now as they view advertising, and they want information as well. People want creativity and innovation, but it all comes down to knowing how to communicate, because there are also certain people that just want facts. A good marketer today knows how to communicate because the audiences will change. The definition of innovation will change. The definition of creativity will change, and all of it will be valued more or less depending upon the way the future changes. I think that something that's always going to be there for a marketer is the ability to communicate to an audience.

The Web's Place in Brand Building

Later in this book we will analyze how marketers communicate their messages through a variety of vehicles including television, radio, print advertising, direct mail, and roadside billboards. Each has pros and cons, including price, reach, and an ability or inability to be targeted to a specific audience. Marketers set their strategies by mixing and matching the marketing vehicles that they expect will be the most effective in communicating their brand to the desired audience for the budget they have available.

Despite the differences between traditional methods, most share two key similarities:

- Promotional efforts are finite; that is, their messages are in some way limited. A 30-second TV commercial can tell a story for only 30 seconds, an 8.5×11-inch print ad can say only as much as can be printed on the page.

- Promotional efforts speak to consumers as a group, not as individuals.

Neither of these characteristics is true of the Web because the Web is not just another traditional marketing tool. The Web is a hybrid medium, in that it is both something to advertise *for* (marketers will often use advertising to drive people to a site) as well as something to advertise *on* (sites, especially B2B sites, are often used as advertising vehicles in and of themselves, with companies using their pages to promote their products and services, etc.).

To understand how the Web plays into the branding picture, we must examine the Web as an isolated entity, offering both increased channels and challenges to the brand-building effort.

The Web's Hybrid Status

Advertising is used to promote a product or service, or increase awareness of a brand. It's a single-effect communication requiring the audience to take action themselves. A reader of a print ad, for example, cannot make a purchase from that print ad. He or she must take some sort of action, such as making a phone call or visiting a store in order to make a purchase. The ad promotes the brand, and the company or the store sells the product.

The Web, however, falls between the promotion and sales processes. A Web site can act in exactly the same way as an ad in a magazine, by promoting the brand and pushing consumers toward a product. In this sense, both the print ad and the Web site exist for the purposes of driving consumers to make a purchase (take action)—they each work to advertise a brand.

The Web is different from other marketing tools in that visiting a Web site is often the very action that other marketing tools want consumers to take. Rather than making the case to consumers to visit a store and purchase a product, a print ad may instead make the case to consumers to visit the brand's Web site and gather more information. In this sense, the Web is not only a means of advertising; it is also the subject that is being advertised. One marketing tool is, in a way, marketing another marketing tool.

The Web offers infinite room for providing information, promoting the brand personality, and offering e-commerce capabilities and social media tools that allow the brand to interact with its market. This offers a far richer experience than a 30-second commercial or one page print ad could possibly provide.

Individual Message Delivery

Traditional mass marketing tools and branding efforts address the audience as a single entity, regardless of how many people that might include. This approach offers no flexibility in speaking to individual members of a target market. It sends messages to large demographics based largely on assumptions made from the shows being watched. The investment firm Charles Schwab can take a calculated risk that they are more likely to reach people interested in their services by running their ads during *The Suze Orman Show* on CNBC than they would by advertising on *The Real World* on MTV. While individual shows can provide a more narrow audience demographic, the message is still sent to the audience as a whole; the commercial has no way of reaching out to a particular member of the audience and saying, "Hi, John. We saw that you've been looking around for tennis equipment lately. You might be interested in this brand."

Because of social media tools, the Web has the ability to speak to each member of a given audience on an individual basis through personalization. Sites like Amazon.com have perfected the art of promotion based on intuitive, one-to-one marketing. Figures 7-7 and 7-8 shows two iterations of Amazon.com—the first screen shot is the site upon initial arrival, as though I had never been there before. The second screen shot shows how the site looks the second time I visited it—after doing some searching on the site. Even though these visits were only a few minutes apart, Amazon changed the products on its home page to reflect what it thinks I would be interested in based on my previous search and/or purchasing history.

248

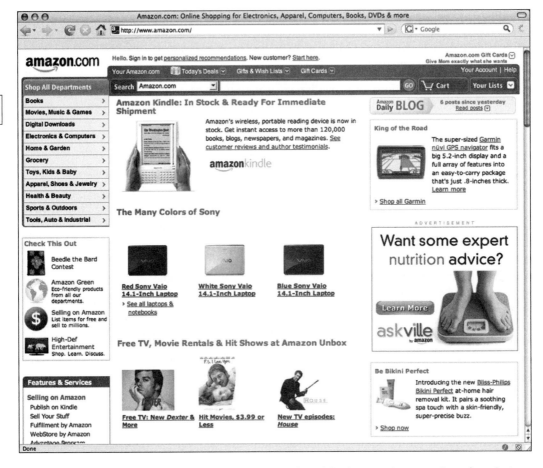

Figure 7-7   The Amazon home page as it looks when first visited, promoting a number of products including Sony laptops and movie rentals.

The ability to market to individuals based on previous buying behavior increases the potential for sales by making brands accessible to the people most likely to buy them. From a brand perspective, this creates significant opportunities for increased revenue and brand recognition from key markets.

Increased Markets

Traditional marketing can be expensive. One full-page print ad can cost anywhere between a few thousand dollars to a few hundred thousand dollars, depending on the publication. Television spots can be even more expensive. Thirty seconds of time can cost between a few hundred dollars to air in a single county on a relatively unpopular cable show, to nearly three million dollars to air during the Super Bowl. This can add up quickly, limiting reach and exposure.

Figure 7-8 The Amazon.com page during a second visit, a few minutes later. The home page now offers me products that other people have purchased after searching for that same item and other books Amazon recommends based on my search.

Technically, the Web's exposure is limitless and easily accessible to anyone, regardless of demographic or geographic boundaries. Of course, this doesn't mean that everyone *will* see it, just that everyone *can* see it. This opens up opportunities to marketers to increase the reach of their brands, by concentrating efforts on driving people to their sites through traditional marketing, word-of-mouth, and links shared between sites. By opening themselves up to new audiences, brands can generate increased exposure and sales.

Reinforcement of the Brand Message

Because the Web is so dynamic, it presents marketers with opportunities for reinforcing their brand image and promise, without the consumer even making a purchase. Pampers.com, shown in Figure 7-9, has developed its Web site specifically to enhance its promise as a brand that cares about kids. For decades, Pampers has been trusted by parents throughout the world, earning that trust by consistently marketing safe, reliable, and high-quality products specifically for babies—an area in which it can be particularly difficult to gain trust.

Figure 7-9   The Pampers Web site provides information for parents about how better to care for their children.

To reinforce parental trust in its products, Pampers uses its site less as a marketing tool and more as a parenting resource. The site presents helpful insights and information for parents regarding child development, growth, activities, expert advice, and more. Much of this information has little or nothing to do with the products it sells.

Why would Pampers bother? After all, the company is in business to sell a product, not provide advice. The reason is the difference between the product (what Pampers *sells*) and the brand (what Pampers *promises*). The promise is the effort taken to show that the company is not just manufacturing diapers; it does, in fact, care about its customers before caring about profit. This is what builds trust. Trust in turn builds loyalty, and loyalty eventually translates to increased sales.

When translating your brand onto the Web, marketers need to ask themselves (or better yet, ask their customers), "what type of information can we provide beyond standard product information that can improve your lives?" The Web offers brands increased opportunities to provide value-added services over and above their product offerings and engage their market in far more personal ways, increasing trust and reinforcing their brand.

Heightened Consumer Interaction

Social media tools have dramatically changed the way people use the Web and the way they interact with the brands that they use. Unlike any other medium, the Web provides marketers with more than just the ability to market on a one-to-one basis; it also provides the ability to create a community of customers. Through blogs, Wikis, social networking, and other tools, brands can interact with consumers more closely than ever before. The Web lets brands learn from customers, gathering opinions, running more effective marketing and promotional campaigns, and giving consumers the opportunity to interact with each other. These efforts help to build trust and strengthen the emotional connection between brand and consumer, providing increased opportunities for the brand to more closely connect itself to its market.

Chapter Summary

- There are many ways to define a brand; however, the most important definition in the mind of the marketer is that that the brand is not a particular product or service, but rather is broken down as *"The sum total of all user experiences with a particular product or service, building both reputation and future expectations of benefit."* This definition positions the brand as intangible and interactive

252

with its audience. While there is a clear distinction between brand and product, there is less distinction between brand and company. Often a company can be a brand unto itself that is perceived differently than its individual products.

- The importance of branding is to aid consumers in recognizing a product or service, and to build up trust and positive expectations of future use. The ideal for any company is to parlay that trust into brand loyalty, which occurs when consumers become so close to a brand that they will go out of their way to seek it out, avoid competing products, and tell other people about the brand, encouraging further use and purchase.

- Brands are made up of numerous elements, both tangible and intangible. These elements include the brand promise, which tell consumers what the brand intends to provide and how it will benefit the consumer; the brand personality, which forges an emotional connection with consumers; and the unique selling proposition, which is something that can differentiate the brand from its competitors. Other more tangible features of a brand include the logo, tagline, colors, and fonts, all of which are detailed in the brand's style guide—a book that houses the important information related to the communication of the brand for consistency purposes.

- In building the brand, the Web provides both increased opportunities and challenges. The Web is a hybrid marketing vehicle, speaking to consumers on a one-to-one basis, increasing geographic and demographic markets, reinforcing the brand promise and heightening consumer/brand interaction.

Key Terms

brand guide/style guide—A book that details all of the elements of a brand. It can vary in length from just one or two pages for a small company to several hundred pages.

brand loyalty—When consumers stay faithful to a given brand and take pains to continue their use of that brand.

brand management—Efforts to promote a brand and ensure it's being used properly and effectively.

brand personality—The aspects of a brand's character that help forge an emotional connection with consumers.

brand promise—The benefit the brand will deliver to consumers.

logo—A unique, visual means by which people can instantly recognize a company and understand its product, promise, and personality.

tagline—A brief statement used by most brands to send a quick message of brand promise or core competency summation to the audience.

unique selling proposition—The aspect of a brand that differentiates it from its competitors.

Review Questions

1. Which of the following is not a primary ingredient in the development of a successful brand?

    a. The brand promise

    b. A global presence

    c. An aspect that makes the brand unique from other brands

    d. Brand recognition

2. The most crucial element to brand success is a:

    a. High marketing budget

    b. History of brand promise fulfillment

    c. Logo that has an interesting story behind it

    d. Memorable tagline

3. Which of the following would best describe the personality of a particular brand?

    a. The brand is fun, lively, and meant to be enjoyed by people who love life.

    b. The branded product is of high quality and will last a very long time without breaking.

    c. The branded product is the top seller in its market.

    d. The brand has an interesting history and has been established over a number of decades.

4. Which of the following is the least likely to qualify as a viable unique selling proposition for a chain that services automobiles?

    a. "We fix cars."

    b. "We always use the best parts."

    c. "We have experience with older vehicles."

    d. "We work on all imports."

5. Ideally, a brand has success as a result of:

   a. Severe price breaks and ongoing promotional rebates

   b. Brand loyalty due to an emotional connection made between the brand and the audience

   c. The repetition of the brand message through exhaustive marketing efforts

   d. The collapse of competing brands

6. A "brand" and a "product" are interchangeable:

   a. Always

   b. Sometimes

   c. Never

7. A tagline can best be described as:

   a. A quick summation of the brand promise or core competency

   b. The most effective means of promoting the brand personality

   c. A marketing tool that has no real relevance to building the brand

   d. The subject line for brand e-mails

8. Consistency of a brand image has to happen:

   a. During the initial rollout of the brand, but may become more loose over time

   b. During the period of translation from traditional brand to online brand

   c. Throughout the life of the brand

   d. Internally for the benefit of brand employees

9. A company that manufactures hair care products could enhance the emotional connection between consumers and the brand by:

   a. Providing hair care tips and style guides for various occasions

   b. Providing a page of printable coupons for its products

   c. Providing a list of stores where the product is sold

   d. Providing biographies of celebrities who use the products

10. Nike is an example of a:

    a. Brand

    b. Company

    c. Both a and b

11. Colors can have an effect on the way people perceive the brand. True or False?

12. USP stands for:

    a. Unique site page

    b. Unique selling proposition

    c. Understated performance

    d. Upside potential

13. Which font style is most likely to come across as modern?

    a. Serif

    b. San Serif

    c. Script

    d. Artistic

14. Which category of consumers is most likely to try another brand should prices adversely change?

    a. Brand loyal

    b. Brand preferred

    c. Brand aware

    d. Brand conscious

15. The most likely reason that a brand site would include helpful tips unrelated to direct sales of the product is:

    a. To increase site traffic to sell more ad space

    b. To eventually sell the information in newsletter subscriptions

    c. To build consumer trust in their brand

    d. To keep people on their site longer—the more time spent on their site, the less time spent on competitors' sites

16. According to Tony Meola, brands should reflect the company's:

a. Personality

b. Experience

c. Values

d. Management

17. The style guide is meant to:

a. Provide the details of the brand elements

b. Give the history of the brand

c. Provide information about the people who build the brand

d. Outlines future marketing strategy

18. Which of the following is not a necessary element of the brand?

a. Personality

b. Promise

c. Unique selling proposition

d. Venture capital

19. Which color can make a brand seem balanced and healthy?

a. Green

b. Blue

c. Orange

d. Yellow

20. A Web is a hybrid marketing vehicle because:

a. It can play both music and video

b. It is a tool used for marketing, while at the same time it is a destination that is often the subject of other marketing tools

c. Television advertisers can show their commercials on their Web site as well as on TV

d. One site can include links to many different sites

Projects

1. Taglines help you form an immediate association between a brand and an idea. Below are taglines from famous brands:

    - Mmmm, Mmmm, Good
    - Just Do It
    - The Quicker Picker Upper
    - Snap, Crackle, Pop
    - We Bring Good Things to Life
    - I'm Lovin' It
    - When You Care Enough to Send the Very Best.

    a. Name the brands that are associated with these taglines. What do the taglines say about the brand?

    b. From your own knowledge of each company (either through use of their products or exposure to their marketing), what do you perceive each brand's promise to be? What about its unique selling proposition? Are they different?

    c. Based on their style and marketing, how would you describe the brand personalities?

2. Northeast Ski has decided to open an e-commerce Web site. The company sells all major brands of skis and ski accessories and has a client base that keeps coming back. Northeast is known for its service and the product knowledge of its salespeople. The shop also has a wide product selection and a great return policy. A fireplace in the center of all Northeast stores is a draw for its customers, who enjoy the lodge-style atmosphere when they shop at this particular retailer.

    a. On a Web site, how can Northeast maintain the warm, homey atmosphere that has been such a draw for its stores?

    b. What steps can the company take to provide online service similar to the service that customers appreciate in the stores?

    c. Using techniques that rely less on direct sales than its current strategy, how else can Northeast further enhance the brand?

    d. What steps can the company take to convert non-skiers into skiers with its Web site?

    e. Assume that this company does not have a name, established brand, or tagline. Come up with a name, brand promise, and tagline that will quickly let customers know what makes this particular chain different from its competitors.

3. In Chapter 2 of this book, we listed a number of sites that failed when the Web bubble of the late-1990s burst. Choose one of these companies and research the reasons why it failed. In a one-page paper, describe the reasons why it failed, referencing problems and consumer disconnects specifically in terms of its branding efforts.

4. Find five name brands around your home that you have purchased in the last few months. For each, explain which category of brand loyalty you fall into, and why. For those brands you are not brand loyal to, explain what it would take for those brands to gain your loyalty.

5. Take the "Mike Hand Challenge." Define your personality in terms of three to five brands. Which ones would you choose to describe you? Get three friends to describe your personality in terms three to five brands. What do their choices tell you about each person?

Endnotes

1. Scott Openshaw, Brian Kennedy, "New Survey Shows National Brand Loyalty High Among American Consumers." Grocery Manufacturers of America, 12 Jun 2002.
2 Ibid.
3 Ibid.
4 MacShane, Nick. Personal Interview. 12 June 2008.
5 "The Man Behind the FedEx Logo." The Sneeze <www.thesneeze.com> 14 Nov 2004.
6 Jennifer Kyrnin, "Color Symbolism." About.com <www.about.com> Sep 2008.

CHAPTER 8

Planning and Developing the Site

In this chapter you will learn about:

◎ The beginning stages of Web site development

◎ The importance of understanding a site's target audience and how that understanding can affect site development

◎ Methods for getting a site developed

◎ Baseline considerations for every site, including navigation, organization, graphic design, and content development

So, here is it—the meat and bones of site development. You have gotten the in-depth analysis on just about every social media tool in popular use and have read more on branding than you ever thought you would as a Web programmer. Finally, we get to the part we have all been waiting for—developing the site.

Sort of.

Before any code gets written, the site owners and developers need to decide on the overall concept for the site—what it will do, why it will exist, and what elements will be needed to make it come to life. Many of these questions can only be answered by undertaking research to develop an understanding of who the target audience is, what they want, and what they will respond to. Furthermore, companies that own and operate a site need to weigh the pros and cons of internal site development versus outsourcing to a third party. Finally, all parties involved need to carefully plan all aspects of the site prior to construction—including how the site will be organized, how it will look, and how the content will be developed.

Getting the Site Started

Web site developers need to take many steps before programming can begin. They must come up with core idea behind the site, and they must develop a general concept for the site. In addition, developers need to have a full understanding of their goals and the required resources in advance of actually building the site.

Developing the Idea

Web sites don't start with a line of code, a body of copy, or even a graphic design. Regardless of the Web site's purpose, all sites start with an idea. Whether it is a B2B site that promotes a company's products or services, a social networking site, an e-commerce site, or a site that supports an advertising campaign, each site stems from a concept or idea that one or more people believe in.

Developing a successful idea for a site can be trickier than you might think. To create a successful site, a developer should start with a concept about which he or she is passionate and knowledgeable. The idea should relate to a subject of interest to the intended audience. It also must be easily translatable into a Web site (given the budget and resources available).

The Web is a rich canvas on which developers can get carried away. It is important that site owners put into action ideas that are exciting and of interest to the target audience while also being realistic for the scope of the project.

Defining the Site Objectives

Every site has a reason for being. Once the developers have finalized the concept, they must establish the objectives of the site. The objectives need to be clear so that the site can be developed to reach the desired goals.

Objectives for a Web site could include one or more of the following:

- To generate direct revenue through e-commerce capabilities
- To generate indirect revenue by enticing visitors to contact the company and engage in a business relationship
- To build brand recognition (which ultimately leads to generating revenue)
- To build traffic for the purposes of generating advertising revenue
- To gather like-minded people
- To express opinions
- To share one's creative talents relating to music, art, etc.

Needs Assessment

Successful Web developers conduct a thorough needs assessment for their projects prior to beginning development. What each site needs in terms of resources ultimately depends on its objectives. The skills and resources required to build a site can be numerous, and can include:

- Graphic design
- Programming
- Marketing
- Content development
- Product inventory
- Site hosting

Graphic designers, programmers, and other staff all need to be paid and have a place to work. Each needs a computer, software licenses, scanners, printers, and other office equipment. Owners must also finance the cost of any necessary product inventory, site hosting services, and a variety of other expenses associated with site development. The level of financial resources needed to develop a site largely depends on the idea behind the site and the level of programming complexity involved. More complicated sites can

262

require multiple servers, sophisticated databases, and other tools. Sometimes, companies can keep costs down through what is known as **boot-strapping**—a slang term that means a company tries to do most of its site development in-house in order to keep costs as low as possible.

Companies with development plans that require heavier financial aid usually seek funding either through a bank loan or from a venture capitalist. Acquiring funding through a venture capitalist usually involves writing a **business plan**, which outlines the site concept, market, anticipated revenue structure, marketing, strategy, and technology plans. Basically, business plans lay out the reasons why the site will work, how it will serve the market, and how it will reach its goals.

Understanding the Audience

Part of establishing a successful brand is promising something that people want. An underarm deodorant that promises to make people smell worse than they already do might be able to live up that promise, but is it a promise that people are interested in? Similarly, in order to develop a successful Web site, developers need to understand the potential audience, what they want, what they are likely to respond to, and what will make them take action.

To develop that understanding, companies work to define their **target market**—the market segment most likely to visit their site and purchase their products or services. In defining the target market, marketers gather as much information as they can about the audience, painting a picture by gathering both demographic and psychographic data:

- **Demographic data** provides information on large groups by specific population characteristics such as:

  - Age (median age and predominant age group)

  - Marital status

  - Family size (marital status, number of siblings, number of offspring, etc.)

  - Education level

  - Income (median income and income range)

  - Gender (percentage male versus percentage female)

  - Occupation (type of work and number of years with same employer)

  - Nationality

- Race

- Religion

- Geographical residence

- **Psychographic data** further defines audiences by personality and lifestyle characteristics, including:

  - Types of hobbies

  - Vacations (places traveled and number of trips taken per year)

  - Recreational sports played

  - Luxury items owned

  - Number of general-use items (cars, sneakers, etc.) purchased last year or over the last three years

  - Hours per day/week spent on the Web

  - Web use location (percentage work versus home)

  - Types of sites visited

  - Top five favorite Web sites

  - Dollars spent on online retail over the last six months and over the last year

  - Social media tools used (blogging, video sharing, social networking sites, etc.)

To appeal to the target market, marketers study the demographic and psychographic data as a basis for developing appropriate content. For example, the personalities and lifestyle similarities of people that would go to a Web site on car racing are likely very different from those of people who would visit a site about opera. Knowledge of the target market translates into a site's ability to devise an effective **marketing strategy** (the strategy that a site or company employs in order to gain more customers and revenue). A successful marketing strategy translates into increased product sales and/or increased **visitor retention** (the measure of how long a visitor remains on your site and how often he or she returns). Further, market research of this nature often provides insight that might not be obvious on the surface. For example, consider an e-commerce site that sells clothing and accessories to an audience of 14- to 19-year-old females. Without doing any market research, site developers might design the site using colors, text, images, and content that they assume would appeal to girls and women in that age category. However, more in-depth research of the target market would likely lead developers to build a site that would appeal to 20- to 25-year-old women, because 14- to 19-year-olds want to look and feel like they are 20 to 25 years old. In addition, the research might also show that the one sure way to lose the audience completely would be to focus too much on the product line. Hard sales won't work with this demographic. Instead, the site needs content and tools that appeal to this market segment, like updated celebrity gossip, product reviews, and relevant blogs. The sales of product will come with the broader appeal of the site. This, in turn will come by creating an emotional connection between the brand and the target market. This connection is nurtured as marketers cultivate a better understanding of who the market is and what they are likely to respond to.

Gathering the Information

Researchers use a number of different methods to collect market data, including conducting personal interviews (either existing clients or random people in a highly populated area, such as a shopping mall), telephone surveys, or **focus groups**. Focus groups are meetings in which a group of individuals (usually between 15 to 20 people) that represent the target market are gathered together and engaged in a discussion about a topic of interest to the marketer. Often, the group is unaware of what company or brand is conducting the meeting.

As the Web has grown, newer methods of research have become popular. Surveys, for example, which used to be conducted mostly over the phone, in person, or via mail, are now made much easier thanks to the Web. Sites like SurveyMonkey (shown in Figure 8-1) have made the creation and distribution of surveys quick and efficient. These sites allow marketers to easily create online surveys that can be posted on a Web site or included in an e-mail. Further, marketers can create surveys that retain the logo, colors, and style of their brand. All of this can be done without users having to program a single line of code.

Marketers also conduct research through careful review of the blogosphere, customer reviews, and social networking sites. These techniques allow brands to see far more than just who is in their market. These alternative methods give brands insight into how the people who make up their target market speak, what they say, and how they feel in a setting where people feel more free to express themselves; freedom they may not feel during an interview or focus group.

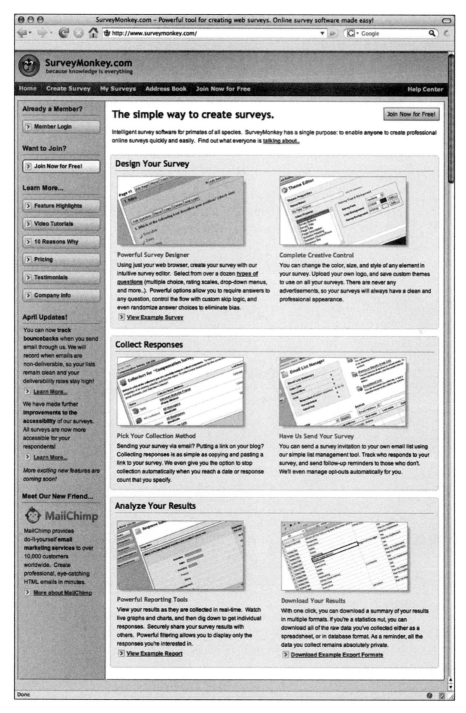

Figure 8-1   Sites like SurveyMonkey make market research over the Web easy and efficient.

How the Target Market Affects the Development of a Web Site

Once gathered, data that defines a target market can be used to shape the choices made during a Web site's development, such as appropriate colors, graphics, photographs, and social media applications. Most importantly, understanding the audience will help shape the core message and personality of the brand for long-term market penetration. In the final analysis, it is the brand's job to sell the product or service, and it is the site's job to help build the brand.

As we first saw in Chapter 1, the current Pepsi Web site (see Figure 8-2) provides an excellent example of a brand that has built its site based on a deep understanding of its audience.

Figure 8-2   The Pepsi Home page acts as a gateway to Pepsi's many other sites and to external sites with whom Pepsi has a relationship. The various links tap into the personality of their target market and reflect interests that Pepsi has come to understand through significant market research.

Pepsi is always focused on reaching out to a core of younger customers. Pepsi knows that its site will not retain visitors for very long or keep them coming back if the main feature of the site is the calorie count for a 20-ounce bottle of Diet Pepsi. Instead, Pepsi has developed a site that serves as a launching pad to sub-sites, including music sites, social networking sites, and a series of sports-related sites.

These Pepsi-branded sub-sites engage visitors far beyond the Pepsi products and connect with consumers on a more personal level. Figures 8-3 through 8-5 shows a number of these Pepsi sites, built to create a community to strengthen brand loyalty.

Figure 8-3   The Pepsi sites that promote the brand through its affiliation with NASCAR racing (left) and through baseball (right).

Figure 8-4   Other Pepsi sites focus on rap music (left), and the Hispanic market specifically (right).

Figure 8-5   One Pepsi site sells clothing. Notice the ages of the people pictured (left). Another site taps into the green movement, and gives information on environmentalism and recycling (right).

INTERVIEW WITH...

LEE RAINIE, DIRECTOR, PEW INTERNET & AMERICAN LIFE PROJECT

The Pew Internet & American Life Project is one of the most oft-quoted research entities on Internet trends, usage, and demographics. A non-profit entity, Pew explores the Internet's impact on families, communities, and more. It has become an authoritative source on the evolution of the Internet.

I was fortunate enough to interview Lee Rainie, the founding director of the Pew Internet & American Life Project, and former managing editor of U.S. News and World Report. In a very open, enthusiastic interview, Lee provided wonderful insight into some of the new demographic categories that marketers need to be aware of when trying to sell to a plugged-in audience.

JASON: Throughout your research, what have you found to be the most remarkable shift in terms of how the Internet has changed society and our personal lives?

LEE: The most striking overall story is the degree to which in the past 12 or 14 years the Internet has gone from being at the periphery of a small number of people's focus and has moved into the center of most American lives. Right now our latest data shows that 75% of adults use the Internet and more than half of Americans now have broadband connections at home. Ninety-four percent of teenagers use the Internet. If you asked those questions 15 years ago the numbers would have been in single digits. So, it's a technology that has been rapidly adopted by the population, and the consequences of that have affected how we live our lives. First, it's changed the communication patterns people have with each other through e-mails and instant messaging. People use the Internet to supplement, complement, and add on to the volumes of communications they already have. The second consequence is that it's changed people's relationship with information. Massive amounts of material have been made available online, and the Internet has enabled people to create their own media and publish information. It's become a go-to place for people who want to learn new things and find out facts.

JASON: In a report you filed on the Pew Web site, you talk about three groups of users: high, middle, and low end. Tell me a little bit more about those groups and how they are distinguished.

LEE: We did a major survey about people and their gadgets. We looked at the kind of technology they had, how they used it, and how they felt about it. When we clustered those three elements together we came up with some very interesting distinctions among people about what they like and don't like, what they do, and what they don't do. There are interesting distinctions based on people's sense about whether they like being connected all the time or whether they disliked it.

We found that the heaviest consumers and users of technology blog, post videos, and use their cell phones to browse the Web and get news updates. These users make up about 8% of the population. It's not a terribly big cohort, but it's an important cohort because these are the early adopters. They lead the way for everybody else, and they are in love with everything about the new technology.

Below them is the group of people who aren't necessarily into blogging or new media tools in general, but they love the communications features of the Internet like e-mail, IM-ing, and the fact that they can interact with others and stay linked to the people that they care about using these methods.

But there are some people who are just annoyed that they have to be online at all. They have technology, and their family members or bosses are encouraging them to use it. But, they don't like it. They don't like always being on the grid, and they don't like the implied pressure that they are at somebody else's beck and call or that they can be interrupted at any moment and any time. So even though they have a lot of this gear, they are not true to it.

About 15% of the population lives on the other end of the spectrum, and are completely off the grid. They don't have cell phones, they don't use the Internet. That's primarily older folks, poorer individuals. It's sometimes hard to remember, in an environment where there is so much "gee whiz" coverage of new technology and so much enthusiasm among heavy users and adopters, that there is a big portion of the population who just isn't into this stuff in the same way that we are.

JASON: Moving forward, will marketers and advertisers have to consider those types of groups and traits as part of their traditional demographic breakdowns?

LEE: It hasn't produced a shift as much as it's added to the complexity of marketing. In other words, there are new things to worry about while understanding that classic demographics still matter. Men are different from women; young people are different from old people; the well-to-do are different from people who have fewer resources; the well-educated are different from people who don't have a lot of education. All those distinctions still hold true in the online world, but our research suggests that there are more market differences to consider.

For example, people who connect to the Internet wirelessly are different from broadband users who are different from dial-up users who are different from non-users. So there's a new cluster of demographic characteristics—sort of techno-demographic characteristics—that now overlay classical demographics and make the job of marketing much harder, because you have to deliver a message to people in ways that they expect it. It's a completely different way of dissecting an audience.

JASON: How are consumer habits being altered by the Internet?

LEE: There are a couple of things to say about that. The first is that there is at least one more step of the consumer experience that didn't exist pre-Internet, and that is the post-consumer moment. We're beginning to see that when people make purchases now, they think that their duty as consumers hasn't ended until they've told other people about what they bought. So they'll post a product review on their blog or on a consumer-oriented Web site or at least post it to a listserv. They'll harass the tech support staff of the company that they just bought the item from if it doesn't serve them right. They'll tag material, take pictures of it, and post it on Flickr. They might even create and post a how-to video on YouTube. So there's sort of this creator-consumer who is different from the industrial age passive consumer that bought a product, hoped that it would work, and didn't have any type of interaction with other consumers or even the company in many cases. Now the Internet facilitates a lot more ongoing communication, conversation, and critiquing of products and services.

That's just one brand new thing that the Internet has introduced to the world of consumer affairs. But, every other step of the consumer process has also changed at least to some degree. The window shopping experience changed, for example. We see a lot of people who do a significant amount of research online before they show up at a brick and mortar facility to make a purchase or to close the deal by talking to a person on the sales staff. The point of sale is even changing, as more companies introduce technology that allows shoppers to interact with live salespeople over the Web, altering the whole purchasing experience from the way it use to be.

At each stage of the process, and clearly at the marketing stage, there are new ways to get information in front of consumers, from the use of specific keywords, through viral campaigns and Web sites that give you information about products, product review sites, recommendation systems, and sites like that. I mean, you go to Amazon, you buy a book and a little screen pops up that says there are other people who bought this book and it tells you what other products they like. So from the beginning to the end of the consumer process, the Internet is a potential actor now in ways that were inconceivable 20 years ago.

JASON: And last thing, tell me what you think is the future of the Internet.

LEE: More. Bandwidth is going to grow, storage capacity is going to grow and become less costly. All of the things that we do online will become even more abundant in the future. There are going to be new applications that come and exploit that.

The virtual world will also grow, though it's hard to know what the future of the virtual world is. People are excited about Second Life right now, but I can't see around the corner enough to know whether that will really be a big deal or not. I think it's safe to say that virtual worlds are going to get more compelling over time as we increase bandwidth, and they begin to look more 3D. They are going to be immersive in ways that they aren't now, and I suspect that it will be compelling to people. I don't know that masses of people will march into Second Life and live in a virtual world, but I do know that we'll start looking there for the creation of new advertising.

Getting the Site Developed

A business can handle development of their Web site internally, meaning that their own employees plan, design, and program the site, or a company can hire another firm to build the site for them. Common sense might suggest that B2B and B2C companies would hire third parties to build their sites, but that companies, such as Amazon or LinkedIn, whose sites represent their entire business, would do the programming themselves. While this seems logical, it is not always the case. As you recall from the interview with Catherine Cook, in Chapter 3, MyYearbook.com outsourced all of the programming to India because the cost of programming there is significantly less expensive.

In other cases, large companies with considerable budgets might have full- or part-time programmers on staff for ongoing needs but still use outside companies to develop sites for them. For example, a B2C company might run an advertising or marketing campaign which needs an accompanying campaign-oriented site. Chances are the ad agency running that campaign will also be responsible for developing the site. After all, they understand and have access to all of the creative concepts, graphics, copy, etc.

Because programmers understand computers and languages on a higher level than most company owners or marketing managers, they are often asked for their opinion as to whether an outside company is needed for a particular site and if so, which company to choose. Once a selection has been made those programmers are often relied upon to interact with the programmers at that company to ensure that all the required tasks are completed.

There are pros and cons associated with developing a site internally, just as there are pros and cons with using an outside agency to develop a site. Table 8-1 outlines each of these. It is important to take a close look at each project and balance all of the benefits and drawbacks before deciding whether to use a third party or keep the work in-house.

Development Option	Pros	Cons
In-house development	• Potentially lower costs. • You have the subject expertise. You know your products and services better than anyone. • You maintain control over all elements, which can be more comforting.	• Building a site takes more than just programming. You must to write copy, design graphics, and organize all of the information, which can be time consuming. • If you have other projects to work on, the site could take a backseat, resulting in an extended launch time. • Sometimes an outside agency is better at developing a message that is clear to your market.
Outsourced development	• Faster time to launch—outside companies are more likely to make you a priority than you might make yourself. • Your site and message will get developed from an outside perspective. • Expertise in all areas, including programming, organization, design and copy writing.	• Potentially more expensive than building the site in-house • Loss of direct control over all aspects of the site. • Outsourced company will not know your company, product, or service as well as you do.

Table 8-1   The pros and cons of building a site internally versus outsourcing development to a third party.

Working with an Outside Company

Both companies involved in a third-party Web site development project have different priorities that they need to ensure are addressed in order for the relationship to work. Marketing or site development agencies often bring unique talents and experiences to the table, and choosing the right partner is vital to getting the site in question built quickly and correctly. We will look at the dynamics of the relationship from the perspective of both the client (the company that wants the site built), and from the third-party developer, as career paths often lead programmers to explore both sides of the marketing divide.

Outsourcing from the Client's Perspective

Successful site development through a third party requires ensuring that the most appropriate third party is selected to complete the project. For the client, there are three main goals that an outside vendor needs to accomplish: get the site done as quickly as possible, get the site done within budget, and get it done right. Accomplishing these goals requires trust between the client and the vendor. This trust comes with time, open communication, experience, and the client's careful selection of the vendor they hire. Once a project has been started by one vendor, it can be difficult and expensive to move the project to another vendor (plus it can set a project back by days, months, or more), so it is important to choose the right resource from the outset.

Because good communication and trust between the two companies is vital, selection of a vendor needs to be based on more than just talent, price, and experience. As with any personal relationship, a client and vendor need to like each other to a certain extent, as they will be working closely together for an extended period of time. A very corporate client that is buttoned up, requires weekly status reports, and wants all communications to be professional and official may not work well with a Web development firm run from a gutted warehouse where the employees wear concert t-shirts to meetings and start each sentence with the word "dude." Usually, these issues will come up during interactions throughout the interview process, and not necessarily from specific or pointed questions.

Among the questions that a company looking to develop a Web site needs to ask when selecting a development partner:

- *What is the extent of the agency's experience?*

  This can be measured in terms of years as well as the number of Web sites on which they have worked. Established companies that have been around for a while may offer benefits in terms of experience, while newer companies may be "hungrier" for the work and pay more attention to your project.

- *What is the agency's general type of experience?*

  In other words, has it generally worked on B2B, B2C, or B2E sites? For what markets has the agency built Web sites? Are these markets consistent with those you are looking to reach? Reviewing their URL list is the best way to determine their experience—more so than having agency representatives answer this question themselves. Remember, agencies are looking to gain business, and it is not uncommon for the seller to exaggerate their experience in the pursuit of new business.

- *What is the agency's proficiency with various programs and languages?*

  Can the agency easily accomplish tasks using multiple language types, or does it have expertise in only a few programming languages? Has the bulk of the agency's experience been with static sites, e-commerce, database-driven sites, or other specialties?

- *Does the agency understand all of the social media tools available and how audiences interact with each other and the marketer through these tools?*

  Many site developers, even those with past site-building experience, may not yet understand the power of social media and how to harness it as they develop new sites.

- *How large is the agency?*

  Large agencies may have more resources but might not give you the attention you require. Small agencies might give you a lot of attention but not have as many resources to handle the job.

- *Does the agency handle all aspects of the site in-house, or does it have to outsource certain tasks, such as the graphic design?*

  Ideally, the resource selected will be able to handle all aspects of your project in-house. There may be times, however, when the agency that is sourced may themselves need to outsource a portion of the project to another firm. Often this does not create any issues; however, the more companies involved in building a site, the greater the likelihood that something will go wrong or the message will be compromised.

- *What is the agency's primary business objective?*

  Is it strictly a Web site development shop, or is it a marketing agency that builds Web sites as one of its marketing services? Different needs call for different types of agencies.

- *Will the agency provide you with client referrals?*

  Whenever possible, it is helpful to speak with a vendor's other clients. You will get a better understanding of how easy it was for the client to work with the vendor, how well the vendor adhered to schedules and budgets, and how creative and proactive the agency was in providing solutions.

- *Has the agency had experience in the same industry as the company hiring it?*

  More experience in a given industry gives an agency greater insight into that market, which can be helpful in developing an effective site.

- *How much will the project cost, and how is that figure derived?*

  Each agency has its own way of setting their prices. Some charge by the hour; others provide a set project fee. While it is the agency's desire to get the highest possible price for a site, it is in the hiring company's best interest to keep prices down. Having the agency break down its pricing into as much detail as possible is typically the most effective way to keep costs down. Agency clients must be vigilant to ensure that their bills do not include "hidden costs" (costs not detailed prior to the agency being selected). Companies utilizing an outside agency also need to pay close attention to the payment terms (when payment is due). Every vendor is different. The way that one vendor structures its payment schedule may conflict with how a company can or wants to pay. For example, some vendors may require a certain percentage of the final price paid before the project starts, with the balance due in equal monthly installments throughout the life of the project or in a lump sum upon completion of the project. Others may allow more flexible terms, such as allowing the client to pay a certain amount 30 or 60 days after the site is complete (expressed as "net 30" or "net 60," respectively).

- *Will the agency fix the site if something goes wrong with it after launch?*

  Even though most sites are thoroughly tested prior to launch, it is not uncommon for problems to be uncovered after the launch. A company needs assurances that the agency it hires will fix problems quickly, even after the last invoice has been paid.

Further, it is a good idea for a client to visit a potential vendor's facility to see firsthand the environment and atmosphere before making a decision.

Outsourcing from an Agency's Perspective

Agencies approach site development and client relationships from a different perspective. Programmers and marketers working on the agency side need to consider different issues before beginning any project. Third-party vendors hired to build a site for a client often simultaneously act as planner, programmer, designer, consultant—and

276

educator. It is not unusual for clients to be sorely lacking any real understanding of the Web, how sites work, what can be done, and what is realistic for certain timeframes and budgets. It often falls to the agency's programmers to explain much of this and field questions throughout the development process.

While conventional wisdom might dictate that agencies should accept any clients that come along in the pursuit of profit, the reality is that not all clients will prove profitable. Some may offer so little money for a project that the project is simply not worthwhile. Other clients might offer a sufficient budget at the outset but cause so many problems throughout the process that eventually they are not worth the money they are spending. Because of this, and because some projects simply might not fall into an agency's core competencies, agencies need to carefully scrutinize the clients and projects they take on.

Among the questions that an agency needs to ask when deciding whether or not to take on a development project:

- *What is the purpose of the client's Web site?*

  It is important to understand what the proposed site's needs are. Does the site include e-commerce, social networking, an underlying database, **static pages** (pages that stay the same regardless of the person visiting the page or the time of visit) or something else entirely? After getting a full understanding of the requirements of the site, agencies should honestly assess whether the project is within the agency's capabilities and can be successfully completed.

- *What is the industry and market that the client is serving?*

  It is often easier to complete sites in industries where there is agency has previous experience. Agencies need to assess on a project by project basis if they have sufficient experience in a potential client's industry. If not, they should carefully evaluate if it is a project they feel comfortable taking on.

- *What is the client's understanding of the Web?*

  As mentioned earlier, clients often do not know much about the Web. They may not have a good understanding of the Web's capabilities, including what is realistic and what isn't. This can translate into many hours spent by the agency and its programmers explaining minor details and answering an inordinate number of questions. Although it may seem trivial, these hours add up, and often go unbilled, eating away at the agency's profits.

- *How creative will the client allow an agency to be?*

An agency needs to understand the boundaries in terms of creative design and features that may be included.

- *Does the client have an organized brand that can be incorporated into the site?*

  An agency needs to learn about a client's brand and how to translate its personality into design. Agencies should also request a style guide to ensure that fonts, colors, and other details are adhered to.

- *Does the client already have some content created?*

  In many cases, the developing agency will not have to start from scratch. Clients often already have some content ready for use, such as a database from which the site can pull information, copy from a printed brochure, digitized photographs, etc. It is important for an agency to ask clients about the availability of these resources because a client that does not have a good understanding of the Web well may not realize how helpful this material can be.

- *Does the client have an established budget for the site?*

  Typically, if a client knows what they want, they can communicate their needs succinctly enough for an agency to provide a price quote. In other instances, clients, especially those who do not understand the full capabilities of the Web, may not know exactly what they want. In these cases, the agency is better off asking the client if there is a budget available and then proposing options that can completed within that budget.

- *How is the client's credit?*

  It goes without saying that regardless of the agreed upon price, it is important for an agency to know that it will get paid. If the agency extends any kind of terms to the client (such as allowing them to pay some of the agreed upon price at a later date), they should also take the time to ensure that the client is credit-worthy.

- *How does the client typically pay?*

  Clients often have predetermined rules for how they pay their bills. Large companies may be mandated by their accounts payable department not to provide down payments for any project and require terms of net 30 or net 60 for all invoices. Smaller companies might not be as strict, but they also may not have the liquidity to pay much up front. Before deciding to take on a new client, vendors need to determine whether or not they can realistically accept the terms by which the potential client is willing to pay. New projects often require the vendor to cover initial costs (such as the purchase of photography or air travel) that might not be reimbursed by the client for a while. If the vendor cannot cover these costs, or has cash flow issues that would make it difficult to function or survive on an extended payment schedule, they should be very careful as to which clients they accept.

Baselines: Design and Development

Learning all of the skills necessary to design a Web site, including developing an understanding all of the intricacies of navigation and graphic design, requires many classes on topics not covered in this textbook. For the purposes of moving ahead with a more marketing-oriented conversation of the Web, we will quickly review the basics of design, content, and organizational issues relating to site development.

Web Site Navigation

Most media tends to be fairly linear. Sunday newspapers have different sections, and news is found by turning from one page to the next. Television is similar. A show is selected, and the viewer watches, scene by scene, in the order that those scenes are presented.

Web sites are quite different. Aside from the interactivity that the Web provides, Web sites allow visitors to review information in a non-linear fashion, jumping from one page to another in any order that they would like. In doing so, visitors are able to find the information in which they are most interested. However, the information that visitors are most interested in does not always coincide with the information that the site's owners most want them to view. Typically, the information that will most assist a company in meeting its goals relates to sales, and it is important that site visitors can easily view that information.

Because of the non-linear nature of the Web, developers face a dual responsibility:

- Create a navigation and hierarchy of content that makes finding information easy for site visitors

- Serve information in such a way that visitors are led to pages that the site's owners most want them to view

Developers must spend a significant amount of time planning a site's navigation prior to design and programming it in order to ensure that these two responsibilities are met. Navigation, however, should not be thought of simply as a menu bar with links from one page to another. While navigation certainly does act as a linking mechanism, the word **link** can refer to any word or image that, when clicked, brings a visitor to a new page. **Navigation** refers to the specific and planned organization of certain links, which provide the organizational structure of a Web site.

Navigation can be provided through a number of different methods, most commonly links within text, graphic buttons, or Flash buttons.

Because navigation is so vital to finding content within a site, buttons are typically found either across the top of a Web site or down the left hand side. These two areas of the site are visible as soon as a page loads, and viewers are most likely to see those areas regardless of how large the browser window is.

Each button within the navigation represents one category within a site. Depending on how many categories will be included on a site and how much content there will be, developing sound site navigation can get confusing. To alleviate this confusion, developers typically establish a **schematic**—a visual map that shows how the content of a site will be organized. Further, sites are broken down into **tiers**—levels of information and sub-categories within a larger category. Figure 8-6 shows a relatively basic schematic with categories of information directly accessible from the Home page. The names of these categories, which represent the top tier navigation, are the names that will later appear on the buttons when the site is designed and built.

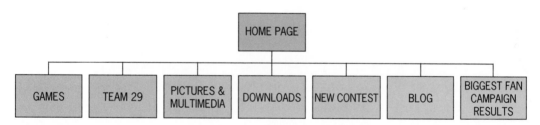

Figure 8-6 A basic schematic that shows the categories of information that are directly accessible from the Home page.

To ease visitor usage, you should include top tier navigation on every page of the site, allowing users to easily leave one category and view another. It is important to maintain consistency in navigation. Best practices dictate that once established the navigation structure remains in exactly the same place with exactly the same size, shape, and color on all pages, to avoid user confusion.

Within each category, other topic-related pages may be required. Figure 8-7 shows the basic schematic as presented earlier, this time presenting each of the pages that are accessible within each category—considered the second tier of the site. In Figure 8-8, the schematic is expanded even further as some second tier pages provide access to a number of pages of their own, considered the third tier.

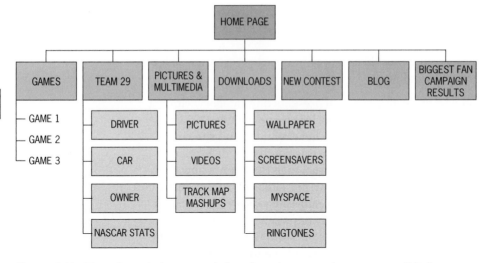

Figure 8-7   The schematic has expanded to show the pages that are accessible from some of the main categories. These are second tier pages.

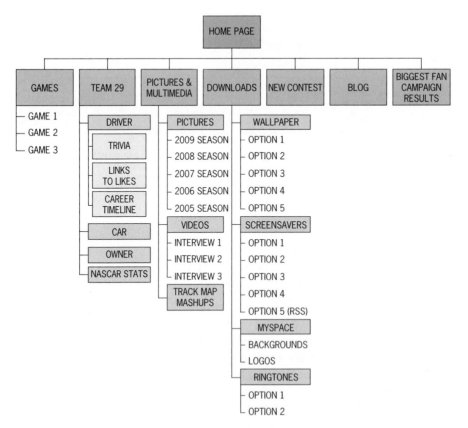

Figure 8-8   The schematic has been expanded even further to show the individual pages that can be accessed through second tier pages. These pages are considered third tier.

Typically these lower tiers are accessed one of two ways:

- They may have their own navigation system which is separate from the main navigation and appears only within the pages of a given category, as illustrated in Figure 8-9.

- They may be accessed as drop-down items from a navigation menu, as shown in Figure 8-10.

No matter which way the navigation is designed, the schematic will provide the architectural foundation for the site organization.

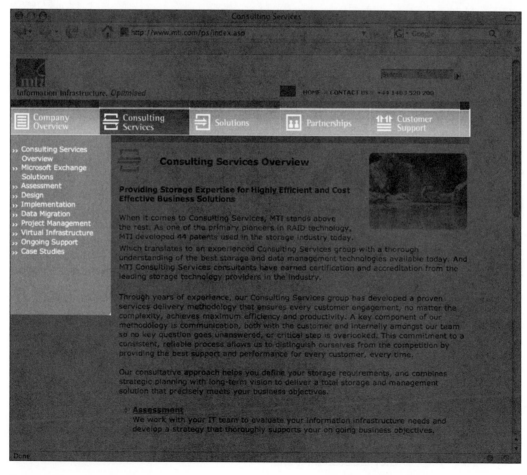

Figure 8-9 The main navigation for this site appears across the top. This page, on consulting services, presents second tier navigation on bar down the left hand side of the page.

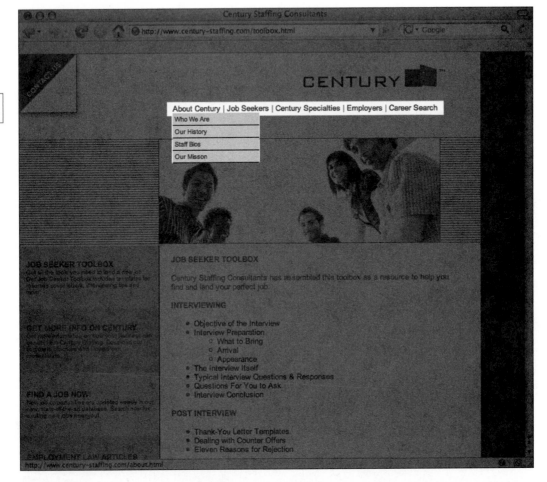

Figure 8-10   This site uses drop-down menus for the navigation, giving easy access to all pages within all categories, from anyplace on the site.

Navigation Elements: Search Engines, Site Maps, Tag Clouds, and Breadcrumbs

Along with the standard navigation, other means of finding information on a Web site are also used to help users find the information they are searching for.

Search Engines

Search engines invite users to type in a word or phrase that they wish to search for within a site. After a search term has been entered into the search engine, the engine scours a database for matches to the word(s) being sought. If the engine does not find any matching words, it returns a message to the user that no results were found. Poorly developed sites will simply display a message that the search was unsuccessful. Better sites will suggest alternative information that the users may be interested in. From a marketing standpoint, search engines also work to give users the impression that the site is quite large—a facade that can become transparent if a user's searches come back with no results too often. Figure 8-11 shows an example of a search engine that offers suggested product categories and individual items based on a user's search.

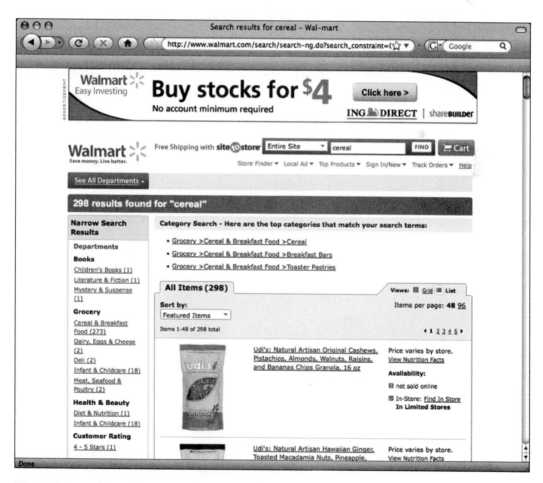

Figure 8-11　The Wal-Mart site provides a search engine for finding products on its site. In this search for the keyword "cereal," the results page includes suggestions on ways to narrow down the available products, and then provides a list of individual products that match the keyword.

Site Maps

Site maps are basically re-creations of the original schematic, existing on the site itself. Each of the pages within the schematic, or site map, are provided as a link for easy access to those pages. This tool can make large or confusing sites easier for users to understand. Figure 8-12 shows a sample of a site map.

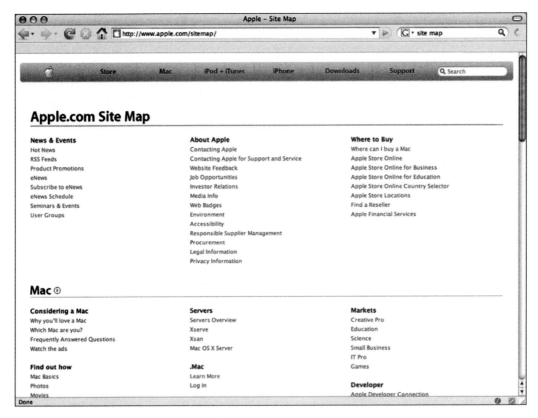

Figure 8-12   The site map on the Apple Web site.

Tag Clouds

Tag clouds are a new innovation born of the social media revolution. When blogs, videos, and other media are posted to a site either by the site developers or by users, they are often tagged with keywords that represent the subject matter of each post, so that they will come up in keyword based searches. A **tag cloud** (shown in Figure 8-13) is a collection of tags that are popular among visitors to a certain site. Tags within the cloud change in size, getting bigger or smaller as they are searched more or less often relative to other tags.

Figure 8-13   The tag cloud on the flickr site.

Breadcrumbs

As Figure 8-14 shows, **breadcrumbs** show the path of links the visitor took to get to the page they are on. Breadcrumbs are not so much a means of navigation as they are an aid to determining one's location within the site. This is especially helpful on sites packed deep with information. As more tiers are explored, breadcrumbs make it easier for a visitor to remember exactly which category they are in or how they found the page they are currently reading.

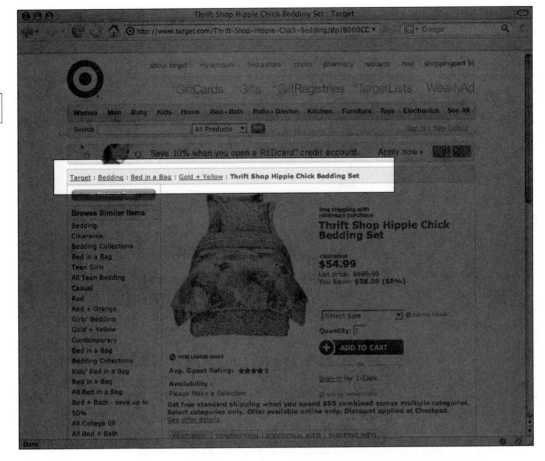

Figure 8-14 The Target site with the breadcrumbs highlighted.

Page Layout

The way a page is laid out can make or break a site, as many site visitors' interest in a site will be based on how the site looks and how it is laid out. Successful site layout will accomplish the following:

- Make the purposes of the site clear, letting the visitor know what they can expect to find there

- Promote the brand

- Provide easy access to information

- Lead the user to specific areas of interest or areas that the site owner wants them to see

- Provide an attractive, aesthetically pleasing environment for the user

Often, a site will have two page layouts: one for the Home page, and a second for all interior pages. As a rule of thumb, sites tend to be more graphic heavy on the Home page, where the pages need to catch the user's eye and entice them to browse further. In the lower tiers, after the visitor has already committed to exploring the site, pages tend to be more copy or content heavy. Visitors who have gone this deep into the site are usually more interested in reviewing information rather than just viewing marketing-style aesthetics.

When designing a page, it is important to consider how information will be presented. Whatever is most immediately visible to the viewer will likely determine whether or not a visitor remains on that page or navigates elsewhere. It can be difficult to know exactly how a site will look to an audience. Some sites will look different depending on the monitor size and resolution settings and the Web browser being used, so developers often try to design sites for the lowest common denominator—the worst viewing conditions that could reasonably be expected. Site designers typically consider the **fold** of the site when deciding how to disperse information. The fold is the part of a Web page that might be cut off by the bottom of the browser window. Information that is seen immediately when a page opens is considered "above the fold." Information that requires scrolling in order to be viewed is considered "below the fold." This is important because information that a marketer considers significant might not be seen at all if it falls below the fold; therefore, the real estate above the fold is the most important space on each page.

With this in mind, developers should design page layouts that make use of this prime real estate to drive traffic to the pages that they want their audience to see. Although the top tier navigation might not give preferential treatment to one content area over another, other areas of a page may have call-outs that drive traffic in a particular direction. Figure 8-15 shows the Home page for a typical B2B site. The large animated graphic in the center draws visitors in, and the four small boxes to the right drive traffic to specific pages based on current campaigns or important, timely information. Figure 8-16 shows an interior page of the same site. Notice how the page layout has changed. The size of the graphics has been reduced, providing more space for content.

288

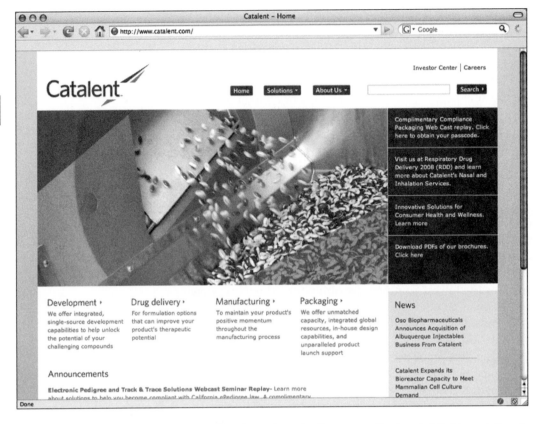

Figure 8-15 The Catalent Home page has the main navigation across the top, but it drives visitors to specific areas through announcements on the right-hand side.

Figure 8-16 The interior page of the Catalent Web site. Notice that the image is smaller, leaving more room for content.

Graphic Design

As with other mediums, such as music, television, and fashion, graphic design styles change over time. In the early days of the Web, sites were overrun with wacky, colorful backgrounds (no one seemed to care if people could not read the copy). Soon Web site designers began putting bevels, embosses, and drop shadows on absolutely everything.

Over time, a cleaner, more streamlined design style gained popularity. As it did, sites changed and adapted to keep up and fit in. Sites often reinvent themselves as the need to update content grows, new tools—such as social media applications—become available, and design styles evolve. This not only helps keep the brand fresh, but it also lets audiences know that the company behind the site is not stagnating.

Regardless of style, however, certain aspects of design have not changed. Good, bad, attractive, or ugly, all Web-based graphic design shares the same commonalities:

- Graphics are typically displayed in one of two **bitmap** (pixel-based) formats:

    - JPGs can use millions of colors to display each image and are static; they cannot be animated.

    - GIFs use far less colors in their representation and can be animated (although animated GIFS are often somewhat crude)

- Bitmap graphics are sized to 72 pixels per inch—which is how computer monitors display information

- Colors in graphics are presented in RGB—a combination of red, green, and blue that combine to create any the millions of colors that can be shown on a computer monitor. The RGB color model is used because computer monitors emit red, green, and blue light to communicate colors to the viewer's eyes. Images that get printed on paper are created in CMYK—cyan, yellow, magenta, and black.

- Vector graphics, which are created from mathematical formulas rather than pixels, cannot recreate photographic quality in an image, but they are good for illustrations and creating smooth animations (such as those that might be created using the Flash program)

- Images will tend to look darker on PC-based computers; they will look lighter and brighter on Macintosh computers.

- File size, which used to be a very important issue in the early days of the Web, has become less of a consideration for designers as more business and homes access the Web through broadband connections.

Content Development

Content for a site can come in the form of copy, images, video, blogs, or a variety of other media. Content creation can be a daunting task. Copywriters and other developers must have an intimate knowledge of the topics that will be covered on the site. They need to be able to express these ideas in a way that accurately represents the brand and its personality and is easily understood by the audience.

Some sites rely heavily on site visitors for content generation for all or portions of their site. Sites such as YouTube, MySpace, and Wikipedia, are made up almost entirely of user-generated content. These sites serve as a platform for visitors to generate and post their own content.

Chapter Summary

- All sites begin with an idea. The site owners and developers should start with an idea about which they are passionate and knowledgeable. They also need an idea that will attract the target audience. It is equally important to define the objectives of the site so that it can be built to meet the stated goals. It is also essential to assess the particular needs of the site, including appropriate financing.

- Understanding the audience is vital for both the site and the brand. Without this understanding, it is practically impossible to build a site specifically for a target market. Marketers have several different tools for collecting market data on a specific audience, which is defined by the demographic and psychographic traits its members share in common. These methods include conducting surveys, organizing focus groups, and tracking usage of the blogosphere and other social media.

- Sites can either be developed in-house or by a third-party developer. Each of these options comes with certain pros and cons, in terms of cost, speed to completion, and knowledge of content. When working with an outside company, the relationship is vital to site success, and each party needs to carefully understand and analyze the other before engagement.

- Basic site design and development issues that all sites need to consider include navigation, which is critical to helping move users from one page to another. Navigation should be planned in advance and be consistent throughout the site. Well-developed sites are organized into tiers, with lower tiers favoring content over aesthetics. Creating a page layout that fully engages site visitors is similarly important, as is developing appropriate content.

Key Terms

bitmap—Pixel-based graphics

boot-strapping—A slang term that means a company tries to do most of its site development in-house in order to keep costs as low as possible.

breadcrumbs—A navigation aid used to show the path of links that the visitor took to get to the page they are currently on.

business plan—A formal document that outlines the site concept, market, anticipated revenue structure, marketing, strategy, and technology plans.

focus groups—Meetings in which a group of individuals (usually between 15 to 20 people) that represent the target market are gathered and are engaged in a discussion about a topic of interest to the marketer.

fold—The part of a Web page that might be cut off by the bottom of the browser window.

link—Any word or image on a Web site that, when clicked, brings a visitor to a new page.

marketing strategy—The strategy that a site or company employs in order to gain more customers and revenue.

navigation—The specific and planned organization of certain links that provide the organizational structure of a Web site.

psychographics data—Data that provides information on large groups based on personality and lifestyle characteristics.

schematic—A visual map that shows how the content of a site will be organized.

site Maps—Recreations of the original schematic, existing on the site itself.

static pages—Pages that stay the same regardless of the person visiting the page or the time of visit

tag clouds—A collection of tags that are popular among visitors to a certain site.

target market—The market segment most likely to visit a company's site and purchase its products or services.

tiers—Levels of information and sub-categories within a larger category on a Web site.

visitor retention—The measure of how long a visitor remains on a site and how often he or she returns.

Review Questions

1. Which of the following is probably not a viable reason for developing a Web site?

   a. To build brand recognition

   b. To build traffic for the purposes of generating advertising revenue

   c. To reduce the number of phone calls a company gets

   d. To meet other like-minded people

2. Which of the following is not among the resources a site needs in order to get developed?

   a. Graphic design

   b. An interesting logo

   c. Content

   d. Programming

3. A target-market can best be defined as:

   a. The market segment most likely to visit a site

   b. The market segment least likely to visit a site

   c. The people that site visitors will tell about the site

   d. The people involved in developing the site

4. Which would not qualify as demographic data for a site?

   a. 45% of visitors are male

   b. 16% of visitors come from the north east

   c. 11% enjoy hiking

   d. 72% have broadband connections

5. Which would not qualify as psychographic data for a site?

   a. 18% of visitors go on cruise vacations

   b. 32% read sports magazines

   c. 9% plan to purchase golf equipment over the next year

   d. 14% are married

6. The main reason to collect data on a target market is:

    a. To better understand how to design and build the site

    b. To know how much to charge them for products

    c. To change their behavior

    d. None of the above

7. Members of a focus group are typically made aware of what brand is conducting the meeting. True or False?

8. One reason that searching social networks and blogs for market information is useful is:

    a. Blogs can be written in a way that users can be led to give information the developer is looking for

    b. People who participate in blogs would never participate in a survey or focus group

    c. It is likely a marketer can get more honest feedback this way

    d. It is not useful because it takes too long

9. According to Lee Rainie, what percentage of the population is considered "heavy users" of the Web?

    a. 8%

    b. 20%

    c. 51%

    d. 92%

10. Which of the following is more likely to have a lower cost associated with development?

    a. In-house development

    b. Outsourced development

11. Which of the following would a marketer most likely want to know about a third-party developer before engaging in a working relationship?

    a. Breadth of experience

    b. Type of experience

    c. Agency size

d. All of the above

e. None of the above

12. In the quest for revenues, Web development agencies should accept all the projects that they are offered. True or False?

13. Which question would be the least useful for an agency to ask a potential client before engaging in new site development?

a. "Do you have an established budget for this site?"

b. "Is any content already developed?"

c. "How much creative freedom do we have?"

d. "Who came up with the idea for the site?"

14. Web sites are fairly linear. True or False?

15. Navigation can best be described as:

a. Specific and planned organization of certain links that provide the organizational structure of a Web site

b. Any links within a site that brings users from one page to another

c. Any link that has been created a graphic on a site

d. Any link that appears in text

16. The map that initially lays out the organization of a site is called the:

a. Blueprint

b. Schematic

c. Footprint

d. Tier

17. Which is most likely to have the most copy and the least graphics?

a. The Home page

b. Tier 1 pages

c. Tier 2 pages

d. Tier 3 pages

18. Which of the following is most likely to have the largest graphics presence and the least copy?

   a. The Home page

   b. Tier 1 pages

   c. Tier 2 pages

   d. Tier 3 pages

19. Which type of graphic cannot be animated?

   a. JPG

   b. GIF

   c. FLASH

   d. None of the above

20. RGB stands for:

   a. Roy G. Biv

   b. Red, Green, Blue

   c. Really Great Blog

   d. None of the above

Projects

1. Find a Web site whose second tier navigation system is separate from the first tier navigation, as shown in the example in Figure 8-9. Access the code for the site by selecting View → Source on your browser menu bar. Copy the code and manipulate it locally to turn the second tier navigation into drop downs off the first tier navigation.

2. Choose a site with at least three tiers of information. Create a schematic that represents the site.

3. Suppose you work for a company that is looking to build a Web site and you have decided to hire a third party to do the development. Choose a Web development company or marketing agency to work with based strictly on the information on their site.

   In a two- to three-page paper, discuss this company and explain why you would select them. Discuss at least two competing companies that you did not choose and why you did not select them.

4. Create a survey that measures 8-10 demographic and psychographic characteristics of any established group of 5 to 7 people that share a particular similarity—for example, people who live in your apartment building or neighborhood or people in one of your classes. Gather the results and in a one-page report, and describe this market based on your findings.

5. Using the same survey that you created in Project #4, program the survey to work on the Web. Use at least three different types of question and answer formats (such as radio buttons, check boxes, and fill-in forms).

CHAPTER 9

E-Commerce Sites

In this chapter you will learn about:

◎ What e-commerce is, who uses it, and how

◎ The various sources of revenue that e-commerce marketers rely on to generate profits

◎ The means and methods of online store development within the context of social media

In Chapter 2, we discussed many of the different types of sites that can be found on the Web, including business-to-consumer, or e-commerce, sites. E-commerce is an extremely important factor in the ongoing development of the Web. It has already proven able to alter consumer habits and generate significant revenue. It also holds the promise of changing the future of retailing. Thus, e-commerce is a topic that any successful Web developer needs to fully understand.

An Overview of E-Commerce

E-commerce is the buying and selling of services through any electronic medium. For our purposes, we focus on e-commerce as it exists on the Web, where sites provide the ability to shop for, research, and purchase products via electronic payment transaction (either directly through their site or through a third-party payment processing site).

The aggressive global growth of e-commerce is captivating. Although media attention has been more squarely focused on social media, the rapid growth of e-commerce is truly remarkable. Over 86% of all Web users worldwide have made at least one online purchase. That represents a 40% increase in the past two years, and it includes a staggering 93% of all Web users in Europe and 92% of Web users in North America.[1] The chart in Figure 9-1 provides a breakdown of how prevalent e-commerce usage is within various world regions, as a percentage of overall Web users.

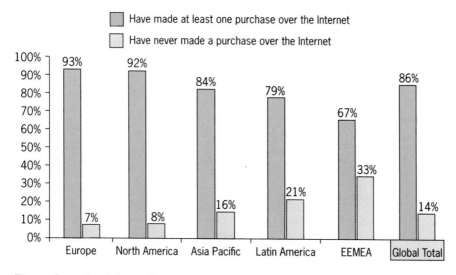

Figure 9-1 Breakdown of e-commerce usage in various world regions, along with the global total. SOURCE: Nielsen Global Online Survey, Nielsen, Jan. 2008.

With virtually everything available online that can be found offline, marketers are particularly interested in understanding which product types are most interesting to shoppers online. As Amazon.com continues to be ranked one of the top ten most visited sites on the Web, it should not be too surprising that books rank among the most popular products being purchased on the Web.

The list of popular online purchases shown in Figure 9-2 provides an interesting insight into the minds of e-commerce shoppers. Books and video games (ranking first and third, respectively) would seem to make sense as online purchases since they can be reviewed online prior to the purchase. However, the fact that the "clothing, accessories, and shoes" category (items that typically need to be tried on prior to purchase) ranks a solid second place makes clear that for many people, the convenience of Web shopping is enough to overcome the inconveniences of not being able to experience the items first-hand.[2]

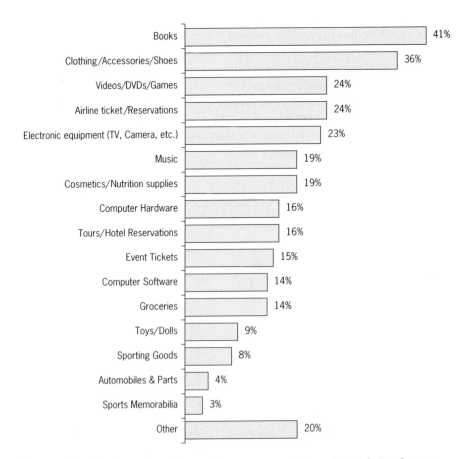

Figure 9-2   Most popular online purchases. SOURCE: Nielsen Global Online Survey, Nielsen, Jan. 2008.

This observation raises the larger question: why do people shop online? What are the benefits and drawbacks when compared to traditional, in-store shopping? Marketers need to understand the pros and cons from the perspective of the shopper, before undertaking an e-commerce effort.

For many shopping, the pros of online shopping include:

- **Convenience**: According to Nielson research, 81% of all online shoppers cited convenience as their number one reason for shopping online. Convenience goes beyond being able to shop in one's pajamas—it includes being able to shop at any time of day, not having to wait in lines or push through crowds. In 2008, as gas prices soared past $4/gallon in most parts of the U.S., convenience also included driving less and saving on gas.

- **Not being bothered**: One of the more annoying parts of shopping is having pushy salespeople constantly interrupting consumers. Shoppers can avoid this by shopping online.

- **Online reviews**: As more online stores add social media components, shoppers can read what other consumers thought of a product before making a purchase and post their own opinion for others.

- **Easy comparison shopping**: Online shopping gives consumers the ability to compare prices and features between retailers far more quickly than they could by going from store to store. Some sites have been established to provide comparison-shopping services for consumers, saving shoppers even more time.

- **Less expensive**: In most cases, retailers would prefer that consumers purchase online, as it helps to reduce the retailer's overhead (fewer sales people means less salary expense). To help promote online shopping, many retailers offer reduced prices for making online purchases. This has been particularly true and successful in the travel industry.

- **Personalized selection**: When a consumer makes a purchase in a store, that is typically the end of the transaction. The next time that person comes to the same store the salespeople are not likely to have any recollection of that shopper's purchasing habits. However, online searching and buying habits can be tracked, stored, and used to offer a more personalized selection.

- **Wider selection**: Retail stores have limited shelf space, so they need to limit the selection they offer. Web retailers do not have to contend with shelf space issues and can therefore offer a wider selection. Plus, if one site does not offer what a consumer wants, that consumer can broaden their selection by visiting other sites.

- **No sales tax**: Most states still do not charge sales tax for online purchases (although this is changing in some states). This makes it less expensive to buy products online.

- **Historical order record**: If shoppers lose their receipts after a purchase from a traditional retailer, they are typically out of luck—especially if they used cash. When purchases are made online, however, an historical record is kept of all transactions.

Marketers also need to have a solid understanding of the aspects of online shopping that consumers might view as drawbacks to purchasing. These can include:

- **Shipping payments**: Online shoppers typically incur a shipping charge, which they would not have to pay when shopping in a store (except for large purchases, such as furniture). Shipping charges can be fairly pricey, and the quicker the desired shipping, the more expensive it usually is.

- **Delivery wait time**: Online shoppers usually have to accept a lag time in receipt of material. Depending on how much they are willing to pay, consumers may have to wait anywhere from 24 hours to a month or more before they get their purchases. This is far different than the immediate gratification that shoppers get when they shop in a store and can take their purchases home with them.

- **Lack of a non-cash payment option**: Cash is not an option for online shoppers, who must pay through credit card or other non-cash methods.

- **Inability to experience**: There is a big difference between touching, feeling, tasting, wearing, and trying products prior to purchase, and simply looking at their picture and reading about them. Online shopping does not give the consumer the ability to try on clothes, smell perfume, or feel a texture before buying, which heavily reduces the product experience.

- **Lack of trust**: Although online transactions are largely secure, online shoppers need to trust that their private information will not be stolen by hackers or sold by the retailer. In the case of less well-known sites, customers need to trust that they will receive their purchases in the time guaranteed (in some cases customers have to worry if they will receive their purchase at all).

- **Wider selection**: How can a wider selection be both a pro and a con? While wider selections give shoppers more to choose from, the additional choices can be overwhelming. Traditional retailers, with their limited shelf space, do part of the selection work for the consumer by offering only the best products available from manufacturers. This helps reduce consumers' confusion and saves them time.

- **Unsocial**: With social media, online shoppers have the ability to interact with other people by leaving comments on products, writing and responding to blog entries, etc. That is still a far different social experience than shopping with friends and interacting with others in real life.

- **Lack of assistance**: Although sales people at traditional retailers can be intrusive, they are also available when shoppers have a question. Even e-commerce sites that have online chat (and not all do) would have a hard time providing the same level of service as traditional stores with in-person sales people.

Without question, online shopping provides compelling reasons for consumers to make their purchases over the Web. In the discussion above, we touched upon the issue of selection, which can be viewed as both a positive and negative aspect of e-commerce. The issue of increased selection applies to the number of products offered by stores as well as the number of stores available to a consumer. A single mall, no matter how large, can only offer as many stores as there is physical space for retailers to rent. Even the Mall of America in Minnesota (by most counts the largest mall in the U.S. at the time of this writing) can only offer a fraction of the retail options available online. As Figure 9-3 shows, there are a number of reasons why shoppers may choose one online store over another when it comes time to make their purchases.

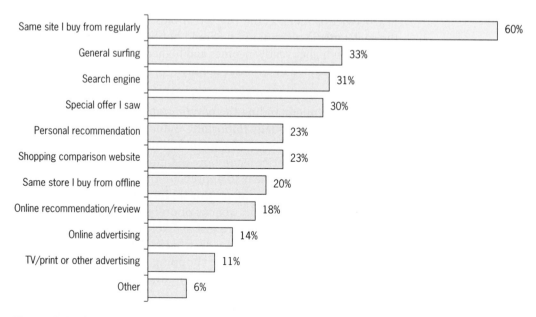

Figure 9-3 A breakdown, as reported by Nielson, of how shoppers decide from which online stores to buy. SOURCE: Nielsen Global Online Survey, Nielsen, Jan. 2008.

Some of these answers should look vaguely familiar. Both the number one reason, "the same site I buy from regularly," which topped the list by a wide margin, and the number five reason, "personal recommendation," reflect back to our discussion of brand building in Chapter 7. For marketers, one of the most important outcomes of developing a brand is building trust among their potential market base. Each time a shopper has a positive experience on an e-commerce site, which includes finding the information they were looking for, being satisfied with the prices, having a relatively easy check-out procedure, and receiving their purchases on time, they build a little more trust equity in that brand. That means they are more apt to revisit the site and purchase there again. Further, as that trust equity evolves into brand loyalty, shoppers are more likely to spread the word of their positive experiences to others, and that word of mouth plays heavily in helping to drive new traffic. As we look more deeply into the specific means by which e-commerce sites engage their visitors and move them to purchase, it is important to consider the importance of how each shopping experience is reflective of the overall brand.

The demographic breakdown of online shoppers, shown in Table 9-1, is also very telling. This breakdown can give marketers an insight into how their specific audience reacts to online shopping. Whereas younger audiences are more likely to be involved in social networking sites, such as video sharing and blogging, it is the slightly older, 30-49 year-old market that is more apt to engage in online shopping—by nearly twice as much as the 18-29 year olds who have dominated the social media revolution.[3] It should not be surprising, then, that people with higher yearly incomes and higher levels of education tend to be more inclined to purchase online.

Of course, as we learned earlier, demographics are only part of the picture. Understanding the psychographic behavioral patterns and similarities is equally important. Table 9-2 presents some of the reasons that people engage in online shopping, broken down by income. Notice again how the more an individual earns, the more likely he or she is to appreciate the positive aspects of online shopping. Now compare this to Table 9-3, which shows how people react to the drawbacks of online shopping. Individuals earning higher incomes are just as likely to be dissuaded from online shopping due to specific drawbacks. This demographic, which is more engaged in online shopping, is more likely to have their behavior more widely swayed by either pros or cons of online shopping.

Armed with this information, marketers can develop their sites in specific ways to deliberately appeal to key audience demographics to more effectively promote their products.

Category	% of Online Purchasers
Gender	
Male	49%
Female	51%
Age	
18–29	26%
30–49	46%
50–64	23%
65+	6%
Race/Ethnicity	
White (not Hispanic)	74%
Black (not Hispanic)	10%
Hispanic (English speaking)	10%
Education	
Less than high school	6%
High school grad	29%
Some college	25%
College+	39%
Annual Income	
Under $25K	13%
$25K–$40K	12%
$40K–$60K	17%
$60K–$100K	22%
$100K+	19%

Table 9-1 Demographic breakdown of online shoppers. SOURCE: Horrigan, John B. "Online Shopping." Pew Internet & American Life Project, 13 Feb. 2008.

Reason for Shopping Online	Less than $25K	$25K–$40K	$40K–$60K	$60K–$100K	$100K+
The Web is the best place to buy hard to find items	26%	23%	25%	28%	32%
Online shopping is convenient	22%	24%	22%	28%	36%
Shopping online saves time	19%	19%	18%	24%	31%
The Web is the best place to find a bargain	12%	10%	8%	8%	13%

Table 9-2 The percentage of online shoppers that strongly agreed with certain positive statements about online shopping, broken down by annual income. SOURCE: Horrigan, John B. "Online Shopping." Pew Internet & American Life Project, 13 Feb. 2008.

Perceived Drawback of Online Shopping	Less than $25K	$25K– $40K	$40K– $60K	$60K– $100K	$100K+
Afraid to provide personal and credit card info online	26%	23%	25%	28%	32%
Prefer to see things before buying them	22%	24%	22%	28%	36%
Shopping cart is complicated	19%	19%	18%	24%	31%

Table 9-3 The percentage of online shoppers that strongly agreed with certain negative statements about online shopping, broken down by annual income. SOURCE: Horrigan, John B. "Online Shopping" Pew Internet & American Life Project, 13 Feb. 2008.

Sources of Revenue

While many of the site categories reviewed in Chapter 2 exist solely for the purposes of providing entertainment or information, business-oriented sites have one end goal upon which all other decisions are ultimately based—that is to generate a profit. Without getting too deep into the business aspect of site development, **profit**, for our purposes, is defined as the difference between the cost of an item and the price for which it is ultimately sold. The cost of any given item may be made up of any number of variables, including the price of any raw materials needed, manufacturing costs, warehousing, energy costs, and salary expenses. Other costs that need to be considered are office and equipment leases, marketing costs, shipping, travel, research and development, etc. While some of these costs might not be directly related to any one particular product (such as the salary expense for administrative assistance), they still represent a cost to the company and need to be recovered through the sales of product or other revenue streams.

In determining prices for products, advertising, or any other revenue stream, businesses need to consider the following:

- The overall cost of doing business

- The volume of business they expect to do

- The overall demand for what they are selling

- Prices set by competing companies

- What the market will bear—how much are consumers willing to pay for what a business is selling

- How well established the brand is—the more people trust the brand, the more they will be willing to pay for it

Business managers consider each of these points in setting their prices, and, because **margins** (the difference between revenue and cost) are often very tight, they are always on the lookout for new ways of generating additional revenue, especially if they can do so with little increase to their own expenditure.

Pricing issues can be far more complex than these points, as issues beyond the cost of doing business often influence pricing. These issues may include the decision by one company to deliberately sustain a loss on the products they sell, in hopes of driving poorer competitors out of business, or the decision to sell one product at a loss (such as a razors) so that the company can make a larger profit later on associated products (razor blades). These issues, while beyond the scope of this book, play an important role in the pricing and promotion of online products and the ability to turn a profit.

Online stores have a number of opportunities to generate revenue—some of which (advertising, in particular) also represent revenue opportunities for non e-commerce sites, such as media content providers or social networks.

Direct Sales

Direct sales represent the largest and most important revenue stream for e-commerce sites. The simple and straight-forward mission of an e-commerce site is to sell as many products to as many online shoppers as possible. Products can be tangible, such as shampoo, sneakers, and groceries, or intangible, such as digital music or the purchase of a reserved seat on a flight. Typically, the direct sale of products is made in numbers of units, with each unit multiplied by the advertised price (three bottles of shampoo at $5 each is a grand total of $15, plus any shipping, taxes, and other charges that may apply).

Typically, consumers who purchase products do so for one of three reasons:

- They have a *need* for a certain type of product. Although they may switch brands from time to time, they have decided in advance that they have a need for a specific product (for example, a new car if their old one is dying, or a tube of toothpaste once the current one is used up).

- They *want* a certain type of product. This want may linger for a while, depending on how expensive or frivolous the product is (such as jewelry), or may be satisfied more quickly depending on how great the want is (such as the latest video game console). In the mind of the consumer, the decision-making process in terms of where and when to buy is less urgent because there is not an absolute necessity to make the purchase.

- They are *compelled* to buy an item at or around the time of purchase. Some of the most valuable real estate in any traditional retailer is the space near the cash register, where consumers may make last-minute purchases of items that are within their line of vision. These items tend to be smaller, lower priced items, such as gum, chocolate bars, bottles of water or soda, batteries, and similar items that people are more likely to decide they want at the last moment.

A successful e-commerce company will consider each of these purchasing reasons in the development of its site. Because online stores do not have floor space for displays, salespeople to point the shopper in a specific direction, or signage hanging from the ceiling, e-commerce marketers have only two means of pushing their products to consumers: the page layout and a compelling presentation of their product. We will discuss the set-up of the page for maximum efficiency later in this chapter.

In the presentation of the product, marketers generally rely on three elements:

- Copy, which can be used to describe the product, its attributes, its value, and any other important information that the marketer feels will be appropriate to boost sales. Copy also includes information such as the price of the product, size, weight, and other such vital info. As Figures 9-4 and 9-5 show, a small amount of copy is provided upfront to entice the buyer to investigate further. As customers dig deeper, more detailed copy is then presented.

Figure 9-4   This e-commerce site sells a variety of health-related products. Notice that each product is shown with only a small amount of information—just enough to interest the shopper.

Figure 9-5 Once a shopper investigates a particular product more closely by clicking on it on the previous page, the store provides more information, including a detailed product description and a list of features.

- Pictures, which are used to provide a visual reference so that shoppers can see what they are buying. In the case of products that might be less familiar, or whose appeal might be in the way they look (picture frames or decorative candle holders, for example), marketers may decide to show the product from a number of different angles. As with copy, smaller images, called **thumbnails**, are shown initially, and larger images are often provided upon further consumer investigation. Other times, application shots are provided to show how the product might look in its final environment or when being used by a representative consumer. Figures 9-6 through 9-8 provide examples.

310

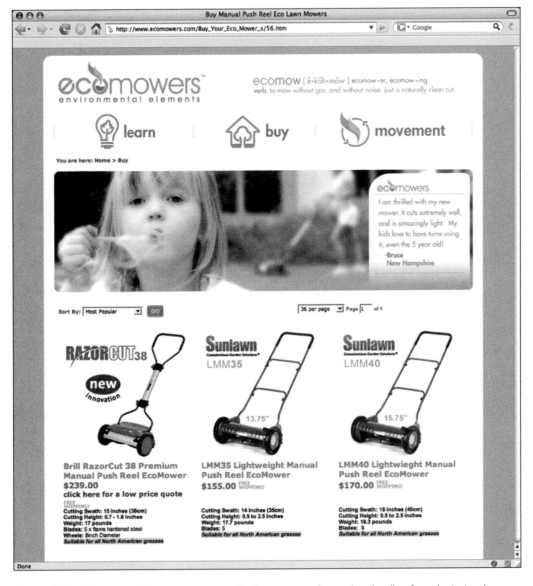

Figure 9-6   This page of the e-commerce site Ecomowers shows thumbnails of products to give shoppers a preview of what the products look like.

Figure 9-7   Once a product's thumbnail is clicked on, a larger picture of the product is shown. Notice that below the main image are other thumbnails of the same product shot from different angles.

Figure 9-8   When a shopper clicks on one of the smaller thumbnails of the product shown from a different angle, that image is enlarged to provide greater detail.

- Video of the product is sometimes used to demonstrate how the product works, market its benefits, or generally build excitement for the product. As we discussed in Chapter 5, online videos can increase audience retention time—a big benefit to e-commerce marketers who want to keep audiences on their site for as long as possible while providing them with valuable and engaging product information.

By effectively managing the presentation of products, e-commerce marketers can capture their audiences' attention, feed them the necessary information, and potentially drive them to take action.

Indirect Sales

E-commerce marketers fall into one of two categories: those that are an extension of traditional offline retailers (such as American Apparel, Sears, and Target), and those that are their own entity and do not have an offline component (such as Amazon.com and CafePress.com). Sites without an offline component need to secure sales from visitors to their sites, either on current or future visits, in order to generate revenue. E-commerce sites that also have an offline retailing extension, however, may serve as a point of research for shoppers to investigate products, promotional offers, and in-stock inventory before going to the retailer and making their purchases offline. According to a February, 2008 report by the Pew Internet & American Life Project, 81% of Internet users have used the Web to do research on a product they are considering purchasing—and a full 20% do this type of research on a daily basis. This means that while online shopping rates are definitely growing, e-commerce stores are even more effective in helping to increase sales at offline entities. The importance that Web-generated information has in the decision to buy increases as the value of the product (such as a home) or the weight of the commitment (such as a long-term cell phone contract) increases.

The relationship between offline and online information in a customer's purchasing decision can be far more complex than a shopper sitting down to review product information online before going to a store and making a purchase. For example, a consumer watching a movie sees one of the main characters using a new Apple laptop model in one of the scenes. He goes home and jumps online to visit the Apple store where he finds more information about that particular laptop. The detailed information, images from different angles, and streaming video pique his interest even further, but rather than buy it online, he decides that he wants to try it out first. He uses the store locator feature on the site to find the closest Apple store, the hours that it is open, and directions to the store. Once there, armed with information gathered from the site, the consumer discusses the computer further with a live sales person who shows him even more features, talks about programs that the consumer should also consider, and explains insurance policies that are available to protect the purchase in case of malfunction. In the end, the consumer makes his purchase, but only after the combination of media, online information, and offline interaction work together to make a compelling case. The epilogue to this story, in some cases, is that the shopper will later post his review of his new laptop on a social shopping site.

Paid Memberships and Subscriptions

Some e-commerce sites sell paid memberships and subscriptions as well as (or instead of) actual physical products. Typically, these subscriptions are for information or usage that can be accessed on a Web site only after payment has been made. Dating sites such as Match.com or eHarmony give users limited access to see other users' profiles, but require a monthly payment in order to contact people. Figure 9-9 shows a page from the Marketwatch.com Web site, which provides free stock-related news and information, with the exception of highly detailed and in-depth investment newsletters, which are available by subscription only. Figure 9-10 shows the subscription page from the JDate. com online dating service. This page pops up when a non-paying user tries to contact another user on the site. Interestingly, while only 17% of Web users have purchased a membership or subscription for online content[4], this is the one area of e-commerce where younger users eclipse older users, and men are far more likely to be customers than women.

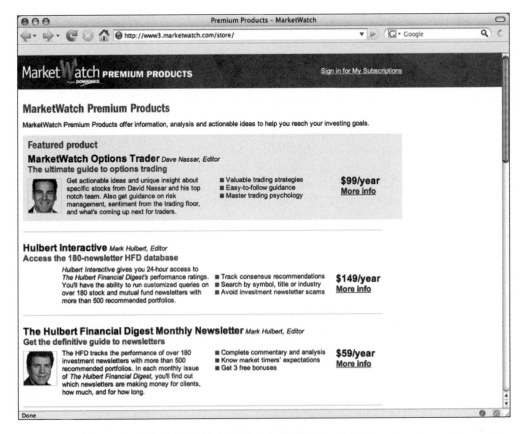

Figure 9-9   Although most of the Marketwatch.com Web site provides free investment information, paid subscriptions offer more in-depth and expert information.

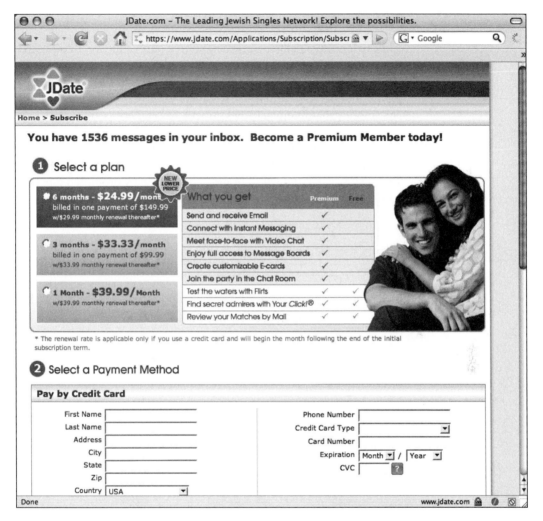

Figure 9-10 The online dating site JDate.com allows users to post a profile and search other user profiles for free, but this subscription screen shows up as soon as a non-paying user tries to contact someone else on the site.

Paid online subscriptions are often tough sells, but they can provide a strong revenue stream. Subscriptions are an ongoing source of income, and the Web site owners typically do not continually incur new costs associated with the subscription. The downside is that savvy Web users can often find similar subscription-based information or services elsewhere on the Web (social networks, for example, can be used for dating purposes and are usually free), so marketers have to make a compelling case for why a user should pay every month or year for a particular service.

Advertising

Although not typically the primary source of revenue for e-commerce sites, online advertising can still provide a strong revenue stream to marketers. Often, this advertising may not be transparent to the online shopper. Big box retailers, for example, may receive co-op dollars (money that manufacturers provide to retailers as an incentive to advertise more aggressively or in specific ways) in exchange for giving certain products better placement on a page or running promotions through the retailer's site. Figure 9-11 shows the bottom part of the Target site, where the Jell-O brand is more heavily promoted due to co-op dollars provided by the manufacturer.

Figure 9-11 The bottom of the Target site features the Jell-O brand front and center, generating co-op revenue from the manufacturer for better, more visible page placement.

In addition, some e-commerce sites may allow banner ads or other ads from outside sources, although this is not a common practice.

Shopping on the Social Web

While the basic premise of shopping in a social media-focused World Wide Web is the same as shopping online in the early days of the Web's commercialization (i.e., consumer logs on, finds the products he or she is looking for, and makes a purchase), there is no question that e-commerce has gone through a maturation process. The Web now offers a far more sophisticated shopping experience. The advent of social media tools has had a significant impact on changing the online shopping experience, and any study of e-commerce needs to be done with these tools in mind. Specifically, consumers expect the online stores they purchase from to go beyond simply offering products to buy. Customers expect Web sites to create an intimate environment with personalized service and peer-to-peer communication tools to aid product research and allow avenues of honest feedback.

The Store Layout

How an online store is laid out will play a large role in the actions that shoppers take while shopping online. Here, organization is the key. There is no floor expanse, no store clerk, no shelves or aisles. There is simply a Web page. The shopper is only able to get as much information as can be seen on his or her computer monitor at any given time.

With this understanding, e-commerce marketers need to design and organize their online stores to do the following:

- Spotlight specific items that the marketer wants to sell, either because they produce a greater profit, there is an overstock, the manufacturer has paid for the item to be more heavily promoted, or some other such reason.

- Promote other saleable items to entice the consumer to make specific purchases.

- Lead customers to other non-product promotional areas (such as pages where a person can sign up for a credit card or newsletter).

- Provide clear and uncomplicated navigation that organizes products into categories (much like the aisles of a supermarket). Remember—if the shopper cannot find a product, then he or she cannot buy it.

- Offer easily accessible help, whether through live chat, e-mail, or another method of contact.

- Give easy access to the shopper's account information.

- Present a shopping cart that can be easily accessed at all times for item inclusion, removal, or purchase.

As discussed earlier, the most valuable space on an e-commerce site (or any site, for that matter) is the Home page above the fold. This is the area that will garner the most attention. Marketers pay particular attention to how this space is presented, because it is the most pivotal point of consumer decision making, and it will typically determine whether or not a person explores the site further or shops elsewhere. Figure 9-12 shows the Home page of BJ's, the big box retailer, with each of the important elements listed above pointed out.

Access to account info

Access to shopping cart

Access to shopping help

Navigation, breaking the products down into categories

Spotlight on specific items that the marketer is more anxious to sell

Non-product promotions

Visible promotion of other important saleable items

Figure 9-12   The layout of the BJ's e-commerce site highlights important products, while also providing access to non-product information, account info, shopping cart, and help.

The Shopping Cart and Check-Out Process

No matter how compelling an online store is, most customers will not buy if they cannot easily make their desired purchase. Every store needs a shopping cart and check-out process that is as efficient and painless as possible.

Just as it would in a supermarket, the shopping cart on an e-commerce site holds the items that the consumer wants to purchase. It will calculate the price times the quantity of each item, add all the items in the shopping cart together, and maintain a running total of all of the items being purchased. A well-organized site will give the user access to his or her shopping cart at all times to review their intended purchases, and a well-executed shopping cart will allow products to be removed as easily as they are put into the cart. Figure 9-13 shows a sample shopping cart from Amazon.com.

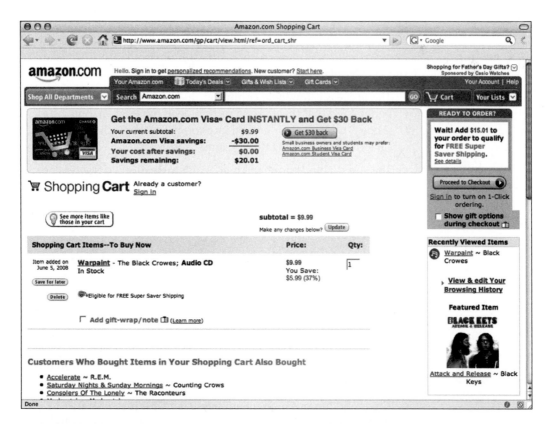

Figure 9-13 The shopping cart on Amazon.com. Like any quality shopping cart, this one shows the shopper the item(s) they have already selected and calculates the subtotal based on the price multiplied by the quantity.

As the figure shows, the shopping cart area of an e-commerce site can be one of the best opportunities to increase sales. Once an item has been placed into the cart, marketers understand that the consumer has already, at least in part, made a decision to purchase that product. The area around the cart gives the marketer a chance to offer a consumer related products or entice customers with discounts if they order more. Notice that in Figure 9-13, the large banner across the top offers a savings if the consumer signs up for the Amazon.com Visa card. Directly above the shopping cart, the light bulb icon offers the chance to see items that are similar to the one currently in the cart. Off to the right, a small display ad prompts the consumer to purchase $15.01 more to qualify for free shipping. The remainder of the space around the cart is dedicated to showing featured items that may be of interest to the consumer—based on what is currently in the shopping cart and what other consumers that have bought the same item have also purchased.

Once satisfied with their order, the consumer then goes on to make their purchase—possibly the most precarious part of the online buying process. According to a 2007 report by DoubleClick, nearly 75% of all online shoppers abandon their shopping carts before making the final purchase. There are a number of reasons why consumers abandon their orders at this stage:

- The process is too long, confusing, and cumbersome. Shoppers understand that there are steps that need to be taken, but if the process is too long or broken into too many steps, the marketer runs the risk of losing the consumer's interest.

- The site requires too much personal information. Marketers need to balance the desire to gather as much consumer information as possible with the reality that many people will resist giving personal information (such as a phone number) that is not relevant to receiving their order.

- The marketer adds too many extra charges to the sub-total before final check-out (such as heavy shipping costs, excessive handling fees, etc.).

- The page layout of the shopping cart and/or the check-out process is poor and disorganized, causing the consumer to question the legitimacy of the site overall. Page design for the check-out process is extremely important, as a disorganized check-out will lead users to feel that the store itself is disorganized.

- The brand has not built up enough trust with the consumer to encourage them to take the risk and purchase the product online.

These last two points are especially important and reflect back not only on early discussions of site design, but also on the importance of building the brand. Recall that building the brand is equivalent to building trust—an important element when you consider that 75% of all Web users do not like to give sensitive personal and credit card information over the Web.[5] However, if this population felt more confident about the security of their information—if they trusted the site or the brand—the amount of people who would use e-commerce as a means of making regular purchases would increase by a full 7%.[6] This is a significant increase that could potentially push millions more dollars into the pockets of online marketers through e-commerce sites.

At a minimum, a successful check-out system needs to gather the following information:

- The shopper's shipping address (where the items should be delivered)

- The method of payment; Web sites typically offer a variety of options, including:

  - Credit or debit card

  - Electronic check (this pulls funds directly from the shopper's checking account and requires customers to provide their personal checking account information)

  - Payment from a third party facilitator, such as PayPal; shoppers can move funds into their PayPal account and use those funds for online payments without having to give sensitive credit card or checking account information to a number of different vendors

- Payment from an invoice sent to the customer; this is not a popular choice, as Web sites typically will not ship items until after payment has been received.

- The desired shipping method (faster shipping options, like overnight delivery, are usually more expensive)

- The billing address, if the shopper intends to pay by credit or debit card, or electronic check (this is for security purposes)

Shipping can be a sticking point for many shoppers, and the shipping charges (a cost that shoppers do not have to incur if they go directly to the store) can quickly turn online shoppers away. In fact, of the 75% of shoppers that abandon their shopping carts, 72% did so because the shipping rates were too high.[7] Savvy marketers will use clever promotions that eliminate shipping costs altogether if the consumer agrees to make purchases over a pre-set amount.

Once all of this information has been submitted, e-commerce sites typically allow the shopper to review all of the information that they have submitted, the list of items ordered, and the grand total one last time. Customers will usually have an opportunity to edit any errors or make changes before finalizing the order. Figure 9-14 shows the pre-purchase summation page on Amazon, which provides the grand total for the order, the products that are being purchased, their quantities, the shipping and billing addresses, shipping method, and how the order will be paid for.

322

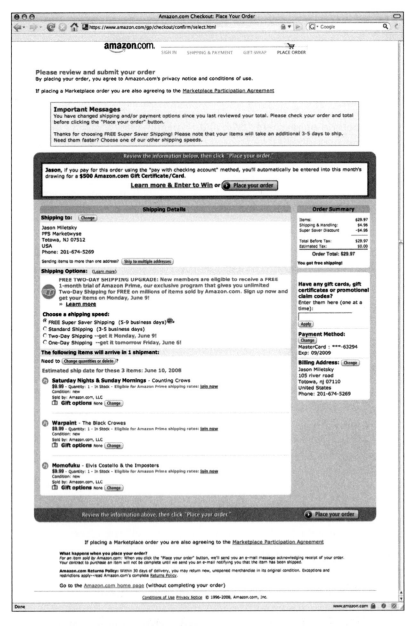

Figure 9-14 The pre-order summation page on Amazon.com gives shoppers the ability to review their order and their account before placing the final order.

Upon completion of the order and processing of the payment, efficient e-commerce sites provide a printable receipt. Most sites then send an e-mail to the shopper thanking them for their purchase, summarizing their order, and providing a tracking number for the shipment.

INTERVIEW WITH...
KEVIN SPROLES: FOUNDER OF VOLUSION.COM

In 1999, Kevin Sproles turned his passion for coding and designing shopping carts and Web sites into Volusion.com, one of the largest and most successful e-commerce providers on the Web. (See Figure 9-15.) Volusion software is the engine behind online stores across a large number of industries, and brands, including the official store for the well-known candy brand Pez (Figure 9-16) and Barack Obama during his 2008 presidential run (Figure 9-17). Volusion's success has been so great that BusinessWeek named Kevin among their "Best 25 Entrepreneurs under 25."

Kevin was good enough to spend some time talking to me about his take on e-commerce, the issues that marketers face reaching their audiences, and what he sees as the future of the online shopping.

JASON: Thanks for talking with me, Kevin. Tell me a little bit about Volusion and how you got started programming shopping carts?

KEVIN: I started programming back when I was in high school and was about 16 when I started Volusion. I started programming Web sites in general. Then I realized that there are a lot of people that really need a shopping cart, so I built the first version of Volusion. It had obviously a very small client base, so we really listened to what our clients needed and grew from there, one client at a time. Now Volusion has over 20,000 customers.

JASON: Tell me more about the Volusion site, how it works, and who it is meant for.

KEVIN: Sure. Clients pay us a low monthly fee and they get everything they need to build and run an entire online business. We provide the software that they use to build their Web site with a particular focus on online stores. So they use our software, which builds their Web site with a shopping cart, the one page check-out system, everything they need to accept payments and to sell their products. We also do a lot of their hosting, and we give them a lot of tools for Internet marketing.

JASON: Talk to me about some of the online marketing tools.

KEVIN: One of the important things for a low budget is that the Web site is SEO [Search Engine Optimized] and our software has a lot of built-in methods that help you link well. Your pages, for example, have to be in a certain format that is attractive to Google and all the other search engines. We also put all the right words in your title tags, which gets you linked well through search engines. I also suggest that store owners get involved with e-mail marketing and even partnering with similar Web sites for cross-promotional purposes.

JASON: As an expert in e-commerce, what advice would you give to a storeowner for increasing sales and discouraging cart abandonment?

KEVIN: Well that's all about the usability of a site. You want to make sure that the site is easy. So, for example, say you're selling a pair of shoes or another product where people are going to need to not only settle on a design and style, but also on a specific size. The site needs to allow users to filter out search responses by your desired shoe size. Having those kind of features makes it easier for a person to find what they want, which is really important. Volusion stores also get to use a feature that zooms in on a product when the user rolls over it. So if you roll over a shoe image, for example, the photo will magnify the image, give the user more details about the product, and provide other information that will help increase the confidence of the customer. Once you've gained the consumer's confidence, store owners should encourage them to add reviews to their store about the products they buy, which encourages other people to buy.

In terms of cart abandonment, that mostly comes down to ease of check-out. The research we've done is that one page check-out, which we use on Volusion stores, reduces cart abandonment. In the past, people had to go through up to five pages on average to check out and make their payment. But, we came up with the one page that includes filling out all vital information, making the payment, and hitting the Submit button. Now you've captured the customer, and after the sale, store owners should do some e-mail marketing to keep bringing that customer back.

JASON: You mentioned consumer confidence. When I think of consumer confidence, I think of brand building. When it comes to online marketing and online store ownership, how important is it for a storeowner to build their brand?

KEVIN: Making sure that your Web site presents a strong brand is really important. You can do that in a lot of ways. Having an organized, attractive Web site is one of the keys—most people decide from the moment they come to your Home page whether or not you're a reputable company just by the look and feel. They also can tell that once they get into the check-out page. If that check-out is too confusing or difficult the brand is going to look incompetent. It's also important to provide some information about the store and the brand behind it, such as an "about us" page with a company history, contact information—anything that legitimizes the brand in the mind of the consumer and gains their trust.

JASON: You also mentioned encouraging customers to leave reviews on products. That gets us into social media. In your opinion, how is online shopping evolving given the social media environment?

KEVIN: Well, social media has quite a large array of definitions. One perspective is about the usability and how social media makes online shopping easier to use. It can put a store owner off balance, of course, because customer reviews aren't always going to be positive. But, the ability for consumers to voice their opinion about a product or brand is great, and it's definitely had a big impact on online shopping. A lot of people look at reviews—whether on a shopping-specific site or just generally on the Net like in the blogosphere.

JASON: Predict the future for me. How is e-commerce going to evolve moving forward?

KEVIN: It's going to become infinitely more convenient. In the past five years, we've seen that convenience improve, and over the next five years it's going to be that much more impressive. It'll be cheaper, more mobile, and it'll be the single most important means that consumers find products and information that they need.

Figure 9-15 The Volusion home page

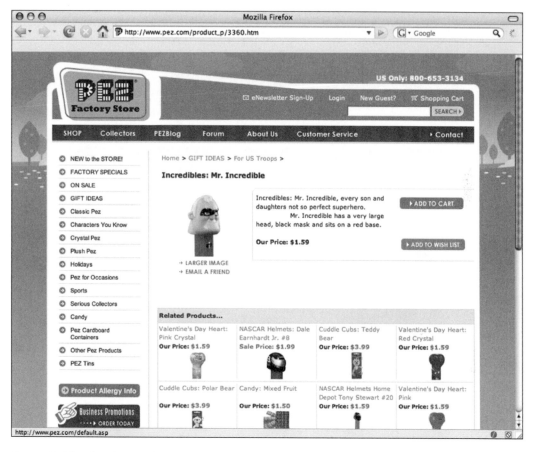

Figure 9-16 Popular candy brand PEZ uses the Volusion software as the foundation for their online store.

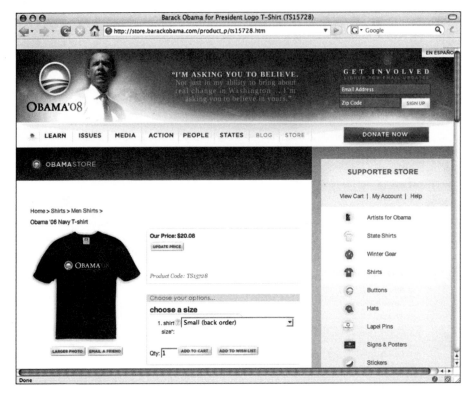

Figure 9-17　Barack Obama's store during his 2008 presidential run also used Volusion software for its store and shopping cart.

Intuitive and Personal Content Provision

Online stores can offer a benefit that traditional offline retail outlets can rarely do: retain an intimate knowledge of each and every customer. Armed with this knowledge—which is housed in massive databases—marketers can gain a significant advantage by arranging the home page of their stores in such a way that the products offered are the products most likely to be desired by individual customers.

The psychology behind personal content provision is fairly simple: A male shopper who has visited a sporting goods site twice before to browse the fishing equipment on the site is more likely to be driven to action if, on his third visit, the Home page features the store's new line of fishing polls or a weekend fishing trip rather than a line of women's tennis sneakers.

Similarly, by understanding where, geographically, a user's search is taking place, online marketers can run purposeful promotions to encourage increased sales. **Geotargeting**, which is the practice of defining of a target audience based on their geographical location, is often used by marketers to offer specific options. Based on the user's IP address, a marketer may determine that a shopper is located in Venice Beach, near Los Angeles. When summertime approaches, the products they push on their home page may be beach-related—sun screen, beach towels, surfing gear—while a shopper in Denver, shopping at the same online store, is offered products that are not beach-related. However, suppose that same Denver shopper searches the store while poolside during his vacation to Orlando. The store understands who the shopper is, but, because the IP address is different, it also now knows that the shopper is on vacation. The site would then likely offer different products, such as discount tickets to a local theme park. If the e-commerce store has a mashup application, it could tap into Google Maps, and provide directions to that theme park or connect with the site for a local bus company to provide information on public transportation.

These methods provide both improved service as well as help increase the potential for increased spending. In addition, personalized attention helps to increase consumer trust in the brand, as it shows technological legitimacy. It also helps to create a stronger, more personal one-to-one connection.

Feedback and Reviews

The social Web has allowed people across all boundaries to interact and provide opinions. Consumers, saturated with marketing, have come to realize that advertising, whether in print, on TV, or on the Web, is a one-sided message, written and produced from the marketer's perspective. While these ads are useful in communicating a message, building brand awareness and promoting the brand's personality, they are rarely a means of establishing trust.

Consumers are more apt to trust their peers than they are to trust marketers—even if those peers are faceless, nameless, and similar only in the sense that they have similar buying habits. With the popularization of social media, e-commerce stores are increasingly compelled to allow users to communicate their feelings about individual products. These opinions are typically expressed in two ways:

- **Ratings**: Users can rate a product or media (such as downloadable songs or movies), usually on a one to five scale, with a five rating being the best. Each person's individual rating is usually displayed along with the average of all the ratings.

- **Reviews**: Users are allowed to leave their reviews of the product or media, expressing their opinions in their own words, whether positive or negative. Many stores will also allow other users to digitally appeal certain reviews by letting readers rate each review as helpful or not helpful or by flagging reviews for removal if they feel one is inappropriate or malicious.

Figure 9-18 provides a sample of a product on Target.com. Notice how the site provides the average rating, along with individual customers' ratings and reviews and other users' feedback as to the helpfulness of those reviews.

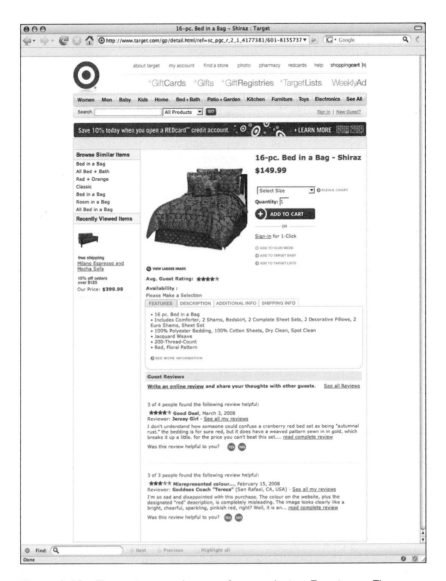

Figure 9-18 The customer review area for a product on Target.com. The average review rating is shown directly below the product picture, and full reviews are shown a bit lower. Each review also shows how many other shoppers found that review helpful.

According to the Pew Internet & American Life Project, a full third of all online shoppers have posted reviews about a product after they have purchased it.[8] This is a significant level of involvement by online shoppers. This statistic paints a picture of how personal the relationship between brands and consumers really is. It also illustrates how important it is for shoppers to have a voice in the future use (or disuse) of the products that are on the market.

Chapter Summary

- E-commerce is used by consumers across practically all demographic boundaries, although adults over age 30 and with higher annual income are more apt to make use of e-commerce tools. Brand and trust equity play a large role in shoppers' decisions about where to make their purchases. These factors are especially important to customers because concerns about providing sensitive information are often a deterrent to shopping online. While there are many pros and cons associated with shopping on the Web, convenience, time savings, and the potential for lower prices are among the biggest reasons why consumers look to the Web to buy their products.

- E-commerce marketers generate revenue online in a variety of ways. While direct sales are the primary means of turning a profit, other avenues also exist. These include indirect sales in the case of consumers visiting an online store to do research before making their purchases at an offline store, the sale of membership subscriptions, and advertising.

- The way an online store is designed is the key to whether or not marketers can move their shoppers to take action. With limited real estate, e-commerce stores need to promote their most important products up front, give consumers access to other key products, and divide all products into easily accessible categories. Marketers can also increase sales through the use of social media applications such as the ability for users to leave and read product reviews, personalizing each store visit based on the individual consumer's shopping history, and making the cart and check-out process as easy and trustworthy as possible.

Key Terms

e-commerce—The buying and selling of services through any electronic medium.

geotargeting—The practice of defining an audience based on their geographical location.

margin—The difference between revenue and cost.

profit—The difference between the cost of an item and the price for which that the item is ultimately sold.

thumbnails—Small images that represent a larger image on a Web site.

Review Questions

1. Which of the following is more likely to make a purchase over the Web?

    a. A 19-year-old male, earning $30,000 per year

    b. A 21-year-old woman with a college degree

    c. A 28-year-old man with a college education

    d. A 48-year-old woman earning $99,000 per year

2. Which of the following regions of the world is least likely to make a purchase online?

    a. North America

    b. Latin America

    c. Asia Pacific

    d. Europe

3. The popularity of clothes and shoes being purchased online is surprising because:

    a. Fashions change faster than sites can be updated

    b. People cannot try them on prior to making a purchase

    c. The government charges higher taxes for clothing

    d. Most people are not interested in clothing

4. What percentage of online shoppers is likely to leave a review about a particular product after they have purchased it?

   a. 33%

   b. 50%

   c. 72%

   d. 92%

5. According to 81% of all online shoppers, the main reason for shopping online is:

   a. Rising cost of gas

   b. Not being bothered by a sales person at the store

   c. Convenience

   d. Lower prices

6. The main reason shoppers will abandon their carts without making a purchase is:

   a. They do not want to wait for delivery

   b. They get a phone call that knocks them offline

   c. They read a bad review of the product

   d. They do not want to pay the high shipping costs

7. Increased selection is:

   a. A positive aspect of e-commerce

   b. A negative aspect of e-commerce

   c. Neither

   d. Both

8. Trust equity in the brand plays an important role in which store people choose to buy from. True or False?

9. People with lower incomes are more likely to see the positive attributes of online shopping. True or False?

10. Which of the following does not usually need to be considered when determining the cost of a product?

    a. Prices set by competitors

    b. The anticipated volume of sales

c. How nicely designed the packaging is

d. How well established the brand is

11. Which product would retail shoppers most likely feel com-pelled to buy without too much thought before purchase?

a. A new car

b. Light bulbs

c. The latest Elvis Costello CD

d. A pack of gum

12. As online shoppers do further research (navigate into lower tiers) on a specific product on a Web site, they will find that the amount of copy on a page typically:

a. Increases

b. Decreases

c. Stays the same

13. As online shoppers do further research (navigate into lower tiers) on a specific product on a Web site, they will find that the size of product photography on a page:

a. Increases

b. Decreases

c. Stays the same

14. Marketers with traditional, offline retail locations have an advantage over retailers that are only online because:

a. A significant number of shoppers use e-commerce site to do research but make their purchases offline

b. Traditional locations can usually offer lower prices

c. People usually enjoy being approached by live salespeople

d. Fewer people can fit into an offline store, so they are promised better attention

15. Which of the following is more likely to be purchased online?

a. A subscription to an online humor magazine

b. A new fiction book

c. A ticket to Europe

d. A pair of sneakers

16. The most important real estate on a shopping site is:

   a. The space directly next to the brand logo

   b. The bottom of the page

   c. The area of the Home page above the fold

   d. The area of the Home page below the fold

17. The shopping cart is a good place to try to increase sales. True or False?

18. If the check-out process is too long, consumers are most likely to:

   a. Struggle through it, but leave a nasty review about their experience somewhere

   b. Abandon their cart

   c. Leave the site for a while and finish their purchase later

   d. Shop for more items—if they have to go through a long check-out process, they may as well buy more

19. Which of the following is the least common method of paying for products online?

   a. Credit card

   b. Debit Card

   c. Electronic check

   d. Being billed for the items

20. Online product ratings are usually done on a scale of:

   a. 1 to 3

   b. 1 to 5

   c. 1 to 7

   d. 1 to 10

Projects

1. One of the topics we discussed in this chapter was how important it is for shoppers to feel safe and secure when providing sensitive personal and credit card information. Research the ways that e-commerce sites provide this security and detail them in a paper no longer than three pages.

2. Choose an online store and spend some time exploring it. In a two-page paper, describe your experience. Make sure you discuss the positives and negatives, how easy it was to find information, and any methods the marketer took to compel you to buy. Would you make future purchases from that store? Why or why not?

3. Using pretend products (copy some images off of your favorite online store), program and design the home page of your own store. You do not need to build a working shopping cart, but create the page in such a way that it would interest shoppers.

4. In a three-page paper, detail how you designed the site in Project #3.

   • Why did you design it the way you did?

   • Who do you consider your target audience?

   • What steps did you take to make that audience buy from your store?

Endnotes

1. Nielsen Global Online Survey, Nielsen, Jan. 2008.
2. Ibid.
3. Horrigan, John B. "Online Shopping." Pew Internet & American Life Project, 13 Feb. 2008.
4. Ibid.
5. Ibid.
6. Ibid.
7. Ibid.
8. Ibid.

CHAPTER 10

Programs and Languages

In this chapter you will learn about:

◎ The programs used by designers for graphic design, blogging, databasing, and site creation

◎ Some of the popular languages Web developers use to make their sites come to life

This chapter finally takes you out of the world of marketing and back into the more familiar, more logical world of Web-related programs and languages. This is the magic that works behind the marketing—the stuff that pulls it all together. As the Web evolves and matures into a richer, more robust arena, the programs and languages that are used to develop sites and applications rise and fall in popularity. These tools are constantly changing to meet the needs of the market and expanding to give programmers greater capabilities to develop effective, dynamic sites.

The number of programs and languages that are used in site development is extensive—far more than we could hope to cover in a book on Web marketing. This chapter will discuss the programs and languages that developers most commonly use in creating sites. We will talk about the situations in which they would most likely be used and the benefits developers get from each one.

One fact that most programmers come to understand early in their careers is that the developer/marketer relationship is seldom a two-way street. Programmers are typically expected to understand Web sites from a marketing standpoint—why the sites are being developed, the intended audience, ways to drive traffic to a site and keep it there. On the other hand, the eyes of most marketers will often glaze over at the first hint of a programming conversation. They may understand what certain programs and languages can do, but most will not have the patience or training to understand Web programming to the depth that a programmer does. This chapter is not meant to be a discussion on how to program a site. Rather, it presents an overview of programs and languages that will be relevant to marketers.

Relevant Programs and Applications

Off-the-shelf programs and Web-based applications are used by professionals for different aspects of site creation, including everything from graphic design to site construction. In the following sections, we will discuss some programs and applications that help developers construct Web sites, create Web graphics, set up blogs, and utilize databases.

Graphic Design

Design programs allow graphic designers to create, edit, and save graphics that provide the visual features on Web sites. Although some designers may choose to use less well-known programs for creating their graphics, Web design is really dominated by two key programs.

Photoshop

Developed by Adobe Systems, Photoshop is the predominant computer-based design program, largely viewed as the Microsoft Word for the design world. Practically any image today in print or on the Web has passed through Photoshop at some point prior to publication. It is unlikely that a professional graphic designer could reach a significant level of success without having at least a partial understanding of this tool. Figure 10-1 shows the Photoshop interface.

Toolbar

Canvas

Layers Palette

Figure 10-1 The Photoshop interface. On the canvas is a Web site being designed in Photoshop. Once final, each graphic element will be extracted and saved separately, and the site will be reassembled using coding.

Photoshop can be difficult to master, but it is exceptionally powerful in creating graphics, manipulating or editing photography, and developing special effects for graphics (such as drop shadows, bevels, and embosses). It gives designers complete control over image sizes, file format, resolution, colors, and even background transparency. Web designers use Photoshop for everything from preparing standard graphics and images for publication to creating customized buttons for their sites to laying out an entire site. Designers often design all elements of a site in Photoshop first, using the program's layers feature to house individual graphics, and then pull each element out individually to build the site once approval has been granted for the overall design. Photoshop also offers powerful tools for compressing images and creating **animated GIFs** (an animation made up of a series of individual graphics, which plays like a flip-book).

Flash

Also produced by Adobe Systems (after their 2005 acquisition of Macromedia, the company that originally developed Flash), Flash has had a resounding impact on the Web's growth. Earlier in this book, we studied how the Flash player has revolutionized Web-based video; it is the driving force behind YouTube and other video-sharing sites. As a graphics application, Flash helps designers create illustration-style animation and interactivity, giving sites more activity and motion. Flash helps designers draw users' attention to key areas. We will discuss Flash again when we look at Action Scripting, a programming language commonly used when entire sites are created in Flash.

Unlike Photoshop, which works primarily with **bitmap** images (images made up of pixels), Flash is a vector-based program. **Vector graphics** are created from lines and shapes, which are generated by mathematical formulas. With vector graphics, designers can create animations that are very smooth and have a very low file size. Animated GIFs are often choppy and usually have a larger file size, since all of the individual graphics in an animation contribute to the total file size.

Flash works with a timeline-based interface. Using this interface, designers can include individual graphic elements, images, and music at various points across the timeline (the Flash interface is shown in Figure 10-2). In addition, Flash can be used to make highly interactive Web graphics. Designers utilizing Flash can create animations and pop-ups that are immediately triggered when users roll-over or click certain areas. Because of its ease of interactivity and the relatively small file size (allowing each Flash file to load and play with extreme speed), many developers of Web-based games use Flash as their program of choice.

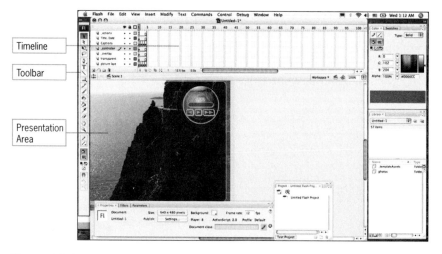

Figure 10-2 The Flash interface. Notice the timeline at the top, which allows designers to create different actions to take place at specific times.

Site Construction

Later in this chapter, we will learn about languages that are used to build larger sites. However, smaller sites with more basic features can be created by someone who does not know any programming at all. The predominant tool for this type of Web site development is a program called Dreamweaver. We will discuss Dreamweaver and other site editors in the sections below.

Dreamweaver and Other WYSIWYG Editors

Anyone want to take a wild guess as to which company makes and markets Dreamweaver? Once again, the company behind one of the most dominant programs within the Web universe is Adobe. Dreamweaver software makes the programming of Web sites simple and straightforward. Dreamweaver is widely considered to be one of the most powerful **WYSIWYG** editors available (WYSIWYG stands for What You See Is What You Get). A WYSIWYG editor is a software application or online editor that allows a designer to see what the final Web page will look like as he or she is creating it.

Dreamweaver allows developers to compile and create Web pages without knowing any programming (although having a basic understanding of HTML certainly helps). Using graphic elements (such as those that can be created in Photoshop or Flash), Dreamweaver users can piece together the pages of their sites, while the program writes the necessary code. Dreamweaver also allows users to create multiple pages and establish the necessary links from one page to another. Users can create an entire multi-page site quickly and easily.

More advanced developers can use Dreamweaver for more complicated sites; although its most popular use is for simple sites developed by non-programmers. Figure 10-3 shows a site being built in Dreamweaver, and Figure 10-4 shows how that same site looks when published on the Web.

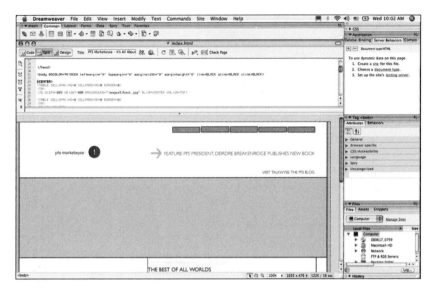

Figure 10-3   The Dreamweaver interface. In this view, the main screen is split, showing the code for the page on top, and a preview of how the page will look on the bottom.

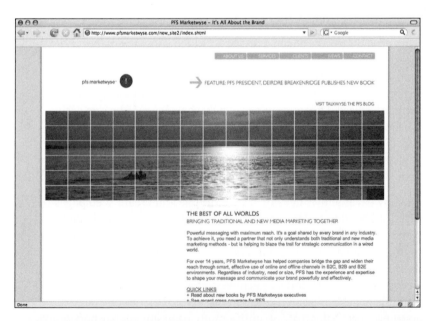

Figure 10-4   The resulting page in a browser after being assembled in Dreamweaver.

Over the years, a number of other WYSIWYG editors have fallen to Dreamweaver's dominance. These include Microsoft's FrontPage, which remained on the market for nearly a decade even though user criticism of the program was strong from its earliest release. Front-Page has since been replaced by two newer products called Share-Point and Expression Web.

Sharepoint has seen increased popularity, particularly among enter-prise corporations with a large and diffuse workforce. SharePoint (shown in Figure 10-5) allows users to create Web sites as well as browser-based collaboration workspaces. These collaborative tools include wikis, blogs, and other social media features.

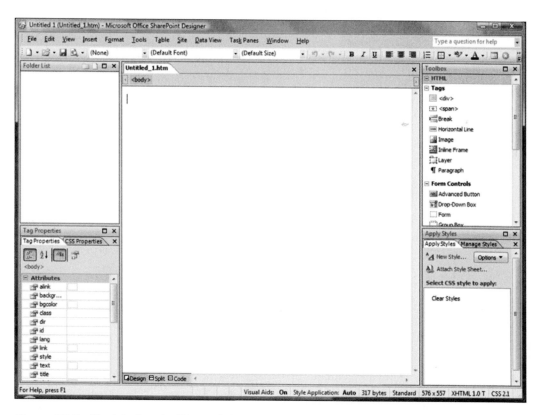

Figure 10-5 The interface for Microsoft SharePoint Designer, used to create SharePoint sites.

Adobe's GoLive is another WYSIWYG editor that has fallen. Adobe halted production of GoLive and recommends that users transition to Dreamweaver. However, there are a number of other WYSIWYG off-the-shelf programs and Web-based applications still available for developers to use. Each comes with its own price and features, and developers need to determine for themselves which one is right for them.

Blogs

Setting up a blog is very simple and typically takes no more than a few minutes. Even better, establishing a blog site is free, and can be done without setting up an external host.

Many different programs can be used to set up a blog. Most of the programs are fairly similar in terms of what users can do with them and how the programs are structured. Because of this similarity, we will review just two of the more popular ones here.

Blogger and WordPress

Blogger, which is owned and operated by Google, and WordPress are each easy to set up and use. Blogger and WordPress provide bloggers with simple interfaces for creating and publishing blogs. While the blog services are free, these sites do reserve the right to place advertising on users' blogs. Users can pay for site upgrades, such as having a more personalized URL, the ability to radically adjust layouts and site designs, more space for image uploads, etc. Once an account has been established with service (the user will need to select a URL, such as miletsky.wordpress.com), a simple management tool, or dashboard, will allow the user to:

- Select the desired blog template (design) from a library of pre-created designs (experienced programmers can manipulate these or create their own)

- Set up their blogroll (links to other blogs)

- Set up their blog categories

- Select **widgets** to include on the blog (widgets are small bits of code that can be inserted into a blog to add specific functionality, such as a calendar or mapping device)

- Upload written content

- Load pictures, videos, or music files

- Create external links

As reader comments are left on each blog entry, blog editors can return to the dashboard to review the comment before approving it and allowing it to be publicly posted. This ensures that very offensive remarks or comments that are spam are not posted to the blog. Figure 10-6 shows a screen shot of the Blogger interface, while Figures 10-7 and 10-8 show screen shots from the WordPress dashboard. Figure 10-9 shows the resulting blog site.

People that want to start new blog sites decide which service to use based on a number of variables, most notably which dashboard they feel most comfortable using. Blog creators can also consider which service provides the most useful site templates and which offers the most cost-effective upgrades.

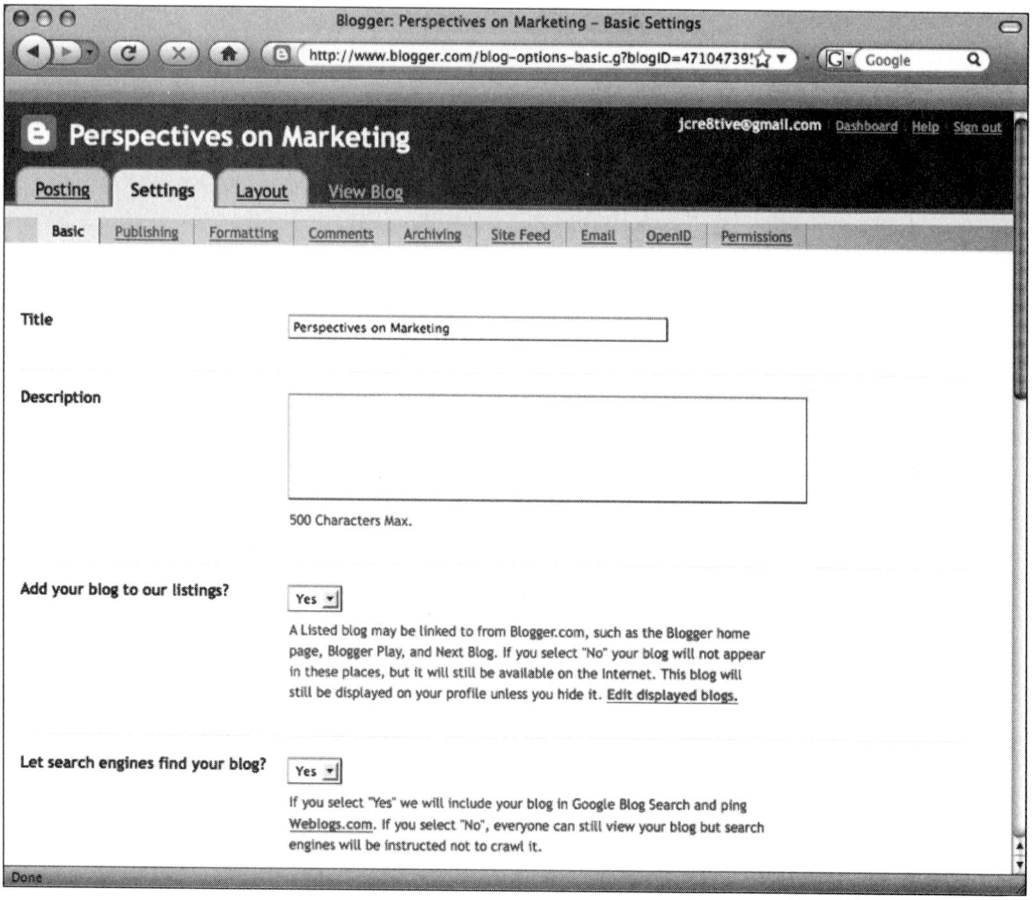

Figure 10-6   The Blogger dashboard.

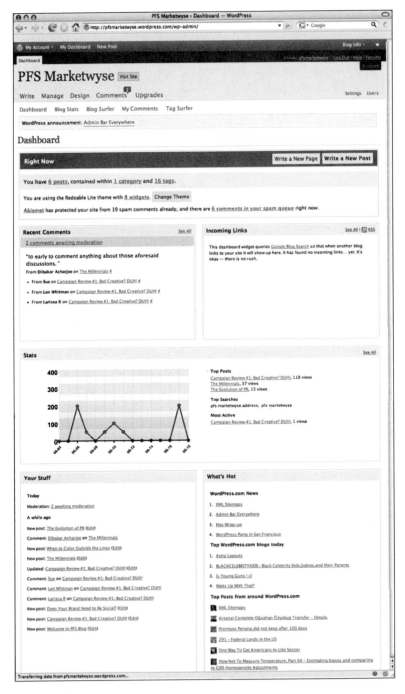

Figure 10-7 The main dashboard of a blog on WordPress shows the blogger the most recent reader comments, top posts, vital statistics (such as how many visitors have visited the blog and the popularity of each blog post), and what other topics have been posted by other WordPress users.

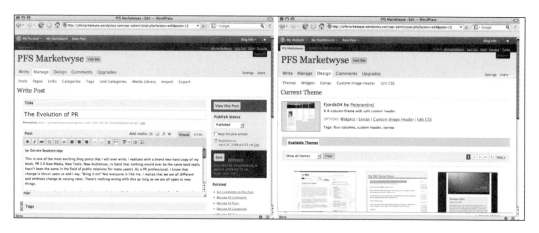

Figure 10-8 On the left, WordPress allows the blogger to create a new post, which can be immediately published or saved. The blogger can add tags to the post and decide whether or not to allow readers to post comments in reply. On the right, users can choose their design, add widgets such as calendars to show when new posts have been uploaded, RSS feeds to show headlines from other blogs and, for those willing to pay a fee, make changes to the layout and look and feel.

Figure 10-9 The resulting blog, after all the setup tasks have been completed in WordPress.

Databases

Like a filing cabinet, databases are used to store data in an organized fashion. Web designers who want to store, save, and organize digital information need to utilize a database. Information that can be stored in a database includes user information, such as name, address, and phone number. Designers also use databases to store site data, such as information on the products in an online store including their descriptions and prices.

Databases are software applications, which each offer different benefits.

MySQL

MySQL was developed by the Swedish company MySQL AB, which is now a subsidiary of Sun Microsystems. MySQL is a popular database choice among Web developers. Although it is more limited in functionality than databases developed by larger competitors such as Oracle, MySQL has gained traction because it is inexpensive, easy to use, and built for speed. MySQL is easy to customize; it allows developers to alter the software to fit their needs. It can also support large databases, is secure, and can run on practically any operating system.

Developers can download MySQL for free if the database will be used for general public use on a Web site—even if the purpose of that site is to generate revenue. Richer versions of the software that include enhanced features, better pre-release testing and optimization, and various levels of technical support are available for a monthly subscription fee.

SQL Server

Developed by Microsoft, SQL Server is one of the leading choices of developers for database software. While SQL Server shares many of the features of MySQL, some fundamental differences are enough to give developers something to think about when deciding between them. There are a number of important differences between them. MySQL is open source, while SQL Server is closed and proprietary. MySQL is cheaper as long as the developer keeps his or her project open source. SQL Server offers more features, but partly because it needs to support so many additional features, SQL Server often does not perform as well as MySQL. Developers decide which option is best for them based on the above factors and their needs for their project.

Microsoft Access

According to Microsoft, Access is the most popular database in the world—and it may very well be. Simple to use and relatively inexpensive, Access maintains the look and feel of most Microsoft software products. Because of this, most developers feel immediately comfortable with the Access database. Access is not really scalable; therefore it is most often used by smaller businesses or Web sites that require limited information in a database.

Access is often compared to Microsoft Excel, the spreadsheet program that is part of Microsoft Office. Each can store information and manage data, but while Excel stores information in worksheets that can be used to create lists (such as a directory of names, telephone numbers, and addresses), Access stores them in tables that look like spreadsheets but can query relational information from other tables in other locations. For example, a simple register of customers would keep first names, last names, and contact information in the same list. For this limited purpose, either Excel or Access can do the job. However, information about what each person has purchased would be kept in a separate table—likely for each individual order. Because it may be important for all of this data to be easily accessible from a single query, Access is the better choice. Different segments of information are kept in distinct tables, but the tables can share information back and forth.

Oracle

The Oracle database is a larger, more robust, and complex database. Companies typically need seasoned developers to properly tackle this software. Because of its security and its ability to handle very large databases, Oracle is typically the choice for larger companies and companies that have a vast amount of information to include in their database.

Relevant Programming Languages

As with programs, different programming languages are designed to perform different functions. Very often, however, the choice of which language to use is based on the preference of a developer, many of whom can be as fanatically dedicated to their favorite language as brand loyalists who prefer Pepsi over Coke or Apple over PCs.

In the following sections, we will discuss some of the most popular languages, what they do, and why developers would choose to work with them. We will begin, however, with an entry that every developer needs to know and nearly every site uses, but which is often not even ranked among the top languages.

HTML

In a 2006 poll, About.com posed the question, "Do you consider HTML a programming language?" Over 50% of all respondents said "No." An online review of more serious programming blogs and articles shows that most programmers agree. However, the depth of the debate proves one thing: there really is no factual answer. To understand some of the issues in this argument, consider the following two comments to the About.com poll question:

HTML is a programming language. How can you say that it is not? Sure, you can't make exquisite things with HTML alone, but it still is a language. Maybe people don't consider it one because they use a program to help them generate the code, but I'm old school and love my notepad! Granted, I do use PHP and CSS with my HTML, because it takes it a step (well, several) farther, but don't deny HTML its right to be called a programming language. We would all be sad if people didn't use HTML, and all we got was text over the Internet.

—Robert M.

HTML is not a programming language, it's a MARKUP language. There's no logic in HTML, it's all about presentation (or semantics), no action at all. Thus, it can never be considered programming.

—Jari V.

It is likely that this debate will rage on as long as the Web exists. In not listing HTML in its top 20 ranking, Tiobe.com has cast its vote that HTML should not be considered a programming language. Whichever argument a developer sides with, one thing is certain: HTML is a vital and life-giving component of the Web as we know it.

HTML stands for HyperText Markup Language. With it, Web developers can tell browsers how to present information to those viewing a Web page. HTML contains codes that allow a designer to determine where an image appears, how large or small the copy will be, which words will be bold or italicized, which colors will be in the background, how the page will lay out, where the links will be placed, and to which pages they will link. Figure 10-10 shows an HTML coded page.

HTML is extremely easy to learn relative to most other languages. Each command is made up of bracketed code that the browser reads and translates. The command <B>, for example, tells the browser to show any copy afterward in boldface, until a second command </B> tells the browser to stop and resume presenting copy in standard non-boldface.

```
news.shtml
<TR>
<TD WIDTH=993 HEIGHT=850 BACKGROUND="images5/back.jpg" ALIGN=CENTER VALIGN=TOP>

<TABLE CELLSPACING=0 CELLPADDING=0 BORDER=0>
<TR>
<TD VALIGN=TOP>

<TABLE CELLSPACING=0 CELLPADDING=0 BORDER=0>
<TR>
<TD WIDTH=971 HEIGHT=170 BGCOLOR=WHITE>
<TABLE CELLSPACING=0 CELLPADDING=0 BORDER=0>
<TR>
<TD WIDTH=415 HEIGHT=170 BGCOLOR=WHITE ROWSPAN=4>
<A HREF="index.shtml"><IMG SRC="images5/logo.jpg" BORDER=0></A>
</TD>
<TD WIDTH=556 HEIGHT=36>
<!--#include file="mainnav.html" -->
</TD>
</TR>
<TR>
<TD WIDTH=556 HEIGHT=45>

</TD>
</TR>
<TR>
<TD WIDTH=556 HEIGHT=32>
<A HREF="features.html"><IMG SRC="images5/feature.jpg" BORDER=0></A>
</TD>
</TR>
<TR>
<TD WIDTH=556 HEIGHT=57>
<A HREF="http://pfsmarketwyse.wordpress.com"><IMG SRC="images5/blog.jpg" BORDER=0></A>
</TD>
</TR>
</TABLE>


</TD>
</TR>
<TR>
<TD WIDTH=971 BGCOLOR=WHITE>
<TABLE CELLSPACING=0 CELLPADDING=0 BORDER=0>
<TR>
<TD WIDTH=10></TD>
<TD WIDTH=371 BGCOLOR=WHITE>
<iframe src="news_movie.html" width="371" HEIGHT="242" align="CENTER" valign="BOTTOM" scrolling=no
frameborder=0></iframe>
</TD>
<TD WIDTH=571 BGCOLOR=WHITE>
<iframe src="news_flash.html" width="571" HEIGHT="242" align="CENTER" valign="TOP" scrolling=no
frameborder=0></iframe>
</TD>
</TR>
```

Figure 10-10 HTML code like this is used to tell browsers how to assemble and present information.

CSS

Cascading Style Sheets (CSS) help make changing elements of Web sites faster and easier. Suppose the developer of a 50-page Web site built entirely in HTML has made the headline font color red, and then, after the site is launched, decides that blue would be better. The developer would then need to open all 50 pages of the site and change the code to tell the browser to change the color from red to blue. That can be tedious and time consuming, and leaves the door open for more error. However, with CSS, the developer would have stored all information such as headline color, font styles, background colors, and any other style decision in a separate document that ends in the .css extension. Each of the 50 HTML documents would then look to the CSS file for information, so when the developer wants to change the headline color from red to blue, one simple change to the CSS document is all it takes for the entire site to be changed.

Java

Developed by Sun Microsystems in the mid-1990s, **Java** is a programming language that allows programmers to develop complex standalone interactive applications (such as games or cross-computer file sharing) for cross-platform usage. This means that PCs, MACs, and UNIX machines can all read the same code with little difference in functionality.

To view a program built in Java, Web users need to have an appropriate plug-in. Most computers and browsers have the plug-in pre-installed; however it can also be downloaded from the Sun Microsystems Web site, if necessary. In addition, developers need a Java runtime environment (which can also be downloaded at Sun's Web site), in order to program in Java.

At one time, Java's popularity on the Web was based on the development of **applets**—small programs, such as stock tickers or interactive weather maps, which can be included in Web sites. More recently, however, Java applets have lost developer support as more have turned to Flash as an easier, lighter, and more effective tool.

JavaScript

Although they share similar names, JavaScript and Java are completely different languages. JavaScript is used as part of **DHTML** (Dynamic HTML—a combination of HTML and other technologies and languages), which creates more dynamic, animated, and interactive Web sites. Designers can use JavaScript to create interactive forms (which help users to correctly fill in each field), enhanced rollovers, image slideshows, animations, and calculation applications (such as mortgage and interest calculators).

Many JavaScripts exist online, and developers can often find code that other developers have written and simply add them to their own Web pages. Along with this accessibility, JavaScript is popular because it is a relatively easy language that produces effective results.

PHP

PHP originally stood for *Personal Home Page tools*, but has come to stand for *PHP: HyperText Preprocessor* as it has grown in functionality. A scripting language specifically created for Web use, PHP allows static Web sites (such as those created with standard HTML) to function more dynamically (interacting with the user rather than simply presenting information to them).

Much of PHP's popularity comes from its ability to interact and communicate with practically any database on the market. PHP is embedded in an HTML page and processed by PHP software that is installed on the host server. The server processes the HTML commands and ignores the PHP language, instead passing those commands on to the PHP software for processing. Because PHP is embedded in HTML, it is read and executed quickly. This is one of the primary reasons why PHP has grown in popularity, along with the fact that it is free. Other reasons include its relative ease of use, security (Web users do not see the PHP code), and the fact that it can run on practically any operating system. In addition, help is easily available through a number of public Web-based user-groups.

Ajax

Surging in popularity, Ajax takes the "clicking" out of the equation. Ajax allows users to pull information from a server without having to click multiple buttons to navigate from one page to another with the reload flicker in between each click.

A developer could make use of Ajax to design a shopping cart that allows users to drag and drop items directly into their shopping cart without having to click the "Add to Cart" button. Shoppers could go through the check-out process without needing to reload each page of the process.

ActionScript

Earlier in this chapter we discussed Flash as a program for creating illustrations and animations for Web sites. While Flash can increase a site's "cool" factor, it is still fairly limited in terms of interactivity. Enter ActionScript, which in June of 2008 appeared on the Tiobe.com top 20 list for the first time. ActionScript is used specifically to increase the functionality of Flash applications.

The code itself is similar to JavaScript, and while it can be a challenge to master, it is not as daunting as many other programming languages. With ActionScript, developers can create multiplayer games, create intuitive navigation and search features, integrate Flash with JavaScript components, and perhaps most importantly, communicate with a database through PHP or another programming language. This means that developers can update and expand upon Flash navigation elements by editing a database or create interactive quizzes and store the results in a database.

INTERVIEW WITH...

MARK SKROBOLA

Mark Skrobola is an entrepreneur with over 20 years of business and programming experience. In 1994, Mark started Pure Performance, a computer consulting firm specializing in Web development and Enterprise Resource Planning (ERP) systems. Pure Performance's clients have included J. Crew, Lucent Technologies, Ernst & Young, LLC, and ADP. Mark's area of expertise is in assisting large corporations with transforming their regional systems into global operations.

JASON: What do you consider to be the most important and effective Web programming languages for today's designers?

MARK: For designers it is important to understand HTML (Hyper-Text Markup Language) and CSS (Cascading Style Sheets) and how these languages are used to build Web site layouts and designs.

HTML is the building block of a Web site. Whether you're building a single page Web site or a highly interactive site, HTML is required to define the content.

CSS is used to separate the style of the site from the content. It defines the style of the HTML elements on your Web site. Simple changes to the CSS will change the look and feel of your site.

JASON: As a programmer, how do you choose which language to use for any given site?

MARK: Most programmers work to become experts in a specific set of Web technologies, so they focus on building sites that fit their competencies. Larger Web site development companies look to have groups of developers for each type of technology required. This gives them the ability to handle nearly all clients' needs.

A common tool set that programmers work in is LAMP (Linux, Apache, MySQL, and PHP). The LAMP solution is free and open source, which keeps cost to the client low. Open source refers to programs whose source code is made available for use or modification; no licensing restrictions exist to limit use. This configuration runs the majority of interactive Web sites in the world today.

There is also a large following for the Microsoft solution (IIS, ASP, .NET). Most sites that run Microsoft's solution are for companies that have a large investment in Microsoft products and have the resources to support these technologies.

Then there is Flash and all the other Adobe solutions that are used to create highly interactive Web sites. If you want a site with animation, video, or high user interaction, Adobe has the solution.

Depending upon the client's needs, a programmer will determine the language to use. When you meet with the client, you should ask a few simple questions. Their answers will help you to determine which technology is best for you to use to provide them with the site that suits their business objectives.

Sample questions include:

* Who will be using this site?
* What type of Internet connection will your users have?
* What is more important response time or style?
* What Web infrastructure do you currently have in place?
* Will the site be highly interactive?

JASON: What are some of the specific challenges you have faced as a programmer, and how have you overcome them?

MARK: Most clients don't understand what is involved in creating a Web site. They want flashy Web sites with animation, video, and large graphics, not knowing the impact on site performance. Some believe a site should cost $100 because they have seen templates for that price on the Web.

Educating the client is the biggest challenge we face. So we need to understand their business. Once we know their business and customer base, we can advise them on what type of site would best meet their needs.

Another challenge is to make sure we advise the client on what they need, not what we think is cool. Developers as well as designers have a knack for adding bells and whistles because they like them, even though they don't provide any value added to the client. So, only give the client what he needs.

JASON: How important do you think it is for programmers to understand Web marketing?

MARK: Creating a Web site that makes a client happy is awesome, but that's only half the battle. Keeping customers is what keeps your business growing. The only way to retain customers is to provide ROI. By knowing Web marketing you are providing your client with a valuable service. Without it, they have a site that no one can find. However, with effective Web marketing, through search engines including Google and Yahoo!, the world will know about your site.

JASON: How has a programmer's job changed with the rise of social media?

MARK: Like everything else in today's Internet world, things are changing rapidly, and you need to stay abreast of these changes. It's important to know about new technologies and solutions before they become mainstream—not after the fact. You should read trade magazines and e-zines daily. There is no sitting back and living on the technology of yesterday. Rather, you should engage and be part of the growth.

JASON: What is the most important thing a programming student should know as he embarks on a Web programming career?

MARK: I believe, in any career, not just Web programming, you need to enjoy what you do. When starting in Web development you should experiment, expand your knowledge, absorb and learn from your peers. I follow many experts and forums on the Web to keep up-to-date and learn new things. Once you have a good base, find a niche, a specialty, and become the expert.

Chapter Summary

- Web development is not all about coding. Depending on the type of site that is being built, designers will make use of a variety of software programs to accomplish certain tasks. Graphic design programs such as Photoshop and Flash help developers create the images that Web site designers use to display products and aesthetically appeal to the audience. Blogging programs give bloggers the ability to easily post their thoughts online. Databases organize files and collect or deliver information. Non-programmers can make use of some software programs to easily create and assemble sites without needing to know any coding.

- Thousands of different programming languages give developers options and opportunities to make their Web pages look and perform the way that the developer, and the client, require. As users' and developers' needs have evolved, certain programs have risen and fallen in popularity. Our review covered just a few of the languages that let programmers create fun online applications, tell the browser how to present a Web page, pull information from a database, or even create a site that doesn't need to refresh between clicks.

Key Terms

animated GIF—An animation made up of a series of individual graphics, which plays like a flip-book.

applets—Small programs written in Java, such as stock tickers or interactive weather maps, which can be included in Web sites.

bitmap—An image made up of pixels.

DHTML—Dynamic HTML. A combination of HTML and other technologies and languages used to create more dynamic and interactive Web sites.

HTML—HTML stands for HyperText Markup Language. HTML is the simple coding that can tell browsers how to present information to those viewing a Web page

Java—A language that allows programmers to develop complex stand-alone interactive applications.

vector graphic—An image created from lines and shapes, which are generated by mathematical formulas.

widgets—Small bits of code that can be added to Web pages to add specific functionality—such as a calendar or mapping device.

WYSIWYG—What You See Is What You Get. A software application or online editor that allows a designer to see what the final Web page will look like as he or she is creating it.

Review Questions

1. Is HTML a programming language?

   a. Yes

   b. No

   c. There is no definitive answer

2. The leading graphic design program is:

   a. SharePoint

   b. Photoshop

   c. Expression Web

   d. Dreamweaver

3. Photoshop is primarily a(n):

   a. Bitmap program

   b. Vector base program

   c. Hybrid between bitmap and vector program

   d. Animation program

4. Which of the following includes a specific programming language to make it come to life?

   a. Photoshop

   b. Flash

   c. Dreamweaver

   d. Blogger

5. Which of the following programs works on a timeline?

   a. Photoshop

   b. Flash

   c. Dreamweaver

   d. Blogger

6. A software application the produces a final output very close to what is developed during editing is called a:

   a. WYSAWYG editor

   b. YSAWAGY editor

   c. YGWISYW editor

   d. WYSIWYG editor

7. Developers using Dreamweaver absolutely must understand basic HTML to get a site built. True or False?

8. Which of the following could be considered a widget on a blog?

   a. A calorie counter

   b. A game of tic-tac-toe

   c. A calendar

   d. All of the above

   e. None of the above

9. The management tool for most blog programs allows users to:

   a. Reformat images

   b. Create animations with vectors

   c. Upload written content

   d. Draw information from a database

10. With ActionScript, developers can draw information directly from a database.

    a. True

    b. False

    c. It depends on the database being used

11. Which database can developers use at no cost?

    a. MySQL

    b. SQL Server

    c. Oracle

    d. Access

12. Which database application is used more often for larger, more complex databases?

    a. MySQL

    b. SQL Server

    c. Oracle

    d. Access

13. LAMP stands for:

    a. Linux, Apache, MySQL, PHP

    b. Linux, Access, MySQL, PHP

    c. Linux, Ajax, MySQL, PHP

    d. Linux, Apple, MySQL, PHP

14. Which of the following is most closely connected to JavaScript?

    a. Java

    b. ActionScript

    c. DHTML

    d. Ajax

15. HTML can tell a browser:

    a. How to present information

    b. How to act in certain situations

c. What information to pull from a database

d. Whether a user has visited any given site before

16. Java was developed by:

a. Oracle

b. MySQL AB

c. Sun Microsystems

d. Microsoft

17. In recent years, Java applets have lost favor to:

a. DHTML

b. PHP

c. Flash

d. Animated GIFs

18. PHP is mostly used for:

a. Creating animations

b. Telling the browser how to present information

c. Creating online forms

d. Communicating with a database

19. Which of the following programs would most likely be used for eliminating the number of page jumps on a Web site?

a. HTML

b. PHP

c. Ajax

d. ActionScript

20. Which of the following is not a characteristic of PHP?

a. It is able to interact and communicate with most databases.

b. It is embedded in an HTML page.

c. It is processed by PHP software that is installed on the host server.

d. It is read and executed slowly.

Projects

1. Is HTML a programming language? In a paper no longer than two pages, give your thoughts on this debate. Make sure you support your opinion with programming-based facts.

2. Suppose you are the developer of a Web site focused on providing news and information and selling products to busy executives. Using one of the many free widget creation sites on the Web, create a widget that the traffic on your site would find useful.

3. In his interview, Mark Skrobola mentions that many programmers work in LAMP—Linux, Apache, MySQL, and PHP. We discussed MySQL and PHP briefly in this chapter. Research and write a page on Linux and a page on Apache. Make sure you include reasons why developers would need to know these.

4. Create a five-page Web site (content does not matter). Use CSS to set the background colors, headline font sizes, and table borders.

5. In a two-page paper, discuss three different database options available to developers and when each should be used.

CHAPTER 11

Driving Traffic: Marketing Strategies

In this chapter you will learn about:

◎ The importance of the Web in an effective marketing campaign and the variety of marketing methods that brands use to drive traffic to their Web sites

◎ Different types of advertising and the major components of an advertising campaign

◎ How public relations helps build market trust through a perceived third-party endorsement

◎ The ways direct marketers bring their messages straight to individuals on a one-to-one basis, especially through highly measurable e-mail blasts

◎ Promotions, especially online contests, and how they can help drive traffic to a site

◎ The power of viral marketing and how word-of-mouth can increase traffic and reduce marketing costs

In the early days of the Web, marketers subscribed to the *Field of Dreams* method of driving traffic to their site, believing that "If you build it, they will come." In other words, most marketers assumed that simply building a site would be enough, and like a lighthouse, its mere existence would beckon audiences and draw them in. Many marketers believed that people from all corners of the world would visit every site published and that the Web would become the great equalizer. They thought the Web would level the playing field to allow small businesses with little or no marketing budgets to gain just as much exposure as their far larger, more richly funded competitors.

Not quite.

Whether these early beliefs were genuine or derived from apprehension (few early marketers really understood how the Web worked or how it could be integrated with other marketing tools), one thing became crystal clear as the Web matured: simply building a site was not going to be enough. As the number of sites grew and users became more savvy and selective, marketers realized that creating a site was only the first step into a complex maze of driving traffic and attracting an audience.

The Individual Segments of Marketing

The word "marketing" is fairly self-descriptive. It refers to the act of bringing a product or service to the market—in other words, enticing prospective audiences to consider and ultimately purchase a specific brand. Given that, any method that helps communicate a message from a brand to its audience fall under the fairly broad marketing umbrella. Standing on a rooftop and shouting "Buy Pepsi!" is technically marketing, as is handing out flyers alerting students to new programming on a university radio station or running a TV commercial. One consumer telling another consumer about a brand they had a good experience with is also marketing.

In today's connected world, the Web has become such a large part of everyday life that consumers rarely make a purchase directly after receiving a marketing message. The Web is often the intermediate step that consumers take before deciding to make a purchase, for reasons that could include any of the following:

- To make sure that a company is legitimate. If the brand is unknown, consumers will typically want to make sure the company behind it is reputable before making a purchase. Consumers are wary of most marketing efforts and often skeptical of messages sent directly from brands—especially lesser known brands—and Web research gives them added comfort.

- To see what other people have to say about their experiences with a brand.

- To get more detailed information about a brand than they might have been able to discern from an advertisement.

The amount of research that consumers conduct on a brand prior to purchase tends to increase along with the price of the product or service being considered. People rarely engage in significant research before buying low-cost items like toothpaste or gum. Less common and more expensive purchases like vacations, furniture, and cars will be researched more heavily. People involved with making a business-to-business purchase are especially likely to do heavy Web research prior to the beginning a relationship and making a purchase from another company.

With this understanding, marketers today typically include the brand's URL with all of their marketing material in order to make it easier for consumers to find the site. These efforts include everything from printing their URL on business cards, letterhead, and invoices, to announcing it on TV, radio, and other forms of advertising.

For the purposes of this book, we'll break marketing efforts into five distinct segments:

- **Advertising**: **Advertising** is marketing in which various media outlets are paid to convey a message from the advertiser to its desired audience. Marketers purchase the ad space or time and control the message that the audience receives. Repetition is an important part of advertising and often necessary in order to penetrate the consumer's consciousness.

- **Public relations**: Public relations concentrates on disseminating a message from a brand to its audience and helping that brand maintain a positive public image. This is often done by establishing trust through the use of third-party, credible sources.

- **Direct marketing**: **Direct marketing** seeks to create a direct link between the brand and its audience, typically on a one-to-one basis, without using mass media (such a television or radio). Direct marketing efforts include telemarketing, direct mail, e-mail blasts, or even more basic efforts, like handing out flyers to passers-by in a crowded mall. Direct marketing almost always has a clear call to action.

- **Promotions**: Technically a subset of advertising, **promotions** are one-time or limited actions such as lowering prices or holding a contest, in an effort to generate more rapid consumer interest.

- **Viral marketing**: Like a cold that moves virally from one person to another, **viral marketing** is a specific form of marketing that aims to use a core audience to spread the word to other consumers, in effect, doing the marketer's work for them.

It can be difficult to understand the subtle differences between each area of marketing, because there is often overlap. Figure 11-1 illustrates each marketing method in the form of a conversation.

Figure 11-1 Marketing methods presented as simple conversation.

We will examine each of these areas in greater detail, although it is important to remember that effective, organized marketing efforts will often use several of the methods in an integrated fashion, thereby gaining greater exposure and increasing the likelihood that their brand and message will be remembered. With any marketing effort, it is important to set clear goals for what the campaign is expected to accomplish. Goals could include increasing revenue, boosting traffic levels for a Web site, launching a new brand, or increasing awareness of an existing brand. It is important to establish quantifiable goals whenever possible. Vague goals, such as "increase Web traffic," don't offer much guidance. How much increase is enough to indicate that the marketing efforts have been a success? Establishing quantifiable goals to reach within a given time frame allows marketers to measure how effective or ineffective their efforts are. For example, if a campaign's purpose is to drive traffic to a Web site, marketers need to determine the realistic traffic rates desired—considering the marketing budget, how much increased traffic will make the financial expenditure worthwhile. The goal should be stated numerically, for instance, "200,000 additional visitors per month over the next six months" or "an increase in traffic of 30 percent over last month's traffic rate." By establishing a numeric goal, marketers can track the success of their efforts and make necessary adjustments. Chapter 13 will examine the importance and methods of measurement in greater detail.

Advertising

Marketers advertise using a variety of media outlets that charge advertising fees based on the amount of space provided or the amount of time allotted to an ad. Advertising rates also take into account the anticipated audience and the quality of the audience that an ad is likely to reach. For example, a company that is selling health food might pay more to advertise in a magazine on jogging that reaches 10,000 people than they would to advertise in a general interest magazine that reaches 50,000. Subscribers to the jogging magazine are more likely to be interested in the message from the health food company.

Marketers typically consider two approaches to advertising: conceptual and direct. **Conceptual marketing** uses a story, a metaphor, an image, a joke, or another indirect means to send a message. The famed Charmin toilet tissue television ad campaign provides a good illustration. In the ads, Mr. Whipple had to beg his customers, "Please don't squeeze the Charmin." Shoppers in the commercial just couldn't help themselves from squeezing the Charmin because it was so soft—a conceptual approach to relaying a message. Alternatively, marketers can take a direct approach—advertising that is a straightforward statement of the facts, such as a TV commercial for a local car dealership, announcing their new line of cars and a special sale on those cars over an upcoming weekend. In comparison, a 30-second TV commercial of text on the screen that says "Charmin bathroom tissue is very soft" is a direct approach. Direct ads get a pointed message out clearly, while conceptual ads serve the dual purpose of selling a product or service and establishing the brand personality at the same time.

There are several different types of advertising that marketers can utilize to convey their message, including:

- **TV and radio commercials**: Commercials usually run in 30-second increments for TV spots and 60-second increments for radio spots. Marketers have the opportunity to make their case in a limited amount of time to a viewing and listening audience.

- **Print advertising**: Marketers advertise their message through ads printed in magazines or newspapers in any number of sizes, including full, half, or quarter page. Figure 11-2 shows a sample print ad as it would appear in a magazine.

Figure 11-2 A print ad for a lacrosse camp, as it would appear in a lacrosse-specific publication.

- **Web banners/display ads**: Many sites—especially media sites and sites that draw heavy traffic—provide space on their pages for marketers to display their advertising message. Banner and display advertising comes in many forms, including ads that run across or along the side of a page, ads that appear in their own boxes within the body of a page, and ads that pop up in front of or behind the browser window. Ads such as these can be static, animated, or created in Flash in such a way that they expand to provide more information when the user rolls over them.

- **Pay-per-click**: Technically, pay-per-click refers to a specific payment method for Web advertising—one in which the marketer only pays for the ad if a Web user clicks on it. Banner ads, for example, could be sold on a pay-per-click basis. However, pay-per-click is most closely associated with the small ads that appear along the side of a search engine such as Google (Google, in fact, with their AdWords program, is by far the largest player in the pay-per-click market). These ads may also appear on Web sites that allow ad feeds from Google or other pay-per-click operators. Figures 11-3 and 11-4 show examples of pay-per-click ads.

Figure 11-3   Google AdWords appear on almost every search page. In this figure, the paid ads appear in the shaded area at the top of the page, and down the column on the right.

Figure 11-4 This site earns additional revenue by featuring Ads by Google, located near the top of the page. The marketers that place the ads know that their ads are being seen by consumers who are interested in a certain topic (in this case, camcorders), and the site is paid a fee every time someone clicks on an ad.

- **Streaming video commercials**: Similar to TV commercials, these commercials play on certain Web sites rather than on television. Run in increments of 15 or 30 seconds, streaming video commercials typically precede content requested by Web users, such as a game or another video clip. As of the writing of this book, YouTube does not inject commercial ads before user-requested video segments, but other popular video-sharing sites like Metacafe and media sites like Fox News do. Typically, these sites will use copy to let the user know that clicking on the commercial (which takes the user to the marketer's Web site) will not interfere with their requested video or game loading to completion.

- **Billboard advertising**: Marketers often promote their messages through large signage in public places such as on the wall of a building, along a highway, or even on the side of a bus. These ads are large and noticeable but also very broad, reaching a fairly general audience.

- **Specialized advertising**: Pretty much any place that has extra space available is a potential advertising medium. A single engine plane flying over a beach, pulling a banner that reads "Eat at Joes" is one avenue that marketers can consider. The wall space in the bathrooms of the men's room at clubs and bars is another, as is the signage space above a taxicab.

Advertising can be very expensive. There are many other marketing options available, many of which are less expensive than advertising. However, there are specific benefits that advertising gives to marketers which makes it an extremely valuable marketing tool:

- **Control over the message**. Marketers can make their case and send their message in any way they want in the space or time provided, and they can craft the language and look and feel of the ads they develop.

- **Control over the audience**. With an uncountable number of media outlets to choose from, marketers can send their ads to the audience demographic that is most suitable for their needs.

- **Brand building**. Advertising can help establish a brand name, increase exposure, and help keep the brand name in the minds of consumers.

Of course, there are drawbacks to this form of marketing as well. Marketers must weigh the pros and cons associated with advertising when considering this tactic for attracting an audience and driving traffic. Some of the drawbacks of advertising include:

- **Expense**. Media outlets may charge outrageous fees for ad space that draws a large or highly targeted audience. *Time* magazine, for example, charges into the six figures for a full page ad, and a 30-second commercial that airs during the Super Bowl costs well over $2,000,000. Smaller ads and local advertising, such as in small town newspapers, may cost far less, but will be seen by fewer people.

- **Hard to measure**. Although there are methods that marketers use to try to measure the effectiveness of an ad, it can be difficult to accurately measure whether an ad has generated enough consumer interest or contributed enough revenue to warrant the expense.

- **Limited consumer visibility**. It's easy for a magazine reader to simply flip the page past an ad, just as it's easy for a TV viewer to change the channel during a commercial. With rare exceptions (such as the Super Bowl, which many people watch specifically to see the commercials), it's unlikely that a single ad will generate tangible results. Ads need to be repeated many times before they sink in and have a lasting effect on consumers.

- **Limited consumer trust**. Consumers understand that an ad contains information that is coming directly from the brand that is trying to sell them something—not exactly an unbiased source. Consumers, therefore, are understandably skeptical, or at least hesitant, to fully trust the information that they see or hear in most ads.

Advertising Campaigns

Although it is not always the case, advertising is often thought of in terms of a **marketing campaign**—an organized effort to promote one or more distinct messages, spread over one or more media outlets, and centered on a conceptualized theme.

A campaign has four primary ingredients: message/purpose, theme/concept, time frame, and media.

Message/Purpose

The message or purpose of a campaign is the idea it is trying to convey. General messages may be used to establish or underscore the brand promise, with the objective of increasing recognition of the brand name. The message behind an advertising campaign could be something like, "We provide the healthiest recipes of any cooking site on the Web" or "You can find the product you are looking for more quickly and easily with our unique online shopping feature." Usually these messages are not articulated as bluntly as these examples; rather, they are communicated more subtly through imagery and copy. Other messages might be less brand-oriented. The message might be intended to highlight one specific idea or promotion, such as "Half-price Wednesdays now through Christmas" or "Refer a friend to our Web site and receive a $50 gift certificate with his or her first purchase."

What the appropriate message is often depends on where the brand is in its lifecycle. The younger and less well known a brand is, the more it needs to be more direct in its messaging. As a brand becomes more universally recognized and trusted, its messaging can be less direct and its approach more conceptual. Table 11-1 provides the general overview for effective messaging at different points within the brand lifecycle.

Stages of the Brand	Appropriate Actions/Messaging
STAGE 1: Brand infancy (Little to no brand recognition)	• Campaign should focus on establishing the brand and building name recognition • Explain the brand promise • Make the Unique Selling Proposition (USP) obvious • Concept should be clear so as not to obscure the message • More marketing dollars should be spent to ensure a Web site is solid, functional, and beneficial to its audience
STAGE 2: Brand growth (Base market established, increasing recognition and expanding growth; trust in the brand is growing)	• Message should reinforce the brand, continuing to seek heightened brand recognition • Benefits of the brand should be highlighted, with the USP taking center stage in most efforts • Concept should be clear, although if research has shown that the company or product already is familiar to the core audience, the concept can begin to show more of the brand personality
STAGE 3: Brand maturity (Significant brand recognition either in a general market or among its desired market demographic; trust is established)	• Message can stray from mere brand recognition to promote particular aspects of the brand, product, or Web site • If research indicates that the USP has been understood and accepted by the market, then the message can promote beneficial aspects of the brand other than the USP • Concept can be largely personality driven, with heavy creative elements • Campaigns should revisit basic brand recognition (as outlined in Stage 1) if direction of the brand changes • Marketing to current customers should be a primary focus

Table 11-1 Stages of the brand, and the appropriate messages to be sending at each stage.

Theme/Concept

A theme is a secondary idea that supports the message, establishes the personality of a brand, and makes the brand more attractive to one audience versus another. Conceptual approaches rely on a theme, which usually evolves over time and is consistent throughout various media.

Popular advertising concepts have included the Geico cavemen (which took viewers from the original ad featuring a caveman feeling insulted by a Geico spokesperson, to an ongoing story in which the Cavemen struggle with everyday issues while continuing to reel from what they feel are degrading Geico advertisements), the MasterCard "Priceless" campaign, the Energizer Bunny campaign (he just kept going, and going . . .), and the popular "Got Milk" campaign, considered by many to be one of the greatest advertising campaigns ever.

Time Frame

Campaigns may continue for a specific, pre-determined period of time, or simply continue until they have run their course. Throughout any extended campaign, however, most marketers will do continuous research and testing to measure its effectiveness. For example, marketers will want to know whether the campaign increased sales or traffic, or whether it increased brand recognition. For longer efforts, marketers will want to know where within the campaign interest piqued, and at what point it fell off. Understanding all of these issues helps marketers to properly adapt the current campaign as well as mold future efforts.

Establishing a time frame is similarly important for proper coordination of the campaign. Each piece within a campaign needs to be planned. A print ad, for example, requires contracting with the desired publication; creating, writing, designing, and proofing the ad; and then submitting it to the publication, often a full month before it will be printed. In all, it can be a two- to three-month process for one print ad. This gets even more complex when there are multiple components to consider. An ad campaign that promotes a special limited time savings by registering on a Web site needs to be coordinated with a message on the site's Home page clearly announcing the same promotion. The site must also be programmed to register people at a lower price, in coordination with the timing of the external campaign.

Media

How the message and concept reach an audience depends on the media that are used in the campaign. Media options are vast, and marketers have to consider each carefully in their effort to reach the largest possible audience with their available budget. The demographics of each media outlet need to be understood. (TV commercials that air on the Lifetime cable network will reach a large concentration of women, while commercials on the Spike network will reach far more men, for example.)

Large-scale campaigns often use a variety of media to reach an audience, and specialized marketers called media planners have the difficult responsibility of managing all of the media outlets in a single campaign.

INTERVIEW WITH...
MICK McCABE, DEUTSCH EXECUTIVE

Deutsch NY has gained legendary status among global agencies, renowned for its creativity and for masterminding some of modern advertising's most memorable campaigns.

Mick McCabe is the Chief Strategy Officer at Deutsch NY, overseeing strategy for clients including IKEA, TYLENOL, Novartis, and Olympus. Prior to that he was Director of Strategic Planning at Leo Burnett, Chicago, where he worked on Nintendo, Morgan Stanley, and Kellogg's.

His work has been recognized with ten Effies, including two Grand Effies by the American Marketing Association for most effective marketing campaign in America, as well as at Cannes International Ad Festival. He has taught at the Michigan and Notre Dame Business Schools, the University of Texas at Austin, and the Miami Ad School. A U.K. native, Mick has resided in the United States for the last 16 years.

JASON: Any worthwhile conversation about marketing should begin with a few words on branding. "Brand" can mean different things to different people. What is your personal philosophy and definition of a brand?

MICK: This is probably the most written-about subject in marketing, and you could fill a small town library on the subject. Here's one definition that gets to the heart of the matter: A brand is the sum of the tangible and intangible, positive and negative associations, beliefs, and impressions people have about a product or service. This is how a customer experiences a brand.

On a more personal level, I think a brand is simply an idea. A living, breathing idea. It represents and takes a point of view that people want to buy, participate in, and share. Some brands are healthy, some are super athletes, and some are in need of exercise. They are not unchanging, immovable, cast in stone, static ideas but dynamic, moving, breathing ideas. When marketers treat them as such, and people view them as such, emotional and financial prosperity happens for all parties. This is how to create a brand.

JASON: Walk me through the creative process of developing marketing campaigns. What are the key things you consider?

MICK: You have to begin with the end in mind. What are the business situations and the conditions we are trying to alter or improve? A clear articulation and diagnosis of why on earth we are conducting the effort is the basis of most effective and successful marketing. A superficial "grow sales" or "get more customers" goal statement won't cut it.

It requires, amongst other things, an analysis of where we will source business from, identifying the consumer behavior and barriers to behavior change, accounting for competitive activity in that category, and looking at the broader cultural forces at work in technology, society, and the economic conditions. All of these, at a bare minimum, should be consulted before the synthesis stage. From there, we articulate a target audience to focus on, the opportunity, a strategy to achieve success, and the execution of the effort from a message and a media standpoint. It is equal parts art and science, and great marketing doesn't force a tough decision between the two.

JASON: How does the brand as you've defined it play a part in the development of a marketing campaign?

MICK: The brand is at the center alongside the target audience. The brand provides a consistent way for marketing to orient itself, for the company to speak, for decisions to be made. It's easy to ask, will this make money? But it takes greater control, patience, and mental acuity to ask if this is something the brand should do or say. New Coke is the classic case study of the wrong question asked and the brand not being at the center of the decision-making process.

JASON: Are there standard goals that you seek to achieve with each marketing effort (such as increased revenue, increased Web traffic, etc.)?

MICK: The goals are specific to the brand. TYLENOL, IKEA, and USAA couldn't be more different. The business models are different; purchase cycles are different; the consumers are different; peer-to-peer recommendations work differently; and their corresponding indicators of success account for this. IKEA may place greater emphasis on same-store sales or foot traffic. USAA might look at likelihood to recommend, customer satisfaction, or consideration to renew a policy. TYLENOL might look at the strength of retail sales year on year at, say, Target or Wal-Mart, or traffic to its site. There's no one silver bullet.

JASON: How has the Internet played a part in the evolution of marketing and brand building?

MICK: It is now almost impossible and probably inadequate to create a marketing campaign without accounting for the role of the Web. It's been statistically proven that the majority of people consult the Web before a purchase, whether that's direct to a brand's Web site, consulting user reviews, third-party information, or through a search engine. And the experience has to account for multiple consumer goals: people's desire for product information, to explore a brand, to communicate with a brand, or to simply transact. A great brand like Amazon enables those experiences to co-exist, simultaneously.

JASON: Would you say that the Web plays an important role in all of your marketing efforts? What role has social media played?

MICK: It's made it intellectually more challenging, but more exciting and surprising at the same time. The control and command way of thinking about brands is dying; telling people what to think, messaging to them, and monologue advertising alone through TV ads has diminishing returns. Social media has made marketers accept (albeit reluctantly) that people control—and ultimately determine—a brand's health (but then again, they always did). One person can tell 10,000 people in one e-mail about their good or bad experience and the next person can be submitting new product ideas.

JASON: From your experiences at Deutsch, what campaign has been your favorite, and why?

MICK: They are all like children, so favorites are hard. And I think the one thing that's true, that agencies don't acknowledge enough, is that effective marketing is done with smart, creative client partners. It isn't just us sitting in a room "brainstorming."

I think uniting a lot of sub-brands under one idea, "Feel Better," and returning a billion-dollar mega brand like TYLENOL to prosperity have been rewarding. The work done on Westin Hotels to articulate a simple, meaningful brand idea around Renewal (with the tagline "This is how it should feel") that the hotel experience, the employees, and the marketing bring to life in meaningful ways. And lastly, the Bronx Zoo has seen tremendous attendance growth from an idea we created for them in 2007.

JASON: What one skill is the most important for future marketers to have to successfully market a brand?

MICK: Good people EQ. (EQ is the emotional intelligence quotient; it describes an ability or skill to perceive, assess, and manage the emotions of one's self, of others, and of groups.) Knowing your audience back to front. I think you can't go wrong if you have an understanding of people. I deliberately said people—not consumers—because I think the latter narrowly and mistakenly casts people as shoppers only. To know and understand people, their motivations, their hopes, their idiosyncrasies, and their relationships with other people is worth its weight in gold. It's not surprising that you've seen a lot of senior executives in the last few years getting out of their ivory towers, trying to get "in touch" with their audience by embarking on high profile, publicized ventures to retail stores or call centers or research, aiming to look their audience in the eye.

Public Relations

Public relations is a set of actions taken to persuade or improve the general public's ideas, opinions, or attitude regarding a particular individual, organization, product, company, or Web site. In many cases, PR is executed through the manufacturing of news. By having a story reported through the media, a company's message becomes news, not advertising. This kind of third-party reporting is seen as unbiased and is often more meaningful to customers than messages delivered through advertising.

A large percentage of the news you read or see is generated through the efforts of PR personnel. When you hear about a new Microsoft product upgrade on CNBC, or an upcoming U2 concert tour discussed on MTV, or even about the mayor of a small town who is planning to run for re-election, chances are that the information began its life as a PR objective.

PR executives use a number of methods to facilitate their work, including:

- Arranging special events, such as parties for product launches or luncheons for media representatives at an industry trade show.

- Writing and distributing **news releases** (summaries of a newsworthy event or information relating to a specific company, product, or brand) to the appropriate media outlets. An example of a press release is shown in Figure 11-5.

- Facilitating interviews between the media and key executives or spokespeople at a given brand.

- Arranging public appearances for key brand executives or spokespeople to present information at a public or industry-specific forum.

- Arranging events or promotions that the media will likely find interesting enough to pick up on and report about. (In 2008, Dr. Pepper made news by announcing that if Guns 'N Roses front man Axl Rose actually released the long-awaited *Chinese Democracy* album before the end of the year, everyone in the U.S. would get a free Dr. Pepper. Silly, but it made news and promoted their brand name.)

- Facilitating and overseeing brand-sponsored research in an effort to help establish the brand as an industry expert.

- Responding to negative events, such as product liability issues and accidents, to help save the brand image in times of peril.

pfs marketwyse   (!)   For Immediate Release

PFS MARKETWYSE PRESIDENT NAMED "WOMEN OF EXCELLENCE" BY NATIONAL ASSOCIATION OF PROFESSIONAL & EXECUTIVE WOMEN

TOTOWA, NJ (March 25, 2008) – PFS Marketwyse, an integrated branding, marketing and communications firm announced that The National Association of Professional & Executive Women (NAPEW) has recognized Deirdre Breakenridge, president, for her commitment to excellence. Her induction into the "Women of Excellence" Registry acknowledges her success and professional achievements. The National Association of Professional and Executive Women is dedicated to providing the networking resources, education, and marketing services necessary to empower professional and executive women nationwide.

Breakenridge's leadership and expertise in business enhances the professional services provided by her organization. In addition to serving as president, Breakenridge also handles hands-on marketing, business development, and financial management for her business. She works diligently to maintain its outstanding reputation and takes pride in the excellent service they provide.

As a leader in her field for 20 years, Breakenridge attributes her personal and professional success to hard work, determination, and perseverance. Her involvement in the public relations industry started in her youth when she realized her love for writing and speaking. Highlights of her career are the books she has authored, *Cyberbranding: Brand Building in the Digital Economy* and *The New PR Toolkit*. Her third book, *PR 2.0* will be released in April.

Breakenridge is affiliated with the Public Relations Society of America, Public Relations Society of New Jersey and the New Jersey Ad Club. She donates charitably to Juvenile Diabetes Research Foundation, Pharmacy Safety Institute and St. Jude Children's Hospital.

About PFS Marketwyse
Headquartered in Totowa, NJ, PFS Marketwyse is an integrated branding, marketing and communication agency that offers "Big Agency" capabilities without the inflated price tag. Whether it's business-to-business or business-to-consumer, PFS Marketwyse offers a unique blend of experience and talent that delivers cost-effective, creative solutions with attitude. For more information on PFS Marketwyse, call Candace Vadnais at 973-812-8883, ext. 430 or visit www.pfsmarketwyse.com.

###

Figure 11-5 A sample news release.

Why PR Works

PR is a behind-the-scenes way to influence public opinion. One of the primary benefits of PR is that in the eyes of the consumer, the marketer's message is coming from neutral sources. Advertising is clearly biased; a print ad for a Web site that says the site offers the widest selection is not necessarily believed by the market. Consumers realize that the claim is likely to be highly exaggerated. Furthermore, empty advertising claims of being "the best" or "the largest" or the "the leading" often fall on deaf ears—consumers have heard it all before.

By comparison, statements that proclaim a site to have the widest selection or a product to be more useful than competing products are far more believable if they come from an impartial news source that reports the information. Most consumers believe that the information they read in newspapers, magazines, media sites, or blogs was deemed newsworthy by a journalist or editor. The praise is therefore seen as unbiased and more believable. This believability factor is one reason that aggressive PR campaigns are a popular marketing method. It should be noted, however, that while the editorial coverage is typically not paid for, marketers often pay PR agencies to ensure that positive news makes its way to the journalists' desk.

Wide exposure is another reason that companies use PR. One event or news release may be covered by any number of media outlets—far more than it might be financially possible to advertise in. For example, a news release announcing the launch of a Web site for music downloads might be picked up by *Billboard*, *Rolling Stone*, *Spin*, *ZDTV*, *Good Morning America*, and other smaller publications and shows. Although some of the mentions may be relatively small (sometimes only a line or two in a "New and Noteworthy" feature), the minimal effort of writing and sending the release has resulted in wide exposure to a large audience. To buy advertising space and time in all the media outlets that carried the story would break the bank. It's because of this that PR is often referred to as "free advertising."

Brands that reach their audience through PR have the added advantage of creating an association between their brand and the brand reputation of the media source. If readers believe *Rolling Stone* is a credible source of music news and a *Rolling Stone* writer discusses a new music site in a positive way, then that reflects positively on the brand.

Because of the potential for wider exposure and increased credibility from third-party sources, PR is a strong weapon in brand building. When integrated with advertising and other marketing tactics, PR has the potential to create a stronger relationship between the Web site and the consumer. This relationship enhancement occurs because the benefits of the site and the value to the user are relayed from a supposedly unbiased source, rather than from the company itself. As discussed earlier, part of the brand is its promise, and building a successful brand involves fulfilling that promise, which translates into trust. Advertising alone can tell the audience what the promise is, but an editorial mention about how that promise is being fulfilled helps build trust.

When reaching out to the media, marketers need to provide the important information that journalists need to make a decision on whether or not to include a story in their reports. With so many brands looking for PR exposure, journalists look for certain information to help them decide what to cover:

- Why is the company or Web site you are promoting better than or different from its competitors? Why is the update so interesting that it needs to be reported? If there is nothing unique about the site, or if the site doesn't do anything that hasn't been done before, why would a publication or program want to report on it?

- What specific trends in the industry does the site address? What services does it perform for its audience?

- Who is the target audience for the site?

- Who are the key executive personnel at the company you are promoting? What are their backgrounds relative to their positions in the company?

How the Web Has Changed PR

Of course, PR can be used to promote a Web site, and, like any other marketing form, it is likely to drive consumers to visit the Web site of a brand they read or hear about and take an interest in. However, the Web has forced traditional PR to evolve as more consumers look to the blogosphere for news and information, and street journalists pass information across the Web through social media tools. Today, PR professionals work to reach their online audiences in different ways, including helping to establish blog sites for their clients and maintaining a scheduled list of appropriate topics for their clients to post blogs about. In addition, PR professionals will seek out already established and well-read blogs that are popular with the brand's target market and look for opportunities to leave comments.

Marketers also have the ability to increase the effectiveness of their PR from within their own site. The **cyber newsroom** is an area of a Web site where a marketer can post current and past news releases so that journalists and broadcasters can research the company.

Often when an editor receives a news release of interest, his or her first action is to visit the company's Web site to gather more information. In addition, the cyber newsroom may also be of interest to non-media visitors, such as potential customers and employees, who want the most recent news about the company.

Cyber newsrooms can vary in complexity. The simplest cyber newsrooms offer little more than a list of news release headlines that act as hyperlinks to the full news release. Other cyber newsrooms can be more interactive, providing more information about a company, bios of its key executives, links to high-resolution images and logos, or even videos of current news releases. All of these resources make the editor's job far easier—a definite plus for the company that is seeking coverage.

Figure 11-6 shows a cyber newsroom for JVC Professional Products, which highlights the company's most recent releases. Figures 11-7 and 11-8 shows other areas of the newsroom, where members of the media can download high resolution logos and images, respectively.

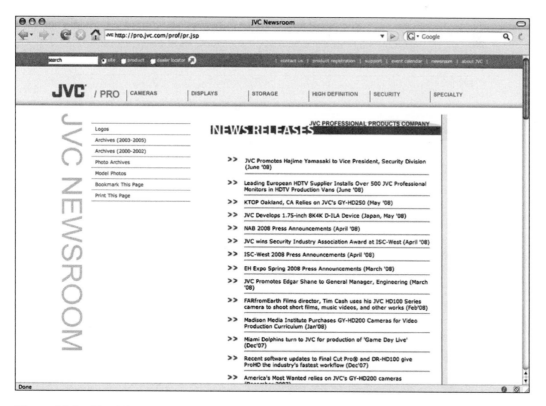

Figure 11-6 The JVC cyber news room gives the media (and prospective clients) a chance to see the most updated information about the company.

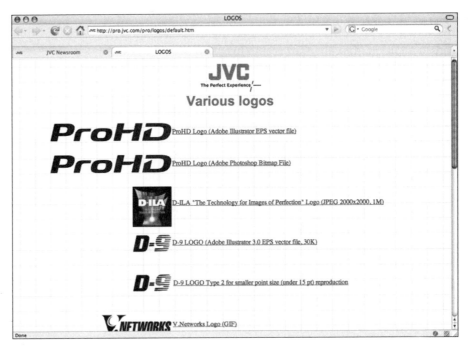

Figure 11-7 To help journalists and entice them to further report about the brand, JVC's cyber news room provides high-resolution logos for downloading.

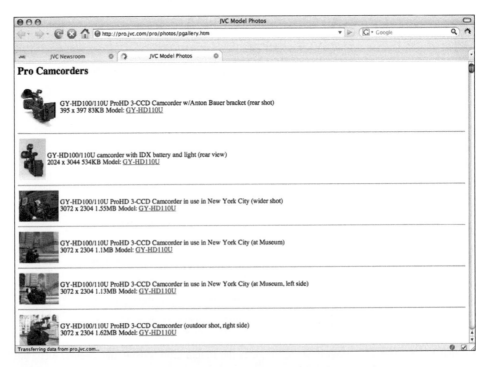

Figure 11-8 Similarly, JVC also provides access to high-resolution images of its products.

Along with helping to promote updated news to the media, cyber newsrooms often feed recent headlines to the site's Home page. This allows visitors to see the most recent news as soon as they come to the site, so that even if they never make it to the cyber newsroom, they will have an idea of the company's latest developments. This also allows the Home page of a site to change on a regular basis, alerting visitors to the fact that there is new information within the site.

INTERVIEW WITH...
DEIRDRE BREAKENRIDGE

Deirdre Breakenridge is the President and Director of Communications for PFS Marketwyse. A veteran in the PR industry, Deirdre leads a creative team of PR and marketing executives strategizing to gain brand awareness for their clients through creative and strategic public relations campaigns. She counsels senior level executives at companies including RCN Metro Optical Networks, Quality Technology Services, JVC, Michael C. Fina, and Kraft.

Deirdre is an adjunct professor at Fairleigh Dickinson University in Madison, New Jersey where she teaches courses on Public Relations and Interactive Marketing for the Global Business Management program.

After having worked with Deirdre for nearly ten years, I can attest to her surpassing ingenuity, knowledge, and communications talent. I consider it a privilege to have her be part of this book.

JASON: Let's start with the basics. Define "PR" for me. How does it differ from "advertising?"

DEIRDRE: The classic definition of public relations is communicating to the public through a credible third-party endorsement to create awareness or to change an opinion or behavior. However, today, public relations has changed tremendously with the technological advancements of Web 2.0 applications. PR 2.0 is a different approach to public relations, in which professionals use social media tools to communicate to new influencers, including bloggers and now directly to their customers. Of course, traditional PR is not going away. On the contrary, PR 2.0 only adds to a brand's arsenal of best public relations practices to help with meaningful conversations and direct communication that leads to strong relationships with stakeholders. I like to think that PR 1.0 plus PR 2.0 all equal great PR.

The difference between PR and advertising is very distinct. Although both fall under the marketing umbrella, advertising is, quite simply, paid-for space. So whether you are looking to place an ad in a magazine, on a print billboard, a mobile advertisement, or on a Web banner, the ad is designed by the brand and the messages are crafted carefully and with creative language to evoke a specific action or behavior from the consumer. However, in PR, you cannot control the message. Because PR works through influencers, whether it's the traditional journalist or a blogger, you only have the ability to communicate with precision and accuracy and intended meaning. However, the perception of the influencer can often shape your message by the time it hits the market. Nonetheless, PR is extremely valuable as it's far more credible to be endorsed by another party. Even though advertising supports and maintains the messages in a PR campaign, many realize that advertising comes directly from the brand.

JASON: How has public relations changed given the Web 2.0 environment?

DEIRDRE: The PR industry has seen tremendous change with the ability to use social media tools to communicate. The Web 2.0 environment alters the way brands communicate. They can use PR to build relationships with groups of people in Web communities that want to engage and have meaningful conversations—the people that need to hear about your brand. This dialog leads to stronger relationships and ultimately the purchase of the brand's products and services. The key to the 2.0 environment is that customers want to hear the voice behind the brand, and brands can no longer hide behind their monikers. Through PR and social media tools, brands are able to tell a more humanized story. So, for example, it's the ability of an executive to blog and to speak directly to a customer. He or she can be engaged in conversations in a community not only to hear what customers are saying but also what customers say to one another. It's a huge focus panel in your backyard and the information is invaluable. The ability to hear the dialog and then use the information to build better products or more attractive and useful services is powerful research.

JASON: Can PR significantly increase traffic to a Web site?

DEIRDRE: Yes, PR along with other Web marketing efforts increases traffic to a Web site. Brands want to drive traffic to their sites so they can track responses to campaigns and analyze the success of an initiative. It's as simple as sending out a news release over the news wire or using a social media release. [Editor note: A social media release is a news release prepared for distribution through social media outlets, with related tools such as links to online photo libraries, blogs, etc.] A brand's Web site is the place for stakeholders to gather additional information. As a matter of fact, companies set up very elaborate interactive newsrooms so that they can track which influencers are interested in viewing more details about their company, executives, and products/services. In my book, *PR 2.0*, I interviewed Ibrey Woodall, Director of Marketing at TEKgroup International. Her organization specializes in setting up interactive newsrooms that are so advanced that brands are able to offer customers, analysts, the media, and other influencers tools to gather information and file articles, links, etc. in a newsroom "brief case" in an effort to build their stories or share the information with other parties. PR, through news releases, blogging, social networking, events, emarketing, etc., can offer information linking to a company's newsroom. It's imperative to have the right materials available for the groups who want to find out more information regarding a product launch, promotion, or event.

JASON: Are there any PR tools that Web developers should consider as they design and develop their sites?

DEIRDRE: Web developers should keep in mind that Web sites should be designed and programmed to promote interaction and one-to-one conversations with stakeholders. Therefore, Web 2.0 applications such as RSS feeds on a Web site help visitors to quickly opt into a newsfeed, so they can receive the latest news from the brand directly and conveniently. Also, there should be interactive areas including blogs so that the brand can interact directly with customers and engage in conversations whether they are product related, or perhaps deal with issues or concerns regarding their industry. Blogs give the company a human voice and allow company executives to take a stand on issues that are pressing.

Other areas of the Web site should include streaming video and podcasts. It's very important to hear and see the people behind the company. This gives the brand personality and lets you know who you are doing business with. Audio and video are a great way to meet the players behind the scenes. In addition, today podcasts and streaming video are viral and can be shared among groups of people advancing the reach of the brand in Web communities.

JASON: Is traditional PR dead, replaced by PR 2.0, or can new media and traditional methods co-exist?

DEIRDRE: No, I wouldn't say that traditional PR is dead. After all, PR is communicating to the public and the public isn't always online. For example, we still gather information through newspapers, magazines, trade journals. Public relations professionals will continue to use grass roots PR and keep enhancing relationships through events and face-to-face interaction. PR 2.0 only enhances what the public relations industry has to offer to brands today. PR 2.0 approaches public relations so that brands can speak intelligently in Web communities. Through PR 2.0 they are able to understand the culture of different groups online rather than spam everyone in a community. If you take traditional PR and PR 2.0, you have the greatest path toward successful communication. PR builds relationships, and this will continue to happen, offline and online as well. With the blending of traditional and this new media PR, we are truly reinventing an industry to show value in every type of communication. No longer do we communicate to the masses, and the PR professionals who were once known for the hype and spin of past years can no longer exist. People today demand meaningful information to make informed decisions; today's PR—both traditional and new media—is able to deliver that information and create incredible loyalty towards brands.

JASON: Do you have a favorite PR campaign that you've spearheaded? What were the results?

DEIRDRE: I have a favorite campaign, but not because it is a ground breaking, revolutionary product launch. Rather, the reason why it's my favorite campaign is because the company has gained a tremendous amount of exposure and the executives, who are the third generation of a family business, are so thrilled with the amount of media attention that they are receiving. Our work with Michael C. Fina, a leader in the global employee recognition industry, has resulted in an unprecedented amount of PR coverage for the organization. Prior to our PR program, Michael C. Fina had only a handful of relationships with the media. We provided them with a strategic thought leadership program that has positioned them as experts in the recognition industry, and they've captured the attention of every trade magazine that covers rewards and recognition. Because of the tremendous amount of exposure and results, we've moved the campaign to the national level, focusing on print and radio. We're also venturing into PR 2.0, which is very exciting for the company. I think the most rewarding campaigns are the ones that create great results and make the executives of the company happy that they chose PR as a means to communicate.

Direct Marketing

Direct marketing brings the message directly to the consumer with little or no outside media intervention. Telemarketing is perhaps one of the most well known—and almost universally scorned—examples of direct marketing. Telemarketing involves calling consumers one at a time in an effort to get them to make a purchase. People standing on a street corner, handing out flyers about local sales are engaging in direct marketing, as are restaurant owners who stand outside their door to try to entice passers-by to come inside.

Direct mail is a commonly used form of direct marketing, in which marketers develop or purchase a list of names and addresses and send out marketing messages to the people on the list through the mail. These messages can take the form of postcards, letters, or even large packages with items inside for the recipient to keep as a way of remembering the brand. The effectiveness of a direct mail campaign will vary based on the type of piece sent—smaller pieces of mail, such as postcards, are more likely to get lost in the shuffle and discarded without being seen. Larger packages are far more likely to be opened, viewed, and remembered. The effectiveness of a direct mail campaign is especially important in a well-organized campaign where the direct mail effort is soon followed up by a sales person pitching the product or service to the recipient over the phone. However, the larger and more complex a mailing is, the more expensive it can be to execute. To mail an item that costs $3, for example, may cost the marketer well over $10 when other costs including the printing of accompanying material, packaging, fulfillment/assembly, addressing, and postage are factored in.

Far less expensive is a newer form of direct mail, particularly useful in driving traffic to a Web site—e-mail blast campaigns. With these campaigns, marketers send their messages to potential consumers through e-mail, putting what they need to say right in the recipient's inbox. There are a number of reasons why more marketers are finding direct marketing through e-mail to be a highly beneficial and effective means of reaching their audience:

- Most e-mail programs such as Microsoft Outlook, Outlook Express, Eudora, Yahoo, and others can read HTML code, giving marketers the freedom and flexibility to design their e-mail in such a way as to catch the recipient's attention (Figure 11-9 provides an example of an HTML e-mail blast).

- E-mail blasts are far less expensive to execute than traditional mail campaigns.

- E-mail campaigns are highly measurable, as discussed in more detail later in this section.

- Links within the blast can drive recipients to a specific page of the marketer's Web site.

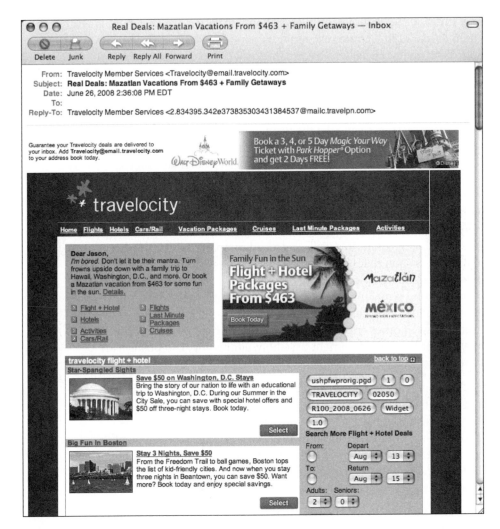

Figure 11-9   An e-mail blast from Travelocity brings flight deals right to the consumer.

As with any other medium, e-mail campaigns do have certain draw-backs that need to be considered. Chief among these is the possibility of losing an audience—not just their attention, but in extreme cases, their trust. Other drawbacks include:

- The potential for the marketing to be seen as spam. Although ide-ally all legitimate e-mail campaigns would market only to recipi-ents on an **opt-in list** (recipients who have pre-agreed to receive e-mail solicitations), this is often not the case. While there is still typically a clear distinction between legitimate companies sending e-mail blasts and spam e-mail offering fake prescription drugs and replica watches, it is possible for potential clients to look unfavor-ably upon any brand that sends unwanted e-mail ads.

- Current e-mail lists can be difficult to assemble, and as of the writing of this book, quality e-mail list brokers are few and far between.

To execute an e-mail blast, marketers need to use special software applications, or third-party online vendors. There are many such vendors in the marketplace, each with different options, functionalities, and pricing structures. Nearly all worthwhile e-mail blast facilitators provide certain basic functionality (all the figures for this section are from a popular e-mail blast facilitation site called iContact):

- The ability for users to upload and manage e-mail lists.

- E-mail creation through a WYSIWYG editor and/or HTML editor (Figure 11-10 shows the page that allows the e-mail to be assembled).

- The ability for the marketer to schedule their blasts in advance or send them out immediately after creation (see Figure 11-11).

- A tracking mechanism that shows the marketer how successful their blast has been. As shown in Figure 11-12, e-mail blasts can be tracked in real time to show the **open rate** (the percentage of recipients who have opened an e-mail) and the **click-thru rate** (the percentage of recipients who have clicked on one of the links within the e-mail and visited the Web site). Marketers can also capture the names of the people who have opened and clicked through and the **bounce rate** (the percentage of e-mails that never made it to the recipient, either due to firewall systems of because the address is not valid). In addition, marketers will be alerted to which, if any, recipients have opted out (requested to no longer receive e-mail blasts from that marketer), or have forwarded the blast on to someone else.

Figure 11-10 The page within iContact that allows the e-mail blast to be assembled. Notice the WYSIWYG editor in the center.

Figure 11-11 Before a blast gets sent, the marketer must certify that people on the e-mail list have granted permission to be sent e-mail blasts. The marketer can then send the blast immediately or schedule it for later execution.

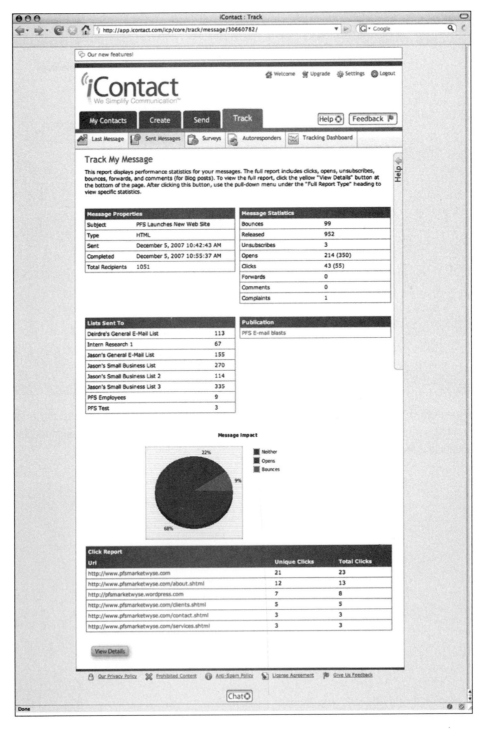

Figure 11-12 Once sent, e-mail blasts facilitators give marketers the ability to track all vital statistics relating to their effort.

Promotions

Promotions are typically used to increase short-term exposure and entice consumers to take immediate action. Promotions can be especially effective on the Web, where e-commerce stores can offer limited-time discounts, free shipping, or free items with purchases over a certain amount as a means of increasing traffic and sales. Often, promotions such as these may be run at a financial loss to the site. Sites sometimes make the choice to temporarily reduce the price of certain products to such a point that money is lost on every sale. This is done in the hopes that by introducing new customers to the Web site, those customers will evolve into dedicated, regular clients.

Contests are also an effective means of promoting a site, as Web users can enter quickly and return to see results. This has been particularly true with the popularization of social media. Using various social media tools, marketers have been able to entice consumers not only to enter a contest, but to participate in a more complete way—by taking their own action plus observing and commenting on the actions of others. Online contests can include concepts such as:

- Supplying only name and contact information

- Achieving the highest score on an online video game

- Writing a short essay to explain why you should win (usually around a specific topic)

- Posting a still picture or video within certain creative guidelines stated by the marketer

Figure 11-13 shows an online video contest promoted by the chocolate milk brand Nesquik. This contest provides a $10,000 prize to the entrant that posts the best video showing "where Nesquik takes you." The contest not only reaches the contest participants, enticing them to interact with the brand, but it reaches non-participants, who visit the site to watch the videos that are posted. In some cases, these casual viewers may come to the site on their own—in other cases, they may be the friends and relatives of contest entrants, who are now helping Nesquik market themselves by passing the word about the site and the brand on to other people. The contest further engages consumers by allowing them to comment and rate each video. After Nesquik judges narrow the finalists down to the top ten, consumers can then help the brand select the ultimate winner (based on ratings and reviews).

393

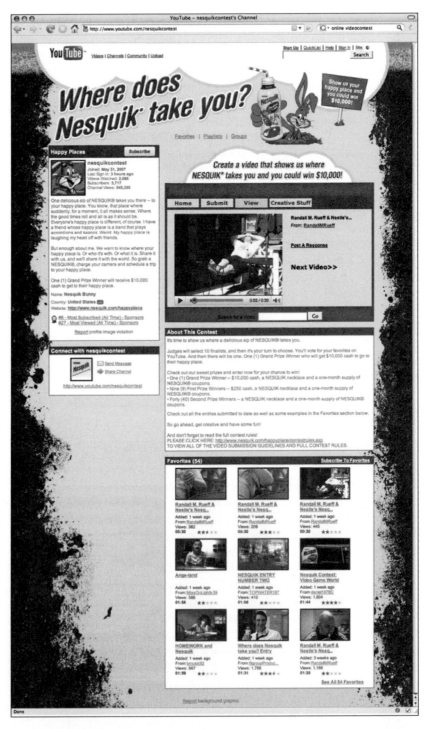

Figure 11-13 This promotion from Nesquik allows consumers to enter a contest by uploading videos. Other viewers can then watch and rate each video, becoming more engaged in the brand while influencing the voting.

The purpose of any promotion is to increase brand visibility and recognition as well as increase sales. As with any site, however, promotions also need to be marketed, whether through advertising, public relations, or other means.

Viral Campaigns

With e-mail making communication between friends, family, and associates as quick and easy as pushing the Forward button, viral campaigns have become a hot topic in marketing circles. Viral campaigns are attractive due to their potential for high visibility rates and their relatively low cost (when compared to other forms of mass media advertising).

In short, a viral campaign is one in which the marketer deliberately creates aspects of the campaign in such a way that the audience will be compelled to pass the message on to others. This is typically done in one of two ways:

- The marketer can offer an incentive to a consumer to pass a message on to others. Often called a "refer-a-friend" program, marketers who use this tactic will offer existing customers anything from a free t-shirt to reduced rates to cash if they refer a someone to a site who then signs on and becomes a paying customer. The consumer who passes the word along is happy, because they stand to profit from passing on the name of a brand to which they already feel connected. The person who receives the information is comfortable that the recommendation of the brand is coming from a trusted, reliable source and not directly from the brand itself. The brand is happy because they have set the referral price at a reasonable cost per each new client acquisition.

- The marketer will try to create a marketing piece that can capture someone's attention—so much so that they feel compelled to pass it on if for no other reason than to show it to other people. Typically, these tend to be videos that are either heavily comedic, extraordinarily shocking, or both.

According to Jupiter Research, over 60% of all Internet users have passed along an e-mail to a friend or colleague that they found interesting or funny. However, with new content infiltrating the Web every day, marketers are finding it more difficult to capture consumers' attention and are increasingly pressed to push the envelope to attract attention.

While the term "viral campaign" refers to any portion of a campaign that gets passed from one person to another, savvy marketers seek to create campaigns that are more complex than single, outrageous videos.

Truly effective campaigns that can maintain audience interest for longer periods of time need to tie back to a single creative concept that helps to reinforce the brand message. In 2004, a campaign considered by many to be one of the greatest examples of a successful viral effort was launched. Only 20 people were initially told about the SubservientChicken.com Web site when it first launched—friends of people at the ad agency that created it. It wasn't long before the site had registered 20 million people according to the Wall Street Journal. The site, shown in Figure 11-14, shows a man in a chicken suit standing in a rather unassuming living room. Visitors who log on can tell the chicken what to do. A command of "Do three pushups" results in the chicken doing three pushups. Although otherwise pointless, people found the site fascinating, spending an average of six minutes with each visit. Throughout the campaign, rumors swirled as people tried to find out who was behind the site (although the site today has a brand logo clearly visible, it was not as obvious when the site first launched). Ultimately, it was revealed, to much publicity, that the site was part of Burger King's marketing effort, underscoring its long held "Have it your way" brand promise.

Figure 11-14 The SubservientChicken.com site was a viral effort by Burger King that underscored their brand promise "Have it your way" by allowing users to command a man in a chicken suit to do various things.

Viral campaigns can be less expensive than mass-media centered efforts and may be seen by far more people, but they can also be uncontrollable and unpredictable. It is practically impossible to target any one demographic with a viral campaign, and there is also no guarantee that any viral effort is going to work. Simply igniting the viral flame will not necessarily produce a raging fire.

Chapter Summary

- Having a Web site simply isn't enough. In order to get visitors to the site, marketers need to take steps to generate interest and awareness among their target demographic. To do so, marketers can make use of a number of efforts that fall under the "marketing" umbrella.

- Advertising is an effective means of reaching an audience by purchasing space or time with a media outlet in an effort to reach consumers. While expensive and sometimes viewed with skepticism, advertising gives the marketer more control over the space and time that they purchase. An advertising campaign has four primary ingredients: message/purpose, theme/concept, time frame, and media.

- Public relations helps brands maintain a positive public image by sending messages to its audience indirectly, by relaying them through journalists and broadcasters, which are seen as more unbiased sources of information.

- Direct marketing takes any form in which the marketer speaks directly to the consumer with little to no media involvement. While telemarketing and direct mail have long been viable options, e-mail blast campaigns are increasing in popularity due to their lower cost and ability to track user interaction.

- Promotions, such as contests and limited-time sales, help brands increase traffic and revenue on a more short-term immediate basis.

- Viral marketing has the potential to help brands reach more people for a lower cost by enticing the market to spread the word to others.

Key Terms

advertising—Marketing in which various media outlets are paid to convey a message from the advertiser to its desired audience.

bounce rate—The percentage of e-mails in an e-mail blast effort that never made it to the recipient, either due to firewall systems or because the address is no longer valid.

click-thru rate—The percentage of e-mail blast recipients who have clicked on one of the links within an e-mail and visited the Web site

conceptual marketing—Marketing that uses a story, a metaphor, an image, a joke, or another indirect means to send a message.

cyber newsroom—An area of a Web site where a marketer can post current and past news releases so that journalists and broadcasters can research the company.

direct marketing—Creating a direct link between the brand and its audience without using any specific media as an intermediary.

marketing campaigns—An organized effort to promote one or more distinct messages, spread over one or more media outlets, and centered on a conceptualized theme.

news release—A summary of a newsworthy event or information relating to a specific company, product, or brand that is released to the media.

open rate—The percentage of e-mail blast recipients who have opened an e-mail.

opt-in list—Recipients who have pre-agreed to receive e-mail solicitations.

promotions—One-time or limited actions taken on the part of the brand, such as lowering prices or holding a contest, in an effort to generate more rapid consumer interest.

viral marketing—A specific form of marketing that aims to use a core audience to spread the word to other consumers, in effect doing the marketer's work for them.

Review Questions

1. Direct marketing is typically considered more effective than advertising.

    a. Always true

    b. Always false—it depend on the situation, need and market

    c. Generally true, but not for driving traffic to the Web

    d. Generally true, but only for driving traffic to the Web

2. After seeing a marketing message that they are interested in, what is the next step consumers typically take?

   a. Make a phone call

   b. Send an e-mail requesting more information

   c. Visit the brand's Web site

   d. Make a purchase

3. Which of the following establishes greater trust in a brand?

   a. Advertising

   b. Public relations

   c. Direct marketing

   d. Viral marketing

4. Which of the following relies on word-of-mouth to get the message to a larger audience?

   a. Advertising

   b. Public relations

   c. Promotions

   d. Viral marketing

5. Which of the following typically requires more repetition in order to be effective?

   a. Advertising

   b. Direct marketing

   c. Promotions

   d. Viral marketing

6. Which of the following is most likely to be measured in length of time or amount or space?

   a. Advertising

   b. Public relations

   c. Direct marketing

   d. Promotions

7.   Which of the following would be an example of a poorly established marketing goal?

a.   An increase in site traffic of 25%

b.   75,000 new site users

c.   Really high site traffic

d.   Inventory clearance of a specified product

8.   Which of the following is not an example of advertising?

a.   Web banners

b.   Blogs

c.   TV commercials

d.   Roadside billboards

9.   Which of the following is a reason why marketers would choose mass media advertising?

a.   It's relatively inexpensive.

b.   It instills greater trust in the audience.

c.   It give marketers control over the message.

d.   It can be fairly simple to measure.

10.   During which stage of a brand's life cycle is it most safe to run highly conceptual advertising?

a.   Stage 1

b.   Stage 2

c.   Stage 3

d.   Stage 4

11.   Throughout an advertising campaign, marketers are constantly:

a.   Researching and testing to measure campaign effectiveness

b.   Blogging about the campaign

c.   Posting news releases in the brand's cyber newsroom

d.   Sitting back and hoping for the best

12. According to Mick McCabe, goals in marketing are:

    a. Specific to the brand

    b. Usually impossible to reach

    c. Nearly impossible to set

    d. Overrated and not always necessary

13. Marketing messages delivered through public relations efforts are typically seen as a more trustworthy way of marketing because:

    a. PR costs more than advertising

    b. PR costs less than advertising

    c. PR relates the message through third-party, supposedly unbiased sources

    d. This is a false statement—messages delivered through public relations efforts are not seen as more trustworthy

14. According to Deirdre Breakenridge, with the coming of social media, traditional public relations is considered dead. True or False?

15. Which of the following is least likely to be considered a promotion?

    a. Advertising a new line of skis at a local ski store

    b. Offering free shipping for all online orders over $50

    c. Creating an online contest where entrants write an essay about why they like a particular brand

    d. Offering 10% off all online orders until Thanksgiving

16. Web contest promotions are beneficial to the brand because:

    a. They can engage the consumer to interact more closely with the brand

    b. They can easily gain consumer trust

    c. They tend to last for years

    d. None of the above

17. An e-mail blast campaign can measure which of the following?

    a. Opt outs

    b. Click-thru rates

    c. Open rates

    d. All of the above

    e. None of the above

18. E-mail blasts can be dressed up with HTML code, which most e-mail programs can read. True or False?

19. In a refer-a-friend type program, which party typically ends up being unhappy?

    a. The brand

    b. The established customer

    c. The referred friend

    d. All of the above

    e. None of the above

20. A negative aspect of viral marketing is that:

    a. It can get wildly expensive.

    b. There is no real control over it once it's out in the cyber world.

    c. Not many people tend to pass e-mails on to others.

    d. There are no negatives to viral marketing.

Projects

1. Choose any Web site that you like. Assume that they have asked you to help market them. Regardless of budget, which marketing methods do you think would be most effective in reaching the site's target audience? In a three-page paper, detail your marketing plan. Make sure you provide sound rationale for your choices, including the site's perceived market demographic.

2. Assume that as part of the campaign in Project #1, the Web site you have selected asks you to include an e-mail blast.

Using the free trial feature on iContact, and your own e-mail address, design, program, and execute an e-mail blast on their behalf.

3. Find a sample of a print ad, banner ad, and public relations for any established company. In a two-page paper, explain how each of these works differently in terms of messaging. How do their messages relate back to their Web site? Is there any one element that ties all of the pieces together?

4. In a two-page paper, explain why public relations builds more trust in consumers than advertising. Provide some real examples.

5. Find a contest online that requires you to post an essay, picture, or video to win. In a one-page paper, describe your efforts. Did it make you engage more closely with the brand? Do you feel you are more aware of the brand after your efforts?

CHAPTER 12

Capturing and Keeping an Audience

In this chapter you will learn about:

◎ Why it is so important to keep visitors coming back to a site

◎ The methods that Web sites utilize to increase customer retention

Imagine you own a restaurant. You take out loans with numerous banks and max out your credit cards in order to rent a building, construct a state-of-the-art kitchen, and get the place up and running. It takes a tremendous amount of work. You carefully select everything from the silverware and plate designs to the furniture and restaurant decor. You make connections with all of the necessary food vendors and establish a line of credit with them. Night after night you practically live in the kitchen, perfecting recipes and setting the menu. You issue a press release to the local paper, which announces the impending opening prominently. You advertise. In the days before opening night, you invite friends and family to a pre-opening party, where they rave about your food, pat you on the back, and wish you the best of luck. And then they spread the word to others.

Finally, opening night comes. It's been a lot of work, and a lot of money, but you did it. And from the looks of things—you are bound to be a huge success! The place is packed to capacity, and reservations have the place booked solid for a month out. Your investment of time and money is going to pay off after all.

Or is it? As the first month winds down, it's no longer that difficult to make a reservation. In fact, even weekends, when you should be your busiest, seem to have slowed. Slowly, you start to realize that you haven't seen many of the same faces twice—there just don't seem to be a lot of repeat customers. As the second month winds down and the restaurant is virtually empty, you come to the frightening conclusion: the business simply cannot survive without repeat customers.

Keeping Visitors Interested, Engaged, and Coming Back

The preceding analogy underscores one of the primary reasons why many Web sites struggle to survive: while external marketing can bring new people to a site, bringing those visitors back to the site is the lifeline that will determine how successful a site becomes—and how expensive the site is to run. According to many studies, the cost of acquiring new customers can be six to eight times the cost of keeping an existing customer. In other words, once a Web user has visited the site, it is far less expensive to encourage that visitor to come back than it is to get new users to visit. This can be a make-or-break statistic for marketers, as the costs associated with providing a continual supply of new customers can be an overwhelming expense that reduces or even eliminates profits.

As competition for viewers increases, marketers are increasingly cognizant of their **churn rate**, which refers to the proportion of customers that discontinue a service or their association with a brand during a given time period. According to a 2008 report by the Chief Marketing Officer (CMO) Counsel, nearly a third of all companies have a churn rate over 10%—an alarmingly high number that can potentially destabilize a brand and negatively impact it through:

● Revenue loss

● Reduced profitability

● Higher marketing costs for customer re-acquisition[1]

Of course, the restaurant analogy detailed earlier in this chapter is not exactly an apples-to-apples comparison. The customers in the restaurant example made the decision to spend money there as soon as they walked through the door. Many visitors coming to an e-commerce site or a standard B2B site may come to browse, not necessarily to shop and spend money. So, is there any value in a site visitor who returns multiple times if he or she is not generating revenue for the site? The answer, of course, is yes. Repeat site visits will help to build consumer confidence and trust and will ultimately lead to increased sales. This is true both for B2B sites, which usually require human contact in order to initiate a sale, and for B2C e-commerce sites. Marketers for these types of sites, in tracking visitor usage (discussed in greater detail in Chapter 13), often concentrate on two key measurements as an average of all users over time:

● **Days to purchase**: The number of days that pass from the day a user first comes to the site to when he or she finally makes a purchase.

● **Visits to purchase**: The number of visits a user makes to a site before he or she makes a purchase.

Every site will rely on different measurements depending on the target market and the products being sold. A customer making a decision to purchase a DVD player will likely require fewer site visits than a customer looking to buy a car. Younger consumers, who are more comfortable with online shopping, are likely to require fewer site visits than older consumers, who approach online shopping with more hesitancy.

Once an initial purchase has been made, future site visits will encourage future sales, with little outside marketing expense on the part of the marketer. Assume, for example, that the average cost per new customer acquisition by an online bookstore is $12. In other words, the total marketing dollars spent divided by the number of new customers that marketing has yielded, equals $12 per customer. Let's further suppose that the average gross sale on the site is $20 per customer, with a net profit (after cost of goods sold, inventory expense and shipping) of $7. In this scenario, the site will have suffered a loss of $5 for every new customer. However, the steps needed to get those users to return again in the future are far less costly—let's say an average of $2 per customer. Now, every future sale by a returning visitor (at an average profit of $7) yields a net gain of $5. As paying customers come back regularly, marketers are able to achieve larger profits from continued sales.

INTERVIEW WITH...

JULIE MATHEWS, INTERNET MARKETING MANAGER, HERSHEY'S

Hershey's has over 40 different brands, including Reese's, Kisses, and KitKat. Each of those brands needs to utilize the Web differently, and brand managers throughout the company turn to Julie Mathews to help them develop online marketing strategies. Over the years, Julie has helped grow a small Internet marketing department into a centralized command center responsible for all of Hershey's Internet efforts in the United States and around the world.

Julie is extremely knowledgeable and passionate about the subject of Internet marketing, and I was very happy to have the opportunity to sit down with her to discuss her work.

JASON: Hershey's is made up of a number of different brands, each with its own marketing strategy. What's the initial protocol when a brand wants to do something on the Web?

JULIE: Practically every brand manager would like to have some sort of Web presence or online strategy to enhance their marketing efforts. When they do, they contact me to discuss it—often times they won't know exactly what they want, just that they need some type of Web presence. The first thing I do is sit down with them and determine what their offline strategy is so that we can determine what the online strategy should be, to complement offline programs and drive sales or increase brand exposure. Then we'll determine which outside vender should manage the project, and set up and design the Web site, based on our needs compared to the vendors' capabilities.

JASON: How important do you think it is for Web programmers to understand marketing and what the marketers are trying to accomplish?

408

JULIE: It's crucial. I believe that it's very important for the Web design company to understand where the brand is coming from. They should be able to understand what that brand is trying to achieve with that particular product. For example, the project managers will likely take different actions and recommend different options if they understand that at this point, that we want to get the word out about a new product to a target audience of females age 18 to 34. I need the vendor then to be thinking for us—that if our audience is 18 to 34, and female, they're probably on MySpace or they're on iVillage—and present to us different ways to tailor any new site to meet our needs. A vendor is less desirable if their solutions are always the same, and they just keep recommending Web sites with downloadable screensavers and wallpapers, and all the basic things a site usually comes with.

JASON: What is it about Web marketing that excites you?

JULIE: I think the thing about it that excites me the most is that it's a growing field. I mean, we have mothers that are switching from TV to computer. They are on the Internet. The TV may be on, but they're not watching it. They're on the computer. The changes that are happening are only the beginning.

As far as Internet marketing, I love the challenge of finding a niche in a growing audience. The Internet is just such a powerful tool to sell your products, and can engage consumers in so many different ways. Couponing is a great example—an offline coupon will typically get one or two percent redemption. An online coupon, though, can get anywhere from 10 to 20 percent redemption based on the offer. There's so much power in online marketing, and if you effectively integrate offline and online methods, you can potentially double or even triple your market.

JASON: Once you draw people to a site, what are some of the methods that you've taken to encourage users to stay on the site, search around, and come back on a regular basis?

JULIE: That's a huge challenge for CPG (consumer products goods) firms, because typically consumers are going to CPG Web sites for product information or information in general. With the introduction of social media, it's important to have interactive elements that keep people engaged, like a customizable blog or a loyalty program. Coke does a great job of keeping people engaged with their rewards program. Their site grew phenomenally from 2006 to 2007, mostly from repeat visitors. About 35 percent of their audience keeps coming back, which is unheard of for a CPG firm. It's because of increased use of online interactivity and 360-degree marketing that utilizes offline and online media to tell the same story. It can be very powerful.

JASON: Have there been any examples where you've integrated the offline and the online efforts for brands, where you have seen a particularly positive result?

JULIE: We did a program a few years ago with Carrie Underwood after she had won American Idol. It was a little Web site, not very big, where users could download music clips of Carrie Underwood singing some of the classic Hershey jingles, like "Give me a Break" for the KitKat brand (we had run a TV commercial of her singing the songs to help drive audiences to the site). We didn't expect the program to be significant, but we got so much traffic that we couldn't keep up with the demand. The t-shirt sales from the site alone blew all of our expectations out of the water. It was amazing—we couldn't have asked for more exposure. The traffic to the promotional site was way beyond what we had hoped for, and, I think, a great example of how offline efforts like TV and the publicity generated from the popularity of American Idol can combine with the interactive power of the Web to create a marketing phenomenon.

JASON: What are some of the specific challenges that you face in trying to get an Internet-based program off the ground?

JULIE: I think the biggest challenge that consumer companies face is the 360-degree marketing program, because many times the outside agencies develop programs and the internal brand managers develop programs. The Internet strategy is the last thought. So everyone is developing a marketing program, but not really paying attention to expanding the program online. This potentially ends up creating a disjointed 360-degree program. What should happen is that all marketing strategies should be developed together, but that's often easier said than done.

JASON: Have you seen your work and ideas change as social media has grown in popularity?

JULIE: We've been able to introduce a lot more interactivity into our Web sites, which we are hoping will keep people coming back. Also, in a social media environment, consumers want brands to interact with them. They want to be asked their opinions. They want to be in on the ground floor when marketers are deciding things.

JASON: How do you see the Web evolving from here?

JULIE: I can only speak from the CPG side. Social media will allow companies to collect more information on consumers' online behavior so they can deliver results that are important to them. Brands become more successful the more we get to know our customers, and the Web will increasingly allow us to know all of our visitors as individuals, and tailor our messaging to each person on a one-to-one basis.

410

Popular Web Retention Techniques

There are many methods that marketers can utilize to decrease churn rates and encourage visitors to return often. Each of these methods requires advanced planning, and often involves numerous people including writers, designers, and programmers.

It is important to remember, however, that some sites are visited by a wide variety of people, and it is impossible to please everyone who comes to a site. This is why it is especially important for marketers to understand who their audience is. Marketers need to make sure that the retention techniques they put in place speak directly to their core demographic to ensure that the most possible people within their target market come back regularly.

Although there are a number of tools and techniques that marketers use to bring people back to a site regularly, the keys to increasing brand loyalty on the Web are the same online as they are offline: striking the best balance of quality customer service, value, and product selection. In fact, the features that contribute to saving the customer time and money and improving the overall shopping experience rank highest among shoppers in terms of heightening site loyalty (see Table 12-1).

Feature	% of Shoppers
Saving money	63%
Saving time	25%
Free shipping	25%
Inventory/selection	18%
Brands	16%
Customer service	15%
Past experience	11%
Rewards programs	11%
Ease of shopping	9%

Table 12-1   The features of a Web site that impact loyalty. SOURCE: "Consumer Loyalty Survey." DoubleClick Performics, 24 May 2007.

While features affecting the site's functionality are integral to building loyalty, internal tools and policies can also contribute to high customer loyalty (see Table 12-2).

Feature	% of Shoppers
Free or flat shipping	92%
Order tracking	88%
Privacy policies	83%
Rebates and coupons	76%
Online outlet	75%
Customer reviews	74%
Comparison capabilities	73%
Price and product alerts	63%
Live help	58%
In-store returns	58%
Express checkout	52%
How to guides	51%
Internet-only specials	50%
Exclusives	49%
Wish lists	48%
Recently viewed items	46%
In-store pickup	37%

Table 12-2 Tools and policies that encourage return visits. SOURCE: "Consumer Loyalty Survey." DoubleClick Performics, 24 May 2007.

Figure 12-1 highlights many of the features that encourage customers to return to the Nordstrom e-commerce site.

412

Access to personal account

Free shipping

In-store pickup

Wish list

Live customer service help

Loyalty program

E-mail list sign-up

Ability to check order status

Privacy policy

Figure 12-1 The Nordstrom e-commerce site incorporates many of the features that help bring consumers back for future visits.

General Design and Organization

Encouraging a visitor to return to a site begins with the design and organization of the site. Attractive design gives users a sense that the site is established and professional, and that a solid, legitimate company is behind it. At the same time, quality design specifically geared toward the target audience will help to establish the brand personality through images, color, and general layout. Quality design can also be used to emphasize specific messages and products that the marketer wants to highlight. Poorly designed sites do not do much to give customers an understanding of the brand or instill the sense of security that an established corporate entity is behind the site. Consumers do not want to spend money on a site if they do not feel comfortable it will be there the next day.

Similarly, the organization of the site plays a key role in bringing consumers back. Poor navigation or content that is difficult to find can quickly become frustrating—not an emotion that is going to keep users clamoring for more. It is essential that marketers take the time before the site is developed to map out the site, segment the content into categories that make sense, and consider how the navigation elements will lead visitors to find what they are looking for.

Regularly Updated Content and Design

Users have limited attention spans, but long memories. Once they visit a site, users expect to see new content upon the next visit. New content is important to a site for a number of reasons:

- It tells site visitors that new things are happening, and that the brand is in constant evolution, rather than growing stagnant.

- It piques users' curiosity and encourages them to come back often to see new changes.

- It gives the marketer a chance to send new messages regularly to repeat visitors.

The frequency with which a site updates its content depends on two primary variables:

- The ability of the site's marketers to create new content quickly. Content can be difficult, time-consuming, and potentially expensive to create. It can require talented writers and proofreaders for copy and professional photographers and graphic designers for product, application, or brand-oriented lifestyle and marketing shots.

- The type of site in question. While updated information is a key method of bringing visitors back and increasing the frequency of visits, it would be unnecessary and cost prohibitive for all sites to maintain an aggressive content update schedule. Table 12-3 shows a rundown of various site types, how often they should be updating and providing new content, and what type of content they need to update. These determinations are made based on general expectations on the part of the audience. For example, consumers would expect media and information sites to be updated with new content daily as news happens. Most online stores can be updated a little less frequently, depending on their size. This is fairly reflective of real life: consumers expect most newspapers to give them new information each day, but don't expect the window displays, sales, or general selection to be updated as frequently.

Type of Site	Minimum Update Frequency
Media/Informational Site	Daily
E-Commerce Site (large selection)	Daily or Weekly
E-Commerce Site (small selection)	Weekly or Monthly
B2B Site (large company)	Monthly
B2B Site (small company)	Quarterly
Entertainment Site	Daily or Weekly

Table 12-3   Guidelines for the minimum frequency of updates based on type of site.

Regardless of the frequency with which new content is added to a site, it is vital for marketers to maintain a regular schedule of updates, so that, over time, visitors will have a clear understanding of when new content will be posted. Uploading new information randomly can cause confusion, make the site and the site owners seem disorganized, and ultimately discourage repeat site visits. To ensure that new content is posted regularly, marketers will often create content well in advance and maintain an ongoing library of content to draw from, sometimes weeks or months in advance.

Updating a site does not mean that an entire site needs to change. Small updates are sometimes enough to get the point across that something new is going on. In order to make content updates work to a site's advantage, the updates should be relevant to the sites purpose and brand message, and should be highly visible to the user—with prominent placement on the Home page. Updates that are irrelevant, such as daily stock quotes on a site that sells tea cups, or that are buried on an interior page do not tell visitors that the site has something new to offer.

Media and e-commerce sites have the most work to do to keep their sites updated. B2B sites can be updated more easily by simply adding a new press release to the cyber newsroom and promoting it on the home page, adding a new blog entry, or simply changing a prominent image on the Home page. It is important to let users know that the site is being taken care of, taken seriously, and that the company behind the site is active and growing.

As sites add new content, they also need to delete old content. Information that is out-of-date or no longer relevant can deter users from returning to a site. Leaving outdated content on a site can cast the same negative shadow as not posting new content—does out-of-date information mean that the site and company behind it are out of touch or disorganized? Is that the kind of company the consumer wants to do business with? These thoughts may not be that literal or conscious in the minds of visitors, but the doubts created in the minds of potential customers can have subtle, and potentially disastrous, impacts for a Web site trying to generate revenue.

Finally, content is not the only part of a site that needs to be updated. Like fashions and home furnishings, graphic design and artistic style evolve over time; sites need to reflect these changes. For most people, it is fairly easy to look at a hairstyle, for example, and know whether it is from the 1980s, 1970s, or even 1950s. Site design is much the same way. As styles and new tools emerge, marketers must update their sites to stay current. Often this means that a site needs to be completely redeveloped every few years.

Blogging

Blogs are meant to be an ongoing stream of thought by a single publisher or organization. Therefore, visitors expect that when a blog is included on a site, new posts will be loaded consistently. As with general content, marketers need to make a commitment to updating a blog regularly.

Maintaining a strict schedule of blogs can be a daunting task, however, because along with writing new posts that are relevant to the brand and interesting to consumers, there also needs to be a certain amount of transparency. Unlike other site content, which usually written by professional copy writers, blogs are meant to be personal. The background of the person writing the blog plays a part in generating interest among readers. This means that, for example, if the CEO of XYZ Inc. maintains a public blog on his or her company's Web site, then he or she must be the one to write each blog post. Users—both consumers and visiting media—will eventually see through the blog if the posts are actually being written by a representative or an outside agency. Ultimately, this will reflect negatively on the brand, because the blog will no longer be seen as an expression of honest opinions but rather as a blatant attempt at marketing. While blogs can keep visitors engaged, higher-level executives may find it difficult to maintain a regular schedule of writing and posting new blog entries.

Ideally, the subject matter of each blog post should reflect issues and current events within the company. For example, a B2B company that is introducing a new product at a national trade show should be posting blog entries that reflect issues surrounding the new product or the show itself. Crafting blog entries that maintain their relevance with respect to current events as well as a parallel path with other brand messaging is more likely to encourage return visits.

Voting, Polls, and Surveys

Voting, polls, and surveys also give users the opportunity to participate in a site and have their voices heard. These tools help stimulate
future visits by heightening user curiosity as to the results, as well as
drawing them closer to the brand by providing a means of interaction:

- **Voting**: Voting can be done by asking users to cast their choice
  for their favorite among two or more distinct items, files, or ideas.
  Social networking sites, such as MyYearbook.com, pit two member
  profiles against each other in a series of categories including "Biggest Nerd" and "Best Smile" and ask users to vote to determine the
  winner. Voting is typically not open-ended, but rather has a pre-set
  time limit after which a winner is declared. In most cases, voting
  results are made public even while voting is still taking place.

- **Polls**: Polls are usually single questions, asked in multiple-choice
  style. Web sites that establish polls typically ask questions that
  directly relate to a specific topic covered on the Web site, such as
  the AOL poll shown in Figure 12-2, or that somehow relates to
  the general topic of the Web site. A site that sells gardening tools
  might have a poll about the best way to make keep weeds under
  control. Polls are usually not limited to a specific time frame (they
  are often just deleted from the site when they are old and no longer
  of interest). Polls do not determine a winner, and they allow users
  to see cumulative results throughout the life of the poll.

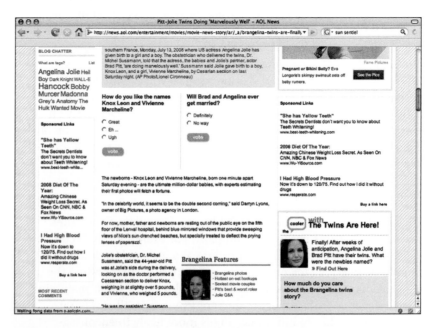

Figure 12-2   AOL asks poll questions about most stories that it features.

- **Surveys**: Online surveys typically ask users a series of questions about themselves, their opinions on a specific topic, or even their feelings about the Web site itself. Very often, surveys are used by marketers to improve a site or gain an understanding of new features and content that should be added. Survey results are aggregated offline for the benefit of the marketer and are usually not posted online.

Although polls and surveys on a Web site are hardly scientific (typically there are few controls over how often people can vote, for example), they do provide a glimpse into the mindset of an audience. They also offer further insight into the type of visitors who frequent a site (which can later be considered as the site and its contents evolve) while creating a strong connection between the user and the brand.

Contests

As discussed in Chapter 11, contests can be a strong tool for bringing new users to a site, luring them in with the possibility of winning cash or prizes. At the same time, contests can entice people to come back and visit the site to see if winners have been posted, or, in the event that the contest requires public postings of video, pictures, or other files, to see how they are stacking up to their competition.

Because they require a winner to be named, contests exist only for a finite period of time (although they may remain posted online indefinitely, to allow people to view the content and see the results). Because there is a limited amount of time to build an audience, marketers will often use the contest registration information to send e-mails and other announcements to entrants throughout the duration of the contest to maintain the participants' interest and draw them back onto the site.

Figure 12-3 shows the home page of the Blue Nile Web site, which is designed so that a contest offer pops up when a user first visits the site.

Figure 12-3 The Blue Nile site entices users to enter a contest with a pop-up window as soon as visitors come to the site.

Loyalty Programs

Loyalty programs provide ongoing incentives for visitors to return to a site often and engage in certain activities (usually that means making online purchases). Although there are a variety of mechanisms for running these types of programs, the most popular tend to be points-based systems, which award a designated number of points to consumers with each purchase, usually based on the total purchase amount.

With these programs, sites maintain a database to track user accounts and cumulative points. Consumers can log into their accounts and review the number of points that they have acquired. Consumers can often earn more by making additional purchases or taking part in limited-time promotions, such as applying for a company-run credit card. As point totals increase, users can "cash in" their points and redeem them for rewards, such as free merchandise, discounts off future purchases, free travel, gift certificates, etc. The theory behind these programs is that once enrolled and earning points, consumers will be motivated to make future purchases from the same site in order to continue building their point totals. In addition, consumers may even increase their pace of purchases in the pursuit of reaching a points-based benchmark, whether consciously or subconsciously.

Points-based programs are widespread and highly popular. According to the report by DoubleClick referenced earlier, 70% of all frequent online shoppers (defined as those shoppers that spend at least $500 online annually) belong to two or more points-based loyalty programs.[2] In addition, while prices are an important factor for online shoppers, those consumers who belong to two or more loyalty programs are less concerned about price, and are less likely to comparison shop, choosing instead to shop at the online stores in which they are earning points.

Of course, simply offering a points-based loyalty program is not enough to encourage a user to return. For a program of this nature to succeed, it needs to have the following:

- **Ease of use**: Points-based programs are notoriously difficult to understand, and they often have fine-print which severely limits how users spend their points. The more difficult a program is to understand and use, the less likely users will be to participate. The most successful and well-known loyalty programs simplify the process by awarding one point per something that is easily measurable. Examples of successful programs include the American Express loyalty program that awards one point for every dollar spent and Continental's OnePass frequent flier program, which gives travelers one point for every mile that they fly.

- **Realism**: Earning points needs to be an obtainable endeavor. Stringent programs that do not award points until the fifth purchase or that have points that expire after a short period of a time create resentment in shoppers and are unlikely to encourage further purchases.

- **Value**: Before enrolling in any points-based loyalty program, a consumer wants to know what rewards are available and how many points they will need to accumulate before being able to redeem them for something of value. With Continental's OnePass program, travelers earn a free round trip ticket to anyplace in the continental United State after they have earned 25,000 points (traveled 25,000 miles). In addition, OnePass allows consumers to earn additional miles when they shop online at partner sites (see Figure 12-4). This has proven to be of tremendous value, especially for business travelers who fly frequently. Conversely, if a consumer signs up for a points-based loyalty program at a furniture retailer and needs to spend the equivalent of a house full of furniture just to earn enough points for a coaster set, the value of the reward will not likely prove worthwhile to many people.

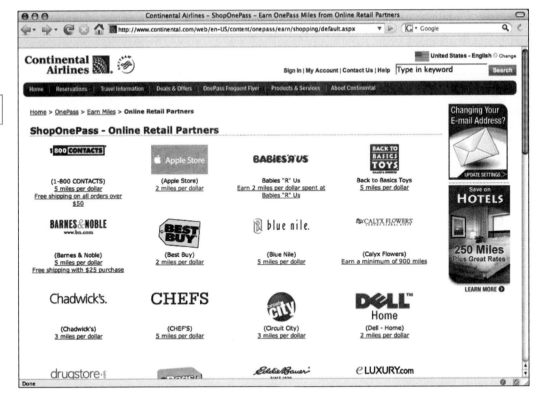

Figure 12-4 The One Pass points-based loyalty program also allows consumers to earn points when they shop at certain partner sites.

INTERVIEW WITH...

JACK BENRUBI, VICE PRESIDENT BUSINESS DEVELOPMENT, ADVERTISING CHECKING BUREAU

Advertising Checking Bureau is one of the powerhouses of trade marketing, specializing in consumer rebate, incentive, and consumer loyalty programs, servicing over 40% of all Fortune 500 companies.

I recently sat down with Jack Benrubi, the Vice President Business Development of ACB, and an industry veteran of 30 years. Jack provided some important insight into the value of loyalty programs.

JASON: How would you define a loyalty program? Are all loyalty programs based on points, or are there other types as well?

JACK: A loyalty program is an incentive to a retailer, consumer, or store salesperson or a combination of all three.

A points program is only one type of program. Another very popular program includes the distribution of reloadable debit cards. These offer an advantage to the marketer as their logo would be on the card with a possible theme and illustration of the product. Gift cards from select retailers are also popular with loyalty programs as they can be used to purchase anything at a given specialty retailer. These debit and gift cards can usually be spent on merchandise in traditional retail outlets or online.

Loyalty programs don't just happen between the brand and the consumer. Very often, a loyalty program will encourage loyalty from the retailer, in an effort to increase sales that way. A "spiff" program is an incentive to the retail salesperson for products sold. The more they sell, the more cash they receive or the more dollars that are loaded on an existing debit card; or the salesperson can choose a gift card from their favorite retail outlet.

JASON: What is the draw that makes consumers enroll in a loyalty program?

JACK: The draw that makes consumers want to enroll is simply high amounts of cash. We have found that if the loyalty program is below $20.00 in total value, participation is normally very low, while $20 or more will generate high participation and excitement.

The communication piece or theme surrounding the loyalty program is very critical. If the program is not adequately communicated, the program will not succeed no matter how high the dollar amount. Programs are usually communicated at the retail level, via the brand's Web site, through local and national advertising campaigns in traditional advertising media, etc.

JASON: In your experience, how successful are these programs? Can they really contribute to increasing a company's revenue and profits?

JACK: The most successful loyalty programs surround themselves with a theme. For example, NASCAR may be the theme. It may be that retail salespeople are competing against each other to sell the most products at the retail level for the manufacturer. The result will be cash based on the product that they have sold or a fully branded debit card that is reloaded every time that a particular sale is made. In this way they are racing against each other with the winner receiving cash or a debit card, but also a bonus cash prize, which is then published on the Web site for all participants to view.

We've been successful in creating Web tools in which the participants register themselves on the Web tool with encrypted Social Security numbers with other pertinent data on themselves and the retailer that they sell from. This is a customized Web tool. This Web site would also include the products that are eligible to be sold in the loyalty program, including details on the program such as sales data, eligibility requirements, eligible retailers, etc. The Web site has the look and feel of the manufacturer's own Web site.

Loyalty programs have been very successful for manufacturers, especially during times of depressed economic times. During these periods, companies refuse to be status quo and see their sales further decrease. Thus, loyalty programs are created in order to help bolster sales during good and especially down economic cycles. Our incentive division has increased by over 50% over the last five years, a clear indication that companies have been successful in running these types of programs, which results in an increase in sales and revenue.

JASON: What advice would you give to a company that wanted to include a loyalty program on their site? What elements should they try to avoid that could cause a loyalty program to fail?

JACK: There are a number of keys to building and maintaining a successful loyalty program. The claiming process needs to be kept simple. The Web site needs to be easy to navigate with simplicity of data entry such as serial numbers, model #'s, sales data, etc. The Web site needs to have easy drop-down boxes with easy access to information. If a Web site is difficult to navigate and information is hard to access, then the loyalty program will be a guaranteed failure.

Wish Lists

Wish lists allow consumers who are not quite ready to make a purchase to keep track of the items and merchandise that they like and may consider purchasing in the future. These lists serve multiple purposes:

- **Encourage repeat visits**: Users are likely to return to a site where they have a wish list because the initial intent in creating the list was to purchase those items at some point in the future.

- **Ease of shopping**: Users who create wish lists have an easier time shopping because once the list is created they no longer have to search for the products in which they were interested.

- **Expand the consumer base**: Items on a wish lists are not always purchased by the individual that compiles the list. Very often, links to those lists are sent to other people such as husbands, wives, parents, friends, etc., to encourage them to buy items as gifts for holidays or just for fun.

Ongoing Marketing to Existing Customers

Keeping a customer coming back to a site may be significantly less expensive than the cost of new customer acquisition, but it is by no means free. While much of the expense of retention is in the development and maintenance of site-specific features such as live help and or content updates, some budget must be made available for marketing to past customers as a means of encouraging return visits.

Marketing to existing customers is often different from the more general marketing done to drive new audiences to a Web site. Because existing customers are already familiar with the store and have already interacted in some way (by registering with the site, making a purchase, or otherwise providing their name and contact information), marketers can be far more specific—and direct—in their messaging. E-mail blasts are especially cost-effective and powerful for directly reaching existing customers. As described in Chapter 11, e-mail blasts can be coded in HTML and designed to reflect the brand. These efforts can be used to nudge customers into coming back simply by putting the site name back in their mind. More effective methods involve providing coupons or limited-time sale announcements to lure consumers back. Further, because databases can record what each shopper has purchased and searched for, e-mail blasts can provide customer-specific offerings with coupons or promotional pricing on products the marketer already knows that customer will be interested in. These efforts are further strengthened when discount pricing or pre-sale opportunities (such as making concert tickets or highly desirable products available before they officially go on sale) are offered only to existing clients. This helps create a sense that by being a customer, the individual is receiving a reward over and above non-customers, further endearing them to the site.

Similarly, e-mail blasts and traditional mail are often used with points-based loyalty programs to remind participants of their current point totals, what they can receive for those points, and how many more points they need to accumulate in order to reach the next plateau of rewards.

Chapter Summary

- Marketing to attract new visitors to a site can cost up to eight times more than the cost of keeping clients coming back to the site repeatedly. Increasing the number of return visits impacts not only marketing expenditures, but overall site revenue and profitability. The number of return visitors is a vital statistic that marketers keep a close eye on. Understanding when and how long it takes for a visitor to make a purchase or take a desired action is vital to keeping revenue up and marketing costs down.

- The most important consumer considerations for returning to a site multiple times relate to price, service, and their overall experience on a given site. Other features such as free shipping, an easy return policy, and the ability to track an order also add value in the mind of the consumer. Further, marketers can encourage return visits by regularly updating site content, blogging, offering polls, surveys, contests, loyalty programs, and wish list functionality. Ongoing marketing to existing customers is another vital part of capturing and maintaining a Web site's audience.

Key Terms

churn rate—The proportion of customers that discontinue a service or their association with a brand during a given time period.

Review Questions

1. The restaurant analogy at the beginning of this chapter explains the importance of return visits, but is not a pure comparison to Web site activity because:

    a. You cannot buy food over the Web.

    b. People going into a restaurant have already decided to spend money there.

    c. Restaurants service a local audience only; Web sites can be accessed by anyone, anywhere in the world.

    d. None of the above

2. Which of the following represents the concept of churn?

    a. A newspaper losing 8% of its subscribers

    b. A credit card company having 11% of its customers cancel their accounts

    c. 7% of an online store's shoppers deciding to shop at another site

    d. All of the above

3. Which of the following is more expensive?

    a. The cost to acquire new site visitors

    b. The cost to keep visitors coming back

    c. It is impossible to measure

    d. They both cost about the same

4. Repeat visits are important for B2C, but not really for B2B sites. True or False?

5. The three most important factors to consumers in building loyalty to a Web site are:

   a. Polls, contests, and videos

   b. Polls, contests, and loyalty programs

   c. Customer service, value, and product selection

   d. E-mail marketing, free shipping, and customer reviews

6. Which of the following is not an important factor in building customer loyalty?

   a. Availability of content in multiple languages

   b. Order tracking

   c. Live help

   d. Wish lists

7. New content is important in bringing consumers back to a site because:

   a. It keeps the site new and not stagnant.

   b. It increases user curiosity.

   c. It gives marketers the opportunity to send new messages.

   d. All of the above

8. Which of the following sites need to be updated most often?

   a. Large B2B sites

   b. Small B2B sites

   c. Small B2C sites

   d. Media/Informational sites

9. One of the most important rules for updating content is:

   a. Keep all new content short

   b. Maintain a regular schedule of updates

   c. Keep new content comical—humor draws more people than serious content

   d. Use video content rather than copy whenever possible

10. A cost-effective way for B2B sites to update content is to:

    a. Post a new press release

    b. Create a whole new section of the site

    c. Redesign the navigation at least once every three months

    d. Don't bother—B2B sites don't need to be updated

11. The best person to write a blog for a business site is:

    a. The company's PR agency

    b. A freelance copywriter

    c. The company CEO

    d. The actual person who is listed as the author of the blog

12. Which of the following is most likely to have its results hidden from public view?

    a. Poll

    b. Survey

    c. Contest

    d. Voting

13. Which of the following is least likely to have a specified end date?

    e. Poll

    f. Survey

    g. Contest

    h. Voting

14. Which of the following is most likely to have more than one question associated with it?

    a. Poll

    b. Survey

    c. Contest

    d. Voting

15. Points programs are primarily used to increase:

    a. The length of time users spend on the site

    b. The potential for users to pass the word about a site on to friends and family

    c. The number of pages users see per visit

    d. Loyalty to the site and brand

16. Which of the following is not considered a key factor in running a successful points-based rewards program?

    a. The value of the rewards users can get

    b. How realistic it is to accumulate enough points before they are worth anything

    c. A catchy marketing name

    d. Making the program easy to use and understand

17. According to DoubleClick, shoppers that belong to two or more loyalty programs:

    a. Are less likely to comparison shop

    b. Would prefer to consolidate all of their points into a single program

    c. Stop visiting a given site after they have cashed their points in

    d. Are unhappy with how difficult the programs are to use and understand

18. Wish lists are meant to be seen only by the people who create them. True or False?

19. Which of the following is a cost effective way to market to existing customers?

    a. E-mail blasts

    b. Television commercials

    c. Billboards

    d. Calling them by phone

20. Giving frequent shoppers benefits such as pre-sale opportunities and coupons that the general public does not have access to tends to:

    a. Annoy the general public, and is likely to keep them from coming to the site

    b. Give the customer a sense that they are being rewarded

    c. Be impossible because of the logistics involved

    d. Be time consuming and usually not worth the effort

Projects

1. Points-based programs are an important part of building loyalty. In a one-page paper, describe what languages and tools you would use to program a points-based loyalty program.

   Research the available off-the-shelf point-based programs a company could use on a Web site. Describe one, and provide an explanation as to whether or not a site would be better off using a pre-written program or a customized one. What would be the pros and cons?

   As an extra credit project, program a simple points system, where points accumulate in a database when a user selects a specific product. Don't worry about attaching this to a shopping cart—simply accumulate points when a user selects an item and pushes a "submit" button.

2. Choose any e-commerce site. In a three-page report, describe the steps they have taken to keep users coming back.

   Which methods work? Which do you think don't work as well?

   What recommendations would you make for increasing repeat visits?

   Visit the site over the course of the next week. How many times do they visibly update content? Do you feel that it's enough?

   Do the same for a B2B site.

3. In the interview with Julie Mathews, she discussed the exceptional work done by Coke with their rewards program. Research and write a two-page paper as to how this program worked, and why it was a success.

4. Find one example each of a survey, poll, and voting mechanism on the Web. For each, describe how, if at all, they tie into the overall site messaging. What effect do you think they are likely to have in increasing repeat visits?

5. You are the lead programmer for a large e-commerce company. One of the key executives asks you for your recommendations for increasing return visits. Other than the examples described in this chapter, what recommendations would you make? Submit your suggestions in a paper no longer than two pages.

Endnotes

1. "Marketers are Flying Blind When it Comes to Leveraging Customer Data and Analytics, Reports the CMO Council." CMO Council, 14 April 2008.
2. "Consumer Loyalty Survey." DoubleClick Performics, 24 May 2007.

CHAPTER 13

Traffic Analysis and Measuring for Success

In this chapter you will learn about:

◎ The importance of setting the right goals and some of the goals often set for Web sites and marketing campaigns

◎ How marketers can track Web sites and what data relating to a Web site they can analyze

Ultimately, every marketing campaign and every Web site is executed to achieve some pre-established objective. Establishing specific goals and continually measuring progress toward those goals allows marketers to zero in on the often elusive, ever-changing recipe for achieving Web site success—however success is defined.

Benchmarks for Success: Setting the Right Goals

The need to set clear objectives might seem obvious, but setting appropriate goals is often tricky. Marketers must set goals that take into account the purpose of the site or campaign, the market, the budget, or a combination of all of these factors. Setting the right goals can make all the difference in whether or not any Web effort is a success.

Large marketing efforts and sites will often set goals for every component. A viral campaign might have one set of goals, while banner advertising might have another. E-mail blasts might be launched with a third goal in mind. Companies also often set different goals for different elements of a Web site. Blogs may be intended to serve a different purpose than a contest, which may serve a different purpose than a limited-time sale. For ease of explanation, we will break possible goals down into two distinct areas: marketing goals and Web site goals.

Marketing Goals

Marketing goals can focus on a variety of different measurements, including:

- **New site traffic**: A marketing campaign is often executed in an attempt to bring new visitors to the site. The goal for this type of campaign is often expressed as either a targeted number of new visitors or as a percentage increase in the number of new visitors from a previous month, quarter, or year.

- **Returning visitors**: Some marketing campaigns are run solely for the purpose of bringing established visitors back to the site. This goal is also expressed as a specific number of visitors or as a percentage increase in the number of returning visitors from a previous time period.

- **Distribution of information**: Sometimes marketers can measure the success of a viral campaign by measuring the amount of times a file or piece of information is passed on from one recipient to another. There are some software programs available that can track how many times an e-mail has been forwarded. However, marketers can also judge the effectiveness of a viral campaign by measuring whether or not traffic to their site is increasing and if it is increasing in geographic areas where they are not engaged in any other marketing efforts.

- **Percentage of e-mail click-throughs**: Goals for e-mail marketing campaigns are often based on the percentage of people who open a given e-mail and click through to the Web site.

- **Increases in specific regional audiences**: Marketing campaigns are often run on a regional or local level to increase audiences in specific geographic territories.

Web Site Goals

Site goals can be fairly expansive as well, including goals relating to one of more of the following areas:

- **Gross revenue**: E-commerce sites often set goals based on gross revenue. These goals are set as a specific target amount or as a percentage increase over a previous time frame.

- **Number of leads gained**: Business-to-business sites that do not generate sales through e-commerce need visitors to take action by calling or e-mailing the company to request more information or to set up an exploratory meeting. These companies will set goals for how many leads are generated from their Web site. This type of goal is usually measured in terms of the number of e-mails generated directly from the site or the number of online forms sent in requesting further information about a company.

- **Number of pages visited**: Sites typically want to maximize the number of pages viewed by each visitor and will set specific goals for this.

- **Length of time spent on the site**: Similarly, Web sites want to keep people on their site as long as possible. Sites will set goals to reach certain time-based benchmarks, often adjusting content to make information more compelling in order to keep visitors on the site longer.

- **Specific pages visited**: Very often, marketers identify certain pages on a site that they most want users to visit. Successful site marketers do not assume that users will find these pages by accident; rather, the marketers create links and visual elements that draw attention to and deliberately drive people to these pages. Marketers set goals relating to how much traffic actually reaches the targeted pages.

- **General brand building**: For some sites, the goal may just be to increase brand recognition. This goal can be difficult and expensive to measure (usually done via pre-launch surveys of brand recognition, which are later compared to post launch surveys of brand recognition). However, long-term success for a company often relies on the market having knowledge of the brand, therefore, raising brand awareness is an important goal for many marketers.

- **Visitor registration**: For sites that want users to register as members, sign up for an online newsletter, or otherwise subscribe to the site, marketers set goals that are based on the number of participating visitors.

Establishing Numbers-Based Goals

Setting goals can be difficult work, and it requires a realistic understanding of what can be achieved through specific marketing efforts. Goals are pointless if they are arbitrary. It would not make sense, for example, for a print advertising campaign to have a goal of increasing the amount of time users spend on a site. External-facing marketing efforts can help increase the number of visitors to a site, but the site must be designed in such a way as to keep people there longer. Similarly, a goal based on leads generated from a Web site is pointless unless a company understands how many leads are required to generate one sale and how many sales are required to compensate for the cost of the site as well as the associated marketing efforts. Therefore, it is vital to set appropriate, realistic goals based on solid figures aimed at achieving a positive **ROI** (return on investment). ROI is the positive or negative return that is generated from any investment, including marketing and Web efforts.

The need for specific, numeric-based goals can be best illustrated through example. Suppose a human resource management company sells its services at an hourly rate of $150 an hour. The company's average billing per client is approximately $10,000 over the lifespan of an account. In reality, a company would need to deduct its expenses from its gross sales to calculate its net sales. However, for the sake of this example, we will assume that the company's gross sales and net sales are equal.

The company has a Web site established, and the site generates fairly steady traffic. Unfortunately, the Web site is not generating many new sales leads. In an effort to increase sales, the company decides to promote itself as an expert in its field by holding a **Webinar**. A Webinar is an online seminar in which a speaker makes a presentation on a given topic to an audience over the Web. A Webinar can include live video, presentation slides, and the ability for the audience to ask public or private questions.

To hold the Webinar, the company will need to pay an outside firm approximately $12,000 for the technology to host the event, which includes setting up a promotional Web page for interested parties to review. The company will also have to spend money to promote the Webinar—it can sometimes be difficult to convince busy executives to take time away from their day to attend a Webinar, even if attendance is free. Costs for marketing and promoting the event will include the following:

- $20,000 to the PR agency the company will hire for a three-month effort to promote the event through online and offline media.

- $3,000 for signage and handouts to promote the Webinar at an upcoming trade show the company will be attending.

- $12,000 to a marketing agency to conduct an e-mail blast campaign, including the following costs:

  - $5,000 to write, design, and program two promotional e-mail blasts along with a third blast to remind registered attendees just prior to the event

  - $1,000 to organize and send the e-mail blast to the company's existing house-list

  - $6,000 for a list of new contacts from an e-mail list broker

- An additional $3,000 in miscellaneous fees, such as the design of the presentation template, updates to the company's home page for promotional purposes, etc.

For the purposes of this example, we will not try to measure the hours spent by company employees writing and rehearsing the presentation and promoting the event to existing clients (who they may want to attend in an effort to sell them additional services). In real life, however, these activities are costly and typically calculated by counting the number of hours that will be devoted to the project, the number of employees working on the effort, and the salary and other expenses that will be incurred.

Given the hard costs in this example, the event will cost the company a total of $50,000. At an average total billings of $10,000 per client, the first goal is fairly straight forward: this Webinar needs to result in five new clients in order to break even; six or more to generate a profit (a positive ROI). However, setting a goal for acquiring a certain number of new clients is not sufficient. The company also needs to set a goal for how many people must attend the Webinar in order to result in five new clients. Historically, the company works on a 10% conversion rate, meaning that for every ten potential clients the company makes contact with, it generates one new paying client. This makes the second goal very clear: the Webinar needs to have 60 companies in attendance if it hopes to sign on the six new clients necessary to generate a positive return.

Unfortunately, having 60 companies attend the Webinar does not mean getting only 60 people to sign up. Even if we make the unrealistic assumption that everyone attending the Webinar will be from a different company (in real life, there may be two or more people from a single company attending, thereby reducing the number of potential new clients), the attendance rate for those who sign up for a Webinar is almost never 100%. In this example, assume the vendor that is going to host the Webinar informs the company that based on its experience hosting Webinars in the HR industry, only about 33% of everyone who signs up for the Webinar will actually attend. The others will forget, have something more important come up, or just change their minds at the last minute. With this statistic in mind, a third goal has been established: in order to get 60 companies in attendance, the company needs about 180 registered attendees.

The list broker that will provide the e-mail contacts is providing them for $.50 per contact, so $9,000 buys 18,000 contact addresses. The company putting on the Webinar also has its own list of about 2,000 contacts, bringing the total number of e-mail contacts to 20,000. Past e-mail efforts for the company have been hit-and-miss—some have really helped drive traffic to the site; others have failed to make a dent. So it is hard to find a good statistic from past efforts on which to base future goals. However, as a point of reference, their past open rate for e-mails was roughly 12% and their click-through rate hovered around 4%. The company does have higher expectations for these blasts, because they are promoting the free Webinar and not just presenting new company information.

With this in mind, the goals are set a little higher—13% for an open rate and 5% for a click-through rate. Based on the total of 20,000 e-mail contacts, that translates into a goal of 2,600 recipients opening the first blast, and 1,000 clicking through to find out more information about the Webinar. If 10% of everyone who clicks through actually registers, the company would have 100 registrants after the first blast.

The goal could be the same for the second blast; however, some of the people (let's say 20%) in the second blast will have already taken some sort of action in the first blast. Thus, the second blast has a lower potential reach of only 16,000 recipients. At the same 5% click-through rate as before, the click-through goal for the second blast is 800 click-throughs. If 10% of those people register, 80 new registrants will be added to the 100 who registered after the first blast—the company would meet is goal for registered attendees. Unfortunately, assuming that 10% of all people who click through would actually register is probably unrealistic. A far more conservative (and somewhat arbitrary) goal of converting 4% of click-throughs to registrants is set.

That means that after two blasts, the company expects 72 registrants (4% of 1,800 total click-throughs).

Since the goal is to get 180 registered attendees, that leaves a lot of work for the PR agency. The PR team will set some goals based on the number of placements and mentions of the Webinar that are made in traditional and online media, but the ultimate goal for the PR efforts is to bring in the remaining 108 registrants needed to make this Webinar profitable.

In order to later assess the value of each component of this campaign, the company must be able to track which registrants responded because of the e-mail blasts, which responded because of the PR efforts, and which responded because they received a flyer at a trade show (no goal was set for this, because it was such a small effort relative to everything else). One of the most popular solutions for analyzing which marketing effort is responsible for which traffic is to set up a series of **landing pages**—one for each different marketing effort. A landing page is a page on a Web site that is set up for certain visitors to access, but the page is usually not accessible from the main site itself. These pages are often used when companies are trying to measure different marketing efforts. Landing pages are typically identical to each other, but they reside at different URLs. For example, the company's main Webinar information page, accessible from their Home page, might be www.company.com/webinar. That page would be duplicated as is, at www.company.com/webinar2, where recipients of the e-mail blast campaign would be sent. It would be duplicated again at www.company.com/webinar3 for people driven to the site by public relations efforts, and again at www.company.com/webinar4 for people who received a flyer at a trade show. By creating these landing pages, the company can assess which efforts were more effective than others and which audience stays on the site longer, converts better, and navigates through the rest of the site more frequently. A company can then make adjustments to their program accordingly while the campaign continues.

Throughout a campaign like the one in this example, benchmarks toward goals are analyzed regularly so that efforts can be adjusted as necessary. If, for example, the first e-mail blast pulled in only half as much as the targeted goal, the company would need to reexamine each part of that campaign before sending the second e-mail blast. Was the list of poor quality with insufficient representation from the target demographic? Were the graphics and copy in the e-mail blast not compelling? By setting and measuring progress toward specific goals, marketers can make sure their budgets and efforts are being spent effectively, and their ROI can be maximized. Further, post-campaign analysis will help determine the best marketing mix for future efforts.

For example, suppose the Webinar was a huge success, with 80 attendees and ten new clients as a result. But while the PR campaign had outstanding results, reaching nearly 30% over goal, the e-mail marketing campaign was disappointing at 17% below goal. When the company plans their next Webinar, they will likely decide to spend less money on e-mail blasts and more money on public relations.

Campaigns and Web sites are rarely done in a vacuum. There will always be future efforts and ongoing evolutions. Setting goals and measuring results against those goals is the best way to set a path toward ongoing positive ROI.

Site Tracking: Breaking Down the Measurements

There are many programs and off-the-shelf software that allow marketers to track and analyze traffic data on a Web site. Software like WebTrends and VisitorVille are popular solutions, and there are a multitude of others. Each option gives the marketer a variety of options to choose from with the more powerful programs costing more but providing more information and greater flexibility.

Google Analytics

As of the writing of this book, one of the most-used tracking mechanisms is Google Analytics. Google Analytics is likely to remain one of the most commonly used tracking programs because:

- Although it is not the most powerful tool available, it provides access to a wide range of information that most marketers need.

- It integrates seamlessly with Google AdWords.

- Google has the ability to promote its Analytics program very aggressively.

- It is free.

Because of its extensive use, and because the information it provides shows up in a fairly similar form in most other tracking programs, we will be using screen shots and references from Google Analytics throughout the remainder of this section.

Programs like Google Analytics typically require developers to include specific lines of code (that the program provides) within each coded page of a site that the developer wishes to track. Depending on the tracking program being used, these lines may need to be installed in a very specific place within the code (for example, Google

Analytics requires that developers put the lines of code directly above the </BODY> at the bottom of the page). Once installed, the tracking software can begin to gather data and report back regarding site traffic.

Figure 13-1 shows the main screen or dashboard for Google Analytics, after it has begun to collect data. While users can customize the information so that data that is most important to them is presented on the dashboard, the information provided in Google's initial dashboard set-up provides a good first glance at what is happening on the site. Users can drill down deeper into each statistic for more information.

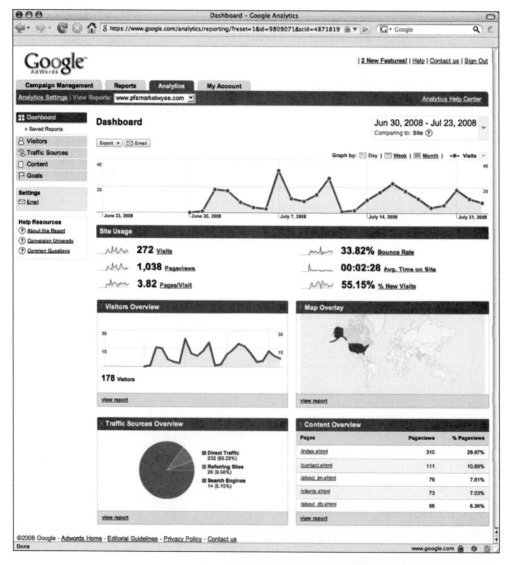

Figure 13-1 The dashboard of Google Analytics provides an overview of important information.

438

Marketers look at all of the information gathered here and analyze its meaning, seeking to gain a better understanding of who is coming to the site, what visitors are doing within the site, and whether or not the site is doing what is expected of it. In most cases, the statistics provided by tracking programs only tell part of the story. In-depth review of all the data can paint a positive or negative picture that marketers use to make recommendations for site evolutions. Appendix A of this book shows a sample traffic analysis report. The report presents vital site statistics, highlights the most and least productive areas of the site, and offers recommended changes.

The Timeline

The timeline, located at the top of the dashboard, shows the activity on the site within a specified time period. Each day is represented by a small dot marking how many visits were made to the site that day (measurement by visits is the default—users can change this to display any number of other analytics).

The timeline is important because it shows users at a glance whether or not there has been steady growth over time; when site usage tends to be at the lowest; if there have been any spikes in usage (for example, after a new press release has been distributed to the media, or a new ad campaign has been launched); or if site traffic levels have hit a plateau.

Users can change the parameters of the timeline to review any one date or date range by using the collapsible calendar menu shown in Figure 13-2. This feature is helpful in reviewing a specific time period during which a campaign ran. Users can also compare one time frame to another such the first quarter of the current year vs. the first quarter of the previous year, to see if growth has been achieved. The date ranges selected will affect the results and data presented throughout the rest of the analytics site.

Figure 13-2   The timeline can be adjusted to any desired date range or set to compare two different timeframes.

Site Usage

All tracking programs provide certain basic information that is vital to understanding site traffic and how visitors are behaving, for a selected time period. Each area can then be researched more deeply for a more complete understanding.

- **Visits**: The number of times people (new and returning) have visited the site. Figure 13-3 shows how the total number of visits can be broken down further by visits per day (or hour, week, or month based on user preference). Understanding which time frame is most popular for visitors can be a key factor in knowing when to upload new content. For example, if the data shows that a significant number of users visit the site between 3pm and 4pm each day, marketers would consider that time frame a desirable time to upload new content in order to gain maximum exposure.

Figure 13-3   Visits to the site can be broken down by hour, day, week, or month.

- **Pageviews**: The total number of pages visited by all of the visitors for the given time period. Like the number of visits, further research within the analytics site breaks down pageviews by hour, day, week, or month.

- **Pages/visit**: The number or pageviews for the given timeframe divided by the number of visits.

- **Bounce rate**: The percentage of visitors who come to the site and leave immediately without visiting any other page. The lower this number is, the better your site. Once again, further inspection shows this rate broken down by hour, day, week, or month.

- **Average time on site**: The total time spent on the site during a given time period divided by the total number of visitors during that time period. The average time users spend on a site is a key statistic that lets marketers know how engaging and interesting visitors find their site to be. Marketers need to understand how long it would reasonably take a user to find and read the information that they want them to read. They can then take the necessary steps toward ensuring that the average time on the site reaches this limit.

- **Percentage of new visits**: The number of visits by new site visitors divided by the total number of visits to the site. Marketers often have a goal for how many new users they want to visit the site vs. how many returning users.

Visitors Overview

The Visitors Overview section provides a much deeper analysis of the visitors that come to the site. While much of the information in this section is repeated from the site usage area in the dashboard, tracking programs like Google Analytics also provide information about users' Internet usage profiles, including in which language they read copy and which browsers they use (shown in Figure 13-4). This section also provides information on screen resolution settings, the operating systems visitors are using, and their ability to support Java or view Flash files.

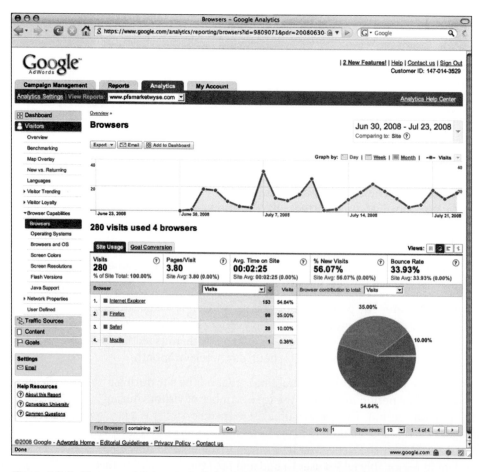

Figure 13-4 Users can drill down to find information about which browsers sites visitors are using. This is helpful to developers, as sites often look and act differently within different browsers.

One particularly interesting feature of tracking programs, especially for B2B sites, is the ability to see patterns in who has been visiting a site. For example, if ABC Company has visited a site, Google Analytics will report that information (assuming ABC Company has its own Internet Service Provider domain; if ABC Company connects through Verizon, Google Analytics would report that visit as Verizon, not as ABC Company). This allows marketers to know which other companies have come to the site. This can be a big help in direct marketing, as site owners have the advantage of knowing which prospects are showing increased interest. Users of Google Analytics can also track how long visitors have stayed on a site, how many pages they have looked at, and how often they come back.

Map Overlay

The map feature breaks down users by geography. Beginning with a map of the world, the map shades the regions where traffic is coming from, with darker shades representing regions with the most traffic. As a country is selected, it is broken down into smaller regions, such as the states within the U.S. (see Figure 13-5). Each state can then be examined to see the cities and towns that have provided the most traffic.

444

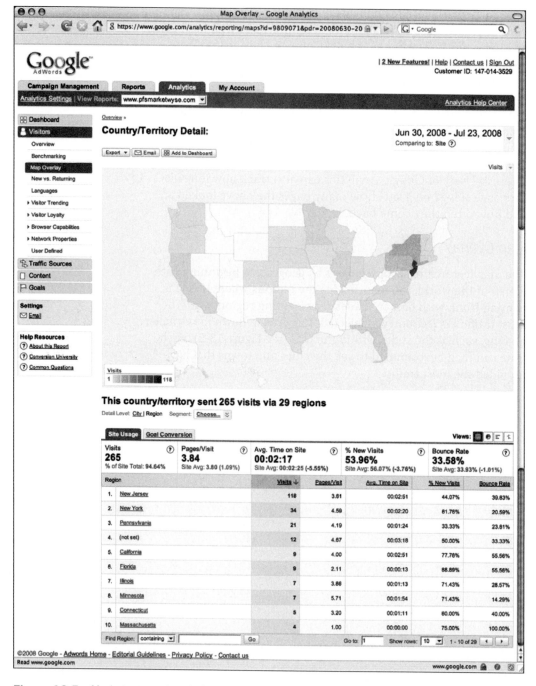

Figure 13-5 Marketers can break down visitor usage by region, right down to the town or city. For each region, data is provided that shows percentage of new visits, bounce rates, and more. This information can be helpful in knowing where to target marketing campaigns.

For each area, the tracking program provides region-specific stats, including the number of visits, pages per visit, average time on the site, percentage of new visits, and the bounce rate. These statistics give a marketer some insights into how users from different parts of the world interact with the site. This helps companies narrow down where to focus their marketing efforts.

445

Traffic Sources Overview

Google's Traffic Sources Overview lets the marketer know how visitors are finding the site (see Figure 13-6), breaking information down by how many people have come to the site directly (by typing the URL into the browser address bar), by finding a link to the site in a search engine, or by clicking onto the site from a link found on another Web site. More in-depth information includes percentage breakdowns of which search engines are most often used to find the site, the most popular keywords used in searches that result in visitors coming to the site, and which other sites visitors have used to find the site.

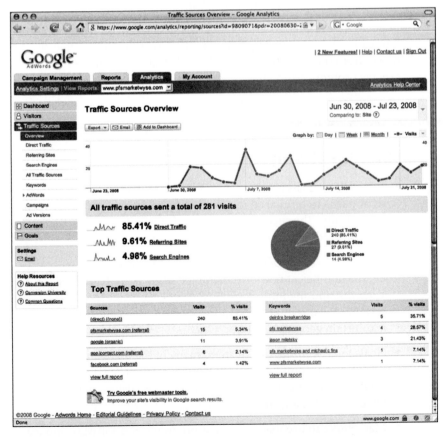

Figure 13-6   Marketers can use metrics applications to understand how traffic is finding their site.

Content Area

The content area gives an in-depth look at the content on a site, how it is being viewed, and which pages connect most strongly with the visiting audience. The tracking program lists every page of the site in order of the most visited, providing information for each page including:

- Total number of pageviews.

- Unique pageviews. This statistic does not count multiple visits to the same page by any one user.

- How much time was spent on each page. This can be helpful if a marketer knows that a certain page should take roughly 30 seconds to read, but the average time spent on that same page is seven seconds. The marketer can target that page for redevelopment.

- Bounce rate. The percentage of visitors who came directly to that page and then left the site completely.

- Percentage exit. The percentage of people who, after traveling through the site, left on any given page.

In addition, tracking programs provide information on traffic patterns. This can be particularly important, as it shows how traffic typically moves from one page to the next through a site, and whether or not specific promotions or links are driving traffic to the desired pages.

Chapter Summary

- Establishing goals is a vital part of knowing what is working and what needs to be altered in a marketing campaign or on a particular Web site. The success of a Web site or marketing campaign can be measured in many ways.

- There are a variety of goals for marketing efforts, including boosting the number of new or returning visitors to a site, increasing sales, distributing information via a viral campaign, achieving a certain level of e-mail click-throughs, and increasing an audience in a certain geographic area.

- Goals for a Web site can relate to many of the following areas: gross revenue, number of leads gained, number of pages visited, length of time spent on a site, targeted pages visited, general brand building, and visitor registration.

- Marketers can use many different programs and software applications to study and analyze site traffic and overall performance.

One of the most popular tools is Google Analytics, which is provided free to any site developer or marketer. Like many other tracking applications, Google Analytics provides vital statistics, such as geographic overviews of traffic sources, the number of pageviews, the time spent on the site, and more. All of this can be studied and analyzed in an attempt to improve the site and reach any pre-set goals.

Key Terms

landing page—A page on a Web site that is set up for certain visitors to access but which is usually not accessible from the main site itself.

ROI—Return on investment. The positive or negative return generated from any investment, including marketing and Web efforts.

Webinar—An online seminar in which a speaker makes a presentation on a given topic to an audience over the Web. This can include live video, presentation slides, and the ability for the audience to ask public or private questions.

Review Questions

1. Web site goals can be based on:

    a. Revenue generated

    b. Unique visitors

    c. Return visitors

    d. All of the above

2. Each component of a marketing campaign should have:

    a. The same goals

    b. Its own goals

    c. No more than two goals

    d. No goals at all

3. If one goal of a marketing campaign is to increase the percentage of new traffic to a site, which of the following should be expected?

    a. Comments left on blogs will increase.

    b. Revenue will grow by the same rate.

c. The number of pageviews will go down.

d. The percentage of returning visitors to a site as part of the overall population will decrease.

4. Which of the following will most likely have a goal relating to the number of consumers who pass along information to other consumers?

   a. A viral marketing campaign

   b. An e-mail blast campaign

   c. An online contest

   d. A new survey question on a Web site

5. E-mail blast campaigns are most likely to have goals based on which of the following?

   a. Gross and net revenue

   b. Open and click-through rate

   c. New and returning traffic

   d. Registration and activity

6. Because of the way most traffic tracking programs work, it is unrealistic to set goals based on specific geography. True or False?

7. Which of the following is most likely to have a goal based on the number of leads generated?

   a. An e-commerce site

   b. A media site

   c. A B2B site

   d. A social network

8. Which of the following goals is of the highest value?

   a. Increasing revenue

   b. Increasing registration

   c. Increasing traffic

   d. It depends on the site and need

9. "ROI" stands for:

    a. Reasonable online integration

    b. Return on inventory

    c. Return on investment

    d. Reasonable online inventory

10. It is possible to have a negative ROI. True or False?

11. Of the following statistics, which would the marketers of a site most likely want to see fall over time?

    a. The bounce rate

    b. The time spent on the site

    c. The number of new users

    d. The percentage of returning visitors

12. It is most useful for goals to be based on which of the following?

    a. What the marketer would like to achieve

    b. Past performance of similar efforts

    c. General ideas of what should be accomplished

    d. None of the above

13. The bounce rate measures:

    a. The number of people that bounce from one page to another

    b. The number of people that never return to a site after their first visit

    c. The number of people who lose their Internet connection while on the site

    d. The number of people who visit a single page and then immediately leave

14. If the percentage of new visitors to a site is 42%, then the percentage of returning visitors is:

    a. 42%

    b. 58%

c. Somewhere between 42% and 58%

d. It is impossible to know

15. Google Analytics is unable to provide information on the type of browser that most visitors to a site are using. True or False?

16. Using Google Analytics, it is possible to break total visits to a site down by:

a. Hour

b. Day

c. Week

d. All of the above

17. A high bounce rate would be most likely to have which of the following effects?

a. Increase the average time spent on a site

b. Decrease the average number of pages viewed per visit

c. Help increase sales

d. Have no effect on other statistics

18. Most tracking programs present data:

a. For the last 30 days

b. For the last quarter

c. For the 24 hours prior to when the information is being reviewed

d. For any timeframe specified by the user

19. Which of the following measurement tracks the number of people who visit a site by typing the URL in the browser address bar?

a. Direct traffic

b. Referring site

c. Search engine

d. None of the above

20. Most tracking programs allow marketers to see which keywords are most often used to find a site. True or False?

Projects

1. In one paragraph for each, discuss some goals that would likely be set for each of the following, and explain why:

    *   A B2B site

    *   An e-commerce site

    *   A social network

    *   A blog

2. For each of the goals that you identified for each type of site in Project #1, describe the statistics that would be most helpful in knowing whether or not each goal was achieved. Use the information discussed in the section on Google Analytics as a basis for your discussion.

3. Research three tracking programs, other than Google Analytics, that are available to Web site marketers. In a two-page report, discuss:

    *   How each differs from Google Analytics

    *   How each differs from the others

    *   The types and sizes of sites that would most benefit from each program

4. In a paper no longer than two pages, discuss how, as a site developer, understanding the goals of a site in advance might change the way you would set out to build a site.

5. You're the Web developer for a large company. Your boss is planning an online, print, and radio advertising campaign to help drive traffic to the company's site. You start talking about landing pages, but your boss seems unconvinced, and doesn't understand why landing pages are important. In a one-page paper, explain why landing pages can be an important part of a marketing campaign and what you would do to convince your boss to change his mind.

Analyzing Site Traffic

Analytics programs like Google Analytics are wonderful tools for seeing how traffic flows through and around a Web site. However, numbers provide only part of the story. Marketers need to analyze the traffic rates for given time periods, taking into account their current marketing initiatives, past performance, and other variables.

The following is an actual report provided by an agency to its client (real name changed to XYZ Corporation for this publication), analyzing the client's Web traffic. The report first collects and parses the numbers from Google Analytics that matter most for this particular report. Then, based on this data, the report presents an assessment of what is going well with the site, where the problems lie, and what steps the agency recommends taking to improve future site performance.

XYZ Corporation: Web Traffic Analysis—March 2008

Analytics Analysis

The Good News

TRAFFIC TRENDING IS STRONG Traffic remains relatively steady from day to day, with an upward trend. Through March 2008, daily traffic (not including weekends or Fridays, when traffic is lowest) averaged about 1,750 visits per day—up from the 1,400 visits per day averaged in November 2007, the last time an analysis was presented. This upward trending has remained consistent throughout each month, signifying increased interest and increased brand recognition over time. Reasons may include an expanded advertising effort, e-mail

ANALYTICS DASHBOARD

TRAFFIC OVERVIEW

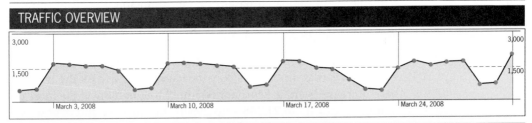

3,000 | 3,000
1,500 | 1,500

March 3, 2008   March 10, 2008   March 17, 2008   March 24, 2008

OVERVIEW VS. FEBRUARY, 2008

MEASUREMENT	RESULT	INC/DEC
TOTAL VISITS	41,222	9.70%
TOTAL PAGE VIEWS	113,731	10.52%
TOTAL UNIQUE VISITORS	21,248	24.95%
PAGES PER VISIT	2.76	0.75%
AVERAGE TIME ON SITE	1:32	1.73%
PERCENTAGE OF NEW VISITS	45.16%	15.89%
BOUNCE RATE	58.62%	-3.59%

CONTENT OVERVIEW

#	PAGE	VIEWS	INC/DEC	TIME
1	INDEX	37568	27%	1:11
2	LOCATIONS	6773	6.38%	2:01
3	DEFAULT	4992	2.72%	:40
4	CONTACT	3660	-10.07%	1:00
5	OVERVIEW	3640	4.45%	:53
6	MANUFACTURING	2,694	2.16%	:32
7	PACKAGING	2,376	9.54%	:48
8	NEWSPUBLICATIONS/NEWS	2,111	-4.22%	:31
9	DEVELOPMENT	1,704	4.48%	:49
10	DRUG	1,367	4.67%	:30
15	STERILEPRODUCTS	1,153	237.13%	1:14
18	ORALDOSEFORMS	782	231.36%	:55
19	MANUFACT/SOFTGEL	686	40.86%	:52
20	VITAMINSMINERALS	663	13.92%	:40
33	DRUG/ORAL/SOFTGEL	379	21.86%	1:07
35	PRINTEDCOMPONENTS	344	135.62%	:45

LOYALTY OVERVIEW

ONE VISIT:	18,603	45.13%	0-10 SECS:	25,807	62.60%

GEOGRAPHY

LOC.	RESULT	INC/DEC
USA	**25,996**	6.61%
NJ	4,143	41.45%
OR	4,021	-15.72%
PA	3,737	-0.03%
NC	2,552	42.09%
IL	2,128	-13.11
BRAZIL	**5,112**	6.06%
U.K.	**2,929**	4.64%
FRANCE	**951**	0.32%
GERMANY	**826**	1.85%
INDIA	**810**	171.81%
ITALY	**554**	8.63%
P.R.	**360**	133.77%

SOURCES

SOURCE	VISITS	INC/DEC
DIRECT	18,887	-3.14%
GGL/ORG	8,631	-0.43%
CAT.COM	3,885	106.87%
GGL/CPC	1,705	N/A
YAHOO	1,247	3.40%
CAT.NET	1,226	119.71%
SRCH.COM	671	-15.70%
CB.COM	412	-16.77%

blast campaigns (although these need to be further standardized, scheduled, and campaign-based), and most notably, the installation of the Google AdWord campaign in the U.S. on February 13, and expanded globally on March 13.

While further improvement is needed in some areas, such as time spent by visitors on the site, key measurements across the board have increased versus February results. Most notably is the increase in unique visitors to 21,248—up 25% from February and over 60% from November 2007. The Google AdWord program, and its expansion to global coverage, is the biggest contributor to this improvement: 13,914 unique visitors came to the XYZ Corporation site between March 13 and March 31, compared to 8,325 between March 1 and March 12—a 67% increase (it should be noted that these figures are adjusted to account for the additional six days between the 13th and the 31st).

Repeat visitor trending remains strong with 55% of all visitors coming back more than once, although this also represents an area for improvement.

Two areas that are particularly encouraging are the pages being visited and the new geographic mix. Although the top ten most highly visited pages increased or decreased in relative moderation (with the exception of the Careers page, which is down nearly 70% from 1,976 pageviews in February to only 616 in March), a very positive story is presented in the upward trending of some of key content pages. Packaging had the biggest increase of the top ten pages, with a 10% increase in traffic, while Sterile Products rocketed up a full 237%, Oral Dose Forms jumped 231%, Manufacturing/Softgel gained nearly 41%, Vitamins/Minerals was up nearly 14%, Drug/Oral/Softgel up almost 22%, and Printed Components gained over 135%. These remarkable gains coincide with the Google AdWords click-thru results, analyzed later in this report.

Geographically, Ohio was almost a non-issue in March, accounting for just 409 visits—down from 1,854 visits in February and nearly 5,000 in November. This is an indication that the reported traffic is increasingly more pure, and not muddied by visits from the ABC Corporation servers, as well as a hint that viewers are clearly seeing the separation between ABC Corporation and XYZ Corporation. Further, while Brazil continues to account for over 5,000 visits per month, and the U.K., France, and Germany continue to take the top spots in terms of visitors, India has jumped up nearly 172% since February to take the number six spot (up from its November ranking of 11). It is likely to knock Germany out of the top five in coming months. Puerto Rico has also shown impressive percentage gains, with an increase of nearly 134% in March.

Areas of Concern

METRIC ADJUSTMENTS Although not as bad as in the first report (November 2007), there are still some adjustments that need to be made to the 41,222 reported visits in order to get a clearer picture:

- Brazil again ranked second in terms of the most visitors at 5,112. As we determined at our last analytics meeting, these are coming from XYZ Corporation facilities in Brazil.

- XYZCorporation.com and XYZCorporation.net accounted for another 5,000 visitors.

- Visits from QRS Corporation, ABC Corporation, CareerBuilder, and other such sources continue to skew the results somewhat.

After accounting for these factors, the number of visits drops to just over 31,000—an almost 25% drop from the 41,222 figure reported by Google Analytics, but almost double November's post-adjustment visitor figure of 16,241.

TIME, LOSS, AND VISIBILITY Although the traffic rates continue to increase, and the efforts being taken to drive traffic to the site are showing positive results, the biggest concern continues to be site usage and retention. While the bounce rate has gone down percentage wise from November and February, it has gone down only marginally, and remains high at 58.62%. This means that the majority of visitors that come to the site leave immediately, without viewing any other page (a small positive note about this—we can assume that the majority of visits from Brazil and XYZCorporation.com and .net are part of the group that never sees more than one page per visit).

Time spent on the site inched upward, but only by a few seconds, and remains uncomfortably low at only 1:32 seconds per visit. This is underscored by the fact that an overwhelming number of visitors (25,807, or 62.6%) stay on XYZCorporation.com for less than 10 seconds per visit. Looking at individual pages, similarly low amounts of time make it questionable that visitors could read all of the content, or get as much out of each page as they should.

Similarly, nearly half of all visitors that came to the XYZCorporation.com site in March only came once (a quick look at the cumulative numbers from November 1 to March 31 shows that this number improves when expanded over a longer period of time, but not by much), and almost 40% (67,104) of all viewers over the five-month period have never returned more than once.

PPV (pages per visit) also continues to crawl upward, although slowly, and not by enough. At 2.77 pages per visit, visitors simply aren't getting the total amount of content that they should be.

Of those 2.77 pages, it was less likely in March that the Contact Us page was among them, as that page fell by nearly 11% from February, and in fact remains flat with the number of visits to that page in November, when true visits were about half of what they were in March.

Recommendations

Online Efforts to Increase Traffic

GOOGLE ADWORDS: REDUCE REACH Because we are already at maximum budget capacity, there is little room to add new campaigns or keywords without diluting the results we are already achieving. To free up funds and allocate them elsewhere, we would recommend reducing the geographic reach. This can be accomplished one of two ways:

- Eliminate the use of AdWords in smaller countries, or countries where XYZ Corporation has less interest. Although these do not account for very much, if enough smaller countries are eliminated, it would make an impact.

- Eliminate some of the larger countries that are more likely to be exposed to XYZ Corporation in other ways, such as e-mail blasts, tradeshows, and print ads. The U.S., France, Germany, and the U.K. all increased in viewership of the XYZ Corporation. Web site in March, but the percentage increases in these regions was smaller, and it is highly likely that growth in these countries would continue without Google AdWords support.

Reducing the reach in certain areas where reach is not needed will help us to maximize click-thru rates in other areas and add more keywords and campaigns.

GOOGLE ADWORDS: ADD SHORT-TERM CAMPAIGNS As of now, the Google AdWords campaign is maximized in terms of monthly budget, yet still remains granular (in the sense that we have chosen fairly detailed keywords, rather than general words, which would be more expensive). Because of this granular approach, we've been able to maintain a high traffic rate, while keeping the average cost-per-click well below $1.00. Therefore, we would not recommend opening keywords up to more general audiences at this time.

We would, however, advocate implementing short-term keyword campaigns that coincide with other marketing efforts, and drive traffic to campaign-specific landing pages. These efforts could include trade shows such as Interphex and Vitafoods, as well as upcoming Insights and Innovation webinars.

INCREASE ADVERTISING IN KEY ONLINE PUBLICATIONS Three online publications combined to account for about 400 unique visitors in the month of March. Although their contribution to site traffic is relatively small, there may be opportunities to better exploit the marketing potential of these publications. Category sponsorship, increased online advertising, direct mail, and e-mail blast partnerships should be explored to better attract their visitors.

Improving the Site

SITE CHANGES AND ADDITIONS Since our last meeting, one major change that we recommended is about to be launched—the reorganization of the XYZCorporation.com Home page. We anticipate that this change, which includes space for three marketing blurbs above the fold, and better visibility to the News section below the fold, will help lead visitors to specific areas throughout the site, and augment overall marketing efforts.

Other changes, however, should also be considered. In our previous meeting, we discussed the following potential changes:

- Search Term Glossary: Having the Search feature on the site is a helpful way to improve site navigation. From the tracking results, in many instances, people might not know exactly what terms they need to use to find what they are looking for. This can be resolved by offering a glossary of search terms link below the search bar, to give users the keyword support they need.

- Headline Color Change: On the interior of the site, the headlines in light blue can be long and difficult to read. We would recommend making each headline shorter and in either a darker blue or black for better readability.

- Interior Quicklinks Navigation: Because there is so much content on the site, we suggest including a "quicklinks" navigation tool to help lead users in the direction we think they should go, to provide an easier means of finding important information relative to their visit.

- Rethinking Sub Navigation: Although the sub navigation is technically interesting, it poses a few problems. It can be difficult to determine the hierarchy, and as the navigation bar expands downward, some of the lower links potentially get lost below the fold. In addition, by being placed along the left side of the page, we lose valuable real estate. By rethinking the sub navigation with a possible move to a horizontal drop down menu, we can gain space across the page and clearly define the hierarchy of information.

- Better Page Titling: This would be strictly to help in the review of traffic and site analytics. As of now, every page title is the title of the category. For example, the title of the XYZ Corporation drug delivery page is "XYZ Corporation - Drug Delivery." Every page within that category shares that same title, so Softgel technology is also titled "XYZ Corporation - Drug Delivery." If each page had an individual title, that would aid in the review of site analytics.

- Creation of a Media Center: Because XYZ Corporation has already compiled a good amount of video, the creation of an online media center would help improve visitor retention and better explain key messages.

- Change the Start-Up Page in Brazil: As part of the effort to get a clearer picture of the analytics, we should consider asking employees in Brazil to no longer use XYZCorporation.com as their start-up page.

Index

Note: Page numbers referencing figures are italicized and followed by an "*f*". Page numbers referencing tables are italicized and followed by a "*t*".